In Other Words

In Other Words is the definitive coursebook for students studying translation. Assuming no knowledge of foreign languages, it offers both a practical and theoretical guide to translation studies, and provides an important foundation for training professional translators.

Drawing on modern linguistic theory, this best-selling text provides a solid base to inform and guide the many key decisions trainee translators have to make. Each chapter offers an explanation of key concepts, identifies potential sources of translation difficulties related to those concepts, and illustrates various strategies for resolving these difficulties. Authentic examples of translated texts from a wide variety of languages are examined, and practical exercises and further reading are included at the end of each chapter.

The second edition has been fully revised to reflect recent developments in the field and new features include:

- A new chapter that addresses issues of ethics and ideology, in response to increased pressures on translators and interpreters to demonstrate accountability and awareness of the social impact of their decisions.
- Examples and exercises from new genres such as audiovisual translation, scientific translation, oral interpreting, website translation, and news/media translation.
- New project-driven exercises designed to support MA dissertation work.
- Updated references and further reading.
- A companion website featuring further examples and tasks.

Written by Mona Baker, a leading international figure in the field, this key text is the essential coursebook for any student of translation studies.

Mona Baker is Professor of Translation Studies at the University of Manchester, UK. She is co-founder and editorial director of St. Jerome Publishing which specializes in translation studies. She is also co-Vice President of the International Association of Translation and Intercultural Studies (IATIS).

In Other Words

A coursebook on translation
Second edition

Mona Baker

Routledge
Taylor & Francis Group

LONDON AND NEW YORK

First published 1992
by Routledge

This edition published 2011
by Routledge
2 Park Square, Milton Park, Abingdon, Oxon OX14 4RN

Simultaneously published in the USA and Canada
by Routledge
711 Third Ave, New York, NY 10017

Routledge is an imprint of the Taylor & Francis Group, an informa business

Typeset in Berthold Akzidenz Grotesk by
Saxon Graphics Ltd, Derby

British Library Cataloguing in Publication Data
A catalogue record for this book is available from the British Library

Library of Congress Cataloging-in-Publication Data
Baker, Mona.
  In other words : a coursebook on translation / Mona Baker. – [2nd ed.].
  p. cm.
  Includes bibliographical references and index.
  1. Translating and interpreting. I. Title.
  P306.B25 2011
  418'.02–dc22
  2010031445

ISBN: 978-0-415-46753-7 (hbk)
ISBN: 978-0-415-46754-4 (pbk)
ISBN: 978-0-203-83292-9 (ebk)

Printed and bound in Great Britain by
TJ International Ltd, Padstow, Cornwall

To Ken

Contents

List of figures	*xi*
List of tables	*xii*
Preface to the second edition	*xiii*
Preface to the first edition	*xv*
Acknowledgements	*xvii*

1 Introduction	**1**
1.1 About the organization of this book	4
1.2 Examples, back-translations and the languages of illustration	6
Suggestions for further reading	8
Note	8

2 Equivalence at word level	**9**
2.1 The word in different languages	9
2.1.1 What is a word?	9
2.1.2 Is there a one-to-one relationship between word and meaning?	10
2.1.3 Introducing morphemes	10
2.2 Lexical meaning	11
2.2.1 Propositional vs expressive meaning	11
2.2.2 Presupposed meaning	12
2.2.3 Evoked meaning	13
2.3 The problem of non-equivalence	15
2.3.1 Semantic fields and lexical sets – the segmentation of experience	16
2.3.2 Non-equivalence at word level and some common strategies for dealing with it	18
Exercises	44
Suggestions for further reading	47
Notes	49

3 Equivalence above word level   **51**

   3.1 Collocation   52
      3.1.1 Collocational range and collocational markedness   54
      3.1.2 Collocation and register   56
      3.1.3 Collocational meaning   57
      3.1.4 Some collocation-related pitfalls and problems in translation   58
   3.2 Idioms and fixed expressions   67
      3.2.1 Idioms, fixed expressions and the direction of translation   68
      3.2.2 The interpretation of idioms   69
      3.2.3 The translation of idioms: difficulties   71
      3.2.4 The translation of idioms: strategies   75
   Exercises   86
   Suggestions for further reading   90
   Notes   91

4 Grammatical equivalence   **92**

   4.1 Grammatical vs lexical categories   93
   4.2 The diversity of grammatical categories across languages   95
      4.2.1 Number   96
      4.2.2 Gender   99
      4.2.3 Person   104
      4.2.4 Tense and aspect   108
      4.2.5 Voice   112
   4.3 A brief note on word order   120
   4.4 Introducing text   121
      4.4.1 Text vs non-text   121
      4.4.2 Features of text organization   123
   Exercises   124
   Suggestions for further reading   127
   Notes   129

5 Textual equivalence: thematic and information structures   **131**

   5.1 A Hallidayan overview of information flow   133
      5.1.1 Thematic structure: theme and rheme   133
      5.1.2 Information structure: given and new   156
   5.2 The Prague School position on information flow: functional
      sentence perspective   170
      5.2.1 Linear arrangement and thematic status in FSP   173
      5.2.2 Linear arrangement and marked structures in FSP   174

5.2.3 The tension between word order and communicative function:
a problem in translation?   175
5.2.4 Suggested strategies for minimizing linear dislocation   176
Exercises   181
Suggestions for further reading   186
Notes   187

6 Textual equivalence: cohesion   **190**

6.1 Reference   190
6.2 Substitution and ellipsis   196
6.3 Conjunction   200
6.4 Lexical cohesion   210
Exercises   223
Suggestions for further reading   227
Notes   228

7 Pragmatic equivalence   **230**

7.1 Coherence   230
7.1.1 Coherence vs cohesion   230
7.1.2 Is coherence a feature of text or situation?   231
7.2 Coherence and processes of interpretation: implicature   234
7.3 Coherence, implicature and translation strategies   239
7.3.1 The conventional meanings of words and structures and the
identity of references   240
7.3.2 The Co-operative Principle and its maxims   244
7.3.3 The context, linguistic or otherwise, of the utterance   249
7.3.4 Other items of background knowledge   255
7.3.5 The availability of all relevant items falling under the
previous headings   259
Exercises   263
Suggestions for further reading   270
Notes   271

8 Beyond equivalence: ethics and morality   **274**

8.1 Ethics and morality   275
8.2 Professionalism, codes of ethics and the law   283
8.3 The ethical implications of linguistic choices   286
8.4 Concluding remarks   290
Exercises   290
Suggestions for further reading   296
Notes   298

Glossary	*300*
References	*305*
Name index	*323*
Language index	*327*
Subject index	*329*

Figures

Figure 1, Chapter 2	Panel from Tronchet's *Jean-Claude Tergal* and its Italian translation, *Domenico Tergazzi*	32
Figure 2, Chapter 2	Lipton Yellow Label tea packet for Arab market	44
Figure 3, Chapter 2	Trados advertisement	45
Figure 4, Chapter 2	Screen shot from Sizism Awareness Campaign video	46
Figure 5, Chapter 3	Title of article in *New Scientist*	74
Figure 6, Chapter 3	Original version of Manchester Museum of Science and Industry leaflet	79
Figure 7, Chapter 3	French translation of Manchester Museum of Science and Industry leaflet	80
Figure 8, Chapter 3	Italian translation of Manchester Museum of Science and Industry leaflet	80
Figure 9, Chapter 3	Spanish translation of Manchester Museum of Science and Industry leaflet	80
Figure 10, Chapter 3	German translation of Manchester Museum of Science and Industry leaflet	80
Figure 11, Chapter 3	Japanese translation of Manchester Museum of Science and Industry leaflet	81
Figure 12, Chapter 3	Original version of Wedgwood leaflet	84
Figure 13, Chapter 3	Japanese translation of Wedgwood leaflet	85
Figure 14, Chapter 6	Caption of article in Wonderlust Guide to Jordan 2010	87
Figure 15, Chapter 6	'Not Beyond Compare', *National Geographic Magazine*, 1 March 2010, p. 26	215
Figure 16, Chapter 6	Homepage of Katha	226
Figure 17, Chapter 6	Sub-page of Katha web site	227

Tables

Table 1, Chapter 3   Unpredictability of collocational patterning   53
Table 2, Chapter 6   Recurrence and collocational cohesion
                       (adapted from Mason 1994/2010:88)   222

Preface to the second edition

This second edition of *In Other Words* comes at a time of increased visibility for translators and interpreters. We only need to look at the extent of reporting on translation and interpreting in the media to appreciate how visible the profession and the activity have become. News of translation and interpreting now pervades our lives: whether it is the lack of qualified court interpreters in a remote part of Australia or Canada, or the fate of translators and interpreters in zones of military conflict; the launching of a national initiative to encourage translation in one region or another, or the decision by the Turkish government to reinterpret Islam through a new translation of the Prophet's sayings; the impending decision by the European Commission to limit the translation of patents to three languages, or the release of a feminist translation of the Bible. Every aspect of our social and political life is now heavily mediated by translators and interpreters, hence their increased visibility. Translation and interpreting are also now firmly part of the professional and academic landscape, with practically every country in the world boasting at least one association that represents the interests of the profession and numerous universities offering full-blown undergraduate and postgraduate programmes in the field. Technological advances in the past two decades have further had a major impact on the profession, resolving old challenges and raising new ones. I have tried to take stock of at least some of these developments in the choice of additional examples and exercises in this new edition. A new chapter on ethics attempts to respond to increased pressures on translators and interpreters to demonstrate accountability and awareness of the tremendous social and political impact of their decisions.

Since the publication of the first edition of *In Other Words*, fortune has continued to favour me with exceptionally gifted and supportive colleagues, students and family whose input into this new edition must be acknowledged. I am grateful to my niece, Hanan Rihan, for support in preparing the text for publication. Colleagues, students and former students at the School of Languages, Linguistics and Cultures, University of Manchester, helped me check the analysis of various examples and key in text that I could not type myself. Luis Pérez-González and James St. André helped with Spanish, French and Chinese examples and Morven Beaton-Thome with German examples. Jonathan Bunt provided extensive support with Japanese, Zhao Wenjing with Chinese, and Sofia Malamatidou with Greek.

I am particularly grateful to Moira Inghilleri, Julie Boéri and Sofia Garcia for their extremely helpful, critical comments on the new chapter on ethics, and to Monika Bednarek and her students at the University of Sydney for critical feedback on several chapters. From Routledge, Russell George, Sophie Jacques, Nadia Seemungal, Anna Callander and Lizzie Clifford have been extremely supportive. Their help is much appreciated.

John Sinclair's departure in 2007 left a considerable vacuum in the lives of those who were fortunate enough to know him and benefit from his immense experience. This new edition of *In Other Words* remains as indebted to his teachings as the first one.

Mona Baker
June 2010

Preface to the first edition

The idea of this book initially grew out of discussions with a number of colleagues, in particular with Dr Kirsten Malmkjaer, formerly of the University of Birmingham and currently at the Centre of English as an International Language, Cambridge. It has been considerably refined during the course of last year through discussions with postgraduate students at the University of Birmingham and students at the Brasshouse Centre and Birmingham Polytechnic.

I am exceptionally lucky to have been able to draw on the outstanding expertise of a number of colleagues, both at the University of Birmingham and at COBUILD, a lexical project run jointly by the University of Birmingham and Collins Publishers. From COBUILD, Stephen Bullon, Alex Collier and Gwyneth Fox provided initial help with Russian, German and Italian texts respectively. From the Shakespeare Institute, Katsuhiko Nogami helped with Japanese and Shen Lin with Chinese texts. From the School of Modern Languages, James Mullen (Russian), Bill Dodd (German), Paula Chicken (French) and Elena Tognini-Bonelli (Italian) helped me work my way through various texts and took the time to explain the structural and stylistic nuances of each language. From the School of English, Tony Dudley-Evans and Sonia Zyngier helped with Brazilian Portuguese and Wu Zu Min with Chinese. Tim Johns read and commented on Chapter 5 ('Thematic and information structures') and kindly allowed me to use much of his own data and report some of his findings on the subject.

Chinese and Japanese texts required additional help to analyse; this was competently provided by Ming Xie (Chinese) and Haruko Uryu (Japanese), both at the University of Cambridge. Lanna Castellano of the Institute of Translation and Interpreting read a substantial part of the draft manuscript and her encouraging comments were timely and well appreciated.

I owe a special debt to three people in particular: Helen Liebeck, Philip King and Michael Hoey. Helen Liebeck and Philip King are polyglots; both kindly spent many hours helping me with a variety of languages and both read and commented on Chapters 2, 3 and 4. Philip King also provided the Greek examples and helped with the analysis of several texts.

Michael Hoey is an outstanding text linguist. In spite of his many commitments, he managed to find the time to read through the last three chapters and to provide detailed comments on each of them. His help has been invaluable. It is indeed a privilege to work with so distinguished a scholar who is also extremely generous with his time and expertise.

Last but not least, I must acknowledge a personal debt to John Sinclair. John has taught me, often during informal chats, most of what I know about language, and his own work has always been a source of inspiration. But I am grateful, above all, for his friendship and continued support.

Mona Baker
May 1991

Acknowledgements

The author and publishers wish to thank the following for permission to reproduce the quotations and illustrations appearing in this book:

Autoworld at the Patrick Collection, 180 Lifford Lane, Kings Norton, Birmingham. Reproduced with permission.

Brintons press release, reproduced with permission.

Euralex (European Association for Lexicography), PO Box 1017, Copenhagen, Denmark for extracts from conference circular. Reproduced with permission.

Stephen W. Hawking, Bantam Press, Space Time Publications and World House Inc. for permission to reproduce extracts from *A Brief History of Time* (1988) by Stephen W. Hawking. © (UK and Commonwealth) Space Time Publications; © (USA) Bantam Books, a division of Bantam Doubleday, Dell Publishing Group, Inc.; © 1988 (Japan) World House Inc. All rights reserved.

Το χρονικό του Χρόνου (Από τη Μεγάλη Εκρηξη έως τις μαύρες τρύπες) (1988) Translated from English by Konstantinos Harakas, Katoptro Publications. Reproduced with permission.

Extracts from *Autumn of Fury: The Assassination of Sadat* © 1983 Mohammed Heikal. Reprinted by permission of André Deutsch Ltd.

John Le Carré and Hodder & Stoughton for extracts from *The Russia House* (1989).

Lipton Export Limited, Stanbridge Road, Leighton Buzzard, Beds.

Lonrho plc (now Lonmin plc) for extracts from *A Hero from Zero*.

The Minority Rights Group, 379 Brixton Road, London, for Lebanon, Minority Rights Group Report by David McDowall, London 1983.

Morgan Matroc – This extract was taken in 1986 from Morgan Matroc which is now Morgan Technical Ceramics.

Museum of Science and Industry promotional leaflet (Manchester), shot reproduced in six languages: English, French, Italian, Spanish, German, Japanese. Reproduced with permission.

National Geographic Magazine, 1 March 2010, page 26.

Article in *New Internationalist* (January/February 2010, special issue on population growth), authored by Vanessa Baird. Reprinted by kind permission of *New Internationalist*. Copyright *New Internationalist* www.newint.org

Do we really know how we translate or what we translate? … Are we to accept 'naked ideas' as the means of crossing from one language to another? … Translators know they cross over but do not know by what sort of bridge. They often re-cross by a different bridge to check up again. Sometimes they fall over the parapet into limbo.

(Firth 1957:197)

Translation is a point of contact between peoples, and since it is rare that two peoples have the same access to power, the translator is in a privileged position as mediator, to make explicit the differences between cultures, expose injustices or contribute to diversity in the world.

(Gill and Guzmán 2010:126)

CHAPTER 1

Introduction

> Writing my own novels has always required a huge effort of organisation and imagination; but, sentence by sentence, translation is intellectually more taxing.
>
> *(Parks 2010)*

Professionals in every walk of life form associations and institutes of various kinds to provide practising members with a forum to discuss and set standards for the profession as a whole, to set examinations, assess competence and lay codes of conduct. The standards set by a given profession may well be extremely high, but this does not necessarily guarantee recognition by those outside the profession. Notwithstanding the length and breadth of one's experience, recognition, in our increasingly qualification-conscious society, comes mostly with proof of some kind of formal education. Every respectable profession (or every profession which wants to be recognized as such) therefore attempts to provide its members with systematic training in the field.

There are two main types of training that a profession can provide for its members: vocational training and academic training. Vocational courses provide training in practical skills but do not include a strong theoretical component. A good example would be a course in plumbing or typing. At the end of a typing course, a student is able to type accurately and at speed and has a piece of paper to prove it. But that is the end of the story; what the student acquires is a purely practical skill which is recognized by society as 'skilled work' but is not generally elevated to the level of a profession. Like vocational courses, most academic courses set out to teach students how to do a particular job such as curing certain types of illness, building bridges or writing computer programs. But they do more than that: an academic course always includes a strong theoretical component. The value of this theoretical component is that it encourages students to reflect on what they do, how they do it and why they do it in one way rather than another. This last exercise, exploring the advantages and disadvantages of various ways of doing things, is itself impossible to perform unless one has a thorough and intimate knowledge of the objects and tools of one's work. A doctor cannot decide whether it is better to follow one course of treatment rather than another without understanding such things as how the human body works, what side effects a given medicine may have, what is available to counteract these effects and so on.

Theoretical training does not necessarily guarantee success in all instances. Things still go wrong occasionally because, in medicine for example, the reaction of the human body and the influence of other factors such as stress will never be totally predictable. But the value of a theoretical understanding of, say, the human apparatus and such things as the nature and make-up of various drugs is that (a) it minimizes the risks involved on any given occasion and prepares the student for dealing with the unpredictable, (b) it gives the practising doctor a certain degree of confidence which comes from knowing that his or her decisions are calculated on the basis of concrete knowledge rather than 'hunches' or 'intuition' and (c) it provides the basis on which further developments in the field may be achieved because it represents a formalized pool of knowledge which is shared and can be explored and extended by the professional community as a whole, not just locally but across the world. Needless to say, this type of theoretical knowledge is itself of no value unless it is firmly grounded in practical experience.

Throughout its long history, translation has never really enjoyed the kind of recognition and respect that other professions such as medicine and engineering have enjoyed. Translators have constantly complained that translation is underestimated as a profession. In summing up the first conference held by the Institute of Translation and Interpreting in Britain, Professor Bellos (reported by Nick Rosenthal) stated that 'The main impetus and concern of this first ITI Conference was the unjustly low status in professional terms of the translator. An appropriate theme, since it was one of the main reasons for the formation of the ITI' (Bellos 1987:163). Today, more than two decades later, the novelist and translator Tim Parks still has to remind us that at least 'for a few minutes every year we really must acknowledge that translators are important' (Parks 2010). There is no doubt that the low status accorded to translation as a profession is 'unjust', but one has to admit that this is not just the fault of the general public. The translation community itself has traditionally been guilty of underestimating not so much the value as the complexity of the translation process and hence the need for formal professional training in the field, though this situation is thankfully changing quite rapidly. Since the first edition of this book was published, in 1992, numerous training programmes have been set up for translators and interpreters across the world. Translation has become a highly attractive career for young people with a love for languages and for engaging with other cultures, as well as a growing area of research. Those entering the profession now have to demonstrate that they can reflect on what they do, that they have invested in acquiring not only the vocational but also the intellectual skills required to undertake such a complex and highly consequential task, one that has a major impact on the lives of the many people who rely on them as mediators.

In the past, talented translators who had no systematic formal training in translation but who nevertheless achieved a high level of competence through long and varied experience tended to think that the translation community as a whole could achieve their own high standards in the same way:

Our profession is based on knowledge and experience. It has the longest apprenticeship of any profession. Not until thirty do you start to be useful as a translator, not until fifty do you start to be in your prime.

The first stage of the career pyramid – the apprenticeship stage – is the time we devote to *investing in ourselves* by acquiring knowledge and experience of life. Let me propose a life path: grandparents of different nationalities, a good school education in which you learn to read, write, spell, construe and love your own language. Then roam the world, make friends, see life. Go back to education, but to take a technical or commercial degree, not a language degree. Spend the rest of your twenties and your early thirties in the countries whose languages you speak, working in industry or commerce but not directly in languages. Never marry into your own nationality. Have your children. Then back to a postgraduate translation course. A staff job as a translator, and then go freelance. By which time you are forty and ready to begin.

(Lanna Castellano 1988:133)

Lanna's recommended career path no doubt worked for many people in the past. Her own case proves that it did: she is a widely respected first-class translator. The question is whether it was ever feasible for most aspiring translators to pursue this career path and whether this approach is or was right for the profession as a whole, bearing in mind that it stresses, at least for the first thirty or forty years of one's career, life experience rather than formal academic training. One obvious problem with this career path is that it takes so long to acquire the skills you need as a translator that your career is almost over before it begins.

Lanna Castellano has never been opposed to formal academic training; on the contrary, she has always encouraged it and recognized its value to the profession. But I have met professional translators in the past, and still come across some very occasionally today, who actually argue strongly against formal academic training because, they suggest, translation is an art which requires aptitude, practice and general knowledge – nothing more. The ability to translate is a gift, they say: you either have it or you do not, and theory (almost a dirty word in some translation circles) is therefore irrelevant to the work of a translator. To take the analogy with medicine a step further: if we accept this line of thinking we will never be seen as anything but witch doctors and faith healers. And while it may well suit some individuals to think that they can heal people because they have magic powers or a special relationship with God, rather than because they have a thorough and conscious understanding of drugs and of the human body, the fact remains that witch doctory and faith healing are not recognized professions and that medicine is.

Most translators and interpreters prefer to think of their work as a profession and would like to see others treat them as professionals rather than as skilled or semiskilled workers. But to achieve this, they need to develop an ability to stand back and reflect on what they do and how they do it. Like doctors and engineers, they have to prove to themselves as well as others that they are in control of what they do; that they do not just translate or interpret well because they have a 'flair' for it, but rather because, like other professionals, they have made a conscious effort to understand various aspects of their work.

Unlike medicine and engineering, translation studies is a relatively young discipline in academic terms, though it is increasingly featuring as a subject of study in its own right in many parts of the world. Like any young discipline, it needs to draw on the findings and theories of numerous related disciplines in order to develop and formalize its own methods – from linguistics to literary theory, from sociology to cognitive science. This is not surprising, given that almost every aspect of life in general and of the interaction between speech communities in particular can be considered relevant to translation, a discipline which has to concern itself with how meaning is generated within and between various groups of people in various cultural settings, and with what impact on society. For translation to gain more recognition as a profession, translators cannot resort to a mixture of intuition and experience to think through and justify the decisions they have to make but must constantly look to developments in neighbouring disciplines to appreciate the varied, complex dimensions of their work. Among the many skills they need to acquire through training is the skill to understand and reflect on the raw material with which they work: to appreciate what language is and how it comes to function for its users.

Linguistics is a discipline which studies language both in its own right and as a tool for generating meanings. It should therefore have a great deal to offer to translation studies; it can certainly offer translators and interpreters valuable insights into the nature and function of language. This is particularly true of modern linguistics, which no longer restricts itself to the study of language *per se* but embraces such sub-disciplines as textlinguistics (the study of text as a communicative event rather than as a shapeless string of words and structures) and pragmatics (the study of language in use rather than language as an abstract system). This book attempts to explore some areas in which modern linguistic theory can provide a basis for training translators and can inform and guide the decisions they have to make in the course of performing their work.

1.1 ABOUT THE ORGANIZATION OF THIS BOOK

The organization of this book is largely hierarchical and is based on a straight-forward principle: it starts at the simplest possible level and grows in complexity by widening its focus in each chapter. Chapter 2, 'Equivalence at word level', initially adopts a naive building-block approach and explores the 'meaning' of single words and expressions. In Chapter 3, 'Equivalence above word level', the scope of reference is widened a little by looking at combinations of words and phrases: what happens when words start combining with other words to form convention-alized or semi-conventionalized stretches of language. Chapter 4, 'Grammatical equivalence', deals with grammatical categories such as number and gender. Chapters 5 and 6 cover part of what might be loosely termed the textual level of language. Chapter 5 deals with the role played by word order in structuring messages at text level and Chapter 6 discusses cohesion: grammatical and lexical relationships which provide links between various parts of a text. Chapter 7, 'Pragmatic equivalence', looks at how texts are used in communicative situations that involve variables such as writers, readers and cultural context. Chapter 8, 'Beyond equivalence: ethics and morality', is new. I have added it to this second edition in order to encourage students to reflect on the wider implications of their decisions and the impact of their mediation on others. Again, like any other profession that strives to be taken seriously, translators and interpreters have to engage reflectively with the ethical implications of their work and demonstrate that they are responsible professionals and citizens of society.

To return to the bulk of this book, namely Chapters 2 to 7, it is important to point out that the division of language into seemingly self-contained areas such as words, grammar and text is artificial and open to question. For one thing, the areas are not discrete: it is virtually impossible to say where the concerns of one area end and those of another begin. Moreover, decisions taken at, say, the level of the word or grammatical category during the course of translation are influenced by the perceived function and purpose of both the original text and the translation and have implications for the discourse as a whole. But artificial as it is, the division of language into discrete areas is useful for the purposes of analysis and, provided we are aware that it is adopted merely as a measure of convenience, it can help to pinpoint potential areas of difficulty in translation and interpreting.

Like the division of language into discrete areas, the term equivalence is adopted in this book for the sake of convenience – because most translators are used to it rather than because it has any theoretical status. It is used here with the proviso that although equivalence can usually be obtained to some extent, it is influenced by a variety of linguistic and cultural factors and is therefore always relative. Kenny (2009) offers an excellent overview of the notion of equivalence and the various ways in which it has been approached in the literature.

The organization followed in this book is a bottom-up rather than a top-down one: it starts with simple words and phrases rather than with the text as situated in its context of culture. This may seem somewhat at odds with current thinking in linguistic and translation studies. Snell-Hornby (1988:69) suggests that 'textual analysis, which is an essential preliminary to translation, should proceed from the "top down", from the macro to the micro level, from text to sign', and Hatim and Mason's model of the translation process (1990, 1997) also adopts a top-down approach, taking such things as text-type and context as starting points for discussing translation problems and strategies. The top-down approach is the more valid one theoretically, but for those who are not trained linguists it can be difficult to follow: there is too much to take in all at once. Moreover, an excessive emphasis on 'text' and 'context' runs the risk of obscuring the fact that although 'a text is a semantic unit, not a grammatical one … meanings are realized through wordings; and without a theory of wordings … there is no way of making explicit one's interpretation of the meaning of a text' (Halliday 1985:xvii). In other words, text is a meaning unit, not a form unit, but meaning is realized through form and without understanding the meanings of individual forms one cannot interpret the meaning of the text as a whole. Translating words and phrases out of context is certainly a futile exercise, but it is equally unhelpful to expect a student to appreciate translation decisions made at the level of text without a reasonable understanding of how the lower levels, the individual words, phrases and grammatical structures, control and shape the overall meaning of the text. Both the top-down and the bottom-up approaches are therefore valid in their own way; I have opted for the latter for pedagogical reasons – because it is much easier to follow for those who have had no previous training in linguistics.

1.2 EXAMPLES, BACK-TRANSLATIONS AND THE LANGUAGES OF ILLUSTRATION

In each chapter, an attempt is made to identify potential sources of translation difficulties related to the linguistic area under discussion and possible strategies for resolving these difficulties. The strategies are not preconceived, nor are they suggested as ideal solutions; they are identified by analysing authentic examples of translated texts in a variety of languages and presented as 'actual' strategies used rather than the 'correct' strategies to use. The examples are quoted and discussed, sometimes at length, to illustrate the various strategies identified and to explore the potential pros and cons of each strategy. Although the discussion is occasionally critical of certain translations, finding fault with published translations is never the object of the exercise. It is in fact virtually impossible, except in extreme cases, to draw a line between what counts as a good translation and what counts as a bad one. Every translation has points of strength and points of weakness, and every translation is open to improvement.

The source language of most examples is English. This is because in both literary and non-literary translation today, English is probably the most widely translated language in the world. And since it also happens to be the language in which this book is written, I feel justified in assuming that all readers will have an adequate command of it. Much as I would have liked to include examples of and exercises on translation into English, I have had to accept that it is not possible to write a general coursebook on translation unless the source language is kept constant. With a few exceptions, the direction of translation is therefore assumed to be from English into a variety of target languages. However, readers – particularly teachers of translation – are invited to adapt the examples and exercises to suit their individual purposes. Once a given topic is discussed and understood, alternative texts can be easily found in other languages to replace the examples and exercises in which English is treated as the source language.

The target languages exemplified are by no means all European. They include major non-European languages such as Arabic, Japanese and Chinese. The emphasis on non-European languages, I hope, no longer seems unusual, although it did when the first edition of this book appeared, in 1992. Since then, much has been done by scholars such as Diriker (2004), Hung and Wakabayashi (2005),

Hermans (2006), Cockerill (2006), Cheung (2006, 2009), Gentzler (2008), Bandia (2008), Curran (2008), Wakabayashi and Kothari (2009) and Selim (2009), among others, to counterbalance the traditional preoccupation with European languages in translation studies. Many more translators as well as teachers and scholars of translation now appreciate that there is life – and indeed translation – outside Europe, and that professional non-European translators use a range of strategies that are at least as interesting and as useful as those used by European translators. The reception of the first edition of this book over the past two decades has confirmed that it is instructive for translators of any linguistic background to explore difficulties of translation in non-European languages, given that the structure of those languages and their cultural settings raise important issues that could otherwise be easily overlooked in discussions of language and translation.

The majority of readers will not be familiar with all the languages illustrated in this book, but they should still be able to follow the discussion of individual examples by using the back-translations provided. **Back-translation**, as used in this book, involves taking a text (original or translated) which is written in a language with which the reader is assumed to be unfamiliar and translating it as literally as possible[1] into English – how literally depends on the point being illustrated, whether it is morphological, syntactic or lexical for instance. I use the term back-translation because, since the source language is often English, this involves translating the target text back into the source language from which it was originally translated. A back-translation can give some insight into aspects of the structure, if not the meaning of the original, but it is never the same as the original. The use of back-translation is a necessary compromise; it is theoretically unsound and far from ideal, but then we do not live in an ideal world – very few of us speak eight or nine languages – and theoretical criteria cease to be relevant when they become an obstacle to fruitful discussion.

All examples are quoted in the original language as well as in back-translation. For instance, an English example is immediately followed by its German or Arabic translation and then a back-translation of the German or Arabic. Technological advances now allow me to manipulate different fonts and languages without too much trouble, a feat that was well beyond my technical abilities in 1992. I have therefore dispensed with appendices in this edition and have embedded all examples in the body of the text – not only French, German, Spanish, Portuguese and Italian, but also Russian, Greek, Arabic, Chinese and Japanese.

Finally, there is no shortage of discussions on the shortcomings and failures of translation as a tool of language mediation across cultures. The literature abounds with theoretical arguments which suggest that translation is an impossible task, that it is doomed to failure because (a) languages are never sufficiently similar to express the same realities, and (b) even worse, 'reality' cannot be assumed to exist independently of language. But in spite of these difficulties, translation remains an inescapable part of our lives – more so today, perhaps, than at any time in the past. Even in these days of aggressive globalization and pervasive violent conflicts, it has brought and continues to bring people of different cultural and linguistic backgrounds closer together, has enabled many to share a more harmonious view of the world, and has built bridges of understanding and appreciation among different societies. We should also be aware that translation and interpreting can be used to sow conflict, support racist agendas, dispossess indigenous populations and manipulate vulnerable groups and individuals (see Fenton and Moon 2003, Baker 2006, 2010b, Inghilleri 2008). The same can be said of all professions, of course. Medicine heals people, but some doctors also use their skills to support torture. The additional chapter on ethics in this edition will hopefully help translators and interpreters who are committed to using their skills in positive rather than negative ways to think of the impact of their decisions on others and to avoid being implicated in unethical practices.

SUGGESTIONS FOR FURTHER READING

Baker, Mona (2000) 'Linguistic Perspectives on Translation', in Peter France (ed.) *The Oxford Guide to Literature in English Translation*, Oxford: Oxford University Press, 20–26.

Baker, Mona (ed.) (2010a) *Critical Readings in Translation Studies*, London: Routledge.

Baker, Mona and Luis Pérez-González (2011) 'Translation and Interpreting', *Handbook of Applied Linguistics*, London: Routledge, 39–52.

Baker, Mona and Gabriela Saldanha (eds) (2009) *Routledge Encyclopedia of Translation Studies*, second edition, London: Routledge.

Munday, Jeremy (2001/2008) *Introducing Translation Studies: Theories and Applications*, second edition, London: Routledge.

Pöchhacker, Franz (2004) *Introducing Interpreting Studies*, London: Routledge.

Venuti, Lawrence (2004) *The Translation Studies Reader*, second edition, London: Routledge.

NOTE

1   It is important to stress that much of the back-translation provided in this book is very literal. The quality of the English that appears in a given back-translation is not meant to reflect the quality of the translation itself. Readers, particularly those who are not native speakers of English, should also be aware that the English used in the back-translations is not necessarily correct and is not to be confused with natural English.

CHAPTER 2

Equivalence at word level

If language were simply a nomenclature for a set of universal concepts, it would be easy to translate from one language to another. One would simply replace the French name for a concept with the English name. If language were like this the task of learning a new language would also be much easier than it is. But anyone who has attempted either of these tasks has acquired, alas, a vast amount of direct proof that languages are not nomenclatures, that the concepts ... of one language may differ radically from those of another. ... Each language articulates or organizes the world differently. Languages do not simply name existing categories, they articulate their own.

(Culler 1976:21–22)

This chapter discusses translation problems arising from lack of equivalence at word level; what does a translator do when there is no word in the target language which expresses the same meaning as the source language word? But before we look at specific types of non-equivalence and the various strategies which can be used for dealing with them, it is important to establish what a **word** is, whether or not it is the main unit of meaning in language, what kinds of meaning it can convey, and how languages differ in the way they choose to express certain meanings but not others.

2.1 THE WORD IN DIFFERENT LANGUAGES

2.1.1 What is a word?

As translators, we are primarily concerned with communicating the overall meaning of a stretch of language. To achieve this, we need to start by decoding the units and structures which carry that meaning. The smallest unit which we would expect to possess individual meaning is the **word**. Defined loosely, the **word** is 'the smallest unit of language that can be used by itself' (Bolinger and Sears 1968:43).[1] For our present purposes, we can define the **written word** with more precision as any sequence of letters with an orthographic space on either side.

Many of us think of the word as the basic meaningful element in a language. This is not strictly accurate. Meaning can be carried by units smaller than the word (see 2.1.3 below). More often, however, it is carried by units much more complex than the single word and by various structures and linguistic devices. This will be discussed in more detail in the following chapters. For the moment, we will content ourselves with single words as a starting point before we move on to more complex linguistic units.

2.1.2 Is there a one-to-one relationship between word and meaning?

If you consider a word such as *rebuild*, you will note that there are two distinct elements of meaning in it: *re* and *build*, that is 'to build again'. The same applies to *disbelieve*, which may be paraphrased as 'not to believe'. Elements of meaning which are represented by several orthographic words in one language, say English, may be represented by one orthographic word in another, and vice versa. For instance, *tennis player* is written as one word in Turkish: *tenisçi*; *if it is cheap* as one word in Japanese: *yasukattara*; but the verb *type* is rendered by three words in Spanish: *pasar a maquina*. This suggests that there is no one-to-one correspondence between orthographic words and elements of meaning within or across languages.

2.1.3 Introducing morphemes

In order to isolate elements of meaning in words and deal with them more effectively, some linguists have suggested the term **morpheme** to describe the minimal formal element of meaning in language, as distinct from **word**, which may or may not contain several elements of meaning. Thus, an important difference between morphemes and words is that a morpheme cannot contain more than one element of meaning and cannot be further analysed.

 To take an example from English, *inconceivable* is written as one word but consists of three morphemes: *in*, meaning 'not', *conceive* meaning 'think of or imagine', and *able* meaning 'able to be, fit to be'. A suitable paraphrase for *inconceivable* would then be 'cannot be conceived/imagined'. Some morphemes have grammatical functions such as marking plurality (*fund**s***), gender (*manager**ess***) and tense (*consider**ed***). Others change the class of the word, for instance from verb to adjective (*like*: *like**able***), or add a specific element of meaning such as negation to it (***un**happy*). Some words consist of one morpheme: *need, fast*. Morphemes do not always have such clearly defined boundaries, however. We can identify two distinct morphemes in *girls*: *girl* + *s,* but we cannot do the same with *men*, where the two morphemes 'man' and 'plural' are, as it were, fused together. An orthographic word may therefore contain more than one formal element of meaning, but the boundaries of such elements are not always clearly marked on the surface.

 The above theoretical distinction between words and morphemes attempts, by and large, to account for elements of meaning which are expressed on the surface. It does not, however, attempt to break down each morpheme or word into further components of meaning, for instance, 'male' + 'adult' + 'human' for the word *man*. Furthermore, it does not offer a model for analysing different types of meaning in words and utterances. In the following section, we will be looking at ways of analysing lexical meaning which will not specifically draw on the distinction between words and morphemes. It is nevertheless important to keep this distinction clearly in mind because it can be useful in translation, particularly in dealing with neologisms in the source language (see section on common problems of non-equivalence below, item (i)).

2.2 LEXICAL MEANING

> every word (lexical unit) has ... something that is individual, that makes it different from any other word. And it is just the lexical meaning which is the most outstanding individual property of the word.
>
> *(Zgusta 1971:67)*

The **lexical meaning** of a word or lexical unit may be thought of as the specific value it has in a particular linguistic system and the 'personality' it acquires through usage within that system. It is rarely possible to analyse a word, pattern or structure into distinct components of meaning; the way in which language works is much too complex to allow that. Nevertheless, it is sometimes useful to play down the complex-ities of language temporarily in order both to appreciate them and to be able to handle them better in the long run. With this aim in mind, we will now briefly discuss a model for analysing the components of lexical meaning. This model is largely derived from Cruse (1986), but the description of **register** (2.2.3 below) also draws on Halliday (1978). For alternative models of lexical meaning see Zgusta (1971: Chapter 1) and Leech (1974: Chapter 2).

According to Cruse, we can distinguish four main types of meaning in words and utterances (utterances being stretches of written or spoken text): **propositional meaning**, **expressive meaning**, **presupposed meaning** and **evoked meaning**.

2.2.1 Propositional vs expressive meaning

The **propositional meaning** of a word or an utterance arises from the relation between it and what it refers to or describes in a real or imaginary world, as conceived by the speakers of the particular language to which the word or utterance belongs. It is this type of meaning that provides the basis on which we can judge an utterance as true or false. For instance, the propositional meaning of *shirt* is 'a piece of clothing worn on the upper part of the body'. It would be inaccurate to use *shirt*, under normal circumstances, to refer to a piece of clothing worn on the foot, such as *socks.* When a translation is described as 'inaccurate', it is often the propositional meaning that is being called into question.

Expressive meaning cannot be judged as true or false. This is because expressive meaning relates to the speaker's[2] feelings or attitude rather than to what words and utterances refer to. The difference between *Don't complain* and *Don't whinge* does not lie in their propositional meanings but in the expressiveness of *whinge*, which suggests that the speaker finds the action annoying. Two or more words or utterances can therefore have the same propositional meaning but differ in their expressive meanings. This is true not only of words and utterances within the same language, where such words are often referred to as synonyms or near-synonyms, but also for words and utterances from different languages. The difference between *famous* in English and *fameux* in French does not lie in their respective propositional meanings; both items basically mean 'well-known'. It lies in their expressive meanings. *Famous* is (normally) neutral in English: it has no inherent evaluative meaning or connotation. *Fameux*, on the other hand, is potentially evaluative and can be readily used in some contexts in a derogatory way (for example, *une femme fameuse* means, roughly, 'a woman of ill repute').

It is worth noting that differences between words in the area of expressive meaning are not simply a matter of whether an expression of a certain attitude or evaluation is inherently present or absent in the words in question. The same attitude or evaluation may be expressed in two words or utterances in widely differing degrees of forcefulness. Both *unkind* and *cruel*, for instance, are inherently expressive, showing the speaker's disapproval of someone's attitude. However, the element of disapproval in *cruel* is stronger than it is in *unkind*.

The meaning of a word or lexical unit can be both propositional and expressive, as in *whinge*, propositional only, as in *book*, or expressive only, for example *bloody* and various other swear words and emphasizers. Words which contribute solely to expressive meaning can be removed from an utterance without affecting its information content. Consider, for instance, the word *simply* in the following text:

> Whilst it stimulates your love of action, the MG also cares for your comfort. Hugging you on the bends with sports seats. Spoiling you with luxuries such as electric door mirrors, tinted glass and central locking. And entertaining you with a great music system as well as a *simply* masterful performance.
> (Today's Cars, *Austin Rover brochure; my emphasis*)

There are many highly expressive items in the above extract, but the word *simply* in the last sentence has a totally expressive function. Removing it would not alter the information content of the message but would, of course, tone its forcefulness down considerably.

2.2.2 Presupposed meaning

Presupposed meaning arises from co-occurrence restrictions, that is restrictions on what other words or expressions we expect to see before or after a particular lexical unit. These restrictions are of two types:

1. **Selectional restrictions**: these are a function of the propositional meaning of a word. We expect a human subject for the adjective *studious* and an inanimate

one for *geometrical*. Selectional restrictions are deliberately violated in the case of figurative language but are otherwise strictly observed.

2. **Collocational restrictions**: these are semantically arbitrary restrictions which do not follow logically from the propositional meaning of a word. For instance, laws are *broken* in English, but in Arabic they are 'contradicted'. In English, teeth are *brushed*, but in German and Italian they are 'polished', in Polish they are 'washed' and in Russian they are 'cleaned'. Because they are arbitrary, collocational restrictions tend to show more variation across languages than do selectional restrictions. They are discussed in more detail in Chapter 3, section 3.1.

The difference between selectional and collocational restrictions is not always as clear cut as the examples given above might imply. For example, in the following English translation of a German leaflet which accompanies Baumler products (men's suits), it is difficult to decide whether the awkwardness of the wording is a result of violating selectional or collocational restrictions:

> Dear Sir
> I am very pleased that you have selected one of our garments. You have made a wise choice, as suits, jackets and trousers eminating from our Company are amongst the finest products Europe has to offer.

Ideas, qualities and feelings typically *emanate* (misspelt as *eminate* in the above text) from a source, but objects such as *trousers* and *jackets* do not, at least not in English. The awkwardness of the wording can be explained in terms of selectional or collocational restrictions, depending on whether or not one sees the restriction involved as a function of the propositional meaning of *emanate.*

2.2.3 Evoked meaning

Evoked meaning arises from **dialect** and **register** variation. A **dialect** is a variety of language which has currency within a specific community or group of speakers. It may be classified on one of the following bases:

1. Geographical (e.g. a Scottish dialect, or American as opposed to British English: cf. the difference between *lift* and *elevator*);
2. Temporal (e.g. words and structures used by members of different age groups within a community, or words used at different periods in the history of a language: cf. *verily* and *really*);
3. Social (words and structures used by members of different social classes: cf. *scent* and *perfume*, *napkin* and *serviette*).

Register is a variety of language that a language user considers appropriate to a specific situation. Register variation arises from variations along the following parameters:

1. **Field** *of discourse*: this is an abstract term for 'what is going on' that is relevant to the speaker's choice of linguistic items. Different linguistic choices are made by different speakers depending on what kind of action other than the immediate action of speaking they see themselves as participating in. For example, linguistic choices will vary according to whether the speaker is taking part in a football match or discussing football; making love or discussing love; making a political speech or discussing politics; performing an operation or discussing medicine.

2. **Tenor** *of discourse*: an abstract term for the relationships between the people taking part in the discourse. Again, the language people use varies depending on such interpersonal relationships as mother/child, doctor/patient or superior/inferior in status. A patient is unlikely to use swear words in addressing a doctor and a mother is unlikely to start a request to her child with *I wonder if you could ...* Getting the tenor of discourse right in translation can be quite difficult. It depends on whether one sees a certain level of formality as 'right' from the perspective of the source culture or the target culture. For example, an American teenager may adopt a highly informal tenor with his or her parents by, among other things, using their first names instead of *Mum/Mother* and *Dad/Father*. This level of informality would be highly inappropriate in many other cultures. A translator has to choose between changing the tenor to suit the expectations of the target reader and transferring the informal tenor to give a flavour of the type of relationship that teenagers have with their parents in American society. What the translator opts for on any given occasion will of course depend on what he or she perceives to be the overall purpose of the translation.

3. **Mode** *of discourse*: an abstract term for the role that the language is playing (speech, essay, lecture, instructions) and for its medium of transmission (spoken, written).[3] Linguistic choices are influenced by these dimensions. For example, a word such as *re* is perfectly appropriate in a business letter or as part of the subject line in an email communication, but it is rarely, if ever, used in spoken English.

Different groups within each culture have different expectations about what kind of language is appropriate to particular situations. The amusement and embarrassment often engendered by children's remarks to perfect strangers testifies to this; more seriously, people unused to highly ritualized situations like committee meetings and job interviews may find it difficult to make their points, and may even be ridiculed because their language appears inappropriate to other participants. Translators would normally wish to ensure that their products do not meet with a similar reaction, that their translations match the register expectations of their prospective receivers, unless, of course, the purpose of the translation is to give a flavour of the source culture or, as advocated by some scholars such as Venuti (1995:20), to deliberately challenge the reader by deviating from target norms in order to 'stage an alien reading experience'.

Of all the types of lexical meaning explained above, the only one which relates to the truth or falsehood of an utterance and which can consequently be challenged by a reader or hearer is propositional meaning. All other types of lexical meaning contribute to the overall meaning of an utterance or a text in subtle and complex ways and are often much more difficult to analyse. To reiterate, it is rarely possible in practice to separate the various types of meaning in a word or utterance. Likewise, it is rarely possible to define even the basic propositional meaning of a word or utterance with absolute certainty. This is because the nature of language is such that, in the majority of cases, words have 'blurred edges'; their meanings are, to a large extent, negotiable and are only realized in specific contexts. The very notion of 'types of meaning' is theoretically suspect. Yet, I believe that the distinctions drawn above can be useful for the translator since one of the most difficult tasks that a translator is constantly faced with is that, notwithstanding the 'fuzziness' inherent in language, he or she must attempt to perceive the meanings of words and utterances as precisely as possible in order to render them into another language. Even a translator who sets out to challenge the reader's expectations cannot do so responsibly without first having understood the source text on its own terms. This requires translators to go beyond what the average reader has to do in order to reach an adequate understanding of a text.

2.3 THE PROBLEM OF NON-EQUIVALENCE

Based on the above discussion, we can now begin to outline some of the more common types of non-equivalence which often pose difficulties for the translator and some attested strategies for dealing with them. First, a word of warning. The choice of a suitable equivalent in a given context depends on a wide variety of factors. Some of these factors may be strictly linguistic (see, for instance, the discussion of collocations and idioms in Chapter 3). Other factors may be extra-linguistic (see Chapters 7 and 8). It is virtually impossible to offer absolute guidelines for dealing with the various types of non-equivalence which exist among languages. The most that can be done in this and the following chapters is to suggest strategies which may be used to deal with non-equivalence 'in some contexts'. The choice of a suitable equivalent will always depend not only on the linguistic system or systems being handled by the translator, but also on the way both the writer of the source text and the producer of the target text, that is the translator, choose to manipulate the linguistic systems in question; on the expectations, background knowledge and prejudices of readers within a specific temporal and spatial location; on translators' own understanding of their task, including their assessment of what is appropriate in a given situation; and on a range of restrictions that may operate in a given environment at a given point in time, including censorship[4] and various types of intervention by parties other than the translator, author and reader.

2.3.1 Semantic fields and lexical sets – the segmentation of experience

> The words of a language often reflect not so much the reality of the world, but the interests of the people who speak it.
>
> *(Palmer 1976:21)*

It is sometimes useful to view the vocabulary of a language as a set of words that refer to a series of conceptual fields. These fields reflect the divisions and sub-divisions 'imposed' by a given linguistic community on the continuum of experience.[5] In linguistics, the divisions are called **semantic fields**. Fields are abstract concepts. An example of a semantic field would be the field of SPEECH, or PLANTS or VEHICLES. A large number of semantic fields are common to all or most languages. Most, if not all, languages will have fields of DISTANCE, SIZE, SHAPE, TIME, EMOTION, BELIEFS, ACADEMIC SUBJECTS and NATURAL PHENOMENA. The actual words and expressions under each field are sometimes called **lexical sets**.[6] Each semantic field will normally have several sub-divisions or lexical sets under it, and each sub-division will have further sub-divisions and lexical sets. So, the field of SPEECH in English has a sub-division of VERBS OF SPEECH which includes general verbs such as *speak* and *say* and more specific ones such as *mumble*, *murmur*, *mutter* and *whisper*. It seems reasonable to suggest that the more detailed a semantic field is in a given language, the more different it is likely to be from related semantic fields in other languages. There generally tends to be more agreement among languages on the larger headings of semantic fields and less agreement as the sub-fields become more finely differentiated. Most languages are likely to have equivalents for the more general verbs of speech such as *say* and *speak*, but many may not have equivalents for the more specific ones. Languages understandably tend to make only those distinctions in meaning which are relevant to their particular environment, be it physical, historical, political, religious, cultural, economic, legal, technological, social or otherwise.

Before we discuss how an understanding of the nature and organization of semantic fields might be useful in translation, let me first spell out the limitations of semantic fields as a concept. The idea of semantic fields is inapplicable in many cases and is an over-simplification of the way language actually works. A large number of words in any language defy being classified under any heading (Carter and McCarthy 1988, Lehrer 1974). Words like *just*, *nevertheless* and *only*, to name but a few, cannot be easily filed under any particular semantic field. The idea of semantic fields works well enough for words and expressions which have fairly well-defined propositional meanings, but not for all, or even most of the words and expressions in a language.

Limitations aside, there are two main areas in which an understanding of semantic fields and lexical sets can be useful to a translator:

(a) appreciating the 'value' that a word has in a given system; and
(b) developing strategies for dealing with non-equivalence.

(a) Understanding the difference in the structure of semantic fields in the source and target languages allows a translator to assess the value of a given item in a lexical set. If you know what other items are available in a lexical set and how they contrast with the item chosen by a writer or speaker, you can appreciate the significance of the writer's or speaker's choice. You can understand not only what something is, but also what it is not. This is best illustrated by an example.

In the field of TEMPERATURE, English has four main divisions: *cold, cool, hot* and *warm.* This contrasts with Modern Arabic, which has four different divisions: *baarid* ('cold/cool'), *haar* ('hot: of the weather'), *saakhin* ('hot: of objects') and *daafi'* ('warm'). Note that, in contrast with English, Arabic (a) does not distinguish between *cold* and *cool*, and (b) distinguishes between the hotness of the weather and the hotness of other things. The fact that English does not make the latter distinction does not mean that you can always use *hot* to describe the temperature of something, even metaphorically (cf. *hot temper*, but not **hot feelings*). There are restrictions on the co-occurrence of words in any language (see discussion of collocation: Chapter 3, section 3.1). Now consider the following examples from Tai Hung-chao's *The Private Life of Chairman Mao*, one of the texts included in the Translational English Corpus:[7]

1. The nights were *cool,* but after an hour or two, I was soaked with perspiration and my body ached all over.
2. He was afraid of the Moscow *cold,* and nothing I said could convince him that the buildings would be so well heated that he would never feel the weather.

Bearing in mind the differences in the structure of the English and Arabic fields, one can appreciate, on the one hand, the difference in meaning between *cold* and *cool* in the above examples and, on the other, the potential difficulty in making such a distinction clear when translating into Arabic.

(b) Semantic fields are arranged hierarchically, going from the more general to the more specific. The general word is usually referred to as **superordinate** and the specific word as **hyponym**. In the field of VEHICLES, *vehicle* is a superordinate and *bus, car, truck, coach* and so on are all hyponyms of *vehicle*. It stands to reason that any propositional meaning carried by a superordinate or general word is, by necessity, part of the meaning of each of its hyponyms, but not vice versa. If something is a bus, then it must be a vehicle, but not the other way round. We can sometimes manipulate this feature of semantic fields when we are faced with semantic gaps in the target language. Translators often deal with semantic gaps by modifying a superordinate word or by means of circumlocutions based on modifying superordinates. More on this in the following section.

To sum up, while not always straightforward or applicable, the notion of semantic fields can provide the translator with useful strategies for dealing with non-equivalence in some contexts. It is also useful in heightening our awareness of similarities and differences between any two languages and of the significance of any choice made by a speaker or writer in a given context. One important thing to bear in mind when dealing with semantic fields is that they are not fixed. Semantic fields are always changing, with new words and expressions being introduced into the language and others being dropped as they become less relevant to the needs of a linguistic community.

For a more extensive discussion of semantic fields, see Lehrer (1974).

2.3.2 Non-equivalence at word level and some common strategies for dealing with it

Non-equivalence at word level means that the target language has no direct equivalent for a word which occurs in the source text. The type and level of difficulty posed can vary tremendously depending on the nature of non-equivalence. Different kinds of non-equivalence require different strategies, some very straightforward, others more involved and difficult to handle. Since, in addition to the nature of non-equivalence, the context and purpose of translation will often rule out some strategies and favour others, I will keep the discussion of types of non-equivalence separate from the discussion of strategies used by professional translators. It is neither possible nor helpful to attempt to relate specific types of non-equivalence to specific strategies, but I will comment on the advantages or disadvantages of certain strategies wherever possible.

2.3.2.1 Common problems of non-equivalence

The following are some common types of non-equivalence at word level, with examples from various languages:

(a) Culture-specific concepts

The source-language word may express a concept which is totally unknown in the target culture. The concept in question may be abstract or concrete; it may relate to a religious belief, a social custom or even a type of food. Such concepts are often referred to as 'culture-specific'. An example of an abstract English concept which is notoriously difficult to translate into other languages is that expressed by the word *privacy*. This is a very 'English' concept which is rarely understood by people from other cultures. *Speaker* (of the House of Commons) has no equivalent in languages such as Russian, Chinese and Arabic, among others. It is often translated into Russian as 'Chairman', which does not reflect the role of the Speaker of the House of Commons as an independent person who maintains authority and order in Parliament. An example of a concrete concept is *airing cupboard* in English which, again, is unknown to speakers of most languages.

(b) The source-language concept is not lexicalized in the target language

The source-language word may express a concept which is known in the target culture but simply not lexicalized, that is not 'allocated' a target-language word to express it. The word *savoury* has no equivalent in many languages, although it expresses a concept which is easy to understand. The adjective *standard* (meaning 'ordinary, not extra', as in *standard range of products*) also expresses a concept which is very accessible and readily understood by most people, yet Arabic has no equivalent for it. *Landslide* has no ready equivalent in many languages, although it simply means 'overwhelming majority'.

(c) The source-language word is semantically complex

The source-language word may be semantically complex. This is a fairly common problem in translation. Words do not have to be morphologically complex to be semantically complex (Bolinger and Sears 1968). In other words, a single word which consists of a single morpheme can sometimes express a more complex set of meanings than a whole sentence. Languages automatically develop very concise forms for referring to complex concepts if the concepts become important enough to be talked about often. Bolinger and Sears suggest that 'If we should ever need to talk regularly and frequently about independently operated sawmills from which striking workers are locked out on Thursday when the temperature is between 500° and 600°F, we would find a concise way to do it' (*ibid.*:114). We do not usually realize how semantically complex a word is until we have to translate it into a language which does not have an equivalent for it. An example of such a semantically complex word is *arruação*, a Brazilian word which means 'clearing the ground under coffee trees of rubbish and piling it in the middle of the row in order to aid in the recovery of beans dropped during harvesting' (*ITI News* 1988:57).[8]

(d) The source and target languages make different distinctions in meaning

The target language may make more or fewer distinctions in meaning than the source language. What one language regards as an important distinction in meaning another language may not perceive as relevant. For example, Indonesian makes a distinction between going out in the rain without the knowledge that it is raining (*kehujanan*) and going out in the rain with the knowledge that it is raining (*hujan-hujanan*). English does not make this distinction, with the result that if an English text referred to going out in the rain, the Indonesian translator may find it difficult to choose the right equivalent, unless the context makes it clear whether or not the person in question knew that it was raining.

(e) The target language lacks a superordinate

The target language may have specific words (hyponyms) but no general word (superordinate) to head the semantic field. Russian has no ready equivalent for *facilities*, meaning 'any equipment, building, services, etc. that are provided for a particular activity or purpose'.[9] It does, however, have several specific words and expressions which can be thought of as types of facilities, for example *sredstva peredvizheniya* ('means of transport'), *naem* ('loan'), *neobkhodimye pomeshcheniia* ('essential accommodation') and *neobkhodimoe oborudovanie* ('essential equipment'). Brennan (1999) discusses a range of interesting examples that demonstrate this type of difficulty in interpreting between English and British Sign Language (BSL):

> An ongoing problem for interpreters is that the speaker often uses an English generic term for which BSL has no direct equivalent: the opposite problem is that BSL is frequently much more specific than English. Some examples of generic English terms ... include: *touch*, *hit*, *murder*, *assault*, *hold*. While the English word *hit* does not specify **how** someone was hit (for example with the flat hand, the fist, the back of the hand, etc.) or **where** someone was hit (on the face, head, legs, back, etc.), a signed version of *hit* would typically be quite specific in relation to how and where.
>
> *(233-234; emphasis in original)*

(f) The target language lacks a specific term (hyponym)

More commonly, languages tend to have general words (superordinates) but lack specific ones (hyponyms), since each language makes only those distinctions in meaning which seem relevant to its particular environment. There are endless examples of this type of non-equivalence. English has many hyponyms under *article* for which it is difficult to find precise equivalents in other languages, for example *feature*, *survey*, *report*, *critique*, *commentary*, *review* and many more. Under *house*, English again has a variety of hyponyms which have no equivalents in many languages, for example *bungalow*, *cottage*, *croft*, *chalet*, *lodge*, *hut*, *mansion*, *manor*, *villa* and *hall*. Under *jump* we find more specific verbs such as *leap*, *vault*, *spring*, *bounce*, *dive*, *clear*, *plunge* and *plummet*.

(g) Differences in physical or interpersonal perspective

Physical perspective may be of more importance in one language than it is in another. Physical perspective has to do with where things or people are in relation to one another or to a place, as expressed in pairs of words such as *come/go*, *take/bring*, *arrive/depart* and so on. Perspective may also include the relationship between participants in the discourse (tenor). For example, Japanese has six equivalents for *give*, depending on who gives to whom: *yaru*, *ageru*, *morau*, *kureru*, *itadaku* and *kudasaru* (McCreary 1986).

(h) Differences in expressive meaning

There may be a target-language word which has the same propositional meaning as the source-language word, but it may have a different expressive meaning. The difference may be considerable or it may be subtle but important enough to pose a translation problem in a given context. It is usually easier to add expressive meaning than to subtract it. In other words, if the target-language equivalent is neutral compared to the source-language item, the translator can sometimes add the evaluative element by means of a modifier or adverb if necessary, or by building it in somewhere else in the text. So, it may be possible, for instance, in some contexts to render the English verb *batter* (as in child/wife battering) by the more neutral Japanese verb *tataku*, meaning 'to beat', plus an equivalent modifier such as 'savagely' or 'ruthlessly'. Differences in expressive meaning are usually more difficult to handle when the target-language equivalent is more emotionally loaded than the source-language item. This is often the case with items which relate to sensitive issues such as religion, politics and sex. Words like *homosexuality* and *homosexual* provide good examples. *Homosexuality* is not an inherently pejorative word in English, although it is often used in this way. On the other hand, the traditional equivalent expression in Arabic, *shithuth jinsi* (literally: 'sexual perversion'), is inherently more pejorative and would be quite difficult to use in a neutral context without suggesting strong disapproval.[10]

(i) Differences in form

There is often no equivalent in the target language for a particular form in the source text. Certain suffixes and prefixes which convey propositional and other types of meaning in English often have no direct equivalents in other languages. English has many couplets such as *employer/employee*, *trainer/trainee* and *payer/payee*. It also makes frequent use of suffixes such as *-ish* (e.g. *boyish, hellish, greenish*) and *-able* (e.g. *conceivable, retrievable, drinkable*). Arabic, for instance, has no ready mechanism for producing such forms and so they are often replaced by an appropriate paraphrase, depending on the meaning they convey (e.g. *retrievable* as 'can be retrieved' and *drinkable* as 'suitable for drinking'). Affixes which contribute to expressive or evoked meaning, for instance by creating buzz words such as *washateria, carpeteria* and *groceteria* (Bolinger and Sears 1968), and those which convey expressive meaning, such as *journalese, translationese* and *legalese* (the *-ese* suffix usually suggests disapproval of a muddled or stilted form of writing), are more difficult to translate by means of a paraphrase. It is relatively easy to paraphrase propositional meaning, but other types of meaning cannot always be spelt out in a translation. Their subtle contribution to the overall meaning of the text is either lost altogether or recovered elsewhere by means of compensatory techniques.[11]

It is important for translators to understand the contribution that affixes make to the meaning of words and expressions, especially since such affixes are often used creatively in English to coin new words for various reasons, such as filling temporary semantic gaps in the language and creating humour. Their contribution is also important in the area of terminology and standardization. Examples of creative use of affixes can often be found in advertisements and other types of promotional literature. One advertisement for the chocolate Toblerone which appeared in many outlets in the mid 1990s showed three chocolate triangles against a larger image of the three pyramids in Egypt, with the caption 'Ancient Tobleronism?' appearing next to the pyramids. Here, the *-ism* ending evokes spirituality (as in Buddh*ism*) and, possibly, tradition – the kind we associate with established schools of thought that have large numbers of loyal followers, such as Marx*ism*, Existential*ism* and so on.

Eating Toblerone is thus likened to a spiritual experience; at the same time, the making of the chocolate, as well as eating it, are presented as part of a tradition, with a long and stable history.

(j) Differences in frequency and purpose of using specific forms

Even when a particular form does have a ready equivalent in the target language, there may be a difference in the frequency with which it is used or the purpose for which it is used. Thus, English uses the continuous -*ing* form for binding clauses much more frequently than other languages which have equivalents for it, for example German and the Scandinavian languages. Consequently, rendering every -*ing* form in an English source text with an equivalent -*ing* form in a German, Danish or Swedish target text would result in stilted, unnatural style.

(k) The use of loan words in the source text

The use of loan words in the source text poses a special problem in translation. Quite apart from their respective propositional meaning, loan words such as *au fait*, *chic*, *Auf Wiedershen* and *alfresco* in English are often used for their prestige value, because they can add an air of sophistication to the text or its subject matter. Japanese in particular tends to use loan words widely, 'just for effect, for example because they sound beautiful or look elegant' (Jüngst 2008:61). This effect is often lost in translation, both into the language from which the loan word is originally borrowed and into other languages, where it is not always possible to find a loan word with the same meaning or associations. *Dilettante* is a loan word in English, Russian and Japanese, but Arabic has no equivalent loan word. This means that only the propositional meaning of *dilettante* can be rendered into Arabic; its stylistic effect would almost certainly have to be sacrificed.

Loan words also pose another problem for the unwary translator, namely the problem of **false friends**, or **faux amis** as they are often called.[12] **False friends** are words or expressions which have the same form in two or more languages but convey different meanings. They are often associated with historically or culturally related languages such as English, French, Spanish and German, but in fact false friends also abound among totally unrelated languages such as English, Japanese and Russian. Mayoral Asensio (2003:95–96) discusses several interesting examples of false friends (which he refers to as 'deceptive cognates') in English and Spanish in the context of translating official documents, including *college/colegio* and *graduate/graduado*.

Once a word or expression is borrowed into a language, we cannot predict or control its development or the additional meanings it might or might not take on. Some false friends are easy to spot because the difference in their meanings is so great that only a very inexperienced translator is likely to be unaware of it. The average Japanese translator is not likely to confuse an English *feminist* with a Japanese *feminist* (*feminist* in Japanese is usually used to describe a man who is excessively soft with women). An inexperienced French or German translator may, however, confuse English *sensible* with German *sensibel* (meaning 'sensitive'), or English *sympathetic* with French *sympathique* (meaning 'nice/likeable').

The above are some of the more common examples of non-equivalence among languages and the problems they pose for translators. In dealing with any kind of non-equivalence, it is important first of all to assess its significance and implications in a given context. Not every instance of non-equivalence you encounter is going to be significant. It is neither possible nor desirable to reproduce every aspect of meaning for every word in a source text. We have to try, as much as possible, to convey the meaning of key words which are focal to the understanding and development of a text, but we cannot and should not distract the reader by looking at every word in isolation and attempting to present him or her with a full linguistic account of its meaning.

2.3.2.2 Strategies used by professional translators

With the above proviso in mind, we can now look at examples of strategies used by professional translators for dealing with various types of non-equivalence. In each example, the source-language word which represents a translation problem is underlined. The strategy used by the translator is highlighted in bold in both the original translation and the back-translated version. Only the strategies used for dealing with non-equivalence at word level will be commented on. Other strategies and differences between the source and target texts are dealt with in subsequent chapters.

(a) Translation by a more general word (superordinate)

This is one of the commonest strategies for dealing with many types of non-equivalence, particularly in the area of propositional meaning. It works equally well in most, if not all, languages, since the hierarchical structure of semantic fields is not language-specific.

Example A
Source text (*Kolestral Super* – leaflet accompanying a hair-conditioning product):

> The rich and creamy KOLESTRAL-SUPER is easy to <u>apply</u> and has a pleasant fragrance.

Target text (Arabic):

> كولسترال سوبر غنى ومكثف فى تركيبته التى تمنح مستحضراً يشبه الكريما، مما يجعله فى
> منتهى السهولة لوضعه على الشعر. . .

> Kolestral super is rich and concentrated in its make-up which gives a product that resembles cream, making it extremely easy to **put** on the hair.

Example B
Source text (*Kolestral Super*):

> Shampoo the hair with a mild WELLA-SHAMPOO and lightly towel dry.

Target text 1 (Spanish):

> **Lavar** el cabello con un champú suave de WELLA y frotar ligera- mente con una toalla.

> **Wash** hair with a mild WELLA shampoo and rub lightly with a towel.

Target text 2 (Arabic):

> يغسل الشعر بشامبو من "ويللا" على أن يكون من نوع الشامبو الملطف . . .

> The hair is **washed** with 'wella' shampoo, provided that it is a mild shampoo ...

Example C
Source text (*A Brief History of Time* – Hawking 1988:1):

> A well-known scientist (some say it was Bertrand Russell) once gave a public lecture on astronomy. He described how the earth orbits around the sun and how the sun, in turn, orbits around the center of a vast collection of stars called our galaxy.

Target text (Spanish):

> Un conocido científico (algunos dicen que fue Bertrand Russell) daba una vez una conferencia sobre astronomía. En ella describía cómo la Tierra **giraba** alrededor del Sol y cómo éste, a su vez, **giraba** alrededor del centro de una vasta colección de estrellas concida como nuestra galaxia.

> A well-known scientist (some say that it was Bertrand Russell) once gave a lecture on astronomy. In it he described how the Earth **revolved** around the Sun and how the latter in its turn **revolved** around the centre of a vast collection of stars known as our galaxy.

Example D
Source text (*China's Panda Reserves* – World Wide Fund for Nature text which accompanied a slide show):

> Today there may be no more than 1000 giant pandas left in the wild, restricted to a few mountain <u>strongholds</u> in the Chinese provinces of Sichuan, Shaanxi and Gansu.

Target text (Chinese):

> 今天，仍处于野生状态的大熊猫可能只有一千只，仅限于中国的四川、陕西和甘肃省内的一些山区。

> Today there may be only 1000 big pandas which still remain in the wild state, restricted to certain mountain **areas** in China's Sichuan, Shaanxi and Gansu.

The above examples illustrate the use of a general word (superordinate) to overcome a relative lack of specificity in the target language compared to the source language. 'Shampooing' can be seen as a type of 'washing' since it is more restricted in use: you can wash lots of things but you can only shampoo hair. Similarly, 'orbiting' is a type of 'revolving' because, unlike 'revolving', it only applies to a smaller object revolving around a larger one in space. What the translators of the above extracts have done is go up a level in a given semantic field to find a more general word that covers the core propositional meaning of the missing hyponym in the target language.

(b) Translation by a more neutral/less expressive word

Example A
Source text: (*Morgan Matroc* – ceramics company brochure):

> Today people are aware that modern ceramic materials offer unrivalled properties for many of our most demanding industrial applications. So is this brochure necessary; isn't the ceramic market already over-bombarded with technical literature; why should Matroc add more?
>
> Because someone <u>mumbles,</u> 'Our competitors do it.' But why should we imitate our competitors when Matroc probably supplies a greater range of ceramic materials for more applications than any other manufacturer.

Target text: (Italian):

Qualcuno **suggerisce**: 'i nostri concorrenti lo fanno.'

Someone **suggests**: 'Our competitors do it.'

There is a noticeable difference in the expressive meaning of *mumble* and its nearest Italian equivalent, *mugugnare.* The English verb *mumble* suggests confusion, disorientation or embarrassment, as can be seen in the following examples:[13]

'Sorry,' she managed to <u>mumble</u> incoherently.
I was doing a three-point-turn manoeuvre to get us back onto the road when he woke up, lifted his hat and <u>mumbled</u>: 'Where are we?'
'I didn't mean to disturb you,' I <u>mumbled</u> apologetically.
'I'm in your hands,' I <u>mumbled</u> and didn't quite know why I said it.
Presented with a hard question, she'll blush, stare at her feet and finally <u>mumble</u> her answer.

The Italian near equivalent, *mugugnare*, on the other hand, tends to suggest dissatisfaction rather than embarrassment or confusion. Possibly to avoid conveying the wrong expressive meaning, the Italian translator opted for a more general word, *suggerisce* ('suggest').

Example B
Source text (*A Study of Shamanistic Practices in Japan* – Blacker 1975:315):

The shamanic practices we have investigated are rightly seen as an <u>archaic</u> mysticism.

Target text (Japanese)

我々が探究してきたシャーマン的行為は、古代の神秘主義として、考察されるべきものであろう。

The shamanic behaviour which we have been researching should rightly be considered as **ancient** mysticism.

The translator could have used a Japanese phrase which means, roughly, 'behind the times' and which would have been closer to both the propositional and expressive meanings of *archaic*. This, however, would have been too direct, too openly disapproving by Japanese standards (Haruko Uryu, personal communication). The expressive meaning of *archaic* is lost in the translation.

Example C
Source text (*China's Panda Reserves*):

> Many of the species growing wild here are familiar to us as plants cultivated in European gardens – species like this <u>exotic</u> lily.

Target text (Chinese):

> 这里野生的许多种类我们很熟悉，是欧洲园林内种植的种类——像这一奇异的百合花等种类。

> We are very familiar with many varieties of the wild life here, they are the kind grown in European gardens – varieties like this **strange unique** lily flower.

Exotic has no equivalent in Chinese and other oriental languages. It is a word used by westerners to refer to unusual, interesting things which come from a distant country such as China. The orient does not have a concept of what is *exotic* in this sense and the expressive meaning of the word is therefore lost in translation.

Example D
Source text (*China's Panda Reserves*):

> The panda is something of a zoological <u>mystery</u>.

Target text (Chinese):

> 熊猫可以被称为动物学里的一个谜。

> The panda may be called a **riddle** in zoology.

There is an equivalent for *mystery* in Chinese, but it is mostly associated with religion. The translator felt that it would be wrong to use it in a zoological context.[14]

Example E
Source text (*China's Panda Reserves*):

   (i)   The panda's mountain <u>home</u> is wet and lush,
   (ii) The panda's mountain <u>home</u> is rich in plant life ….

Target text (Chinese):

熊猫的山区栖息地是潮湿、茂盛的。
熊猫的山区定居地有着丰富的植物种类，有着欧洲园林所珍视的
许多树木、灌木和草本植物的种类。

The mountain **habitat** of the panda is wet and lush,
The mountain **settlements** of the panda have rich varieties of plants

---

Home has no direct equivalent in Chinese; in fact, it is difficult to translate into many languages. In the examples above, it is replaced by Chinese near-equivalents which are both less expressive and more formal.

It is sometimes possible to retain expressive meaning by adding a modifier, as in the following example.

Example F
Source text (Soldati, 'I passi sulla neve'):[15]

Ma già, oltre i tetti carichi di neve, a non più di duecento metri dalla parte di Torino, si vedevano altissimi, geometrici, tutti quadrettati in mille finestre luminose e balconcini, i primi palazzi condominiali, case a riscatto, <u>falansteri</u> di operai e di impiegati.

Target text (English: 'Footsteps in the Snow'):

But already, beyond the snow-laden roofs, and no more than two hundred metres in the direction of Turin, there were to be seen towering, geometrical, chequered by a thousand lighted windows and balconies, the first joint-owned buildings, houses under mortgage, workers' and clerks' **ugly** blocks of flats.

The adjective 'ugly' does not actually appear in the source text. The following translator's footnote explains why *ugly* was added in the target text:

Falansteri: communal dwellings which formed part of an ideal cooperative life preached by the French philosopher and socialist writer Charles Fourier (1772–1837). In Italian the word has a pejorative connotation.

(c) Translation by cultural substitution

This strategy involves replacing a culture-specific[16] item or expression with a target-language item which does not have the same propositional meaning but is likely to have a similar impact on the target reader, for instance by evoking a similar context in the target culture. The main advantage of using this strategy is that it gives the reader a concept with which he or she can identify, something familiar and appealing. On an individual level, the translator's decision to use this strategy will largely depend on (a) how much licence is given to him or her by those who commission the translation; (b) the purpose of the translation; and (c) the translator's own judgement of the desirability or otherwise of obscuring the cultural specificity of the source text. On a more general level, the decision will also reflect, to some extent, the norms of translation prevailing in a given community.[17] Tolerance of strategies that involve significant departure from the propositional meaning of the text varies considerably across different communities and temporal locations.[18]

Example A
Source text (*A Brief History of Time* – Hawking 1988:1):

A well-known scientist (some say it was Bertrand Russell) once gave a public lecture on astronomy. He described how the earth orbits around the sun and how the sun, in turn, orbits around the center of a vast collection of stars called our galaxy. At the end of the lecture, a little old lady at the back of the room got up and said: 'What you have told us is rubbish. The world is really a flat plate supported on the back of a giant tortoise.' The scientist gave a superior smile before replying, 'What is the tortoise standing on?' 'You're very clever, young man, very clever,' said the old lady. 'But it's turtles all the way down!'

Target text (Greek):

Η Αλίκη στη Χώρα των Θαυμάτων έδινε κάποτε μία διάλεξη για την αστρονομία. Έλεγε ότι η Γη είναι ένας σφαιρικός πλανήτης του ηλιακού συστήματος που κινείται γύρω από το κέντρο του, τον Ήλιο, και ότι ο Ήλιος είναι ένα άστρο που, με τη σειρά του, κινείται γύρω από το κέντρο του αστρικού συστήματος, που ονομάζουμε Γαλαξία. Στο τέλος της διάλεξης, **η Ντάμα** την κοίταξε θυμωμένη με επιτιμητικό ύφος. «Αυτά που λες είναι ανοησίες. Η Γη δεν είναι **παρά ένα μεγάλο Τραπουλόχαρτο**.

Είναι λοιπόν επίπεδη σαν όλα **τα Τραπουλόχαρτα.**» της είπε, και στράφηκε περήφανα προς τα μέλη της συνοδείας της, που έδειχναν ικανοποιημένα από την εξήγησή της. **Η Αλίκη** χαμογέλασε υπεροπτικά. «Και σε τι στηρίζεται αυτό **το Τραπουλόχαρτο;**» ρώτησε με ειρωνεία. **Η Ντάμα** δεν έδειξε να αιφνιδιάζεται. «Είσαι έξυπνη, πολύ έξυπνη», απάντησε. «Μάθε λοιπόν **μικρή μου** πως αυτό **το Τραπουλόχαρτο** στηρίζεται σε ένα άλλο, και εκείνο το άλλο σε ένα άλλο άλλο, και εκείνο το άλλο άλλο σε ένα άλλο άλλο άλλο…». Σταμάτησε λαχανιασμένη. «Το Σύμπαν δεν είναι παρά **μια Μεγάλη Τράπουλα**», τσίριξε.

Alice in Wonderland was once giving a lecture about astronomy. She said that the earth is a spherical planet in the solar system which orbits around its centre the sun, and that the sun is a star which in turn orbits around the centre of the star system which we call the Galaxy. At the end of the lecture **the Queen** looked at her angrily and disapprovingly. 'What you say is nonsense. The earth is just **a giant playing card**, so it's flat like all **playing cards**,' she said, and turned triumphantly to the members of her retinue, who seemed clearly satisfied by her explanation. **Alice** smiled a superior smile, 'And what is this **playing card** supported on?' she asked with irony. **The Queen** did not seem put out, 'You are clever, very clever,' she replied, 'so let me tell you, **young lady**, that this **playing card** is supported on another, and the other on another other, and the other other on another other other …' She stopped, out of breath, 'The Universe is nothing but a **great big pack of cards**,' she shrieked.

The above example illustrates a very interesting use of the strategy of cultural substitution. It is the opening passage in Stephen Hawking's popular book *A Brief History of Time from the Big Bang to Black Holes* (1988). Like Hawking in the original text, the Greek translator sets out to capture the undivided attention of the reader immediately. He decides that this is best achieved by introducing the reader to characters which are familiar and interesting rather than to foreign characters and stereotypes with which the reader may not identify. Alice in Wonderland is apparently well known in Greece; the average educated Greek is clearly expected to know the story and to be familiar with the characters of Alice and the Queen, as well as the playing-card characters. For anyone who has read the story, the association with Alice recalls an image of a topsy-turvy paradoxical world, which is particularly apposite in this context. *A little old lady at the back of the room* is an English stereotype of someone who is endearing but tends to get the wrong end of the stick, that is, to misunderstand what is being said. This stereotype image is not likely to be accessible to people from other cultures. It is replaced by 'the Queen', and this is then followed by a series of interesting substitutions, such as 'giant playing card' for *flat plate* and 'a great big pack of cards' for *turtles all the way down*.

Example B
Source text (*The Patrick Collection* – a leaflet produced by a privately owned museum of classic cars):

> The Patrick Collection has restaurant facilities to suit every taste – from the discerning gourmet, to the <u>Cream Tea</u> expert.

Target text (Italian):

> ... di soddisfare tutti i gusti: da quelli del gastronomo esigente a quelli dell'esperto di **pasticceria**.

> ... to satisfy all tastes: from those of the demanding gastronomist to those of the expert in **pastry**.

In Britain, *cream tea* is 'an afternoon meal consisting of tea to drink and scones with jam and clotted cream to eat. It can also include sandwiches and cakes'.[19] *Cream tea* has no equivalent in other cultures. The Italian translator replaced it with 'pastry', which does not have the same meaning (for one thing, *cream tea* is a meal in Britain, whereas 'pastry' is only a type of food). However, 'pastry' is familiar to the Italian reader and therefore provides a good cultural substitute.

Example C
Source text (Italian – Gadda, 'La cenere delle battaglie'):[20]

> Poi, siccome la serva di due piani sotto la sfringuellava al telefono coll'innamorato, assenti i padroni, si imbizzì: prese a pestare i piedi sacripantando '<u>porca, porca, porca, porca</u> ...': finché la non ismise, che non fu molto presto.

Target text (English: 'The Ash of Battles Past'):

> Then, because the servant-girl two floors down was chattering at the telephone with her young man, her employers being away, he lost his temper: and began to stamp his feet, bellowing '**Bitch, bitch, bitch** ...' until she gave up, which was not very soon.

Porca is literally the female of *swine.* A translator's footnote explains that the Italian word 'when applied to a woman, ... indicates unchastity, harlotry' (Trevelyan 1965:196). *Bitch* represents a straightforward cultural substitute. Although the literal meanings of *porca* and *bitch* are different, both items are used chiefly for their expressive value. Their literal meanings are not relevant in this context.

An interesting example of cultural substitution in the translation of comics is discussed in Celotti (2008:40–41). In one panel from Didier Tronchet's comic series *Jean-Claude Tergal* (Figure 1), the translator adapts a sign above the door of a bar which reads *Chez Raoul* (literally 'At Raoul', or 'Raoul's' – Raoul being a familiar French name), to read *Bar Juventus* in the Italian translation (*Juventus* is the name of a well-known Italian football club).

Figure 1 Panel from Tronchet's *Jean-Claude Tergal* and its Italian translation, *Domenico Tergazzi*

(d) Translation using a loan word or loan word plus explanation

This strategy is particularly common in dealing with culture-specific items, modern concepts and buzz words. Following the loan word with an explanation is very useful when the word in question is repeated several times in the text. Once explained, the loan word can then be used on its own; the reader can understand it and is not distracted by further lengthy explanations.

Example A
Source text (*The Patrick Collection*):

> The Patrick Collection has restaurant facilities to suit every taste – from the discerning gourmet, to the <u>Cream Tea</u> expert.

Target text (German):

> … vom anspruchsvollen Feinschmecker bis zum **'Cream-Tea'- Experten**.

> … from demanding gourmets to **'Cream-Tea'-experts**.

The Patrick Collection leaflet is translated for the benefit of tourists visiting this privately owned motor museum in the United Kingdom. As mentioned above, the English cream-tea custom is culture-specific; Germans have coffee and cakes. The German translator could have used the strategy of cultural substitution. 'Coffee and cakes' could have replaced *cream tea* (cf. the Italian version of the same text in (c) above), but the translator seems to have decided that the kind of educated German who has access to this type of literature will know of the English cream-tea custom. This also explains the use of the loan word on its own, without an explanation. Note that the transferred English expression is, as is often the case with loan words in translation, in inverted commas. In addition, compounding is much more common in German than it is in English. 'Tea expert' would normally be one word in German (as would, presumably, 'cream tea expert' if such a person existed). The use of a loan word has restricted the German translator, however, since combining a loan word, *cream tea*, with a German word, the equivalent of 'experts', would confuse the reader. Likewise, combining two English words, *cream* and *tea,* would conflict with normal English usage. The use of hyphens is a compromise between the norms of the two languages.

Compare the strategies used by the German and Italian translators with those used by the French and Japanese translators of the same text:

Target text (French):

> … – de la table gourmande au **Salon de Thé à l'anglaise**.

> … from the gourmet table to the **English style tea salon**.

Target text (Japanese):

> パトリック・コレクションは、認識の鋭いグルメからクリーム
> 菓子とお茶の専門店に至るまであらゆる好みに合ったレストラ
> ン施設を有しています。

> … from the gourmet with keen recognition to a shop specializing in **cream cakes and tea**.

Example B
Source text (*A Study of Shamanistic Practices in Japan* – Blacker 1975:315):

> The <u>shamanic</u> practices we have investigated are rightly seen as an archaic mysticism.

Target text (Japanese):

> 我々が探究してきたシャーマン的行為は、古代の神秘主義とし
> て、考察されるべきものであろう。

> The **shamanic** behaviour which we have been researching should rightly be considered as ancient mysticism.

Shaman is a technical word used in religious studies to refer to a priest or a priest doctor among the northern tribes of Asia. It has no ready equivalent in Japanese. The equivalent used in the translation is made up of *shaman* as a loan word, written in katakana script (the script commonly used to transcribe foreign words into Japanese) plus a Japanese suffix which means 'like' to replace the *-ic* ending in English. The Japanese suffix is written in the Kanji script (the Chinese system used to transcribe ordinary Japanese).

Example C
Source text (*Kolestral Super*):

> For maximum effect, cover the hair with a plastic <u>cap</u> or towel.

Target text (Arabic):

للحصول على فعالية مطلقة، يُغطى الشعر بواسطة "كاب" أى قبعة بلاستيكية تُغطى الشعر، أو بواسطة منشفة.

For obtaining maximum effectiveness, the hair is covered by means of a **'cap', that is a plastic hat which covers the hair**, or by means of a towel.

Note that the explanation which follows the loan word is based on modifying a superordinate/general word, namely the equivalent of 'hat'. Note also the use of inverted commas as in the German translation quoted above (from *The Patrick Collection*).

Example D
Source text (*The Patrick Collection*):

Morning coffee and traditional cream teas are served in the conservatory.

Target text (Japanese):

朝のコーヒーと伝統的午後のお茶とクリーム菓子類は来んサーヴァトリー（温室）で楽しめます。

Morning coffee and traditional afternoon tea and cream cakes can be enjoyed in the **conservatory (green house)**.

Example E
Source text (*The Patrick Collection*):

A UNIQUE MOTOR MUSEUM
TERRACED GARDENS AND GOURMET
RESTAURANT COMBINE TO MAKE

THE ULTIMATE ATTRACTION

Target text (back-translated from Japanese):[21]

Unique Motor Museum
Terraced Gardens **Gourmet Restaurant**
are gathered

THE ULTIMATE ATTRACTION

The underlined words in the source text in both examples (D and E) are used as loan words in the Japanese text, not because they have no equivalents in Japanese but because they sound more modern, smart, high class. The emphasis here is on expressive and evoked rather than propositional meaning.

Eirlys Davies (2003:77) discusses an interesting example from the French translation of *Harry Potter and the Philosopher's Stone*, by Jean-François Ménard, where the translator overcomes the lack of equivalent for *prefect* in French by using a cognate word (*préfet*) and integrating an explanation of it in the dialogue rather than placing it in a footnote. The English back-translation that follows the French text is provided by Davies:

> **Préfet**? Qu'est-ce que c'est que ça ? demanda Harry.
> – C'est un élève chargé de maintenir la discipline, répondit Ron. Une sorte de pion … Tu ne savais pas ça?
> – Je ne suis pas beaucoup sorti de chez moi, confessa Harry.

> 'A **prefect**? What's that?' asked Harry. 'It's a pupil whose job is to keep order', replied Ron. 'A kind of "pion" (member of staff at a French school whose role is to keep order). Didn't you know that?' 'I haven't been around much', confessed Harry.

As with the strategy of cultural substitution, the freedom with which translators use loan words will often depend on the norms of translation prevailing in their societies. Arabic and French, for instance, are much less tolerant of the use of loan words in formal writing than Japanese, which may explain the preference for the use of a cognate rather than a loan word in the French translation above.

(e) Translation by paraphrase using a related word

This strategy tends to be used when the concept expressed by the source item is lexicalized in the target language but in a different form, and when the frequency with which a certain form is used in the source text is significantly higher than would be natural in the target language (see section on common problems of non-equivalence above, items (i) and (j)).

Example A
Source text (*The Patrick Collection*):

> Hot and cold food and drinks can be found in the Hornet's Nest, <u>overlooking</u> the Alexick Hall.

Target text (German):

> Im Hornet's Nest, **das** die Alexick-Halle **überblickt**, bekommen Sie warme und kalte Speisen und Getränke.

> In the Hornet's Nest, **which overlooks** the Alexick-Hall, you can have hot and cold meals and drinks.

Example B
Source text (*Kolestral Super*):

> The rich and <u>creamy</u> KOLESTRAL-SUPER is easy to apply and has a pleasant fragrance.

Target text (Arabic):

> كولسترال سوبر غنى ومكثف فى تركيبته التى تمنح مستحضراً يشبه الكريما . . .

> Kolestral-super is rich and concentrated in its make-up which gives a product **that resembles cream** …

The paraphrase in the Arabic text uses comparison, a strategy which can be used to deal with other types of non-equivalence.

Example C
Source text (*China's Panda Reserves*):

> There is strong evidence, however, that giant pandas are <u>related</u> to the bears.

Target text (Chinese):

但是，也有较强的证据表明大熊猫与熊有亲属关系。这一亚洲黑熊分享熊猫在中国境内的活动区域。

But there is rather strong evidence that shows that big pandas **have a kinship relation** with the bears.

Example D
Source text (*The Patrick Collection*):

As well as our enviable location, other facilities include an excellent Conference and Arts Centre, gourmet restaurant, and beautiful terraced gardens.

Target text (French):

Outre une situation enviable, le Musée prévoit également un Centre de Conférence et des Arts, un restaurant gourmand et de magnifiques jardins **implantés en terrasse**.

Besides its enviable location, the museum equally provides a Conference and Arts Centre, a gourmet restaurant and magnificent gardens **created in a terrace**.

(f) Translation by paraphrase using unrelated words

If the concept expressed by the source item is not lexicalized at all in the target language, the paraphrase strategy can still be used in some contexts. Instead of a related word, the paraphrase may be based on modifying a superordinate or simply on unpacking the meaning of the source item, particularly if the item in question is semantically complex.

Example A
Source text ('A Secret Best Seller', the *Independent*, November 1988):[22]

In the words of a Lonrho affidavit dated 2 November 1988, the allegations ...

Target text (Arabic):

وحسب النص الوارد فى إفادة كتابية مشفوعة بيمين قدمتها مؤسسة لونرو بتاريخ 2 نوفمبر 1988 ، فإن الإدعاءات ...

According to the text of a **written communication supported by an oath** presented by the Lonrho organization and dated 2 November 1988, the allegations ...

Example B
Source text (*Palace and Politics in Prewar Japan* – Titus 1974:11):

If the personality and policy preferences of the Japanese emperor were not very relevant to prewar politics, social forces certainly were. There are two reasons for giving them only the most <u>tangential</u> treatment here.

Target text (Japanese):

だが、日本の天皇の人柄や政策上の好みが戦前の政治に大した関係がなかったとしても、社会勢力の側は明らかにそうではない。社会勢力に対して本書がわずかにふれる程度の扱いしかしなかったのには、二つの理由がある。

... There are two reasons for <us> not having treated social power in this book except **to a very slight degree of referring <to it>**.

Example C
Source text (*Brintons* – press release issued by carpet manufacturer, 1986):

They have a totally <u>integrated</u> operation from the preparation of the yarn through to the weaving process.

Target text (Arabic):

هذا وتقوم الشركة بتنفيذ جميع خطوات الإنتاج بمصانعها، من إعداد الخيوط الى نسجها . . .

The company **carries out all steps of production in its factories**, from preparing the yarn to weaving it …

Example D
Source text (*The Patrick Collection*):

You can even dine '<u>alfresco</u>' in the summer on our open air terrace.

Target text (German):

Im Sommer können Sie auch auf der Terrasse **im Freien** sitzen und essen.

In the summer you can also sit and eat on the terrace **in the open**.

Alfresco, 'in the open air', is a loan word in English. Its meaning is unpacked in the German translation. The two expressions, *alfresco* and 'in the open', have the same 'propositional' meaning, but the German expression lacks the 'evoked' meaning of *alfresco*, which is perhaps inevitable in this case. Note that the loan word is placed in inverted commas in the source text.

Example E
Source text (*A Study of Shamanistic Practices in Japan* – Blacker 1975:315):

On the basis of the world view uncovered by the shaman's faculties, with its vision of another and miraculous plane which could <u>interact</u> causally with our own, the more advanced mystical intuitions of esoteric Buddhism were able to develop.

Target text (Japanese):

シャーマンの機能によって覆いをとられた世界観を基盤にし、
日常の世界と因果的にい影響し合うことができる他界の、奇跡

的な次元の幻影を伴って、より進歩した密教の秘教的な組織が
発展し得た。

… with the image of another miraculous dimension which can
causally **influence each other mutually** with the daily world …

Example F
Source text (*China's Panda Reserves*):

… the lower mixed broadleaf forests … are the areas most <u>accessible</u>
to and disturbed by Man.

Target text (Chinese):

偶尔也见于较低地区的混合阔叶森林之中，因为这些地区是人类
最容易进入、干扰最多的地方。

… the mixed broadleaf forests of the lowland area … are the places
where human beings enter most easily and interfere most.

The main advantage of the paraphrase strategy is that it achieves a high level of precision in specifying propositional meaning. One of its disadvantages is that a paraphrase does not have the status of a lexical item and therefore cannot convey expressive, evoked or any kind of associative meaning. Expressive and evoked meanings are associated only with stable lexical items which have a history of recurrence in specific contexts. A second disadvantage of this strategy is that it is cumbersome and awkward to use because it involves filling a one-item slot with an explanation consisting of several items. In certain types of environment, such as subtitling and the translation of advertising and packaging material, there are often severe restrictions on space that preclude the use of any strategy that involves this type of expansion. Similarly, a paraphrase is not normally practicable to use in book or film titles, which need to be sharp and snappy. The main title of Brian Whitaker's (2006) book about homosexuality in the Arab World, *Unspeakable Love*, inevitably loses something of its propositional and expressive meanings when translated into Arabic as *Al-Hubb Al-Mamnu'* (literally: Forbidden Love). But Arabic has no equivalent for *unspeakable*, and a paraphrase would render the title unwieldy and unattractive.

(g) Translation by omission

This strategy may sound rather drastic, but in fact it does no harm to omit translating a word or expression in some contexts.[23] If the meaning conveyed by a particular item or expression is not vital enough to the development of the text to justify distracting the reader with lengthy explanations, translators can and often do simply omit translating the word or expression in question.

Example A
Source text (*The Patrick Collection*):

> This is your chance to remember the way things were, and for younger visitors to see <u>in real-life detail</u> the way their parents, and their parents before them lived and travelled.

Target text (French):

> Voici l'occasion de retrouver votre jeunesse (qui sait?) et pour les plus jeunes de voir comment leurs parents et grands-parents vivaient et voyageaient.

> Here is the chance to rediscover your youth (who knows?) and for the younger ones to see how their parents and grandparents used to live and travel.

Example B
Source text (*China's Panda Reserves*):

> The panda's mountain home is rich in plant life and <u>gave us</u> many of the trees, shrubs and herbs most prized in European gardens.

Target text (Chinese):

> 熊猫的山区定居地有着丰富的植物种类，有着欧洲园林所珍视的许多树木、灌木和草本植物的种类。像这一山杜鹃花等种类为十九世纪的植物学家所集采，然后运回欧洲作为园林收藏品。

> The mountain settlements of the panda **have** rich varieties of plants. There are many kinds of trees, shrubs and herbal plants that are preciously regarded by European gardens.

The source text addresses a European audience, and the use of *gave us* highlights its intended orientation. The Chinese translation addresses a different audience and therefore suppresses the orientation of the source text by omitting expressions which betray its original point of view.

Example C
Source text (*Brintons*):

> The recently introduced New Tradition Axminster range is <u>already</u> creating great interest and will be on display at the Exhibition.

Target text (Arabic):

> أثارت مجموعة "نيو تراديشين أكسمنستر" درجة عالية من الإهتمام منذ أن قامت الشركة بتقديمها حديثا، وهى من ضمن أنواع السجاد التى سيتم عرضها بالمعرض.

> The 'New Tradition Axminster' collection has aroused a high degree of interest since the company introduced it recently, and it is among the types of carpets which will be displayed in the exhibition.

There is inevitably some loss of meaning when words and expressions are omitted in a translation. For instance, *already* in the last example conveys the idea that the New Tradition Axminster range is creating great interest 'earlier than anticipated', and this is lost in the translation. It is therefore advisable to use this strategy only as a last resort, when the advantages of producing a smooth, readable translation clearly outweigh the value of rendering a particular meaning accurately in a given context.

(h) Translation by illustration

This is a useful option if the word which lacks an equivalent in the target language refers to a physical entity which can be illustrated, particularly if there are restrictions on space and if the text has to remain short, concise and to the point.

Figure 2 appeared on a Lipton Yellow Label tea packet prepared for the Arab market. There is no easy way of translating *tagged*, as in *tagged teabags*, into Arabic without going into lengthy explanations which would clutter the text. An illustration of a tagged teabag is therefore used instead of a paraphrase.

Figure 2 Lipton Yellow Label tea packet for Arab market

The examples discussed in this chapter do not, by any means, represent an exhaustive account of the strategies available for dealing with non-equivalence at word level. You are encouraged continually to study and analyse texts prepared by professional translators in order to discover more strategies and learn to assess the advantages and disadvantages of using each strategy in various contexts.

exercises

1. Comment on any differences in meaning between the items in each of the following sets. The differences may relate to expressive or evoked meaning. For instance, some items may be register-specific or dialect-specific, others may be derogatory or neutral. If you are not familiar with a particular word or expression, consult a good dictionary of English before you comment on its meaning.

    car, auto, automobile, motor, limousine, limo, banger, jalopy
    comfortable, comfy, homely, cosy, snug (of a place)
    dad, daddy, pa, papa, pop, father, pater, sire, old man

    Now list all the words and expressions you can think of which are available in your target language for *car, comfortable* and *father*. Comment on any differences in meaning between (a) the individual items in each set, and (b) the English items above and the items in the corresponding sets in your target language.

2. Make a list of all the English verbs you can think of which have to do with speech, such as *say, suggest, complain, mumble, mutter, murmur, whisper, speak, tell* and so on. Try to group them into sets, starting with the more general ones.

    Now list all the verbs of speech you can think of in your target language, starting with the more general ones. Comment on the presence or absence of any semantic gaps in your target language *vis-à-vis* English.

Repeat this exercise using nouns which may come under the general heading of PUBLICATIONS. In English, this would include *book, newspaper, magazine, newsletter, bulletin, journal, report, pamphlet, periodical* and so on.

3. Make a list of ten English words which you feel are particularly difficult to translate into your target language. Comment on the source of difficulty in each case.

4. Make a list of some loan words that are used in your language, and comment on the types of text in which such loan words tend to be used freely (for instance in advertisements). Now consider how you might translate the main text in Figure 3, an advertisement by Trados which appeared in various magazines in 2001, and what loss of propositional, expressive and/or evoked meaning might be involved if you cannot render *Dinero* using a similar loan word in your target text.

Once You Translate the Word "Money" into "Dinero," You Won't Have to Spend More "Dinero" Translating "Money" Again.

Every year you waste time and money re-translating company documents. With **TRADOS**, once you translate the words and sentences that describe your products or services, you won't have to backtrack and re-translate those same words again. **TRADOS** memorizes key words and sentences, making the translation process fast and accurate. So you're able to get to international markets in half the time and half the cost.

Call Trados at 1-800-4-TRADOS ext. 5000 or visit us online at www.trados.com to find out how simple translating your multilingual documents and products can be.

■ **TRADOS**®
Global Leader in Translation Technology

Alexandria · Bern · Beijing · Bruxelles · Dublin · Hannover · Paris · Stuttgart · Tokyo · Vaxjo

© 2001 TRADOS, Inc. All rights reserved.

Figure 3 Trados advertisement

5. Make a list of three English affixes which systematically produce forms that have no direct equivalents in your target language. Suggest suitable paraphrases for each affix.

6. Make a list of all the English words you can think of that end in *-ism* or *-ist* (such as *racism/racist, sexism/sexist, ageism/ageist, extremism/extremist, fanaticism/fanaticist*). Comment on what these words have in common and on the propositional and expressive meanings of the suffix. Now attempt to translate the screen shot in Figure 4, from a video released by the Sizism Awareness Campaign (www.youtube.com/watch?v=IOxbi53J5SU).

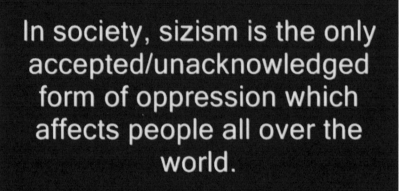

In society, sizism is the only accepted/unacknowledged form of oppression which affects people all over the world.

Figure 4 Screen shot from Sizism Awareness Campaign video

7. Produce two translations in your target language of the following extract from Stephen Hawking's *A Brief History of Time* (1988:1–2). One translation should aim at giving the target reader a straightforward account of the contents of the text. In producing the second translation, assume that Professor Hawking, or his publisher, has authorized you to use whatever strategies are necessary to ensure that the reader's attention is captured in these opening passages.

A well-known scientist (some say it was Bertrand Russell) once gave a public lecture on astronomy. He described how the earth orbits around the sun and how the sun, in turn, orbits around the center of a vast collection of stars called our galaxy. At the end of the lecture, a little old lady at the back of the room got up and said: 'What you have told us is rubbish. The world is really a flat plate supported on the back of a giant tortoise.' The scientist gave a superior smile before replying, 'What is the tortoise standing on?' 'You're very clever, young man, very clever,' said the old lady. 'But it's turtles all the way down!'

exercises

Most people would find the picture of our universe as an infinite tower of tortoises rather ridiculous, but why do we think we know better? What do we know about the universe, and how do we know it? Where did the universe come from, and where is it going? Did the universe have a beginning, and if so, what happened *before* then? What is the nature of time? Will it ever come to an end? Recent breakthroughs in physics, made possible in part by fantastic new technologies, suggest answers to some of these longstanding questions. Someday these answers may seem as obvious to us as the earth orbiting the sun – or perhaps as ridiculous as a tower of tortoises. Only time (whatever that may be) will tell.

Comment on the different strategies used in each translation.

SUGGESTIONS FOR FURTHER READING

On words and morphemes

Bauer, Laurie (2001) *Morphological Productivity*, Cambridge: Cambridge University Press.

Bolinger, Dwight and Donald Sears (1968) *Aspects of Language*, New York: Harcourt Brace Jovanovich. Chapter 4: 'Words and Their Make-up'.

Carter, Ronald (1987) *Vocabulary: Applied Linguistic Perspectives*, London: Allen & Unwin. Chapter 1: 'What's in a Word?'.

Fawcett, Peter (1997) *Translation and Language*, Manchester: St. Jerome Publishing. Chapter 2: 'Sub-Word Components'.

Katamba, Francis (1993) *Morphology*, Basingstoke: Macmillan Press.

Katamba, Francis (1994) *English Words*, London: Routledge.

Palmer, Frank Robert (1976) *Semantics*, Cambridge: Cambridge University Press. Chapter 4, section 4.4: 'The Word'.

On lexical meaning and semantic fields

Bolinger, Dwight and Donald Sears (1968) *Aspects of Language*. Chapter 6: 'Meaning'.

Carter, Ronald and Michael McCarthy (1988) *Vocabulary and Language Teaching*, London: Longman. Chapter 2: 'Lexis and Structure'.

Cruse, D. A. (1986) *Lexical Semantics*, Cambridge: Cambridge University Press. Chapter 12: 'Synonymy', sections 12.1 and 12.2.

Fawcett, Peter (1997) *Translation and Language*. Chapter 3: 'Semantics'.

Palmer, Frank Robert (1976) *Semantics*. Chapter 4: 'Lexical Semantics: Fields and Collocation', sections 4.1–4.3.

On dialect and register

Assis Rosa, Alexandra (2001) 'Features of Oral and Written Communication in Subtitling', in Yves Gambier and Henrik Gottlieb (eds) *(Multi)Media Translation*, Amsterdam: John Benjamins, 213–221.

Findlay, Bill (2000) 'Translating Standard into Dialect: Missing the Target?', in Carole-Anne Upton (ed.) *Moving Target: Theatre Translation and Cultural Relocation*, Manchester: St. Jerome Publishing, 35-46.

Hale, Sandra (1997) 'The Treatment of Register Variation in Court Interpreting', *The Translator* 3(1): 39–54.

Hatim, Basil and Ian Mason (1990) *Discourse and the Translator*, London: Longman. Chapter 3: 'Context in Translating: Register Analysis'.

Leppihalme, Ritva (2000) 'The Two Faces of Standardization: On the Translation of Regionalisms in Literary Dialogue', *The Translator* 6(2): 247–269.

Miller, Katrina R. and Vernon McCay (2001) 'Linguistic Diversity in Deaf Defendants and Due Process Rights', *Journal of Deaf Studies and Deaf Education* 6(3): 226–234.

Pettit, Zoë (2005) 'Translating Register, Style and Tone in Dubbing and Subtitling', *JosTrans: The Journal of Specialised Translation* 4. Available at www.jostrans.org/issue04/art_pettit.php.

Queen, Robin (2004) '"Du hast jar keine Ahnung": African American English Dubbed into German', *Journal of Sociolinguistics* 8(4): 515–537; reprinted in Mona Baker (ed.) (2009) *Translation Studies*, Volume III, London: Routledge, 169–192.

On the concept of equivalence

Hatim, Basil (2001) *Teaching and Researching Translation*, Harlow: Pearson Education. Chapter 2: 'From Linguistic Systems to Cultures in Contact', and Chapter 3: 'Equivalence: Pragmatic and Textual Criteria'.

Kenny, Dorothy (2009) 'Equivalence', in Mona Baker and Gabriela Saldanha (eds) *Routledge Encyclopedia of Translation Studies*, London: Routledge, 96–99.

Munday, Jeremy (2001) *Introducing Translation Studies: Theories and Applications*, London: Routledge. Chapter 3; 'Equivalence and Equivalent Effect'.

On non-equivalence and translation strategies

Barnwell, Katherine (1974) *Introduction to Semantics and Translation*, High Wycombe: Summer Institute of Linguistics. Chapter 9: 'Transferring Lexical Meaning from One Language to Another'.

Beekman, John and John Callow (1974) *Translating the Word of God*, Michigan: Zondervan. Chapters 12 and 13: 'Lexical Equivalence across Languages'.

Chesterman, Andrew (1997) *Memes of Translation*, Amsterdam: John Benjamins. Chapter 4: 'Translation Strategies', section 4.2: 'A Classification'; pages 92–112.

Li, Chris Wen-Chao (2007) 'Foreign Names into Native Tongues: How to Transfer Sound between Languages – Transliteration, Phonological Translation, Nativization, and Implications for Translation Theory', *Target* 19(1): 45–68.

Pedersen, Jan (2007) 'Cultural Interchangeability: The Effects of Substituting Cultural References in Subtitling', *Perspectives: Studies in Translatology* 15(1): 30–48.

Tortoriello, Adriana (2006) 'Funny and Educational Across Cultures: Subtitling Winnie the Pooh into Italian', *JosTrans: The Journal of Specialised Translation* 6. Available at www. jostrans.org/issue06/art_tortoriello.php.

NOTES

1   Bolinger and Sears do not in fact adopt this definition. They prefer to define **words** as 'the least elements between which other elements can be inserted with relative freedom' (1968:43).
2   I use 'speaker' as shorthand for 'speaker and/or writer'.
3   Gregory (1980:464) suggests that 'distinctions amongst modes of discourse, if they are to be useful and revealing, have to be more delicate than the simple spoken–written dichotomy'. He distinguishes, for instance, between speaking spontaneously and non-spontaneously, and within spontaneous speech between conversing and monologuing. In non-spontaneous speech, he distinguishes between reciting (i.e. performing in the oral tradition) and the speaking of what is written. For a detailed discussion of these and other distinctions in mode, see Gregory and Carroll (1978).
4   On issues of censorship in the context of translation, see Gutiérrez Lanza (2002), Sturge (2002), Dunnett (2002), Linder (2004), Billiani (2006) and Chan (2007).
5   Some linguists would not accept this view, or at least not totally. See, for instance, Lyons (1977:260): 'The external world or reality is not just an undifferentiated continuum'. I tend to agree with Lowe (1985:4):

> Reality, the world of experience, consists of a *continuous*, uninterrupted flow of impressions of all sorts which man can perceive with his physical senses. Human language, by categorizing these impressions through the various representational systems it has developed, has introduced some sort of *discontinuity* into this flow of impressions – hence the expression 'to split' the world of experience – by providing man with a mental vision or representation of experience. In fact, by providing man with a certain conceptualization of reality, every language proposes an original, discontinuous vision of the universe of experience. And in a sense, every mean-ingful unit of a given language participates in some way in the creation of the global mental vision of the world this particular language proposes to its speakers.

6   The notion of **lexical set** has a more specific definition in the study of lexis. Briefly, a **lexical set** consists of items which have a like privilege of collocation (see Chapter 3, section 3.1 for a discussion of collocation).
7   The Translational English Corpus, or TEC for short, is a computerized collection of trans-lated English text held at the Centre for Translation and Intercultural Studies, University of Manchester, UK. See www.llc.manchester.ac.uk/ctis/research/english-corpus/.
8   *ITI News*, vol. 3, no. 3, December 1988. ITI is the Institute of Translation and Inter-preting, United Kingdom. See www.iti.org.uk.
9   As defined by the *COBUILD Dictionary of English* (Sinclair 1987b).

10 A less judgemental and pejorative neologism has now been introduced in Arabic and is gaining considerable currency: the word *mithliyuun*, from *mithl*, meaning 'alike' or 'similar'. Whitaker (2006:13–15) discusses this terminology in some detail.

11 For a detailed discussion and illustration of different types of compensatory technique, see Harvey (1995, 1998)

12 For a detailed discussion of false friends and their implications for translators, see Chamizo Domínguez and Nerlich (2002). Nilsson (2005) discusses false friends in the context of sign language interpreting.

13 From the British National Corpus. See www.natcorp.ox.ac.uk/.

14 Ming Xie, translator (personal communication).

15 'I passi sulla neve' ('Footsteps in the Snow'), a short story by Mario Soldati, translated by Gwyn Morris, in Trevelyan (1965).

16 For a detailed analysis and examples of culture-specific items and strategies for translating them, see Nedergaard-Larsen (1993), Aixelá (1996), Kwieciński (1998), Desmet (2001) and Hagfors (2003).

17 The notion of 'norms' has received considerable attention in the years that followed the publication of the first edition of this textbook, particularly through the work of Gideon Toury (see Toury 1995). For an accessible summary of the literature on norms, see Baker (2009a).

18 The section on different historical traditions in Baker (1998/2001) and Baker and Saldanha (2009) reveals the extent to which forms of radical adaptation were not only tolerated but also valued in different traditions in the past. They also continue to be widely practised in some genres today, most notably drama translation; see Aaltonen (2000), Hardwick (2001) and Anderman (2009).

19 As defined by the *COBUILD Dictionary of English* (Sinclair 1987b).

20 'La cenere delle battaglie' ('The Ash of Battles Past'), a short story by Carlo Emilio Gadda, translated by I. M. Rawson, in Trevelyan (1965).

21 I have unfortunately lost the scan of the first page of the Japanese leaflet, on which the analysis was based for the first edition of this book, and hence cannot reproduce the original in this instance.

22 Article published in the *Independent* newspaper (8 November 1988) – copy attached to Tiny Rowland's *A Hero from Zero*, a document describing the acquisition of the House of Fraser by Mohamed Fayed.

23 On the pros and cons of omission as a translation strategy, see E. Davies (2007).

CHAPTER 3

Equivalence above word level

No book was ever turned from one language into another, without imparting something of its native idiom; ... single words may enter by thousands, and the fabrick of the tongue continue the same, but new phraseology changes much at once; it alters not the single stones of the building, but the order of the columns.

(Samuel Johnson, Preface to the Dictionary, *1755:xii)*

much of what we say and write in our own language is both routine and predictable because of what we and others have already said and written. Routine is not a bad thing, however. It is what allows the creative use of language to be identified as such.

(Kenny 1998:515)

In the previous chapter, we discussed problems arising from non-equivalence at word level and explored a number of attested strategies for dealing with such problems. In this chapter, we will go one step further to consider what happens when words start combining with other words to form stretches of language.

It goes without saying that words rarely occur on their own; they almost always occur in the company of other words. But words are not strung together at random in any language; there are always restrictions on the way they can be combined to convey meaning. Restrictions which admit no exceptions, and particularly those which apply to classes of words rather than individual words, are usually written down in the form of rules. One of the rules of English, for example, is that a determiner cannot come after a noun. A sequence such as *beautiful girl the* is therefore inadmissible in English.[1] Some restrictions are more likely to admit exceptions and apply to individual words rather than classes of words. These cannot be expressed in terms of rules, but they can nevertheless be identified as recurrent patterns in the language. In the following sections, we will concentrate on this type of lexical patterning. We will discuss, for instance, the 'likelihood' of certain words occurring with other words and the naturalness or typicality of the resulting combinations. In particular, we will address the difficulties encountered by translators as a result of differences in the lexical patterning of the source and target languages.

Lexical patterning will be dealt with under two main headings: **collocation** and **idioms and fixed expressions**.

3.1 COLLOCATION

> Why do builders not *produce* a building or authors not *invent* a novel, since they do invent stories and plots? No reason as far as dictionary definitions of words are concerned. We don't say it because we don't say it.
>
> *(Bolinger and Sears 1968:55)*

> There are virtually no impossible collocations, but some are much more likely than others.
>
> *(Sinclair 1966:411)*

When I discussed **lexical meaning** in Chapter 2, I made a brief reference to **collocation** under **presupposed meaning** and defined it tentatively as 'semantically arbitrary restrictions which do not follow logically from the propositional meaning of a word'. Another way of looking at **collocation** would be to think of it in terms of the tendency of certain words to co-occur regularly in a given language.

At one level, the tendency of certain words to co-occur has to do with their propositional meanings. For example, *cheque* is more likely to occur with *bank*, *pay*, *money* and *write* than with *moon*, *butter*, *playground* or *repair*. As Sinclair explains (1987a:320), 'To some extent, the nature of the world around us is reflected in the organization of language. ... Things which occur physically together have a stronger chance of being mentioned together'. However, meaning cannot always account for collocational patterning. If it did, we might expect *carry out*, *undertake* or even *perform* to collocate with *visit*. Yet, English speakers typically *pay a visit*, less typically *make a visit* and are unlikely to *perform a visit*. We do not speak of *grilling bread*, even though we put it under the grill (Newman 1988). When butter or eggs go bad they are described in English as *rancid* and *addled*, respectively. Both *rancid* and *addled* mean 'stale/rotten', but *addled butter* and *rancid eggs* are unacceptable or at least unlikely collocations in English (Palmer 1976). Moreover, words which we might think of as synonyms or near-synonyms will often have quite different sets of collocates. English speakers typically *break rules* but they do not *break regulations*; they typically talk of *wasting time* but not of *squandering time*. Both *deliver a verdict* and *pronounce a verdict* are acceptable collocations in English. Likewise, *pronounce a sentence* is acceptable and means more or less the same as *deliver/pronounce a verdict*. And yet, *deliver a sentence* is an unlikely collocation. Cruse gives a similar example (1986:281). The adjectives *unblemished*, *spotless*, *flawless*, *immaculate* and *impeccable* can be thought of as synonyms or near-synonyms, and yet they do not combine freely with the same set of nouns (see Table 1).

When two words collocate, the relationship can hold between all or several of their various forms, combined in any grammatically acceptable order. For example, *achieving aims*, *aims having been achieved*, *achievable aims* and *the achievement of an aim* are all equally acceptable and typical in English. On the other hand, it is often the case that words will collocate with other words in some of their forms but

Table 1 Unpredictability of collocational patterning

	unblemished	spotless	flawless	immaculate	impeccable
performance	-	-	+	+	+
argument	-	-	+	-	?
complexion	?	?	+	-	-
behaviour	-	-	-	-	+
kitchen	-	+	-	+	-
record	+	+	-	?	+
reputation	?	+	-	?	?
taste	-	-	?	?	+
order	-	-	?	+	+
credentials	-	-	-	-	+

+ = common/acceptable collocation
- = unacceptable/unlikely collocation
? = questionable/may be acceptable in some idiolects

not in others. We *bend rules* in English but are unlikely to describe *rules* as *unbendable.* Instead, we usually talk of *rules* being *inflexible.*

It would seem, then, that patterns of collocation are largely arbitrary and independent of meaning. This is so both within and across languages. The same degree of mismatch that can be observed when comparing the collocational patterns of synonyms and near-synonyms within the same language is evident in the collocational patterning of dictionary equivalents/near equivalents in two languages. For example, the English verb *deliver* collocates with a number of nouns, for each of which Arabic uses a different verb. The Arabic 'dictionary equivalent' of *deliver* is *yusallim.*

English	**Arabic**	
deliver a letter/telegram	*yusallimu*	khitaaban/tillighraafan
deliver a speech/lecture	*yulqi*	khutbatan/muhaadaratan
deliver news	*yanqilu*	akhbaaran
deliver a blow	*yuwajjihu*	darbatan
deliver a verdict	*yusdiru*	hukman
deliver a baby	*yuwallidu*	imra'atan

The last Arabic expression, *yuwallidu imra'atan,* literally means something like 'deliver <u>a woman</u>' or 'assist <u>a woman</u> in childbirth'. In the process of childbirth,

Arabic focuses on the woman, whereas English prefers to focus on the baby; it would be unacceptable, under normal circumstances, to speak of *delivering a woman* in Modern English. This suggests that differences in collocational patterning among languages are not just a question of using, say, a different verb with a given noun; they can involve totally different ways of portraying an event. Patterns of collocation reflect the preferences of specific language communities for certain modes of expression and certain linguistic configurations; they rarely reflect any inherent order in the world around us. As Sinclair so aptly puts it, 'there are many ways of saying things, many choices within language that have little or nothing to do with the world outside' (1987a:320). This is not to say that collocations do not often reflect the cultural setting in which they are embedded. Some collocations are in fact a direct reflection of the material, social or moral environment in which they occur. This explains why *bread* collocates with *butter* in English but not in Arabic. *Buy a house* is a frequent collocation in English, but in German it is rare because the practice of house-buying is very different in the two cultures (Alexander 1987). *Law and order* is a common collocation in English; in Arabic a more typical collocation would be *al-qanuun wa altaqaalid* ('law and convention/tradition'). The English collocation reflects the high value that English speakers place on order and the Arabic collocation reflects the high respect accorded by Arabs to the concept of tradition.

3.1.1 Collocational range and collocational markedness

Every word in a language can be said to have a **range** of items with which it is compatible, to a greater or lesser degree. **Range** here refers to the set of collocates, that is other words, which are typically associated with the word in question. Some words have a much broader collocational range than others. The English verb *shrug*, for instance, has a rather limited collocational range. It typically occurs with *shoulders* and does not have a particularly strong link with any other word in the language. *Run*, by contrast, has a vast collocational range, some of its typical collocates being *company, business, show, car, stockings, tights, nose, wild, debt, bill, river, course, water* and *colour*, among others.

Two main factors can influence the collocational range of an item (Beekman and Callow 1974). The first is its level of specificity: the more general a word, the broader its collocational range; the more specific, the more restricted its collocational range. The verb *bury* is likely to have a much broader collocational range than any of its hyponyms, such as *inter* or *entomb*. Only *people* can be *interred*, but you can *bury people*, a *treasure*, your *head, face, feelings* and *memories*. The second factor which determines the collocational range of an item is the number of senses it has. Most words have several senses and tend to attract a different set of collocates for each sense. For example, in its sense of 'manage', the verb *run* collocates with words like *company, institution* and *business*. In its sense of 'operate or provide', it collocates with words like *service* and *course*. It is, of course, perfectly reasonable to argue that the opposite is also true, that it is the collocational patterning of a word that determines its different senses (see 3.1.3 below). Either way, it is clear that there is a strong relationship between the number of senses a word has and its collocational range.

It will be obvious from our discussion of collocation so far that, unlike grammatical statements, statements about collocation are made in terms of what is typical or untypical rather than what is admissible or inadmissible. This means that there is no such thing as an impossible collocation. New and unusual combinations of words occur frequently and we do not necessarily dismiss them as unacceptable. The reason for this is that collocational ranges are not fixed. Words attract new collocates all the time; they do so naturally, through processes of analogy, or because speakers create unusual collocations on purpose. But how does this work in practice and what do unusual patterns of collocation achieve?

Patterns of collocation which have a history of recurrence in the language become part of our standard linguistic repertoire and we do not stop to think about them when we encounter them in text. By contrast, collocations which have little or no history of recurrence catch our attention and strike us as unusual. In wording his or her message, a speaker or writer has two broad options. He or she can reinforce the patterns of collocation which already exist in the language by adhering to them:

> Herman J. Mankiewicz had been a fine screenwriter ... , a *compulsive gambler*, a famous drunk, a slashing wit, and a man who was almost ferociously accident prone.
> > (Shirley MacLaine, You Can Get There From Here, 1975:66–67; my emphasis)

Alternatively, a speaker or writer can create variations on an existing pattern by, for instance, extending the range of an item:

> I first met Hugh Fraser in 1977. Charming, rather hesitant, a heavy smoker and *heavy gambler*, he had made such headway through his fortune that he had decided to sell his last major asset, the controlling shares in the business which his father had built up and named Scottish and Universal Investments.
> > (Lonrho, A Hero from Zero:1; my emphasis)

The difference between *compulsive gambler* and *heavy gambler* is that the first is a common collocation in English, whereas the second represents an attempt to extend the range of *heavy* to include *heavy gambler*, by analogy with *heavy smoker* and *heavy drinker*. The collocation *heavy gambler* does not strike us as particularly unusual because it only involves a slight extension of an existing range. This kind of natural extension of a range is far less striking than **marked** collocations which involve deliberate confusion of collocational ranges to create new images – a **marked** collocation being an unusual combination of words, one that challenges our expectations as hearers or readers.[2] Marked collocations are often used in fiction, poetry, humour, news reporting and advertisements precisely for this reason:

because they can create unusual images, produce laughter or irony, and catch the reader's attention. Moon (1998:161) offers a good example from the Bank of English corpus:

> President Clinton fanned the flames of optimism in Northern Ireland.

The expression 'to fan the flames' is normally associated with very negative collocates such as 'racial tension' and 'hatred'. As Louw (2000) explains, what we understand from this line is that the author is ironically suggesting that the peace process in Northern Ireland is 'almost as aggressive as the war it is designed to end'. See also the discussion of semantic prosodies in Chapter 7, section 7.3.1.

The following example of marked collocation is from John Le Carré's *The Russia House* (1989:102; my emphasis):

> Some tout at the book fair wanted me to take UK rights in a book on *glasnost* and the crisis of peace. Essays by past and present hawks, reappraisals of strategy. Could real *peace break out* after all?

War normally *breaks out*, but *peace prevails*. These unmarked collocations suggest that war is a temporary and undesirable situation and that peace is a normal and desirable one. The deliberate mixing of collocational ranges in the above extract conveys the unexpected image of peace being an abnormal, temporary and possibly even an undesirable situation.

To sum up, we create new collocations all the time, either by extending an existing range or by deliberately putting together words from different or opposing ranges. As well as being reinforced, the established patterns in a language can therefore be used as a backdrop against which new images and new meanings can be invoked. New collocations often catch on, are reinforced by usage and eventually become part of the standard repertoire of the language. In turn, they can be used as a backdrop for communicating new meanings by creating new collocations, and so the cycle continues.

3.1.2 Collocation and register

Collocational patterns are not always typical/untypical in relation to the language system as a whole. You may have noted that all the examples used so far have been of common, everyday collocations which are more or less familiar to all of us, regardless of our occupations, special interests or hobbies. Some collocations may seem untypical in everyday language but are common in specific registers. Sinclair (1966) explains that *dull highlights* and *vigorous depressions* may sound odd in everyday English but are common collocations in the fields of photography and meteorology, respectively. In statistics, collocations such as *biased error* and *tolerable error* are common and acceptable. A reader who is not familiar with the register of statistics may wrongly assume that these collocations are marked.

However, collocational markedness is not an absolute quality; it always depends on what the norm is in a given register.

Register-specific collocations are not simply the set of terms that go with a discipline. They extend far beyond the list of terms that one normally finds in specialized dictionaries and glossaries. It is not enough, for instance, to know that *data* in computer language forms part of compound terms such as *data processing* and *data bank* and to become familiar with the dictionary equivalents of such terms in the target language. In order to translate computer literature, a translator must, among other things, be aware that in English computer texts, *data* may be *handled*, *extracted*, *processed*, *manipulated* and *retrieved*, but not typically *shifted*, *treated*, *arranged* or *tackled*. A translator of computer literature must also be familiar with the way in which the equivalent of *data* is used in his or her corresponding target texts, that is, with the set of collocates which are compatible with the equivalent of *data*. Being a native speaker of a language does not automatically mean that the translator can assess the acceptability or typicality of register-specific collocations. This is largely why courses in specialized and technical language form an important component of translation training syllabuses.

3.1.3 Collocational meaning

In Chapter 2, meaning was discussed almost as if it was a property that each word possesses in its own right. It is, however, disputable whether a word on its own can 'mean' anything. What we do when we are asked to give an account of the meaning of a word in isolation is to contextualize it in its most typical collocations rather than its rarer ones. Asked to explain what *dry* means, we are likely to think of collocations such as *dry clothes*, *dry river* and *dry weather*, which would prompt the definition 'free from water'. As we move away from the most common collocations of *dry*, it becomes clear that the meaning of *dry* depends largely on its pattern of collocation and is not something that the word possesses in isolation.

Try paraphrasing the meaning of *dry* in each of the following combinations:

dry cow	dry sound	dry book
dry bread	dry voice	dry humour
dry wine	dry country	dry run

Most, if not all of the above collocations have unique meanings. This suggests that what a word means often depends on its association with certain collocates. When the translation of a word or a stretch of language is criticized as being inaccurate or inappropriate in a given context, the criticism may refer to the translator's inability to recognize a collocational pattern with a unique meaning different from or exceeding the sum of the meanings of its individual elements. As Hunston and Francis explain, even in the case of a straightforward collocation such as *start a family*, where both *start* and *family* retain their basic dictionary meaning as isolated words, 'the meaning of the whole … includes also a further meaning: "have one's first child"' (2000:9). Collocations that involve one or both items being used in other than their discrete dictionary meaning raise similar issues. A translator who renders *dry voice* for instance as 'a voice which is not moist' would be mistranslating *dry* in this context, having failed to recognize that when it collocates with *voice* it means 'cold', in the sense of not expressing emotion. Likewise, a translator who renders *run a car* as 'drive a car fast' would be misinterpreting *run* in this context. Taking account of collocational meaning rather than substituting individual words with their dictionary equivalents is therefore crucial at the first stage of translation, that is when the translator is interpreting the source text.

Note that even when there appears to be a close match between collocational patterns in two languages, they may not carry the same meaning. For example, *to run a car* in English means 'to own, use, and be able to maintain a car financially'. In modern Greek, to speak of a car 'running' simply means that it is being driven fast or with excessive speed.

3.1.4 Some collocation-related pitfalls and problems in translation

Differences in the collocational patterning of the source and target languages create potential pitfalls and can pose various problems in translation. Some of these problems are more difficult to handle than others. The following are some of the more common pitfalls and problems that are often encountered in translating non-literary texts. Where applicable, examples are given of strategies used by professional translators to overcome the problems under discussion. The English collocation which poses a translation problem is underlined. The collocation or expression which substitutes it in the target text is highlighted in bold.

3.1.4.1 The engrossing effect of source text patterning

It is easy to assume that as long as a collocation can be found in the target language which conveys the same or a similar meaning to that of the source collocation, the translator will not be confused by differences in the surface patterning between the two. For example, *strong tea* is literally 'dense tea' in Japanese; *break the law* is an unacceptable collocation in Arabic, the common collocation being, literally, 'contradict the law'; likewise, *keep a dog/cat* is unacceptable in Danish, where the usual expression is 'hold a dog/cat'. A Japanese, Arabic or Danish translator, one might assume, would not hesitate to make the necessary adjustment since, to all intents and purposes, the English/Japanese, English/Arabic and English/Danish collocations have the same meanings, respectively. There are, nevertheless, many published translations which testify to the contrary. Translators sometimes get quite engrossed in the source text and may produce the oddest collocations in the target language for no justifiable reason. Here is an example from *A Hero from Zero* (p. iv).

Back at the dull mahogany tables of the Commission, I found myself again seated opposite the familiar, tall, languid figure of Sir Godfray Le Quesne, rocking gently on his chair, with his hands clasped behind his head, and his eyes closed as he listened or slept through the hearings. He'd been looking into us for four years, and knew our business backwards. What am I doing here, I thought, as I gazed by the hour and by the month at the hole in the sole of his leather shoe, and wondered why Lonrho's bid was in the hands of a man who couldn't organise his own <u>shoe repairs</u>.

The French translator of *A Hero from Zero* (a document produced by Lonrho plc about the acquisition of the House of Fraser by Mohamed Fayed) rendered *shoe repairs* as *réparer ses chaussures* ('to repair his shoes'), which is a literal translation from English. In French, *réparer* collocates with things like 'fridges', 'cars' and machines in general, but it does not collocate with *chaussures.* The translator should have used *ressemeler ses chaussures* ('resole his shoes'), which is a far more natural collocation in French.[3]

Confusing source and target patterns is a pitfall that can easily be avoided once the translator is alerted to the potential influence that the collocational patterning of the source text can have on him or her. A good method of detaching oneself from the source text is to put the draft translation aside for a few hours. One can then return to the target text with a better chance of responding to its patterning as a target reader eventually would, having not been exposed to and therefore influenced by the source-text patterning in the first place. At any rate, translators are well advised to avoid carrying over source-language collocational patterns which are untypical of the target language, unless there is a good reason for doing so.

3.1.4.2 Misinterpreting the meaning of a source-language collocation

A translator can easily misinterpret a collocation in the source text due to inter-ference from his or her native language. This happens when a source-language collocation appears to be familiar because it corresponds in form to a common collo-cation in the target language. I am assuming here that many professional translators would normally work from a foreign language into their native language or language of habitual use, but see Beeby Lonsale (2009) for a detailed overview of this contro-versial issue, and Pokorn (2005) for a defence of translating into the foreign language. The following example is also from *A Hero from Zero* (p. 59):

All this represents only a part of all that Forbes Magazine reported on Fayed in the March issue mentioned before. In 1983, he had approached the industrialist Robert O. Anderson under the cover of a commission agent. The industrialist had been struck by his appearance as someone with <u>modest means</u>. Mr. Anderson was therefore astonished by his sudden acquisition of a considerable fortune.

Target text (Arabic, p. 69):

وقد رأى فيه رجل الصناعة شخصاً ينم مظهره عن التواضع والبساطة. . . .

The industrialist saw in him a person whose appearance suggests **modesty and simplicity**.

The collocation *modest means* suggests lack of affluence in English. The equivalent of 'modest' in Arabic (*mutawaadi'*) can suggest a similar meaning in some collocations such as *dakhl mutawaadi'* ('small income'). However, both the adjective *mutawaadi'* ('modest') and the noun *tawaadu'* ('modesty') used in connection with a person usually mean that he or she is unassuming. This interpretation is further reinforced by the addition of *basaata* ('simplicity'). The translator of the above extract seems to have confused the collocational patterns of English and Arabic, thus misinterpreting the source collocation and communicating the wrong meaning in the target text.

3.1.4.3 The tension between accuracy and naturalness

In rendering unmarked source-language collocations into his or her target language, a translator normally aims to produce a collocation which is typical in the target language while preserving the meaning associated with the source collocation.[4] This cannot always be achieved. Translation often involves a tension – a difficult choice between what is typical and what is accurate.

The nearest acceptable collocation in the target language will often involve some change in meaning. This change in meaning may be minimal, or not particularly significant in a given context. On the other hand, it may be significant; for example, a *good/bad law* in English is typically a 'just/unjust law' in Arabic. The significance of this difference in meaning depends on whether the issue of 'justice' is in focus in a given text or whether the context favours avoiding explicit reference to justice. Similarly, the nearest acceptable collocation which can replace *hard drink* in Arabic is 'alcoholic drink'. But *hard drink* refers only to spirits in English, for example whisky, gin and brandy. It does not include other alcoholic drinks such as beer, lager or sherry. The Arabic collocation, however, refers to any alcoholic drink, including beer, lager, sherry, as well as spirits. The meanings of the two collocations therefore do not map completely. Whether the translator opts for the typical Arabic collocation or tries to translate the full meaning of *hard drink*, possibly by a circumlocution, will depend on whether the distinction between hard and soft alcoholic drinks is significant or relevant in a given context. A certain amount of loss, addition or skewing of meaning is often unavoidable in translation; language systems tend to be too different to produce exact replicas in most cases. The degree of acceptability or non-acceptability of a change in meaning depends on the significance of this change in a given context. Accuracy is no doubt an important aim in translation, but it is also important to bear in mind that the use of common target-language patterns which are familiar to the target reader plays an important role in keeping the communication channels open. The use of established patterns of collocation also helps to distinguish a smooth translation that does not require readers to labour unproductively over irrelevant linguistic infelicities from a clumsy translation which might leave readers with the impression that the translator is simply inexperienced or incompetent.

Here are some examples of translations which have opted for naturalness at the expense of accuracy. The change in meaning involved in the following examples is not significant enough to justify cluttering the text with additional explanations or using untypical target collocations:

Example A
Source text (*Brintons* – press release, 1986):

> New Tradition offers a fascinating series of traditional patterns in miniature using <u>rich</u> jewel-like <u>colours</u> that glow against dark backgrounds.

Target text (Arabic):

> تقدم مجموعة "نيو تراديشين" عدد من التصميمات التقليدية الممتعة بحجم مصغر، فى ألوان باهرة كألوان الجواهر، تزيد الخلفيات الداكنة من توهجها.

> The 'New Tradition' collection presents a number of fascinating designs in a reduced size, in **dazzling colours** like the colours of gems, the glowing of which is enhanced by the dark backgrounds.

Rich colours are vivid and deep. The Arabic collocation suggests brightness rather than depth of colour.

Example B
Source text (*China's Panda Reserves* – World Wide Fund for Nature text which accompanied a slide show):

> These young pandas in Bejing Zoo are great <u>crowd pullers</u>.

Target text (Chinese):

> 对大多数人来说，能看见大熊猫的唯一机会便是在动物园里。北京动物园里的这些幼熊猫吸引着大量的观众。

> These young pandas in the Bejing Zoo **attract** a lot of **spectators**.

Crowd pullers is not an acceptable collocation in Chinese. In addition, the expression is quite informal. Chinese does not favour informal style in written discourse. Although much of the expressive and evoked meaning of *crowd pullers* is lost in the Chinese translation, the collocation used to replace it is more natural and stylistically more acceptable.

Example C
Source text (*China's Panda Reserves*):

> The Chinese people have already made substantial efforts to protect the giant panda, which is considered to be a national treasure. Nevertheless, we are at a <u>critical time</u> for this species.

Target text (Chinese):

> 中国人民已经做了许多工作来保护被视为国宝的大熊猫。但是，我们正处在熊猫生死存亡的关键时刻。如果没有对大熊猫极其仅剩的栖息地进行及时的、有效的保护和管理，这样的景象就将会越来越难看到——这对中国和整个世界都将是个损失。

> The Chinese people have already done a lot to protect the big panda which is regarded as a national treasure. However, we are at the **crucial moment** when the panda is **in the condition of life-death-existence-extinction**.

Critical time is replaced by a more typical Chinese fixed expression which has a similar, though perhaps more emphatic meaning.

The following examples involve a more significant change in meaning. You may or may not agree with the translator's decision to opt for a typical target collocation in each case:

Example D
Source text (the *Independent*):

> Tiny Rowland is a <u>crisper writer</u> than Peter Wright and has an even stranger story to tell.

Target text (Arabic):

و تاينى رولاند أحدّ "قلماً" من بيتر رايت، كما أن الحكاية التى يرويها أغرب بكثير.

Tiny Rowland has a **sharper pen** than Peter Wright's, and also the story which he is narrating is much stranger.

Crisp writing is clear, concise writing. The collocation suggests approval. In Arabic, 'sharp pen' is a common and typical collocation. However, both its propositional and expressive meanings are quite different from those of *crisp writing* in English. A writer is described as having a 'sharp pen' in Arabic if he or she is a fierce critic. The collocation does not suggest approval.

Example E
Source text (*A Hero from Zero*, Lonrho:13):

In fact, the money came from the Sultan of Brunei, a naive individual, easily romanced and seduced by the <u>oily charm</u> of Mohamed Fayed.

Target text (Arabic, p. 27):

ولكن الواقع أن هذه الأموال قد جاءت من سلطان بروناى وهو إنسان ساذج يصدق القصص الخيالية الملفقة، وأغراه السحر الزائف لمحمد فايد.

But the fact is that this money had come from the Sultan of Brunei and he is a naive person who believes imaginary, fake stories, and the **false charm** of Mohammed Fayed tempted him.

To describe someone as having *oily charm* in English means not only that they are insincere, but also that there is something particularly unpleasant, even sickening, in the way they show excessive politeness or flatter people. In Arabic, 'false charm' merely suggests that someone who appears charming at first glance may not turn out to be as good as they think or claim to be.

3.1.4.4 Culture-specific collocations

Some collocations reflect the cultural setting in which they occur. If the cultural settings of the source and target languages are significantly different, there will be instances when the source text will contain collocations which convey what to the target reader would be unfamiliar associations of ideas. Such culture-specific collocations express ideas previously unexpressed in the target language. Like culture-specific words, they point to concepts which are not easily accessible to the target reader.

Example A
Source text (Euralex conference circular, 1987):

> Papers relating to <u>the lesser-known languages</u> will be particularly welcome.

Target text (Russian):

> **Мы намереваемся отдельно обсудить вопросы соотношения так называемых «малых», т.е. менее распространенных и «больших», т.е. более распространенных языков.**

> We intend to discuss separately questions concerning the **so-called 'small', i.e. less widespread and 'big', i.e. more widespread languages**.

In English academic writing, it is common and acceptable to talk about 'lesser-known languages', as well as 'major languages' and 'minor languages'. Russian has no equivalent collocations. Furthermore, the political and social setting of Russian makes it potentially offensive to draw a distinction between better-known and lesser-known, or major and minor languages. The translator of the above extract seems to be aware of the oddity of such associations in Russian and their potential for causing offence. Hence, inverted commas are used around 'small' and 'big', they are each followed by a paraphrase, and the whole expression is preceded by 'so-called', which serves to distance the writer/translator from the associations made.

Note that the translation of culture-specific collocations involves a partial increase in information. This is unavoidable inasmuch as unfamiliar associations of ideas cannot simply be introduced in a target text without giving the reader some hint as to how to interpret them.

Example B
Source text (*Kolestral Super* – leaflet accompanying a hair-conditioning product):

> KOLESTRAL-SUPER is ideal for all kinds of hair, especially for <u>damaged,</u> dry and <u>brittle hair</u>.

Target text (Arabic):

كولسترال سوبر هو مثالى لجميع أنواع الشعر خصوصاً للشعر المقصف، المتأذى أو التالف
وأيضا للشعر الجاف أو الضعيف البنية والقابل للتكسر.

Kolestral-super is ideal for all kinds of hair, especially for **the split-ends hair, harmed or damaged hair and also for hair which is dry, of weak structure or liable to breaking**.

The above extract is taken from an instruction leaflet which accompanies a hair conditioner. Common collocates of *hair* in English include *dry*, *oily*, *damaged*, *permed*, *fine*, *flyaway* and *brittle*, among others. These collocations reflect cultural reality in the English-speaking world. A large number of English speakers have fine, flyaway hair, which also tends to be brittle. Common collocates of 'hair' in Arabic are mainly 'split-ends', 'dry', 'oily', 'coarse' and 'smooth'. These collocations also reflect the cultural reality of the Arabic-speaking world. The collocations *damaged hair* and *brittle hair* have no close equivalents in Arabic. The translator of the above extract nevertheless feels obliged to reproduce every possible aspect of meaning conveyed in the source text, regardless of whether the source collocations are likely to have any significance in the Arabic context. The collocations and the lengthy explanations given in Arabic 'mean' very little to the Arab reader. Moreover, it is doubtful whether 'damaged hair' and 'brittle hair' would in fact be seen as problems by the average Arab. It is reasonable to assume that people only seek solutions for problems they are aware of or which they are likely to have.

3.1.4.5 Marked collocations in the source text

Unusual combinations of words are sometimes used in the source text in order to create new images (see 3.1.1 above). Ideally, the translation of a marked collocation will be similarly marked in the target language. This is, however, always subject to the constraints of the target language and to the purpose of the translation in question.

Example A
Source text (*Language and Society* – a bilingual journal published in Canada (1985), 15:8):[5]

Canada has chosen to '<u>entrench</u>' its dual cultural <u>heritage</u> in its institutions and, as a result, official translation has taken firm root.

Target text (French, p. 8):

Canada a choisi **«d'enchasser»** – le mot est hélas! à la mode – son double **héritage** culturel dans ses institutions et la traduction officielle y est, par conséquent, solidement enracinée.

Canada has chosen to **'insert'** – the word is alas in fashion! – its double cultural **heritage** in its institutions and official translation is, as a consequence, solidly rooted there.

The reader of the source text is alerted to the writer's wish to communicate an unusual image by the inverted commas around *entrench*. In the target text, the marked collocation is further highlighted by means of an interjection from the translator ('the word is alas in fashion').

Example B
Source text (*Language and Society* (1985), 15:22):

The young ethnic child begins to lose the first language mainly because of impoverishment of reference. What this means is that as the child becomes more and more exposed to English outside the home, he lacks the linguistic resources to deal with many topics in the first language, which tends to become restricted to household matters. We call this phenomenon 'kitchen German', from the observation among many adults of European background in Western Canada whose only remembrance of their parents' language consists of a few words or phrases to do with household chores.

Target text (French, p. 22):

... Nous inspirant de la désignation **«kitchen German»**, nous dirons qu'il y a là une **langue «popote»** comme on a pu l'observer chez nombre d'adultes d'origine européenne établis dans l'Ouest canadien. La compétence langagière est toujours lieé par des associations habituelles à des contextes particuliers.

... Inspiring us from the name **'kitchen German'**, we shall say that there is a **'cooking' language** as one has been able to observe among a number of adults of European origin established in Western Canada. The language competence is always connected by habitual associations to particular contexts.

Note again the use of inverted commas around marked collocations in the source and target texts.

To conclude our brief discussion of collocation, I would reiterate that language is not made up of a large number of words which can be used together in free variation. Words have a certain tolerance of compatibility. Like individual words, collocational patterns carry meaning and can be culture-specific. This, in addition to their largely arbitrary nature, gives rise to numerous pitfalls and problems in translation.

3.2 IDIOMS AND FIXED EXPRESSIONS

Generally speaking, collocations are fairly flexible patterns of language which allow several variations in form. For example, *deliver a letter*, *delivery of a letter*, *a letter has been delivered* and *having delivered a letter* are all acceptable collocations. In addition, although the meaning of a word often depends on what other words it occurs with, we can still say that the word in question has an individual meaning in a given collocation. Thus, *dry cow* means a cow which does not produce milk. We can still identify a particular meaning associated with the word *dry* in this collocation, and, of course, *cow* still retains its familiar meaning of 'a farm animal kept for its milk'. Idioms and fixed expressions are at the extreme end of the scale from collocations in one or both of these areas: flexibility of patterning and transparency of meaning. They are frozen patterns of language which allow little or no variation in form and, in the case of idioms, often carry meanings which cannot be deduced from their individual components.

An idiom such as *bury the hatchet* ('to become friendly again after a disagreement or a quarrel') or *the long and the short of it* ('the basic facts of the situation') allows no variation in form under normal circumstances. Unless he or she is consciously making a joke or attempting a play on words, a speaker or writer cannot normally do any of the following with an idiom:

1. change the order of the words in it (e.g. *'the *short* and the *long* of it');
2. delete a word from it (e.g. *'spill beans');
3. add a word to it (e.g. *'the *very* long and short of it'; *'face the *classical* music');
4. replace a word with another (e.g. *'the *tall* and the short of it'; *'bury *a* hatchet');
5. change its grammatical structure (e.g. *'the music was faced').

As their name suggests, fixed expressions such as *having said that*, *as a matter of fact*, *Ladies and Gentlemen* and *all the best*, as well as proverbs such as *practise what you preach* and *waste not want not*, allow little or no variation in form. In this respect, they behave very much like idioms. Unlike idioms, however, fixed expressions and proverbs often have fairly transparent meanings. The meaning of *as a matter of fact* can easily be deduced from the meanings of the words which constitute it, unlike the meaning of an idiom such as *pull a fast one* or *fill the bill*. But in spite of its transparency, the meaning of a fixed expression or proverb is somewhat more than the sum meanings of its words; the expression has to be taken as one unit to establish meaning. This is true of any fixed, recurring pattern of the language. A fixed expression evokes in the mind of the reader or hearer a range of associations connected with the typical contexts in which the expression is used. It is precisely this feature which lies behind the widespread use of fixed and semi-fixed expressions in any language. They encapsulate stereotypical aspects of experience and therefore perform a stabilizing function in communication. Situation- or register-specific formulae such as *Many happy returns*, *Merry Christmas*, *Further to your letter of* ..., and *Yours sincerely* are particularly good examples of the stabilizing role and the special status that a fixed expression can assume in communication.

3.2.1 Idioms, fixed expressions and the direction of translation

Although most idioms resist variation in form, some are more flexible than others. For example, a BBC radio reporter once quoted a conference speaker as saying 'There was too much *buck passing*' (Baker and McCarthy 1988). The common form of the idiom is *pass the buck* ('refuse to accept responsibility for something'). And yet, we would not expect to hear *There was too much way giving* for *give way* ('allow someone to do something you disapprove of').

A person's competence in actively using the idioms and fixed expressions of a foreign language hardly ever matches that of a native speaker. The majority of translators working into a foreign language cannot hope to achieve the same sensitivity that native speakers seem to have for judging when and how an idiom can be manipulated. This lends some support to the argument that translators should only work into their language of habitual use or mother tongue, at least in genres which are characterized by creative or playful use of language (but see Beeby Londsdale 2009 and Pokorn 2005 for alternative arguments). The Code of Professional Ethics of the Translators' Guild of Great Britain[6] states:

> A translator shall work only *into* the language (in exceptional cases this may include a second language) of which he has native knowledge. 'Native knowledge' is defined as the ability to speak and write a language so fluently that the expression of thought is structurally, grammatically and *idiomatically* correct.
>
> *(quoted in Meuss, 1981:278; my emphasis)*

Assuming that a professional translator would, under normal circumstances, work only into his or her language of habitual use, the difficulties associated with being able to use idioms and fixed expressions correctly in a foreign language need not be addressed here. The main problems that idiomatic and fixed expressions pose in translation relate to two main areas: the ability to recognize and interpret an idiom correctly; and the difficulties involved in rendering the various aspects of meaning that an idiom or a fixed expression conveys into the target language. These difficulties are much more pronounced in the case of idioms than they are in the case of fixed expressions.

3.2.2 The interpretation of idioms

As far as idioms are concerned, the first difficulty that a translator comes across is being able to recognize that he or she is dealing with an idiomatic expression. This is not always so obvious. There are various types of idiom, some more easily recognizable than others. Those which are easily recognizable include expressions that violate truth conditions, such as *It's raining cats and dogs*, *throw caution to the wind*, *storm in a tea cup*, *jump down someone's throat* and *food for thought*. They also include expressions which seem ill-formed because they do not follow the grammatical rules of the language, for example *trip the light fantastic*, *blow someone to kingdom come*, *put paid to*, *the powers that be*, *by and large* and *the world and his friend*. Expressions which start with *like* (simile-like structures) also tend to suggest that they should not be interpreted literally. These include idioms such as *like a bat out of hell* and *like water off a duck's back*. Generally speaking, the more difficult an expression is to understand and the less sense it makes in a given context, the more likely that a translator will recognize it as an idiom. Because they do not make sense if interpreted literally, the highlighted expressions in the following text are easy to recognize as idioms (assuming one is not already familiar with them):

> This can only be done, I believe, by a full and frank **airing of the issues**. I urge you all to **speak your minds** and not to **pull any punches**.
>
> (Language and Society (1985), 14:6)

Provided a translator has access to good reference works and monolingual dictionaries of idioms, or, better still, is able to consult native speakers of the language, opaque idioms which do not make sense for one reason or another can actually be a blessing in disguise. The very fact that he or she cannot make sense of an expression in a particular context will alert the translator to the presence of an idiom of some sort.

There are two cases in which an idiom can be easily misinterpreted if one is not already familiar with it:

(a) Some idioms are 'misleading'; they seem transparent because they offer a reasonable literal interpretation and their idiomatic meanings are not necessarily signalled in the surrounding text. A large number of idioms in English, and probably all languages, have both a literal and an idiomatic meaning, for example *go out with* ('have a romantic or sexual relationship with someone') and *take someone for a ride* ('deceive or cheat someone in some way'). Such idioms lend themselves easily to manipulation by speakers and writers who will sometimes play on both their literal and idiomatic meanings. In this case, a translator who is not familiar with the idiom in question may easily accept the literal interpretation and miss the play on idiom. The following example illustrates how easy it is to accept a literal interpretation that seems plausible in a given context. The text from which the extract is taken is quoted in the *Translator's Guild Newsletter* (January 1985, 10:1).

> I'd just done my stint as rubber duck, see, and pulled off the grandma lane into the pitstop to **drain the radiator**.

This is an extract from a highly idiomatic passage of Citizen Band (CB) Radio special 'trucking talk'. *Rubber duck* is the first trucker in a convoy, *grandma lane* is the slow lane, and *pitstop* refers to services or a place where one stops for a rest. In the context of trucks, motorways and stopping at a service station, a literal interpretation of *drain the radiator* seems highly plausible. It is, however, a special idiom used by CB drivers and means 'to urinate; use the toilet'.

(b) An idiom in the source language may have a very close counterpart in the target language which looks similar on the surface but has a totally or partially different meaning. For example, the idiomatic question *Has the cat had/got your tongue?* is used in English to urge someone to answer a question or contribute to a conversation, particularly when their failure to do so becomes annoying. A similar expression is used in French with a totally different meaning: *donner sa langue au chat* ('to give one's tongue to the cat'), meaning to give up, for example when asked a riddle. *To pull someone's leg*, meaning to tell someone something untrue as a joke in order to shock them temporarily and amuse them when they find out later that it was a joke, is identical on the surface to the idiom *yishab rijlu* ('pull his leg') which is used in several Arabic dialects to mean tricking someone into talking about something he or she would have rather kept secret. In French, a similar expression: *tirer la jambe* ('pull the leg') means to drag one's steps. Instances of superficially identical or similar idioms which have different meanings in the source and target languages lay easy traps for the unwary translator who is not familiar with the source-language idiom and who may be tempted simply to impose a target-language interpretation on it.

Apart from being alert to the way speakers and writers manipulate certain features of idioms and to the possible confusion which could arise from similarities in form between source and target expressions, a translator must also consider the collocational environment which surrounds any expression whose meaning is not readily accessible. Idiomatic and fixed expressions have individual collocational patterns. They form collocations with other items in the text as single units and enter into lexical sets which are different from those of their individual words. Take, for instance, the idiom *to have cold feet. Cold* as a separate item may collocate with words like *weather, winter, feel* or *country. Feet* on its own will perhaps collocate with *socks, chilblain, smelly* and so on. However, *having cold feet*, in its idiomatic use, has nothing necessarily to do with *winter, feet* or *chilblains* and will therefore generally be used with a different set of collocates.

The ability to distinguish senses by collocation is an invaluable asset to a translator working from a foreign language. It is often subsumed under the general umbrella of 'relying on the context to disambiguate meanings', which, among other things, means using our knowledge of collocational patterns to decode the meaning of a word or a stretch of language. Using our knowledge of collocational patterns may not always tell us what an idiom means, but it could easily help us in many cases to recognize an idiom, particularly one which has a literal as well as a non-literal meaning.

3.2.3 The translation of idioms: difficulties

Once an idiom or fixed expression has been recognized and interpreted correctly, the next step is to decide how to translate it into the target language. The difficulties involved in translating an idiom are totally different from those involved in interpreting it. Here, the question is not whether a given idiom is transparent, opaque or misleading. An opaque expression may be easier to translate than a transparent one. The main difficulties involved in translating idioms and fixed expressions may be summarized as follows:

(a) An idiom or fixed expression may have no equivalent in the target language. The way a language chooses to express, or not express, various meanings cannot be predicted and only occasionally matches the way another language chooses to express the same meanings. One language may express a given meaning by means of a single word, another may express it by means of a transparent fixed expression, a third may express it by means of an idiom and so on. It is therefore unrealistic to expect to find equivalent idioms and expressions in the target language as a matter of course.

Like single words, idioms and fixed expressions may be culture-specific. Formulae such as *Merry Christmas* and *say when* which relate to specific social or religious occasions provide good examples. Bassnett-McGuire (1980:21) explains that the expression *say when* is 'directly linked to English social behavioural patterns' and suggests that 'the translator putting the phrase into French or German has to contend with the problem of the non-existence of a similar convention in either TL culture'. Less problematic, but to some extent also culture-specific, are the sort of fixed formulae that are used in formal correspondence, such as *Yours faithfully* and *Yours sincerely* in English. These, for instance, have no equivalents in Arabic formal correspondence. Instead, an expression such as *wa tafadalu biqbuul fa'iq al-ihtiraam* (literally: 'and be kind enough to accept [our] highest respects') is often used, but it bears no direct relationship to *Yours faithfully* or *Yours sincerely*. The same mismatch occurs in relation to French and several other languages.

Idioms and fixed expressions which contain culture-specific items are not necessarily untranslatable. It is not the specific items an expression contains but rather the meaning it conveys and its association with culture-specific contexts which can make it untranslatable or difficult to translate. For example, the English expression *to carry coals to Newcastle*, though culture-specific in the sense that it contains a reference to Newcastle coal and uses it as a measure of abundance, is nevertheless closely paralleled in German by *Eulen nach Athen tragen* ('to carry owls to Athens').

Both expressions convey the same meaning, namely: to supply something to someone who already has plenty of it (Grauberg 1989). In French, the same meaning can be rendered by the expression *porter de l'eau à la rivière* 'to carry water to the river'. Palmer (1976) explains that in Welsh it rains 'old women and sticks' rather than 'cats and dogs', and yet to most intents and purposes both expressions mean the same thing.

(b) An idiom or fixed expression may have a similar counterpart in the target language, but its context of use may be different; the two expressions may have different connotations, for instance, or they may not be pragmatically transferable. *To sing a different tune* is an English idiom which means to say or do something that signals a change in opinion because it contradicts what one has said or done before. In Chinese, *chang-dui-tai-xi* ('to sing different tunes/to sing a duet') also normally refers to contradictory points of view, but has quite a different usage. It has strong political connotations and, in certain contexts, can be interpreted as expressing complementary rather than contradictory points of view.[7] *To go to the dogs* ('to lose one's good qualities') has a similar counterpart in German, but whereas the English idiom can be used in connection with a person or a place, its German counterpart can only be used in connection with a person and often means to die or perish. Fernando and Flavell (1981) compare *to skate on thin ice* ('to act unwisely or court danger voluntarily') with a similar Serbian expression: *navuci nekoga na tanak led* ('to pull someone onto the thin ice'). The Serbian idiom differs from the English one in that it implies <u>forcing</u> someone into a dangerous position. Though similar in meaning, the contexts in which the two idioms can be used are obviously different.

(c) An idiom may be used in the source text in both its literal and idiomatic senses at the same time (see 3.2.2 (a) above). Unless the target-language idiom corresponds to the source-language idiom both in form and in meaning, the play on idiom cannot be successfully reproduced in the target text. The following extract is from a passage which constituted part of the British Translators' Guild Intermediate Examinations for all languages (1986).

> In creating Lord Peter Wimsey, Dorothy L Sayers demonstrated all the advantages of the amateur private eye. As a wealthy dilettante he was able to pursue the clues without the boring necessity of earning a living. His title as the younger son of a duke pandered to reader snobbery and to the obsessive fascination of some readers with the lifestyle of the aristocracy, or with what they imagined that lifestyle to be. He had sufficient influence to be able to **poke his nose into** the private affairs of others where less aristocratic **noses** might have been speedily bloodied.

The above play on idiom can only be reproduced in languages such as French or German which happen to have an identical idiom, or at least an idiom which refers to interfering in other people's affairs and which has the equivalent of *nose* in it.

Another example comes from *Arab Political Humour* by Kishtainy (1985). Although this book was originally written in English, the writer quotes jokes and anecdotes of Arab origin, so that English is in fact the target language here. The following joke emerged after the defeat of the Arab forces in 1967, which resulted in the annexation of Arab territory by Israel:

> Egypt's Commander-in-Chief, Field Marshal Amin, was horrified to see President Nasser ordering a tattoo artist to print on his right arm the names of all the territories seized by Israel like Sinai, Gaza, Sharm al-Shaykh, Jerusalem, the Golan Heights.
> 'Why are you doing this?'
> 'Lest I should forget them.'
> 'But why tattooed? What will you do if we get them back?'
> 'If we get them back **I'll cut off my right arm**.'
> *(Kishtainy 1985:157–158; my emphasis)*

Unless you are an Arab speaker, you will find it difficult to appreciate the humour of the above passage, which relies totally on the manipulation of literal and idiomatic meanings. To cut off one's arm, or cut off one's right arm for emphasis, is an idiom which is similar in meaning to *pigs might fly* in English. It means that something is impossible or at least highly unlikely to happen. Neither this English expression nor any other English idiom with a similar meaning can be used to replace 'I'll cut off my right arm' in the above passage, because the literal meaning of the Arabic expression is as important as its idiomatic meaning in this context. The literal translation that the author gives above is just as ineffective since the non-Arab reader has no access to the idiomatic meaning. This book was translated into Arabic by Al-Yaziji in 1988 and, not surprisingly, the jokes work much better in the Arabic version.

It is also possible, and with more recent technological developments increasingly common, to produce plays on idiom by drawing on the visual and verbal channels simultaneously. Chaume Varela (1997:323) discusses an example from Quentin Tarantino's *Pulp Fiction*, where the following exchange takes place:

> Vincent: Come on, Mia. Let's go get a steak.
> Mia: You can get a steak here, daddy-o. Don't be a …
> (Mia draws a square with her hands. Dotted lines appear on the screen, forming a square. The lines disperse.)

Used idiomatically, as part of expressions such as 'don't be square' and 'you're so square', *square* means 'old-fashioned', 'boring'. Mia plays on both meanings, the literal and the idiomatic, but uses a combination of verbal and visual channels to communicate her message. According to Chaume Varela (*ibid.*), the Spanish dubbed version of the film adopts the following solution (back-translation added; italics in original):

Vincent: *Vayamos a comernos un filete.*
Mia: *Puedes comerte uno aquí, colega. No me seas ...*

Back-translation:
Vincent: Let's go and grab a steak.
Mia: You can eat one here, mate. Don't be ...

A better solution for Mia's line, Chaume Varela argues, would have been 'Puedes comerte uno aquí, mente cuadriculada' (lit.: You can eat one here, grid-mapped/ square mind). Someone who is described as 'mente cuadriculada' in Spanish is understood to be very rigid and unwilling to accommodate other people's sugges-tions – a meaning that overlaps to some extent with 'old-fashioned' and 'boring' as signalled by *square* in English.[8] The play on idiom can be reproduced in this instance, but not without some shift in meaning.

This type of verbal-cum-visual play on idioms is not restricted to multimodal envi-ronments such as film, web pages and television advertisements. In Figure 5, the title of an article which appeared in *New Scientist* on 5 February 2000 (p. 41) makes use of the same strategy. It plays on the idiomatic meaning of 'It's a funny old world', an expression normally used when something doesn't make sense, when some aspect of the world seems strange and incomprehensible, or when we wish to communicate, more graphically, that 'the world is upside down', as it were.

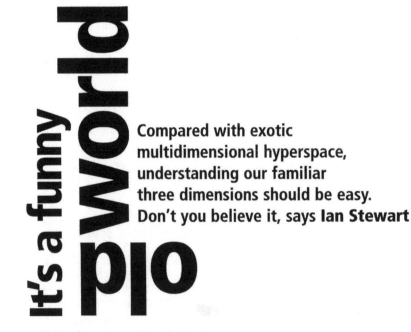

It's a funny old world

Compared with exotic
multidimensional hyperspace,
understanding our familiar
three dimensions should be easy.
Don't you believe it, says **Ian Stewart**

Figure 5 Title of article in *New Scientist*

(d) The very convention of using idioms in written discourse, the contexts in which they can be used, and their frequency of use may be different in the source and target languages. English uses idioms in many types of text, even in serious, international magazines such as *New Scientist* (see Figure 5), and especially frequently in advertisements, promotional material and the tabloid press. The following example from a glossy brochure released in 1989 by the former car manufacturer Austin Rover illustrates the heavy use of idioms in this type of English written discourse. The whole passage is highly idiomatic and very informal in style. The main idioms are highlighted in bold:

> METRO
> Your own sense of style is all your own. Brilliant. Colourful. Original.
> With loads of **get up and go**.
>   There's a car **after your own heart**. The new 1989 Metro. Sporty new models which look great – and **don't hang around**. A new range. With vivid new colours and trim. Full of fresh ideas. Luxurious. And wickedly stylish.
>   **Get going** in the new Metro GTa. Where else would you find 73PS performance, alloy wheels and looks like that – at such a price?
>   Or **show what you're made of** at the wheel of the new Metro Sport. It's got style. And a performance engine that says **it's a lot more than just a pretty face**.
>   Fancy something really special in the sports luxury department? With a sunroof, central locking, tinted glass and a lot more, the new Metro 1.3GS **is just the ticket**. And so is the price.
>
> (Today's Cars, *Austin Rover, 1989*)

Using idioms in English is thus very much a matter of style. Languages such as Arabic and Chinese, which draw a sharp distinction between written and spoken discourse and where the written mode is associated with a high level of formality, tend, on the whole, to avoid using idioms in written texts. Fernando and Flavell (1981:85) discuss the difference in rhetorical effect of using idioms in general and of using specific types of idiom in the source and target languages and quite rightly conclude that '[t]ranslation is an exacting art. Idiom more than any other feature of language demands that the translator be not only accurate but highly sensitive to the rhetorical nuances of the language.'

3.2.4 The translation of idioms: strategies

The way in which an idiom or a fixed expression can be translated into another language depends on many factors. It is not only a question of whether an idiom with a similar meaning is available in the target language. Other factors include, for example, the significance of the specific lexical items which constitute the idiom, that is whether they are manipulated elsewhere in the source text, whether verbally or visually, as well as the appropriateness or inappropriateness of using idiomatic language in a given register in the target language. The acceptability or non-acceptability of using any of the strategies described below will therefore depend on the context in which a given idiom is translated. The first strategy described, that of finding an idiom of similar meaning and similar form in the target language, may seem to offer the ideal solution, but that is not necessarily always the case. Questions of style, register and rhetorical effect must also be taken into consideration. Fernando and Flavell are correct in warning us against the 'strong unconscious urge in most translators to search hard for an idiom in the receptor-language, however inappropriate it may be' (1981:82).

(a) Using an idiom of similar meaning and form

This strategy involves using an idiom in the target language which conveys roughly the same meaning as that of the source-language idiom and, in addition, consists of equivalent lexical items. This kind of match can only occasionally be achieved.

Example A
Source text (*A Hero from Zero*, Lonrho:21):

> The Sultan's magnificent income was distributed impulsively at his command. <u>The rain fell on the just and on the unjust</u>.

Target text (French, p. 21):

> Le revenue fabuleux du Sultan était distribué sur un simple ordre de sa part. **La pluie tombait aussi bien sur les justes que sur les injustes**.

> The fantastic income of the Sultan was distributed on a simple order on his part. **The rain was falling on the just as well as on the unjust**.

Example B
Source text (*Language and Society* (1985), 16:7):

> Five days into what would be the final clash, Pawley tried <u>to force Speaker Jim Walding's hand</u> into calling a vote with or without the Tories.

Target text (French, p. 7):

Au cinquième jour de ce qui allait se révéler l'affrontement final, M. Pawley tenta **de forcer la main au** président de la chambre Jim Walding pour qu'il décrète une mise aux voix, avec ou sans la participation des conservateurs.

On the fifth day of what was going to prove to be the final confrontation, Mr. Pawley tried **to force the hand of** the president of the Chamber, Jim Walding, to declare a placement of the vote, with or without the participation of the conservatives.

Example C
Source text (*A Hero from Zero*, Lonrho:85):

The Fayeds have <u>turned</u> the pre-bid House of Fraser strategy <u>on its head</u>.

Target text (Arabic, p. 94):

وبذا يكون الإخوة فايد قد قلبوا استراتيجية هاوس أوف فريزر السابقة على عرض الإمتلاك، رأساً على عقب.

And with this the Fayed brothers have **turned** the strategy of the House of Fraser previous to the offer of ownership **head over heel**.

The Arabic expression, which means 'upside down', is similar in form only to another English idiom, *head over heels*, meaning 'very much in love'.

Example D
Source text (*Masters of the Universe*):

Perhaps Granamyr wanted to show us that <u>things aren't always what they seem</u>.

Target text (French):

> Peut-être Granamyr voulait-il nous montrer que **les choses ne sont pas toujours ce qu'elles paraissent**.

> Perhaps Granamyr wanted to show us that **things are not always what they seem**.

(b) Using an idiom of similar meaning but dissimilar form

It is often possible to find an idiom or fixed expression in the target language which has a meaning similar to that of the source idiom or expression, but which consists of different lexical items. For example, the English expression *One good turn deserves another* and the French expression *À beau jeu, beau retour* ('a handsome action deserves a handsome return') use different lexical items to express more or less the same idea (Fernando and Flavell 1981).

Example A
Source text (*China's Panda Reserves*):

> The serow, a type of wild mountain goat, is <u>very much at home</u> among the rocky outcrops of Sichuan.

Target text (Chinese):

> **喜马拉雅山羚羊，是野生山羊的一种，在四川的多岩断层露头之间十分自在。**

> The serow, a type of wild mountain goat, is **totally at ease** in Sichuan's many rocky levels.

The Chinese idiom used to replace *very much at home* is *shi fen zi zai*. It consists of a measure word based on a ten-point scale, plus 'self at ease'. The measure word means '100 per cent', but the scale used is out of 10 rather than out of 100.

Example B
Source text (*Masters of the Universe*):

> <u>Feel the force of my fist</u>, frozen fiend!

Target text (German):

Dir werde ich einheizen, du Scheusal!

I will make things hot for you, monster!

The above statement is addressed to an ice monster. The German expression *Dir werde ich einheizen* means literally, or as near literally as possible, 'I will put the heating on to you'.

(c) Borrowing the source language idiom

Just as the use of loan words is a common strategy in dealing with culture-specific items (see Chapter 2), it is not unusual for idioms to be borrowed in their original form in some contexts. In Figure 6, taken from a promotional leaflet available to visitors to the Museum of Science and Industry in Manchester (UK), *Out of this World* refers to a space gallery that is signposted as such throughout the Museum. It is of course a play on the idiomatic meaning of *out of this world* ('fantastic', 'superb'), and the more concrete meaning of 'from another galaxy, beyond the earth environment', referring to what a visitor might expect to see in a space gallery.

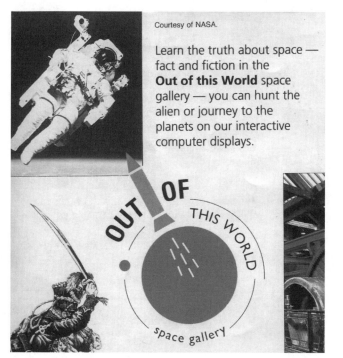

Figure 6   Original version of Manchester Museum of Science and Industry leaflet

All versions of this promotional leaflet (French, Italian, Spanish, German and Japanese) retain the idiom/name of the space gallery in English, in the image as well as the main text (see Figures 7–11).

(d) Translation by paraphrase

This is by far the most common way of translating idioms when a match cannot be found in the target language or when it seems inappropriate to use idiomatic language in the target text because of differences in stylistic preferences of the source and target languages. You may or may not find the paraphrases accurate; the examples below are quoted as they appear in the original documents to illustrate the strategy of paraphrase rather than to explain the meanings of individual idioms.

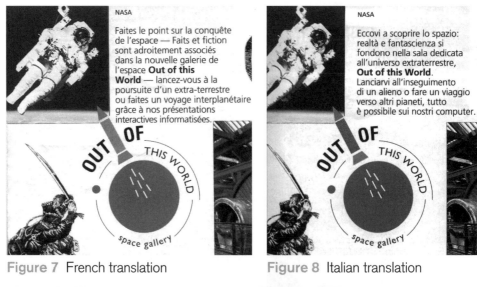

Figure 7 French translation

Figure 8 Italian translation

Figure 9 Spanish translation

Figure 10 German translation

NASA

宇宙についての真実を学ぼう。
事実とフィクションが知りた
かったら Out of this World
(宇宙空間館) へ。コンピュー
ター・ゲームで宇宙人をつかま
えることができるかな。それと
も惑星への宇宙旅行にトライ
してみますか。

OUT OF THIS WORLD

space gallery

Figure 11 Japanese translation

Example A
Source text (*Austin Montego* – car brochure):

The suspension system has been fully uprated to <u>take</u> rough terrain <u>in its stride</u>.

Target text (Arabic):

وقد رفعت طاقة نظام التعليق بحيث يتغلب على وعورة الأرض.

The capacity of the suspension system has been raised so as to **overcome** the roughness of the terrain.

Example B
Source text (*Language and Society* (1985), 15:22):

Programmes to teach heritage languages to ethnic youngsters in upper elementary or high school are all quite laudable, but if it is merely a question of trying to reinforce or replant first language competence already lost for all practical purposes, then this is rather like <u>shutting the stable door when the horse has bolted</u>.

Target text (French, pp. 22–23):

Ces cours, qui seraient dispensés dans les dernières classes de l'élémentaire ou au secondaire constituent certes une initiative louable; mais c'est peut-être **trop peu trop tard**, car dans bien des cas ces jeunes n'ont plus qu'un vague souvenir de leur langue ancestrale.

These courses, which would be given in the last classes of elementary or to the secondary, certainly constitute a laudable initiative; but it is perhaps **too little too late**, because in a good many cases these youngsters have no more than a vague memory of their ancestral language.

Example C
Source text (*A Hero from Zero*, Lonrho:iii):

Lonrho's directors then agreed not to bid without the prior permission of the Department of Trade. We were to regret signing that undertaking, and I do not think that any public company should agree to open-ended ad hoc restraints of this kind. It was subsequently used by Norman Tebbit, as Secretary of State at the Department of Trade and Industry, to unfairly restrain a Lonrho bid while he pushed another pony past the post.

Target text 1 (French, p. iii):

… Cela fut, par la suite, utilisé par Norman Tebbit, alors ministre du Commerce et de l'Industrie, afin de repousser injustement une offre de Lonrho et dans le même temps **favoriser un autre candidat**.

… This was used afterwards by Norman Tebbit, then minister of Commerce and Industry, in order to reject unfairly an offer from Lonrho and at the same time **to favour another candidate**.

Target text 2 (Arabic, p. 9):

وقد أستغل هذا التعهد فيما بعد من قبل نورمان تيبيت باعتباره وزيراً للتجارة والصناعة، حين أعاق دون عدل عرض لونرو بينما أعان متسابقاً آخر على بلوغ نهاية السباق.

… This undertaking was later exploited by Norman Tebbit in his capacity as Minister of Trade and Industry when he unjustly restrained Lonrho's offer while **helping another competitor to reach the end of the race**.

Example D
Source text (*Language and Society* (1985), 16:4):

One frequent criticism of the Manitoba Government throughout the language controversy was that it never seemed to <u>get a handle on</u> the issue.

Target text (French, p. 4):

Tout au long de la controverse linguistique, on reprocha fréquemment au gouvernement du Manitoba de ne pas réussir, selon toute apparence, à **maîtriser** la situation.

For the whole length of the linguistic controversy, the government of Manitoba was reproached frequently for not succeeding, by all appearances, in **mastering** the situation.

Example E
Source text (*Saving China's Tropical Paradise* – World Wide Fund for Nature text which accompanied a slide show):

<u>Best news of all</u> is the decision to develop a system of five nature reserves totalling 2000 sq.kms. where representative examples of the region's unique ecosystems will be protected for the future.

Target text (Chinese):

最好的消息是决定发展一个由五个自然保护区组成的共2000平方公里面积的体系。在这一体系中该区独特生态系统中有代表性的动植物得到保护。

> **The best news is** a decision to develop a system of 2000 sq.kms. consisting of five reserves. In such a system representative animal and plant species within the unique ecosystem of this area will be protected.

'The best news is' does not have the status of a fixed expression in Chinese. Although it looks very similar in back-translation to *Best news of all*, it is just a paraphrase of the English expression.

(e) Translation by omission of a play on idiom

This strategy involves rendering only the literal meaning of an idiom in a context that allows for a concrete reading of an otherwise playful use of language. The example in Figure 12 comes from a promotional leaflet handed out to visitors at the Wedgwood factory and exhibition – home of the famous British brand of pottery and ornamental china, in Stoke-on-Trent, UK.

Something that comes or is handed *on a plate* is made easy to acquire. The English text plays on the idiomatic meaning of the expression as well as the concrete meaning of *plate*, which is particularly salient here given that Wedgwood are famous for producing crockery. This play on idiom is very difficult to reproduce in other languages. The Japanese translation (Figure 13) opts for sacrificing the idiomatic meaning in this instance.

Centuries of craftsmanship on a plate.

He not only created unique designs that are still produced today but he revolutionised the manufacturing process. In addition, Josiah Wedgwood built a village, Etruria, to provide good housing for his potters and a modern factory for them to work in.

Figure 12   Original version of Wedgwood leaflet

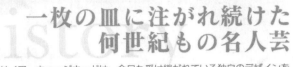

Figure 13 Japanese translation

The caption in Japanese literally reads: 'The craft of famous people has been continually poured for centuries into a single plate'.

(f) Translation by omission of entire idiom

As with single words, an idiom may sometimes be omitted altogether in the target text. This may be because it has no close match in the target language, its meaning cannot be easily paraphrased, or for stylistic reasons. Here is an example from *A Hero from Zero* (p. vi):

> It was bitter, but funny, to see that Professor Smith had doubled his own salary before recommending the offer from Fayed, and added a pre-dated bonus <u>for good measure</u>.

Target text (Arabic, p. 12):

> وكان من المؤسف، بل ومن المضحك، أن يتمكن البروفسور سميث من مضاعفة راتبه مرتين قبل أن يتقدم بتوصيته لقبول عرض فايد، وأن يضيف الى ذلك مكافأة يتحدد سلفاً موعد حصوله عليها.

> It was regrettable, even funny, that Professor Smith had been able to double his salary twice before offering his recommendation to accept Fayed's offer, and that he added to this a bonus, the date of which had been previously decided on.

One strategy which cannot be adequately illustrated, simply because it would take up a considerable amount of space, is the strategy of compensation. Briefly, this means that one may either omit or play down a feature such as idiomaticity at the point where it occurs in the source text and introduce it elsewhere in the target text. This strategy is not restricted to idiomaticity or fixed expressions and may be used to make up for any loss of meaning, emotional force or stylistic effect which may not be possible to reproduce directly at a given point in the target text. Mason (1982:29) explains that, because they were unable to translate specific puns at the points at which they occurred in the text, the translators of *Astérix* 'have sometimes resorted to inserting English puns (of equivalent impact rather than equivalent meaning) in different frames of the cartoon'. For a detailed discussion of compensation as a translation strategy, see Harvey (1995, 1998).

Using the typical phraseology of the target language – its natural collocations, its own fixed and semi-fixed expressions, the right level of idiomaticity, and so on – will greatly enhance the readability of your translations. Getting this level right means that you will avoid unintentionally producing a text that feels 'foreign'.[9] But naturalness and readability are also affected by other linguistic features, and these will be discussed at various points in the following chapters.

exercises

1. Choose one English word and find its first dictionary equivalent in your target language. Make a list of some common collocations of the English word. Make an independent list of the most typical collocations of your target-language equivalent. Compare the two lists and comment on the differences and similarities in the collocational patterning of the two items.

2. Make a list of some common collocations of an English word of your choice.
   (a) Suggest some common collocations in your target language which convey similar meanings to those of the English collocations. Comment on any difference in meaning.
   (b) If there are no common collocations in your target language which express meanings similar to those conveyed by the English collocations, suggest circumlocutions which can be used either as paraphrases or footnotes to convey the meanings of the English collocations in question (if necessary) to a target reader.

3. Make a list of some English idioms with which you are familiar and which have close counterparts in your target language. Comment on any differences in meaning, form or context of use between each English idiom and its 'equivalent' in your target language.

4. Make a list of some common English expressions or idioms that you feel would be difficult to translate into your target language, for example because they relate to specific English habits or social occasions. Try, to

the best of your ability, to paraphrase each expression twice: the first time as briefly as possible so that it can be inserted in a text, and the second time more elaborately so that it can be included as a footnote to a text.

5. Try your hand at translating this challenging title and header which introduce an article promoting visits to the Dead Sea. The article appeared in a Wonderlust Guide to Jordan, published in 2010 (p. 22). The caption under 'Mud, glorious mud' reads: 'As every schoolchild worth their salt knows, the Dead Sea is the briniest lake on earth. But its waters and mud offer unique spa experiences, as Gail Simmons discovers.'

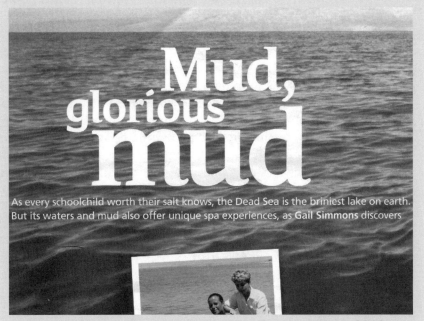

Figure 14   Caption of article in Wonderlust Guide to Jordan 2010

6. *The Chronicle Review*, a section of the US-based *Chronicle of Higher Education*, published an article by Evan Goldstein on the renowned, outspoken historian Tony Judt on 6 January 2010. Entitled 'The Trials of Tony Judt', the article begins by explaining that 'a little more than a year ago, Judt was diagnosed with a progressive variant of amyotrophic lateral sclerosis, better known as Lou Gehrig's disease, a fatal condition that gradually destroys a person's ability to move, breathe, swallow, and talk'.

Imagine that you have agreed to translate this article for one of the many activist websites that provide multiple translations of such material. The full article is available at http://chronicle.com/article/The-Trials-of-Tony-Judt/63449/. Comment on any collocations in the following stretch that might prove difficult to translate into your target language and the strategies you have used to overcome these difficulties, paying particular attention to the play on *life/death sentence* at the end of the second paragraph.

> At bedtime, having been maneuvered from his wheelchair to his cot and positioned upright, his glasses removed, Judt is left alone with his thoughts. In recent months, they have turned to his youth – the charms of a curmudgeonly grade-school German-language instructor, the shifting cultural mores of Cambridge in the mid-60s, the comforting solitude of a train ride. At the encouragement of his friend Timothy Garton Ash, a professor of European studies at Oxford, he has crafted those 'little vignettes from my past' into a series of autobiographical sketches.
>
> In one moving essay, recently published in *The New York Review*, Judt addresses directly his life with ALS. 'Helplessness,' he writes, 'is humiliating even in a passing crisis – imagine or recall some occasion when you have fallen down or otherwise required physical assistance from strangers. Imagine the mind's response to the knowledge that the peculiarly humiliating helplessness of ALS is a life sentence (we speak blithely of death sentences in this connection, but actually the latter would be a relief).'

7. Imagine that you have been asked by a client to translate the following text into your target language. The text appeared in *The Economist* (UK Edition, 6–12 February 2010, p. 68). Your target reader works in the banking business and needs to follow international developments in this field.

> How firms fool equity analysts
> Stockpilers suckered
>
> NEW YORK
> Chief executives pull the wool over analysts' eyes, again
>
> How do you pump up the value of your company in these difficult times? One tried and tested way is to hoodwink equity analysts, according to a new study of 1,300 corporate bosses, board directors and analysts.
>   The authors found that chief executives commonly respond to negative appraisals from Wall Street by managing appearances, rather than making changes that actually improve corporate

governance: boards are made more formally independent, but without actually increasing their ability to control management. This is typically done by hiring directors who, although they may have no business ties to the company, are socially close to its top brass. According to James Westphal, one of the study's co-authors, some 45% of the members of nominating committees on the boards of large American firms have 'friendship' ties to the boss – though this varies widely from company to company.

...

Why do analysts swallow this self-interested narrative? Respondents acknowledged that social ties could undermine independence, but most said they do not have the time to look into such issues. ...

Depressingly, these market-distorting shenanigans are part of a pattern. An earlier study found that public companies enjoy lasting share-price gains from plans that please analysts, such as share buybacks and long-term incentive schemes for executives, even when they fail to follow through on announcements.

When you have translated the text, comment on the strategies you used to deal with various collocations such as *pump up value*, *tried and tested*, *managing appearances*, *top brass* and *swallow a narrative*, including register-specific collocations such as *share buybacks*. Comment also on your strategy for translating the idiom in the subtitle (*pull the wool over analysts' eyes*).

8. Try your hand at this challenging extract from an Austin Rover brochure (*Today's Cars*, 1989). Imagine that you have been asked to translate the passage below into your target language, for distribution in your local market. Do not be distracted by unfamiliar car terminology; this is not the object of the exercise. If necessary, leave a gap if you cannot find an equivalent for a specialized term.

You will note that the passage includes several idioms and is highly informal in style. Whatever strategies you decide to use in translating it, remember that idioms are not just used for the meanings they convey but also for the effect they produce on the reader, for their stylistic value.

METRO SPORT

The new Metro Sport. Terrific looks. Loads of go. For a lot less than you think.

The Sport looks just what it is – a hot little hatchback that knows how to handle itself. With an aerodynamic tail spoiler;

exercises

all-white sports wheel trims; and special graphics and paint treatment.

Under the bonnet is a 73 PS1.3 engine with a real sting in its tail. (Relax – it's also remarkably economical.)

You won't have to put up with a spartan cockpit in return for sparkling performance. Just try those stylishly trimmed sports seats for size.

Now tune into the electronic stereo radio/stereo cassette player. Four speakers, great sound. *And* a built-in security code theft deterrent.

There's a wealth of driving equipment too – including a tachometer of course.

Right up your street? Choose your Sport in one of five selected colours. And paint the town red.

When you have translated the text, comment on any difficulties involved, the strategies you used and any change in the level of informality in your target version.

SUGGESTIONS FOR FURTHER READING

On collocation

Barnwell, Katherine (1974) *Introduction to Semantics and Translation*, High Wycombe: Summer Institute of Linguistics. Chapter 6, section 6.8: 'Collocation'.

Beekman, John and John Callow (1974) *Translating the Word of God*, Michigan: Zondervan. Chapter 11: 'Collocational Clashes'.

Carter, Ronald and Michael McCarthy (1988) *Vocabulary and Language Teaching*, London: Longman. Chapter 2, section 7: 'Linguistic Goings-on'.

Hoey, Michael (2005) *Lexical Priming: A New Theory of Words and Language*, Abingdon, Oxon: Routledge.

Mackin, R. (1978) 'On Collocations: Words Shall Be Known by the Company They Keep', in P. Strevens (ed.) *In Honour of A. S. Hornby*, Oxford: Oxford University Press, 149–165.

Sinclair, John (1991) *Corpus Concordance Collocation*, Oxford: Oxford University Press.

On idioms and fixed expressions

Carter, Ronald (1987) *Vocabulary: Applied Linguistic Perspectives*, London: Allen & Unwin. Chapter 3, section 3.6: 'Idioms Galore', and section 3.7: 'Fixing Fixed Expressions'.

Fernando, Chitra (1996) *Idioms and Idiomaticity*, Oxford: Oxford University Press.

Moon, Rosamund (1998) *Fixed Expressions and Idioms in English*, Oxford: Clarendon.

On the translation of collocations, idioms and fixed expressions

Al-Wahy, Ahmed Seddik (2009) 'Idiomatic False Friends in English and Modern Standard Arabic', *Babel* 55(2): 101–123.

Gottlieb, Henrik (1997) 'Quality Revisited: The Rendering of English Idioms in Danish Television Subtitles vs. Printed Translations', in Anna Trosborg (ed.) *Text Typology and Translation*, Amsterdam: John Benjamins, 309–338.

Laviosa, Sara (2007) 'Learning Creative Writing by Translating Witty Ads', *The Interpreter and Translator Trainer* 1(2): 197–222.

Sheridan, Sarah (2009) 'Translating Idiomatic Expressions from English to Irish Sign Language (ISL): Theory and Practice', *The Sign Language Translator and Interpreter* 3(1): 69–84.

NOTES

1   Rules are generally described in terms of grammatical statements; see Chapter 4.

2   Markedness is an important concept in language study. For a good treatment of different types of markedness, see Lyons (1977:305–311). For a discussion of the relationship between markedness, choice and meaning, see Chapter 5, section 5.1.1.3.

3   I am grateful for this information to Paula Chicken, formerly of French Studies, University of Birmingham.

4   Much has been written in defence of literalism and various exoticizing and foreignizing strategies since the first edition of this book appeared. For an accessible overview and an opportunity to rehearse some of the arguments for and against literalism and foreignization, see the editorial apparatus accompanying the articles by John Sturrock and Lawrence Venuti in Baker (2010a).

5   In all the examples from *Language and Society,* I am not actually sure whether the source language is English or French, but I am assuming it is English for convenience.

6   Superseded by the Code of Professional Conduct of the Institute of Translation and Interpreting. The wording which features in the current Code for individual members, available on the ITI website, is: 'members shall translate only into a language which is either (i) their mother tongue or language of habitual use , or (ii) one in which they have satisfied the Institute that they have equal competence' (article 4.1). See www.iti.org.uk/.

7   I am grateful to Ming Xie, University of Cambridge, for this information.

8   I am grateful to Luis Pérez-González for assistance with the analysis of this example.

9   As explained in Chapter 2, section 2.2.3, a translator may deliberately wish to communicate the foreign feel of the text to the target readership. The issue here is ultimately one of awareness of the effect that a given choice might have on the intended recipients of the translation.

CHAPTER 4

Grammatical equivalence

Even the simplest, most basic requirement we make of translation cannot be met without difficulty: one cannot always match the content of a message in language A by an expression with exactly the same content in language B, because what can be expressed and what must be expressed is a property of a specific language in much the same way as *how* it can be expressed.

(Winter 1961:98)

language ... gives structure to experience, and helps to determine our way of looking at things, so that it requires some intellectual effort to see them in any other way than that which our language suggests to us.

(Halliday 1970:143)

In Chapters 2 and 3 we saw that the lexical resources of a language exercise considerable influence on what can be said in that language as well as how it can be said. The lexical structure of a language, its stock of words and expressions and its established patterns of collocation, provides its speakers with ready-made ways of analysing and reporting experience. We do find new ways of reporting experience when necessary, but on the whole, we tend to rely heavily on existing lexical resources in order to communicate successfully and easily with other members of our language community.

Lexical resources are not the only factor that influences the way in which we analyse and report experience. Another powerful factor which determines the kind of distinctions we regularly make in reporting experience is the grammatical system of our language. In the course of reporting events, every language makes a different selection from a large set of possible distinctions in terms of notions such as time, number, gender, shape, visibility, person, proximity, animacy and so on. There is no uniform or objective way of reporting events in all their detail, exactly as they happen in the real world; the structure of each language highlights, and to a large extent preselects, certain areas which are deemed to be fundamental to the reporting of any experience.

Grammar is the set of rules which determine the way in which units such as words and phrases can be combined in a language and the kind of information which has to be made regularly explicit in utterances. A language can, of course, express any kind of information its speakers need to express, but the grammatical system of a given language will determine the ease with which certain notions such as time reference or gender can be made explicit. Centuries ago, the Greeks and Romans assumed that notional categories such as time, number and gender existed in the real world and must therefore be common to all languages. All languages, they thought, must express these 'basic' aspects of experience on a regular basis. With greater exposure to other languages, it later became apparent that these so-called 'basic' categories are not in fact universal, and that languages differ widely in the range of notions they choose to make explicit on a regular basis. In this chapter, we will take a brief look at the variety of grammatical categories which may or may not be expressed in different languages and the way this area of language structure affects decisions in the course of translation. But before we do so, it may be helpful to outline some of the main differences between lexical and grammatical categories.

4.1 GRAMMATICAL VS LEXICAL CATEGORIES

> the grammatical pattern of a language (as opposed to its lexical stock) deter-mines those aspects of each experience that must be expressed in the given language.
>
> *(Jakobson 1959:235–236)*

Grammar is organized along two main dimensions: **morphology** and **syntax**. **Morphology** covers the structure of words, the way in which the form of a word changes to indicate specific contrasts in the grammatical **system**.[1] For instance, most nouns in English have two forms, a singular form and a plural form: *man/men*, *child/children*, *car/cars*. English can therefore be said to have a grammatical category of number. The morphological structure of a language determines the basic information which must be expressed in that language. **Syntax** covers the grammatical structure of groups, clauses and sentences: the linear sequences of classes of words such as noun, verb, adverb and adjective, and functional elements such as subject, predicator and object, which are allowed in a given language.[2] The syntactic structure of a language imposes certain restrictions on the way messages may be organized in that language.

Choices in language can be expressed grammatically or lexically, depending on the type and range of linguistic resources available in a given language. Choices made from closed systems, such as the number system (singular/plural) or the pronoun system in English, are grammatical; those made from open-ended sets of items or expressions are lexical. Grammatical choices are normally expressed morphologically, as in the case of the singular/plural contrast in English. They may also be expressed syntactically, for instance by manipulating the order of elements in a clause to indicate certain relations between them or to signal the function of the clause (cf. the difference between the order of elements in a statement and a question in English: *She had forgotten about the party./Had she forgotten about the party?*).

The most important difference between grammatical and lexical choices, as far as translation is concerned, is that grammatical choices are largely obligatory while lexical choices are largely optional. Languages which have morphological resources for expressing a certain category such as number, tense or gender have to express these categories regularly; those which do not have morphological resources for expressing the same categories do not have to express them except when they are felt to be relevant. Because a grammatical choice is drawn from a closed set of options, it is (a) obligatory, and (b) rules out other choices from the same system by default. The fact that number is a grammatical category in English means that an English speaker or writer who uses a noun such as *student* or *child* has to choose between singular and plural. Apart from a few nouns which allow a choice of singular or plural concord (e.g. *The committee is/are considering the question*), the choice of singular in English rules out the possibility of plural reference by default, and vice versa. The same is not true in Chinese or Japanese, where number is a lexical rather than a grammatical category (see 4.2.1 below). A Chinese or Japanese speaker or writer does not have to choose between singular and plural, unless the context demands that this information be made explicit. Where necessary, number is indicated in these languages by means of adding a word such as 'several' or a numeral such as 'one' or 'five' to the noun, rather than by changing the form of the noun itself.

Grammatical structure also differs from lexical structure in that it is more resistant to change. It is much easier to introduce a new word, expression or collocation into a language than to introduce a new grammatical category, system or sequence. The grammatical structure of a language does, of course, change, but this does not happen overnight. Grammatical change occurs over a much longer time scale than lexical change. On the whole, the grammatical structure of a language remains fairly constant throughout the lifetime of an individual, whereas one encounters new words, expressions and collocations on a daily basis. Grammatical rules are also more resistant to manipulation by speakers. A deviant grammatical structure may occasionally be accepted in very restricted contexts, for instance in order to maintain rhyme or metre in poetry. A very small number of text types, such as poems, advertisements and jokes, will occasionally manipulate or flout the grammatical rules of the language to create special effect. The well-known poet e. e. cummings does precisely that; he achieves special effect by using unusual grammatical configurations, as he does in his poem 'a pretty a day', which starts as follows:

> a pretty a day
> (and every fades)
> is here and away
> (but born are maids
> to flower an hour
> in all, all)

Likewise, modelled on Louis Jordan's 1944 song 'Is You Is or Is You Ain't My Baby', the following advertisement by Access, a former credit card company, provides an example of a similar type of manipulation in non-literary contexts:

> Does you does or does you don't take access?
> 7 million outlets worldwide does.

On the whole, however, deviant grammatical configurations are simply not acceptable in most contexts. This means that, in translation, grammar often has the effect of a straitjacket, forcing the translator along a certain course which may or may not follow that of the source text as closely as the translator would like it to.

4.2 THE DIVERSITY OF GRAMMATICAL CATEGORIES ACROSS LANGUAGES

It is difficult to find a notional category which is regularly and uniformly expressed in all languages. Even categories such as time and number, which many of us take as reflecting basic aspects of experience, are only optionally indicated in some Asian languages such as Chinese and Vietnamese. On the other hand, a number of American Indian languages such as Yana and Navaho have grammatical categories which in many other languages would hardly ever be expressed even by lexical means. These languages, for instance, have a category of 'shape', which means that an object must be classified according to whether it is long, round or sheet-like (Sapir and Swadesh 1964). Some languages, such as Amuesha of Peru, regularly indicate whether a person is dead or alive by adding a suffix to the name of any person referred to after his or her death (Larson 1984). The absence of the suffix indicates that the person concerned is alive, in much the same way as the absence of a plural suffix such as -s in English indicates a choice of singular as opposed to plural reference.[3] Languages therefore differ widely in the way they are equipped to handle various notions and express different aspects of experience, possibly because they differ in the degree of importance or relevance that they attach to such aspects of experience. Time is regarded as a crucial aspect of experience in English, so that it is virtually impossible to discuss any event in English without locating it in the past, present or future. In Aztec, the notion of deference is regarded as crucial. Consequently, according to Nida, 'it is impossible to say anything to anyone without indicating the relative degree of respect to which the speaker and hearer are entitled in the community' (1964:95). Korean and Japanese similarly draw on a complex system of honorifics to signal the relative status of participants in an interaction.

Differences in the grammatical structures of the source and target languages often result in some change in the information content of the message during the process of translation. This change may take the form of adding to the target text information which is not expressed in the source text. This can happen when the target language has a grammatical category which the source language lacks. In translating from English or French into an American Indian language such as Yana or Navaho, one would have to add information concerning the shape of any objects mentioned in the text. Likewise, in translating into Amuesha, one would have to indicate whether any person mentioned in the text is dead or alive. Details which are ignored in the source text but which have to be specified in the target language can pose a serious dilemma for the translator if they cannot be reasonably inferred from the context.

The change in the information content of the message may be in the form of omitting information specified in the source text. If the target language lacks a grammatical category which exists in the source language, the information expressed by that category may have to be ignored. Jakobson suggests that 'no lack of grammatical device in the language translated into makes impossible a literal translation of the entire conceptual information contained in the original' (1959:235). This is true in theory, but in practice the lack of a grammatical device can make the translation of 'the entire conceptual information' very difficult indeed. First, the lack of a grammatical category in a given language suggests that the indication of information associated with that category is regarded as optional. The frequency of occurrence of such optional information tends to be low, and a translation which repeatedly indicates information that is normally left unspecified in the target language is bound to sound unnatural. Second, because such information would have to be expressed lexically, it is likely to assume more importance in the target text than it does in the source text. The fact that lexical choices are optional gives them more weight than grammatical choices.

The following discussion of some major categories, with examples, is intended to illustrate the kinds of difficulty that translators often encounter because of differences in the grammatical structures of source and target languages.

4.2.1 Number

The idea of countability is probably universal in the sense that it is readily accessible to all human beings and is expressed in the lexical structure of all languages. However, not all languages have a grammatical category of number, and those that do do not necessarily view countability in the same terms. As explained above, English recognizes a distinction between one and more than one (singular and plural). This distinction has to be expressed morphologically, by adding a suffix to a noun or by changing its form in some other way to indicate whether it refers to one or more than one: *student/students*, *fox/foxes*, *man/men*, *child/children*. Some languages, such as Japanese, Chinese and Vietnamese, prefer to express the same notion lexically or, more often, not at all. The form of a noun in these languages does not normally indicate whether it is singular or plural. For example, *my book* and *my books* are both *wo-de-shu* in Chinese (Tan 1980).

Unlike Japanese, Chinese and Vietnamese, most languages have a grammatical category of number, similar but not necessarily identical to that of English. Arabic, Inuit and some Slavonic languages formally distinguish between one, two and more than two. These languages have a dual form in addition to singular and plural forms. In most European languages today, dual is a lexical rather than a grammatical category; it can only be indicated by the use of a numeral. And so English regularly expresses a meaning contrast between *house* and *houses*, whereas Inuit regularly expresses a meaning contrast between *iglu*, *igluk* and *iglut* ('one/two/more than two houses'). A small number of languages, such as Fijian, even distinguish between singular, dual, trial (covering three or a small number) and plural (Robins 1964). Such additional refinements to a system can sometimes pose problems in translation.

A translator working from a language which has number distinctions into a language with no category of number has two main options: he or she can (a) omit the relevant information relating to number, or (b) encode this information lexically. The following examples illustrate how information relating to number is often left out in languages such as Chinese and Japanese. The source language in both examples is English. Items in angle brackets are not specified in the target text but they are not ruled out either since Chinese and Japanese do not have a category of number. The first example is from *China's Panda Reserves* (World Wide Fund for Nature text which accompanied a slide show):

China's Panda <u>Reserves</u>.

Target text (Chinese):

中国的熊猫保护区

China's Panda **Protection-zone<s>**.

'Protection-zone' is a literal rendering of the accepted Chinese translation of *reserve*. It is not marked for number. The reader of the Chinese text has no way of knowing, from this title, whether China has one or more than one panda reserve.

The following example is from *The Fix: The Inside Story of the World Drug Trade* (Freemantle 1985:142):

Enforcement officials – particularly the front-line US Customs Service – have produced a series of recognisable profiles in order to identify and intercept drug runners. It is a system that works particularly well with the Yakuza because of the bizarre but rigid code of ethics by which the Japanese Mafia conducts itself, quite different from any other criminal society in the world. It concerns <u>fingers</u>, or rather the lack of <u>them</u>. And <u>tattoos</u>.

Target text (Japanese):

アメリカの取締当局は、とくに合衆国関税局の第一線は、麻薬の運び屋（ランナー）を識別、摘発するために一種の手配台帖を作成してきた。日本のヤクザを対象とした場合に、ことのほ

か有効なシステムである。日本のマフィアが自らに課している
不気味だが峻厳なヤクザ道の掟は、世界のいかなる犯罪社会の
それとも異なっているからだ。それは指と、つまり指の欠損に
関連する。さらに刺青とも。

… This concerns **finger\<s\>**, or rather the lack of **finger\<s\>**. And
tattoo\<s\>.

Here again the highlighted nouns are not marked for number in any way, and the
Japanese reader can only guess whether the writer is talking about one or several
fingers and tattoos. This apparent lack of interest in the difference between one and
more than one is no more surprising than the lack of interest in duality in English and
most European languages. Chinese and Japanese speakers are not too concerned
with establishing in each case whether there is one or more than one of a given
referent, just as English speakers are not particularly interested in establishing
whether there are two or more than two persons or objects.

It may sometimes be necessary or desirable in certain contexts to specify
plurality or duality in languages which do not normally specify such information
because they do not have a category of number or a dual form. In this case, the
translator may decide to encode the relevant information lexically, as in the following
examples. The first example is from *Palace and Politics in Prewar Japan* (Titus
1974:17); the source text is English:

> The <u>heads of the ministries</u> created in 1869 were not directly
> responsible for 'advising and assisting' (*hohitsu*) the emperor, though
> they were to become so in 1889.

Target text (Japanese):

> 明治二年につくられた諸省の長は、天皇「輔弼」の直接責任者
> ではない。そうなったのは明治二二年なのである。

> The head\<s\> of **various** ministry\<ies\> created in Meiji 2nd are not
> directly responsible for 'hohitsu' the emperor.

A Japanese word meaning 'various' is added in the translation to indicate that
reference is made to more than one ministry and, by implication, more than one
head of ministry.

The second example is from an unpublished document about arbitration procedures in Cairo. The source text is Arabic.

عندما يراد تعيين ثلاثة محكمين، يختار كل طرف محكماً واحداً، ويختار المحكمان المعينان
على هذا النحو المحكم الثالث وهو الذى يتولى رئاسة هيئة التحكيم.

> When the appointment of three arbitrators is required, each party chooses one arbitrator, and the <u>arbitrators-dual appointed-dual</u> in this way choose the third arbitrator and it is he who takes on the presidency of the arbitration authority.

English target text:

> When the appointment of three arbitrators is required, each party selects one arbitrator, and the **two arbitrators** thus appointed select the third arbitrator who then heads the Arbitration Committee.

Where it is felt to be important, information on number can therefore be encoded lexically. However, as with any grammatical category, a translator working from a language with a category of number into one without such a category must be careful not to overspecify this type of information in the target text. Unless the context specifically demands it, regular reference to information normally left unspecified in a given language will only make the translation awkward and unnatural because it will not reflect normal ways of reporting experience in the target language.

4.2.2 Gender

Gender is a grammatical distinction according to which a noun or pronoun is classified as either masculine or feminine in some languages.[4] The distinction applies to nouns which refer to animate beings as well as those which refer to inanimate objects. For example, French distinguishes between masculine and feminine gender in nouns such as *fils/fille* ('son'/'daughter') and *chat/chatte* ('male cat'/'female cat'). In addition, nouns such as *magazine* ('magazine') and *construction* ('construction') are also classified as masculine and feminine respectively. Determiners,[5] adjectives, and sometimes verbs (as in the case of Arabic and Swahili), usually agree with the noun in gender as well as in number.

English does not have a grammatical category of gender as such; English nouns are not regularly inflected to distinguish between feminine and masculine. The gender distinction nevertheless exists in some semantic areas and in the **person** system. Different nouns are sometimes used to refer to female and male members of the same species: *cow/bull, sow/boar, doe/stag, mare/stallion, ewe/ram*. A small number of nouns which refer to professions have masculine and feminine forms, with the suffix *-ess* indicating feminine gender. Examples include *actor/ actress, manager/manageress, host/hostess* and *steward/stewardess*. These, however, do not always reflect straightforward gender distinctions as in the case of other European languages; some carry specific connotations. For instance, the distinction between *author* and *authoress* may carry more expressive than propositional meaning: *authoress* tends to have derogatory overtones, with *author* being the unmarked form for both sexes.[6] In addition to gender distinctions in specific semantic areas, English also has a category of **person** (see 4.2.3 below) which distinguishes in the third-person singular between masculine, feminine and inanimate (*he/she/it*). This distinction does not apply to the third-person plural (*they*). Russian and German make similar gender distinctions in the third-person singular pronouns and, like English, do not apply these distinctions to the third-person plural. On the other hand, languages like French and Italian maintain the gender distinction in the third-person plural: for example, *ils* vs *elles* in French. In some languages, such as Arabic, gender distinctions apply to second- as well as third-person pronouns. In addition to gender distinctions in the third-person singular and plural, Arabic has different forms for 'you', depending on whether the person or persons addressed is/are male or female. Other languages such as Chinese and Indonesian do not have gender distinctions in their person systems at all.

In most languages that have a gender category, the masculine term is usually the 'dominant' or 'unmarked' term. In French, *elles* is used only when all persons or things referred to are feminine; if one or more persons or things in a group are masculine the form used is *ils*, even if the feminine referents outnumber the masculine ones. Similarly, if the sex of a referent is not known, the masculine rather than the feminine form is used. In effect, this means that the use of feminine forms provides more specific information than the use of masculine forms can be said to provide; it rules out the possibility of masculine reference, whereas the use of masculine forms does not rule out the possibility of feminine reference.

There is now a conscious attempt to replace the unmarked masculine form *he* in English with forms such as *s/he*, *he or she* and *him or her*. This is particularly true of academic writing. But even among the general public, overtly masculine nouns such as *chairman*, *spokesman* and *businessman* are consciously and systematically being replaced by more neutral ones such as *chairperson* and *spokesperson*, or by specifically feminine nouns such as *businesswoman* when the referent is clearly feminine. Viaggio (1996:189) reports an incident in a debate on linguistic sexism at the United Nations where the delegates variously addressed the British female presiding officer as *Madam Chairman*, *Madam Chairperson*, *Madam Chairwoman* and *Madam Chairlady*. When one of the delegates finally addressed her as *Madam Chair*, she responded 'I'd rather you called me a man than a piece of furniture'. Viaggio (*ibid.*) offers several possible strategies for dealing with this type of gender-based humour in the context of simultaneous interpreting, including retaining the key English nouns as loan words, and possibly adding an explanation. In Spanish, the result would be:

> Llámeme **man** pero no **chair**, **que no soy un meuble**.

> Call me **man** but not **chair**: **I'm no piece of furniture**.

Gender-based humour and wordplay aside, another challenge comes from a growing trend to use the feminine form as the unmarked form, especially in academic writing. Diane Blakemore, for instance, uses *she* and *her* to mean any person, male or female:

It is clear that because of the role of the context in all aspects of utterance interpretation, a speaker who intends *her* utterance to be taken in a particular way must expect it to be interpreted in a context that yields that interpretation.

(1987:27; my emphasis)

This ideological stance is somewhat difficult to transfer into languages in which gender distinctions pervade the grammatical system. It is fairly easy to make the switch from *he* to something like *s/he* or *him/her* in English because the change affects these items only. But in a language such as Arabic, where gender distinctions are reflected not only in nouns and pronouns but also in the concord between these and their accompanying verbs and adjectives, the resulting structures would clearly be much more cumbersome than in English. With all the good will in the world, an Arab writer or translator cannot side with this admittedly more enlightened approach to gender without sacrificing the readability of the target text. By contrast, the syntax of other languages offers much more flexible ways of avoiding sexist language. In revising the Irish and English versions of the Constitution of Ireland, for example, in order to eliminate traces of sexist language, the Irish text posed much fewer problems than the English (Ó Cearúil 1999:47):

> While the clause 'such resolution shall operate to remove the President from his office' in Article 12.10.7° is gender-proofed in the version published by the All-Party Oireachtas Committeee on the Constitution to 'such resolution shall operate to remove the President from his **or her** office', ... the Irish text needs no gender-proofing, reading '... is é is feidhm don rún sin an tUachtarán a chur as oifig', literally 'such resolution shall operate to remove the President from office'.

Ó Cearúil thus concludes that '[g]ender-proofing the English text from "from his office" to "from office", following the Irish text, would appear to be the better course rather than emending to read 'from his or her office'' (*ibid.*:47–48).

Gender distinctions are generally more relevant in translation when the referent of the noun or pronoun is human. Gender distinctions in inanimate objects such as 'car' or 'ship' and in animals such as 'dog' and 'cat' are sometimes manipulated in English to convey expressive meaning, particularly in literature, but they do not often cause difficulties in non-literary translation.[7] Making the necessary adjustments, for instance by adding the gender dimension in the target text (English *table* : French *la/une table*) is usually straightforward and automatic because the distinctions themselves are largely arbitrary. But gender distinctions in the case of human referents are not arbitrary, and this is why Lyons (1968), for instance, suggests that what is important in communication is the pronominal function of gender rather than the category of gender in general. The pronominal function of gender reflects a genuine, non-arbitrary distinction between male and female. Although languages differ in the extent to which they regularly specify the gender of human referents (cf. English *they* and French *ils/elles*), we all readily recognize the distinction and expect it to reflect a genuine aspect of experience.

The following text illustrates the kind of problem that the pronominal function of gender can pose in translation. As in previous examples, the problematic items in the source text are underlined and the items which replace them in the target text are highlighted in bold. Only those strategies used to overcome difficulties arising from gender distinctions will be commented on.

Source text (English: *Kolestral Super* – leaflet accompanying a hair-conditioning product):

Instructions for use:
– <u>Shampoo</u> the hair with a mild WELLA-SHAMPOO and lightly <u>towel dry</u>.
– <u>Apply</u> KOLESTRAL-SUPER directly onto the hair and <u>massage</u> gently.
– For maximum effect, <u>cover</u> the hair with a plastic cap or towel.
– KOLESTRAL-SUPER can be left on the hair for 10–20 minutes.
– After the developing time <u>rinse off</u> thoroughly before styling – no shampooing required.
– <u>Style</u> the hair as usual.

Target text (Arabic):

تعليمات وارشادات الإستعمال:

– يُغسل الشعر بشامبو من "ويللا" على أن يكون من نوع الشامبو الملطف، ثم يُجفف الشعر بواسطة المنشفة وذلك تجفيفاً بسيطاً ليُترك الشعر رطباً.

– يُوضع كولسترال سوبر مباشرة على الشعر ويُدلك بنعومة ورقة.

– للحصول على فعالية مطلقة، يُغطى الشعر بواسطة "كاب" أى قبعة بلاستيكية تُغطى الشعر، أو بواسطة منشفة.

– يُترك كولسترال سوبر مدة 10 دقائق الى 20 دقيقة.

– بعد انتهاء مدة التفاعل، يجب أن يشطف (يُفوّح) الشعر جيداً وبعمق قبل البدء بالتسريحة المرغوبة. لا حاجة للشامبو فى هذه المرحلة النهائية.

– يُسرّح الشعر ويُشطف كالعادة وبالاسلوب المرغوب وتكون النتيجة مثالية ورائعة.

Instructions and guide to use:
– The hair **is washed** with 'Wella' shampoo, provided that it is a mild shampoo. Then the hair **is dried** by means of a towel, a simple drying so that the hair is left damp.
– Kolestral-Super **is put** directly on the hair and **massaged** with softness and gentleness.

- For obtaining maximum effectiveness, the hair **is covered** by means of a cap, that is a plastic hat which covers the hair, or by means of a towel.
- Kolestral-Super is left for a period of 10–20 minutes.
- After the end of the reaction period, the hair **should be rinsed** well and in depth before starting on the desired hair-do. No need for shampoo in this final stage.
- The hair **is styled** and **combed** as usual and in the desired fashion and the result is ideal and marvellous.

I mentioned earlier that the gender distinction in Arabic applies to the second as well as third person. An Arabic speaker or writer has to select between 'you, masculine' (*anta*) and 'you, feminine' (*anti*) in the case of the second-person singular. Moreover, this type of information must be signalled in the form of the verb itself: an Arabic verb has different forms depending on whether its subject is, for instance, second-person singular feminine or third-person plural masculine. In fact, pronouns such as 'she' and 'I' are usually redundant in Arabic and are used mainly for emphasis, since all the information they carry is incorporated in the form of the verb.

In translating the imperative verbs in the above text into Arabic, the translator would normally have to choose, as far as gender is concerned, between a masculine and a feminine form for each verb. As is the case in most languages which have a gender category, the masculine form is the unmarked form in Arabic and is therefore normally selected in most advertisements, leaflets and in wording general instructions. However, the *Kolestral Super* text is a leaflet which accompanies a hair conditioner, the sort of product which is predominantly used by women rather than men. In the Arab context, it is likely to be used exclusively by women. This situation would make the use of the masculine form in this instance highly marked. The translator could have used the feminine form of the verb, but he or she possibly felt that it would also have been marked or that it might have unnecessarily excluded potential male users. The gender distinction is avoided by using a totally different structure throughout the whole set of instructions. The use of the **passive voice** (see 4.2.5 below) instead of the imperative form of the verb allows the translator to avoid specifying the subject of the verb altogether.

Although gender is also a grammatical category in French, gender distinctions are only expressed in nouns, articles and adjectives, and in third-person pronouns; they do not affect the form of the verb. The French translation of the *Kolestral Super* leaflet can therefore follow the source text more closely than the Arabic translation. The infinitive form of the verb is used, as is the norm in wording instructions in French. The first few lines of the instruction section are quoted below for illustration:

Laver le cheveux avec un shampooing doux Wella et bien les essorer.

Appliquer KOLESTRAL-SUPER directement sur les cheveux et bien faire pénétrer.

Finally, von Flotow (1991:75) discusses a very interesting example of an English translation by Howard Scott of Louky Bersianik's feminist novel *L'Euguélionne*. Referring to a woman who is punished for aborting a baby, Bersianik writes:

> Le ou la coupable doit être punie.
> Literally: The **masculine or feminine** [*le* or *la*] guilty party must be **punished-feminine**.

As von Flotow explains (*ibid.*), the 'e' at the end of the verb *puni* ('punished') makes it clear that irrespective of whether the guilty party is male or female, it is the woman who is ultimately punished for aborting. Given that English does not mark verbs for gender, this information cannot be signalled in the same way. Scott's creative solution is to add the third-person feminine pronoun *she* and embed it in a semantically incongruous clause that further strengthens Bersianik's critique of the politics of abortion in a male-dominated society:

> The guilty one must be punished, **whether she is a man or a woman**.

4.2.3 Person

The category of person relates to the notion of participant roles. In most languages, participant roles are systematically defined through a closed system of pronouns which may be organized along a variety of dimensions.

The most common distinction is that between first person (identifying the speaker or a group which includes the speaker: English *I/we*), second person (identifying the person or persons addressed: English *you*), and third person (identifying persons and things other than the speaker and addressee: English *he/she/it/they*). A number of languages spoken in North America have four rather than three distinctions in the category of person. In these languages, the fourth person refers to 'a person or thing distinct from one already referred to by a third person form' (Robins 1964:264). Russian similarly uses a form of the pronominal adjectives *svoj* (masculine), *svoja* (feminine), *svojo* (neuter) and *svoi* (plural) to refer to a participant already referred to in the same clause, but in Russian this is not restricted to third-person forms; the participant referred to by the pronominal adjective may be first, second or third person. For instance, in *I'm meeting my teacher*, *my* would be translated by *svoj* or *svoja* (depending on the gender of the following noun). Likewise, in *He's meeting his teacher*, *his* would be translated by the appropriate case form of *svoj/svoja* provided the referent of *his* is the same as the referent of *he*; otherwise the pronoun used is *jego* (Halliday 1964).

In addition to the main distinction based on participant roles, the person system may be organized along a variety of other dimensions. As mentioned earlier, the person system in some languages may have a gender or number dimension which applies to the whole system or to parts of it. Although number is not a grammatical category in Chinese (see 4.2.1 above), the pronoun system in Chinese features a number distinction (e.g. *Wo* 'I' vs *Wo-men* 'we'; *Ni* 'you' singular vs *Ni-men* 'you' plural). On the other hand, it does not feature any gender distinctions at all in speech (e.g. *Ta* 'he/she/it' vs *Ta-men* 'they'), though it does in writing, where different characters are used for 'he', 'she' and 'it' and their plural forms.[8] In Japanese, the person system features distinctions in gender as well as social status and level of intimacy (Levinson 1983). Some languages have rather elaborate person systems. Catford (1965) explains that Bahasa Indonesia has a nine-term pronoun system where English has only seven. The gender dimension is absent from Bahasa Indonesia, but two other dimensions are of relevance:

1. the inclusive/exclusive dimension: English *we* has two translations in Bahasa Indonesia, involving a choice between *kami* and *kita*, depending on whether the addressee is included or excluded;
2. the familiar/non-familiar dimension, which necessitates a choice between, for instance, *aku* and *saja* for English *I*, depending on the relationship pertaining between speaker and hearer.

A large number of modern European languages, not including English, have a formality/politeness dimension in their person system.[9] In such languages, a pronoun other than the second-person singular, usually the second- or third-person plural, is used in interaction with a singular addressee in order to express deference and/or non-familiarity: French *vous* as opposed to *tu*; Italian *lei* (third-person singular) and in certain regions, classes and age groups *voi* (second-person plural) as opposed to *tu*; Spanish *usted* as opposed to *tu*; German *Sie* as opposed to *du*; Greek *esi* as opposed to *esis*; and Russian *vy* as opposed to *ty*. Some languages also have different forms of plural pronoun which are used to express different levels of familiarity or deference in interaction with several addressees.[10]

All languages have modes of address which can be used to express familiarity or deference in a similar way: compare the difference between *you*, *mate*, *dear*, *darling* and *Mr Smith*, *Sir*, *Professor Brown*, *Mrs Jones*, *Madam*. The difference between modes of address and pronouns is that the use of pronouns is unavoidable, particularly since pronominal reference is coded in the inflection of verbs in many languages, whereas one can often avoid addressing a person directly (Brown and Gilman 1960/1972).

What all this amounts to, among other things, is that in translating pronouns from English to, say, French, Italian, Greek, Spanish, Russian, German or Bahasa Indonesian, decisions may have to be made along such dimensions as gender, degree of intimacy between participants, or whether reference includes or excludes the addressee. This information may or may not be readily recoverable from the context. Translating in the other direction, from one of the above languages into English, will frequently involve loss of information along the dimensions in question. It is possible in theory to encode all the relevant information in an English translation, for example by using a circumlocution such as 'he and I but not you' for an exclusive 'we', but this kind of detail would be too cumbersome in most contexts.

The following examples illustrate the more problematic situation of having to make decisions in the target language along dimensions which are not explicitly stated in the source text. The examples are taken from a French translation of one of Agatha Christie's thrillers, *Crooked House* (1949/1989). The events of the novel involve a number of key characters who are related to one another in a variety of ways. In the French translation, the nature of each relation has to be reflected in the choice of pronouns that various characters use in addressing each other. The characters in the following dialogue are a young man, Charles, and a young lady, Sophia. They have worked together and have been friends for some time. Charles has just asked Sophia to marry him.

English source text (p. 9):

> 'Darling – don't <u>you</u> understand? I've tried *not* to say I love <u>you</u>—'
> She stopped me.
> 'I do understand Charles. And I like <u>your</u> funny way of doing things …'

French translation (p. 9):

> – Mais **vous** ne **comprenez** donc pas? **Vous** ne **voyez** donc pas que je fais tout ce que je peux pour ne pas **vous** dire que je **vous** aime et
> …
> Elle m'interrompit.
> – J'ai parfaitement compris, Charles, et **votre** façon comique de presenter les choses m'est très sympathique …

Note the use of the *vous* form in the French translation, indicating a level of formality and politeness which are not overtly conveyed in the English original. Compare the level of formality in the above dialogue with that in the following extract from another dialogue where Charles is talking to his father, who happens to be the Assistant Commissioner of Scotland Yard:

English source text (p. 16):

> 'But <u>your</u> police force is fully efficient,' I said. 'A nice Army type tracked her to Mario's. I shall figure in the reports <u>you</u> get.'

French translation (p. 16):

> – Mais **ta** police a l'oeil et un de **tes** hommes l'a suivie jusqu'au restaurant. Je serai mentionné dans le rapport qui **te** sera remis.

The selective use of *vous* and *tu* forms in dialogues involving different characters suggests that the French translator had to make conscious decisions about the nature of the relationships among different characters in the story and about the social standing of these characters as reflected in their adoption of certain conventions to do with approved/non-approved expression of familiarity and/or deference. You may agree or disagree with these decisions; the important thing is that we learn to appreciate the influence that the grammatical system of a language has on the way events are presented in that language. The difficulties that arise from the different demands made by the grammatical systems of different languages in translation should not be underestimated.

The familiarity/deference dimension in the pronoun system is among the most fascinating aspects of grammar and the most problematic in translation. It reflects the tenor of discourse (see Chapter 2) and can convey a whole range of rather subtle meanings. The subtle choices involved in pronoun usage in languages which distinguish between familiar and non-familiar pronouns is further complicated by the fact that this use differs significantly from one social group to another and that it changes all the time in a way that reflects changes in social values and attitudes. Brown and Gilman suggest that the Gujarati and Hindi languages of India have very strict norms of pronoun usage, reflecting asymmetrical relations of power between, for example, husband and wife. And yet, they explain, 'the progressive young Indian exchanges the mutual *T* with his wife'[11] (1960/1972:269).

Pronominal shifts in translation and interpreting can also have ideological implications, for example in terms of strengthening institutional presence and constructing in-group and out-group identities. Some simultaneous interpreters working between English and German in the European Parliament have been shown to introduce the inclusive *we* where it is not used by the speaker, partly by turning passive constructions into active ones, as in the following example (Beaton-Thome 2010:133):

English speaker:

However, it <u>was agreed</u> last week that a common political response would be desirable and that the possibility of coordinated European action <u>could be explored</u> further.

German interpretation:

Aber letzte Woche haben **wir gesagt**, dass es natürlich wünschenswert wäre, eine gemeinschaftlich politische Antwort zu finden und, dass wir uns überlegen können, wie **wir handeln** wollen.

But last week **we said** that it would of course be desirable to find a common political answer and that **we could think** about how we want to act.

They also tend to replace some instances of *they* with *we*, as in the following example (*ibid.*:133):

English speaker:

> Ministers at last week's Council discussed ways in which the member states might be able to offer practical assistance to the US and, in particular, whether <u>they</u> might accept former detainees.

German interpretation:

> Die Frage ist natürlich, sind **wir** bereit ehemalige Häftlinge zu übernehmen?

> The question is of course, are **we** prepared to take on former detainees?

Cumulatively, these choices tend to strengthen the institutional presence of the European Parliament and to enhance in-group identification with it.

These and similar examples suggest that in addition to developing strategies for dealing with challenges posed by differences in pronominal systems, translators and interpreters must also be alert to the overall impact of their cumulative choices, whether or not these are made in response to local linguistic challenges.

4.2.4 Tense and aspect

Tense and aspect are grammatical categories in a large number of languages. The form of the verb in languages which have these categories usually indicates two main types of information: time relations and aspectual differences. Time relations have to do with locating an event in time. The usual distinction is between past, present and future. Aspectual differences have to do with the temporal distribution of an event, for instance its completion or non-completion, continuation or momentariness.

In some languages, the tense and aspect system, or parts of it, may be highly developed, with several fine distinctions in temporal location or distribution. Bali, for instance, has a rather precise system of time reference. Apart from indicating past, present and future reference, each past or future reference is marked to show whether the event in question is immediately connected to the present, is separated from it by a period of time but taking place on the same day, or is separated from the present by at least one night. Wishram, an American Indian language, makes no fewer than four distinctions in reference to past events alone, each distinction expressing a certain degree of remoteness from the moment of speaking (Sapir and Swadesh 1964). In some languages, it is obligatory to specify more unusual types of temporal and aspectual relations. For instance, in the Villa Alta dialect of Zapotec (Mexico), it is necessary to distinguish between events which take place for the first time with respect to particular participants and those which are repetitions (Nida 1959).

Some languages, such as Chinese, Malay and Yurok, have no formal category of tense or aspect. The form of the verb in these languages does not change to express temporal or aspectual distinctions. If necessary, time reference can be indicated by means of various particles and adverbials. The following examples show how time relations are typically signalled in Chinese when the context demands that such information be made explicit:

> ta *xian-zai* zai bei-jing gong-zuo (lit.: 'he *now* in Peking work', i.e. 'he is working in Peking')
> ta *dang-shi zai* bei-jing gong-zuo (lit.: 'he *at that time* in Peking work', i.e. 'he was working in Peking')

(from Tan 1980:111)

Because tense and aspect are not grammatical categories in Chinese, their specification is largely optional. Context is relied on much more often than in English or Bali to establish time reference. If the adverbials in the above examples were not included in the clause, one would have to rely entirely on the context to establish the time of the event. The following examples from *China's Panda Reserves* illustrate (a) the use of adverbials to indicate time reference where necessary and feasible in a Chinese translation, and (b) the omission of time reference altogether where it can be inferred from the context or where the information is not judged to be important.

Example A

This attractive black and white mammal has widespread human appeal and <u>has become</u> a symbol for conservation efforts both within China and internationally as the symbol of The World Wide Fund for Nature (WWF).

Target text (Chinese):

这一吸引人的黑白哺乳动物为人们所广泛地喜爱。作为世界自然基金会（WWF）的标记，熊猫已经成为中国和国际性自然保护努力的象征。

This attractive black-white mammal widely liked by people and **already become** a symbol of conservation efforts …

The adverbial *yi-jing*, meaning 'already', is added to the equivalent of *become* to give the effect of the present perfect in English *has become*.

Example B

Species like this mountain rhododendron <u>were</u> collected by 19th century botanists and then transported back to Europe for horticultural collections.

Target text (Chinese):

像这一山杜鹃花等种类为十九世纪的植物学家所集采，然后运回欧洲作为园林收藏品。

Species like this mountain rhododendron **collect**<ed> by 19th century botanists and then **transport**<ed> back to Europe for horticultural collections.

The connotations of pastness in the above extract can be inferred from the context, because of the reference to nineteenth-century botanists. There is therefore no need to signal the past overtly in the Chinese text.

Although the main use of the grammatical categories of tense and aspect is to indicate time and aspectual relations, they do not necessarily perform the same function in all languages. For instance, the main function of the tense system in Hopi is to signal modal meanings such as certainty, uncertainty, possibility and obligation. Hockett (1958) describes Hopi as having three main 'tenses': the first is used to express timeless truths, as in 'The sun is round'; the second is used in connection with events which are either known or presumed to be known, as in 'Paris is the capital of France'; and the third is used for events which are in the realm of uncertainty, as in 'They will arrive tomorrow'.

Tense and aspect distinctions may also take on additional, more subtle meanings in discourse. In a brief discussion of the use of tense in English and Brazilian academic abstracts, Johns (1991) points out that some verbs refer to what is stated in the academic paper itself (these he calls **indicative verbs**), while other verbs refer to what was actually done in the research on which the paper reports (these he calls **informative verbs**).[12] Johns suggests that in both English and Brazilian academic papers, the indicative/informative distinction correlates with the choice of tense: the present tense is used for indicative and the past tense for informative statements. Verbs such as *present*, *mention*, *propose* and *refer to*, which relate to what the writer is doing in the paper itself, are usually in the present tense, while verbs such as *determine*, *record*, *select* and *detect*, which have to do with actual research, are usually in the past tense. This regular correlation influences the way we interpet statements in academic papers. As Johns points out, 'the fact that the results of an experiment *are* analyzed reports the contents of the paper, but that they *were* analyzed reports one of the procedures undertaken in the research' (1991:5).

Johns (personal communication) also suggests that in English science and engineering academic abstracts, the present perfect is specifically used to refer to the work of other scientists. For example, *It is proposed that* ... suggests that the writer of the abstract is doing the proposing, but *It has been proposed that* ... suggests that the proposing is done by someone other than the writer. This signalling system is apparently more or less the same in Brazilian Portuguese. However, Johns found that translated Brazilian abstracts tend to follow textbook rules of grammar which favour 'consistent' use of tense and aspect. Many translators, for instance, use the present perfect or the simple past throughout the abstract in order to achieve 'consistency', thereby disrupting the natural signalling system of the target language.

Signalling systems such as those outlined above can be significantly different in the source and target languages, even when the basic tense and aspect systems are very similar. Japanese has a grammatical category of tense which is not too dissimilar to that of English. The suffixes *-ru* and *-ta* are regularly added to verbs to indicate non-past and past reference respectively.[13] However, this does not mean that every past tense in an English text can be translated into Japanese with a *-ta* form or that every present or future tense can be translated using a *-ru* form. A translator has to bear in mind the additional meanings that these forms can assume in a Japanese text. In the following example, the past tense in the English text is rendered by a non-past form in the Japanese translation because the non-past is often used in Japanese to express personal judgement.

Source text (*Palace and Politics in Prewar Japan,* Titus 1974:17):

The heads of the ministries created in 1869 <u>were</u> not directly responsible for 'advising and assisting' (*hohitsu*) the emperor, though they were to become so in 1889.

Target text (Japanese):

明治二年につくられた諸省の長は、天皇「輔弼」の直接責任者ではない。そうなったのは明治二二年なのである。

The head<s> of the various ministr<ies> which were created in Meiji 2nd **are** not directly responsible for 'hohitsu' the emperor. It was in Meiji 22nd that it became so.

In this instance, the use of the non-past suggests that the statement made about the role of the heads of the ministries prior to 1889 is based on the author's personal assessment of the situation, as opposed to the statement concerning their role from 1889 onwards, which, presumably, is supported by hard facts. (Meiji 2nd and Meiji 22nd refer to the equivalents of 1869 and 1889 respectively in the Japanese calendar.)

4.2.5 Voice

> A Chinese translator ... uses a preposition bei 'by' whenever he sees a passive voice in the original verb, forgetting that Chinese verbs have no voice. ... Once this sort of thing is done often enough, it gets to be written in originals, even where no translation is involved. ... Such 'translatese' is still unpalatable to most people and no one talks in that way yet, but it is already common in scientific writing, in newspapers, and in schools.
>
> *(Chao 1970; in Li and Thompson 1981:496)*

The use of the passive voice is extremely common in many varieties of written English and can pose various problems in translation, depending on the availability of similar structures, or structures with similar functions, in the target language. Because of its widespread use in technical and scientific English in particular, it has had a strong influence on similar registers in other languages through translation. The tendency to translate English passive structures literally into a variety of target languages which either have no passive voice as such or which would normally use it with less frequency is often criticized by linguists and by those involved in training translators.

Voice is a grammatical category which defines the relationship between a verb and its subject. In active clauses, the subject is the agent responsible for performing the action. In passive clauses, the subject is the affected entity, and the agent may or may not be specified, depending on the structures available in each language.

Active: (a) Nigel Mansell opened the Mansell Hall in 1986.
Passive: (b) The Mansell Hall was opened in 1986.
  (c) The Mansell Hall was opened by Nigel Mansell in 1986.

Note that the form of the verb changes in a passive structure to indicate that its subject is the affected entity rather than the agent. Chao's comment above about Chinese verbs having no voice refers to the fact that the form of the verb in Chinese does not change to indicate its relationship with the subject of the clause.

The structure illustrated in (c), where the agent is specified in a passive clause, is much less frequent than the structure illustrated in (b), where the agent is left unspecified. This is because the main function of the passive in most languages is to allow the construction of 'agentless' clauses.[14] In some languages, such as Turkish, this seems to be its only function (Lyons 1968). In other languages, the use of the passive is obligatory in certain contexts; for instance, the passive has to be used in Yana, an American Indian language, when the agent is a third person acting upon a first or second person (Sapir and Swadesh 1964).

Most languages have a variety of mechanisms for constructing 'agentless' clauses; for instance, the French statement *On parle anglais* and the German *Man spricht Englisch* leave the agent unspecified by using a 'dummy' subject, *on* and *man* respectively. They can be translated into English either by using a similar 'dummy' subject, *They speak English*, where *they* does not refer to a specific agent, or by using the passive voice, *English is spoken* (Lyons 1968).

Languages which have a category of voice do not always use the passive with the same frequency. German uses the passive much less frequently than English. The same is true of Russian and French, where reflexive structures[15] are relied on much more heavily to fulfil similar functions. The frequency of use of the passive in languages which have a category of voice usually expresses a stylistic choice and, in some registers, may be a question of pure convention. Scientific and technical writing in English, for instance, relies heavily on passive structures. This is done to give the impression of objectivity and to distance the writer from the statements made in the text.[16] It has, however, come to represent the 'norm' in technical writing to such an extent that, even if a writer was not particularly interested in giving an impression of objectivity, he or she might find it difficult to break away from the convention of using predominantly passive structures in technical writing. The more pervasive a structure becomes in a given context, the more difficult it becomes for speakers and writers to select other structures or to depict events differently.

Some languages use the passive more frequently than English in everyday contexts. In Tjolobal of Mexico, passive structures are the norm, with active structures being used very rarely (Beekman and Callow 1974). Nida similarly explains that 'in some Nilotic languages the passive forms of verbs are so preferred that instead of saying "he went to town", it is much more normal to employ an expression such as "the town was gone to by him"' (1975:136).

Rendering a passive structure by an active structure, or conversely an active structure by a passive structure in translation can have implications for the amount of information given in the clause, the linear arrangement of semantic elements such as agent and affected entity, and the focus of the message.[17] However, one must weigh this potential change in content and focus against the benefits of rendering a smooth, natural translation in contexts where the use of the passive might, for instance, be stylistically less acceptable than the use of the active or an alternative structure in the target language. The conference circular (in English and Russian) and the back-translated version of the Russian text that follow are quoted at length to illustrate that, in some contexts, professional translators may decide to replace passive structures in the source text with stylistically more acceptable alternative structures, such as the active and reflexive in the case of Russian. The relevant structures are highlighted in the English and back-translated Russian texts for ease of comparison.

Source Text (Euralex Conference Circular, 1987):

CALL FOR PAPERS

<u>Papers are invited</u> for the
EURALEX Third International Congress
4–9 September 1988
Budapest, Hungary.

<u>Papers are invited</u> on all aspects of lexicography, theoretical and practical, diachronic and synchronic. <u>The main fields of interest reflected</u> in the Congress programme will be:

general (monolingual or bilingual), computational
terminological and specialized translation
lexicography.

Papers relating to the lesser-known languages will be particularly welcome.

The format of the Congress will embrace plenary sessions, symposia, section meetings, workshop sessions, project reports and demonstrations of computational and other work; there will also be ample time for discussion.

<u>Individual presentations should be timed</u> to last 20 minutes, with a discussion period to follow.

<u>Abstracts</u> (approximately 1,000 words) in any of the Congress languages, English, French, German or Russian, <u>should be sent</u> to the Lecture Programme Organizer, Dr. Tamas Magay, at the above address by 15 November 1987. <u>A response will be sent</u> before the end of February 1988. <u>Any other correspondence should be addressed</u> to the Congress organizer, Ms Judit Zigany.

<u>It is</u> confidently <u>expected</u> that <u>a volume of collected papers from this Congress will</u> subsequently <u>be published</u> by Akademiai Kiado in Budapest.

This Congress will, like its predecessors at Exeter and Zurich, be a meeting place for lexicographers, academics and publishers. It will also offer a unique opportunity for participants from the East and from the West to strengthen professional and personal contacts and thus to lay the foundations of further exchanges and cooperation in the future.

We look forward to seeing you at BUDALEX '88.

Russian translation

Первый циркуляр

Приглашаем принять участие на
Третьем международном конгрессе EURALEX
в Будапеште (ВНР)
4-9 сентября 1988 г.

Тематика конгресса охватывает все важнейшие аспекты лексикографии. Особое внимание мы намереваемся обратить на следующие области лексикографической науки:

общая (одно- и двуязычная) лексикография,
компьютерная лексикография,
терминологическая и специальная лексикография.

Мы намереваемся отдельно обсудить вопросы соотношения так называемых «малых», т.е. менее распространенных и «больших», т.е. более распространенных языков.

В рамках конгресса мы намереваемся проводить пленарные заседания, симпозии, рабочие заседания, а также обсудить аннотации проектов. Кроме того состоятся заседания секций конгресса и демонстрации использования компьютерной техники в лексикографии.

Предусмотренная длительность индивидуальных докладов составляет 20 минут, не учитывая дополнительных выступлений и дискуссий.

Краткие конспекты рефератов (с объемом до 1000 слов или до 100 строк) просим до 15 ноября 1987 г. на любом из официальных языков конгресса, т.е. на русском, английском, немецком или французском языках, высылать по вышеуказанному адресу главному координатору конгресса Юдит Зигань или научному организатору конгресса д-ру Тамашу Магаи. Последующую корреспонденцию просим адресовать гл. редактору Юдит Зигань.

Издательство Академии наук ВНР намеревается издать в форме сборника весь научный материал конгресса.

Надеемся, что этот конгресс, как и его предшественники в Эксетере и Цюрихе, станет не только местом встречи лексикографов, филологов и работников издательств, но и на то, что участникам, прибывающим с востока и запада предоставится возможность посредством личных и профессиональных контактов положить основы дальнейшего сотрудничества.

До встречи на BUDALEX '88

We invite you to take part in the
Third International Congress of EURALEX
in Budapest (PRH)
4–9 September 1988.

The overall theme of the congress will include all the most important aspects of lexicography. **We intend** to pay particular attention to the following areas of lexicographical science:

general (mono- and bilingual) lexicography,
computational lexicography,
terminological and special lexicography.

We intend to discuss separately questions concerning the so-called 'small', i.e. less widespread and 'big', i.e. more widespread languages.

In the frames of the congress we intend to hold plenary sessions, symposia, workshops, and also to discuss project reports. In addition there will be section meetings of the congress and demonstrations of the use of computer technology in lexicography.

The envisaged length of individual papers is 20 minutes, not counting supplementary speeches and discussions.

We ask for a short abstract of papers (up to 1000 words or up to 100 lines) by 15 November 1987, in any of the official languages of the conference, i.e. Russian, English, French or German, to be sent at the above address to the chief coordinator of the congress Judit Zigany or to the academic organizer of the congress Dr Tamas Magay. **We ask** you to send further correspondence to Chief Editor Judit Zigany.

The Press of the Academy of Sciences of the PRH intends to publish in the form of a collection all the academic material from the congress.

We hope that this congress, like its predecessors in Exeter and Zurich, will be not only a meeting place for lexicographers, philologists and publishers, but that also **the opportunity will make itself available** to the participants coming from East and West by means of personal and professional contacts to lay the foundations for further collaboration.

Till we meet in BUDALEX '88

English has many formulae or semi-fixed expressions in formal correspondence which rely heavily on using the passive for distancing, to project the writer as an agent of an objective process. Russian, on the whole, does not favour this strategy. Common fixed and semi-fixed phrases in Russian make use of the active voice. An expression such as 'we invite you to ...' is more natural in Russian than 'you are invited to ...', although both are possible. The last highlighted expression in the Russian back-translation, 'the opportunity will make itself available', illustrates the use of the reflexive, which is particularly common in Russian and is generally considered stylistically equivalent to the passive in English (James Mullen, personal communication).

As already mentioned, the main function of the passive in English and in a number of other languages is to avoid specifying the agent and to give an impression of objectivity. This is not necessarily the function of the passive in all languages which have a category of voice. Larson explains that in Aguaruna, a language of Peru, 'the passive is used almost exclusively in introductions and conclusions, but not in the body of the text. A shift to passive would indicate that the author is now giving a summary statement' (1984:226). In some languages, notably Japanese, Chinese, Vietnamese and Thai, the main function of the passive, or passive-like structures as in the case of Chinese, is to express adversity. In these languages, the passive is traditionally used to report unfortunate events;[18] for instance, one would say something like 'I was rained on' in Japanese, rather than 'It rained on me' or 'I got wet in the rain'. Even events which would never be passivized in English because they involve only one participant and therefore cannot 'logically' be passivized are expressed in passive structures in these languages if they are unpleasant, for example 'I was died on by my father' in Japanese.

The regular association of passive structures with adversity in certain languages means that the passive can often carry connotations of unpleasantness even when the event depicted is not normally seen as unpleasant. Thus, using the passive in Japanese can imply that a certain event is viewed by the speaker or writer in unfavourable terms, as the following example illustrates. The source text, *Palace and Politics in Prewar Japan* (Titus 1974:20), is English. However, the example used here is originally a quotation from Japanese, translated into English and used in the source text. The Japanese translator of the English book seems to have recovered the original Japanese text (written in Classical Japanese) and quoted it in the Japanese translation. The English text will still be quoted first as this will hopefully make it easier for the reader to follow the back-translation from Japanese. Items in angle brackets in the back-translation do not actually occur in the Japanese text; grammatical subjects are often suppressed in Japanese clauses (see Chapter 6, section 6.1). Possible subjects are nevertheless inserted in the back-translation to make the text readable.

English/Target text:

> Komeda Torao, *Jiho* of the third rank, was the most blunt: 'If in the past [Your Majesty] had shown as much care for politics as he had passion for horsemanship, no such **criticism** from the public as "politics by two or three Ministers" would have occurred'.

Japanese/source text:

> いちばんむきつけだったのは、三等侍補の米田虎雄だった。「平素御馬術を好ませてもうほどに政治上に叡慮を注がせたまわば、今日のごとく世上より二三大臣の政治などいわるることはあるまじくとつねに苦慮つかまつりおれり」。

> The most blunt one was Komeda Torao who was the third Jiho. 'If <Your Majesty> pours his wise consideration into politics as much as <he> likes riding in his daily life, <I> would not think that <he/the government> <u>would have been said</u> as two or three ministers' politics <u>by the public</u>. So <I am> sincerely concerned.'

Because it is used in the passive, 'said' in the Japanese text is understood to mean something like 'criticized', and this meaning is correctly rendered in the English translation. Note that it is the use of the passive structure rather than the lexical item 'said' which signals this 'adverse' meaning of criticism.

The fact that the passive can and often does communicate adverse meanings in languages such as Japanese and Chinese must be borne in mind by translators working from or into these languages. Here are some examples which confirm that professional Japanese and Chinese translators are sensitive to the difference in function of the passive in English and in their target languages and generally tend to replace a large number of English passive structures with active structures in their target texts in order to avoid negative connotations.

Example A
Source text (*A Study of Shamanistic Practices in Japan,* Blacker 1975:315):

> … there is no <u>barrier to be crossed</u>, no mysteriously <u>other kind of being to be met and placated</u>.

Target text (Japanese):

> そこには越えるべき障壁もなく、神秘的な異種の生きものに出合い、なだめることもない。

> There is no **barrier that <one> should go over**, and **<we> do not meet or placate a mysterious different being**.

Example B
Source text (*Palace and Politics in Prewar Japan,* Titus 1974:11):

> If the personality and policy preferences of the Japanese emperor were not very relevant to prewar politics, social forces certainly were. There are two reasons for giving them only the most tangential treatment here. First, <u>this study simply had to be controlled in scope</u>. Obviously <u>not everything relevant to Japanese political development could be encompassed</u>.

Target text (Japanese):

> だが、日本の天皇の人柄や政策上の好みが戦前の政治に大した関係がなかったとしても、社会勢力の側は明らかにそうではない。社会勢力に対して本書がわずかにふれる程度の扱いしかなかったのには、二つの理由がある。第一は、研究範囲を抑えねばならなかった、という単純な理由である。日本の政治的発展に関係のあることすべてをとりあげる、などというのは明らかに不可能事である。

> … The first reason was a simple reason which is <we> **had to limit the area of research. It is** obviously **impossible to take up all the matters which are related to Japan's political development**.

Example C
Source text (*China's Panda Reserves*):

... <u>many have been nursed back to health</u> from the brink of starvation.

Target text (Chinese):

该中心的成年熊猫睡于笼子里，供应的食物匀称、营养丰富；许多熊猫已从饿死的边缘被护理恢复了健康。它们还享有一个大型的户外院子，可以漫游于半野生状态的自然植物中。

... **many pandas have** already through nursing **recovered** health from the brink of starvation and death.

The most important things to bear in mind as far as voice is concerned are the frequency of use of active, passive and similar structures in the source and target languages, their respective stylistic value in different text types, and – most important of all – the function(s) of the passive and similar structures in each language. The idea is not to replace an active form with an active one and a passive form with a passive one; it is always the function of a category rather than the form it takes that is of paramount importance in translation.

The categories discussed and exemplified above are among the most problematic in translation but are by no means the only ones that cause difficulty. The expression of modal meanings, for instance, can vary widely from language to language and has to be handled sensitively and carefully in translation. Modality has to do with the attitude of the speaker to the hearer or to what is being said; in other words, it has to do with such things as certainty, possibility and obligation. The expression of modal meanings can take quite a different form in each language. In an article on political interviews on Israeli television, Blum-Kulka (1983) explains that English tends to use expressions such as *Let's* ... and *Shall we* ... in directing the actions of others, in controlling talk, and in making polite requests that have the force of commands. Hebrew, on the other hand, expresses similar modal meanings by 'addressing a question about the possibility of getting something done. For example, "Perhaps you'll go to sleep" (*ulay telex li[scaron]on*) from a mother to a child simply means "go to sleep"' (*ibid.*:147). Throughout her article, Blum-Kulka renders Hebrew expressions used by the interviewer to direct each talk with natural-sounding English expressions which are not literal renderings of the Hebrew but which express similar modal meanings. For example, she uses *Let's go on to another topic* where a literal translation of the Hebrew would be 'Perhaps we shall/should go on to another topic', and *Let's begin with the question of defence policy* where the Hebrew is literally 'Perhaps we shall start with the question of defence policy'. Becker (2009) offers a similar analysis of differences in the use of modality in German and British political interviews; Kim and Thompson (2010) analyse the use of modal expressions of obligation in English and Korean newspaper science popularization texts and relate the findings to cultural norms characteristic of the two groups: individualism and task-orientatedness in the case of English and collectivism and relation-orientatedness in the case of Korean.

Other grammatical categories which can pose difficulties in translation include mood, direct and indirect speech, and causativity, among many others. Translators should find it useful to investigate and compare the expression of such categories and the meanings associated with various structures in their source and target languages.

For a good overview of a number of grammatical categories and their expression in various languages, see Robins (1964) and Lyons (1968). For a detailed discussion of the main categories and their realization and function in English, see the *Collins COBUILD English Grammar* (Sinclair 1990).

4.3 A BRIEF NOTE ON WORD ORDER

The syntactic structure of a language imposes restrictions on the way messages may be organized in that language. The order in which functional elements such as subject, predicator and object may occur is more fixed in some languages than in others.[19] Languages vary in the extent to which they rely on word order to signal the relationship between elements in the clause. Compared to languages such as German, Russian, Finnish, Arabic and Eskimo, word order in English is relatively fixed. The meaning of a sentence in English, and in languages with similarly fixed word order such as Chinese, often depends entirely on the order in which the elements are placed (cf. *The man ate the fish* and *The fish ate the man*).

Some languages have **case inflections** which indicate the relationship between the elements in a clause, for instance who does what to whom. In such languages, the form of a noun changes depending on its function in the clause. In Russian, both *Ivan videl Borisa* and *Borisa videl Ivan* mean 'John saw Boris' (Lyons 1968), because *-a* marks *Boris* as the object, regardless of its position with respect to the subject and verb.

Languages which have elaborate systems of case inflection tend to have fewer restrictions on word order than languages like English, which have very few case inflections. In languages with elaborate case inflections, word order is largely a matter of stylistic variation and is available as a resource to signal emphasis and contrast and to organize messages in a variety of ways. Word order is extremely important in translation because it plays a major role in maintaining a coherent point of view and in orientating messages at text level. Because of its particular importance to the overall organization of discourse, the next chapter will be devoted to discussing word order at length from a purely textual point of view. But before we move from discussing the lower levels of language – words, phrases, grammatical categories – to talking about the text as a unit of meaning, it would perhaps be useful to explain briefly what a text is and why we identify a given stretch of language as a text rather than assume that it is a set of unrelated words and sentences.

4.4 INTRODUCING TEXT

So far in this book we have attempted to deal with some of the basic 'building blocks' of language: its lexical stock and grammatical structures. In order to make some headway in describing and analysing language, we have had to treat linguistic units and structures temporarily as if they had an independent status and possessed 'meaning' in their own right. We now need to take a broader look at language and to consider the possibility that, as part of a language system, lexical items and grammatical structures have a 'meaning potential'. This 'meaning potential' is only realized in communicative events, that is, in **text**. Following Brown and Yule (1983:6), **text** is defined here as 'the verbal record of a communicative event'; it is an instance of language in use rather than language as an abstract system of meanings and relations.

4.4.1 Text vs non-text

> The nearest we get to non-text in actual life, leaving aside the works of those poets and prose writers who deliberately set out to create non-text, is probably in the speech of young children and *in bad translations*.
>
> *(Halliday and Hasan 1976:24; my emphasis)*

As translators, we have to operate with lexical items and grammatical structures at various stages of the translation process. It is nevertheless imperative that we view the text as a whole, both at the beginning and at the end of the process. With the exception of extremely repetitive and predictable texts such as computer manuals, a conscientious translator does not begin to translate until he or she has read the text at least once and got a 'gist' of the overall message. But this is only the first step. Once the source text is understood, the translator then has to tackle the task of producing a target version which can be accepted as a text in its own right. Depending on the type of text being translated (e.g. an experimental novel vs a set of instructions for operating a machine) and the purpose assigned to the translation by the translator or the commissioner,[20] the phraseology and the collocational and grammatical patterning of the target version may – and usually do – have to conform to target-language norms, but even then the translation may still sound foreign or clumsy. Worse still, it may not even make sense to the target reader. Acceptable collocational patterns and grammatical structures can only enhance the readability of individual sentences, but they do not in themselves ensure that sentences and paragraphs add up to a readable or coherent text. In an unpublished manuscript, 'Ingredients of good, clear style', Wilson comments as follows on the difference between an old and a revised version of the Bible in Dagbani:

> For a native speaker it was difficult to express what was wrong with the earlier version, except that it was 'foreign'. Since superficially there seemed to be no obvious grammatical blunders, and the vocabulary was not obviously faulty, the ingredients of this foreignness were not at first apparent. Now, however, a comparison ... has made clear that what the older version mainly suffers from are considerable deficiencies in 'discourse structure', i.e., in the way the sentences are combined into well-integrated paragraphs, and these in turn into a well-constructed whole. The new version, on the contrary, shows native-speaker mastery over the means of signposting the text into a coherent, clear prose, which is ... a real pleasure to read.
>
> *(quoted in Callow 1974:10–11)*

A text, then, has features of organization which distinguish it from non-text, that is, from a random collection of sentences and paragraphs. Just like collocational and grammatical patterning and a host of other linguistic phenomena, these features of text organization are language- and culture-specific. Each linguistic community has preferred ways of organizing its various types of discourse. This is why target readers can often identify what appears to be a lexically and grammatically 'normal' text as a translation, or as 'foreign'.

A translation may be undertaken for a variety of purposes. However, in the chapters that follow we will assume that the ultimate aim of a translator, in most cases, is to achieve a measure of equivalence at text level, rather than at word or phrase level.[21] More often than not, a translator will want the reader to accept a given translation as a text in its own right, if possible without being unduly alerted to the fact that it is a translation. To achieve this, the translator will need to adjust certain features of source-text organization in line with preferred ways of organizing discourse in the target language. The following chapters will attempt to outline some of the main features of discourse organization by looking at a number of factors which constrain or aid the way we produce and understand text.

This area of language study is somewhat 'messier' than the study of lexis and grammar. Texts may be organized in a variety of ways, the naturalness or otherwise of their organization being determined by a multitude of factors. De Beaugrande and Dressler rightly point out that it is 'much more straightforward to decide what constitutes a grammatical or acceptable sentence than what constitutes a grammatical or acceptable sentence sequence, paragraph, text, or discourse' (1981:17). More importantly, text studies are a relatively recent development in linguistics. There is, admittedly, a long tradition both in linguistics and in literary studies of analysing the works of individual writers, particularly literary writers, but relatively little work has been done on such areas of text studies as the conventions of non-literary writing within a community or the preferred patterns of organization in different types of discourse. Moreover, of the studies now available, most are concerned with describing the patterning and conventions of spoken and written English. Very little is available in the way of describing the types of text available in, say, Chinese or

Spanish, or of how such texts are organized. Readers will note that the rest of this book will sometimes raise more questions than it answers, but they will, I hope, agree that raising questions is at least a step towards providing answers and solving problems.

4.4.2 Features of text organization

Any text, in any language, exhibits certain linguistic features which allow us to identify it as a text. We identify a stretch of language as a text partly because it is presented to us as a text – and we therefore do our utmost to make sense of it as a unit – and partly because we perceive connections within and among its sentences. These connections are of several kinds. First, there are connections which are established through the arrangement of information within each clause and the way this relates to the arrangement of information in preceding and following clauses and sentences; these contribute mainly to topic development and maintenance through **thematic** and **information structures** (Chapter 5). Second, there are surface connections which establish interrelationships between persons and events; these allow us to trace participants in a text and to interpret the way in which different parts of the text relate to each other (**cohesion**; Chapter 6). Finally, there are underlying semantic connections which allow us to 'make sense' of a text as a unit of meaning; these are dealt with under the heading of **coherence** and **implicature** in Chapter 7 ('Pragmatic equivalence').

Another important feature of text organization derives from the overlapping notions of **genre** and **text type**. Both relate to the way in which textual material is packaged by the writer along patterns familiar to the reader. Texts have been classified in two main ways to capture this type of 'packaging'. The first and more straightforward classification is based on the contexts in which texts occur and results in institutionalized labels such as 'journal article', 'science textbook', 'newspaper editorial' or 'travel brochure'. The second is a more subjective, less institutionalized and therefore much vaguer classification which does not normally apply to a whole text but rather to parts of it. Typical labels used in this type of classification include 'narration', 'exposition', 'argumentation' and 'instruction'. The first classification abstracts across contexts, the second abstracts across such factors as the nature of the messages involved or the addresser/addressee relationship. Both types of classification are useful in defining translation problems and in justifying specific strategies to overcome them. Reference to institutionalized genres, such as 'religious texts' and 'newspaper editorial', is made wherever applicable throughout this book. For an interesting discussion of translation problems which makes frequent references to the second type of classification, see Hatim and Mason (1990). For a broader discussion of the issue of text type and genres, see Trosborg (1997).

exercises

1. Choose a notional category such as time reference, gender, countability, visibility, modality or animacy and compare the way it is expressed in your target language with the way it is expressed in English. Comment in particular on the sort of problems that could arise in translation from differences in the way the notion in question is expressed in the two languages. You may find it helpful to refer to grammars of your source and target languages and to base your discussion on an analysis of authentic translated texts.

2. Imagine that you have been provisionally asked to translate John Le Carré's *The Russia House* (1989) into your target language. Before you can sign the translation contract, the publishers insist that you provide a sample translation of a couple of pages to allow them to assess your competence as a translator of this type of literature. They choose the following extract and ask you to submit a target version of it, stating that they appreciate that you may not have had time to read the whole novel but that they just want to see how you might handle Le Carré's distinctive use of language. They provide you with a short summary of the context to help you assess the tone of the extract.

> Note to the translator:
> John Le Carré's *The Russia House* is a spy thriller which revolves around the then new era of glasnost in the Soviet Union. The general feeling that one gets from reading this novel is that nothing much has changed and that the cold-war machinations are still at play and are as irrelevant and as brutal as ever. The narrator in the following extract is Palfrey, legal adviser to the British secret service or, in his own words, 'Legal adviser to the illegals' (p. 47). In this passage, which is very near the end of the book, he ironically sums up the manner in which the hypocritical bureaucrats of Whitehall and Washington dealt with their own inadequacies when their major spying operation went wrong. The various people mentioned, such as Ned and Barley, had all been involved in the operation in one way or another.

> Extract for translation:

> Oh, and note was taken. Passively, since active verbs have an unpleasant way of betraying the actor. Very serious note. Taken all over the place.
> Note was taken that Ned had failed to advise the twelfth floor of Barley's drunken breakout after his return from Leningrad.
> Note was taken that Ned had requisitioned all manner of resources on that same night, for which he had never accounted,

exercises

among them Ben Lugg and the services of the head listener Mary, who sufficiently overcame her loyalty to a brother officer to give the committee a lurid account of Ned's high-handedness. Demanding illegal taps! Imagine! Faulting telephones! The liberty!

Mary was pensioned off soon after this and now lives in a rage in Malta, where it is feared she is writing her memoirs.

Note was also taken, if regretfully, of the questionable conduct of our Legal Adviser de Palfrey – I even got my *de* back* – who had failed to justify his use of the Home Secretary's delegated authority in the full knowledge that this was required of him by the secretly agreed Procedures Governing the Service's Activities as Amended by etcetera, and in accordance with paragraph something of a deniable Home Office protocol.

The heat of battle was however taken into account. The Legal Adviser was not pensioned off, neither did he take himself to Malta. But he was not exonerated either. A partial pardon at best. A Legal Adviser should not have been so close to an operation. An inappropriate use of the Legal Adviser's skills. The word injudicious was passed around.

It was also noted with regret that the same Legal Adviser had drafted a glowing testimonial of Barley for Clive's signature not forty-eight hours before Barley's disappearance, thus enabling Barley to take possession of the shopping list,** though presumably not for long.

In my spare hours, I drew up Ned's terms of severance and thought nervously about my own. Life inside the Service might have its limitations but the thought of life outside it terrified me.

(pp. 412–413)

* Palfrey's full name is Horatio Benedict de Palfrey, but, as he explains earlier (p. 47), 'you may forget the first two [names] immediately, and somehow nobody has ever remembered the "de" at all'.
** A document detailing information required by Whitehall and Washington from the informant/potential defector on the Russian side.

When you have translated the above text into your target language, discuss any differences between the source and target versions in terms of grammatical meaning, paying particular attention to the use of passive structures[22] and the reflexive *take himself to Malta* (paragraph 6). You may also wish to use this opportunity to consolidate your

exercises

knowledge of other areas covered so far, namely semantics and lexis. Consider, for instance, the evoked meaning of an expression such as *all over the place* (paragraph 1), or the impact of an unusual collocation such as *lives in a rage* (paragraph 4); how well do these expressions translate into your target language?

Comment at length on the strategies you used to overcome difficulties at the grammatical level in particular.

3. *Miss Smilla's Feeling for Snow* is the title of one of two English translations of an award-winning novel by the Danish author Peter Høeg, which first appeared in 1992. On the surface, the story revolves around Smilla Qaaviqaaq Jaspersen, daughter of a Greenlandic Inuit mother and a rich Danish dentist, who becomes suspicious about the death of a Greenlandic child in Copenhagen and decides to investigate it. At a deeper level, the story is about Denmark's colonial history and the relationship between different groups in Danish society today.

In the following extract (Høeg 2005:262–263), Smilla switches from reflecting on her current situation to remembering aspects of her past life.

> I put on my tracksuit. I knot the steel ball into a long white bath towel that I've folded double. Then I hang it back on its hook. And I sit down to wait.
>
> If you have to wait for a long time, you have to seize hold of the waiting or it will become destructive. If you let things slide, your consciousness will waver, awakening fear and restlessness, then depression strikes, and you're pulled down.
>
> To keep up my spirits I ask myself, What is a human being? Who am I?
>
> Am I my name?
>
> The year I was born my mother travelled to West Greenland and brought home the girl's name Millaaraq. Because it reminded Moritz of the Danish word *mild*, which didn't exist in the vocabulary of his love relationship with my mother, because he wanted to transform everything Greenlandic into something that would make it European and familiar, and because I apparently had smiled at him – the boundless trust of an infant, which comes from the fact that she still doesn't know what's in store for her – my parents agreed on Smillaaraq. With the wear and tear that time subjects all of us to, it was shortened to Smilla.

Imagine that Peter Høeg and the English publisher of this novel have commissioned you and various other translators to render a number of exercises passages, including this one, into your target language(s) in order to establish whether the English translation can serve as a source text in situations where translators from Danish (for example into languages like Ukranian or Kurdish) are unlikely to be available. When you have translated it, comment on the relevant difficulties and the strategies you used to convey the function(s) of each tense and the impact of the switch in tenses. Your comments need to be clear and accessible, because they will be passed on to the translators who will eventually be commissioned to render the full novel into a range of languages. These translators will need to be sensitized to the impact of the interplay of tenses, among other things, in the English translation – because they will use this English translation as a source text.

SUGGESTIONS FOR FURTHER READING

Beekman, John and John Callow (1974) *Translating the Word of God*, Michigan: Zondervan; Chapter 3: 'Implicit and Explicit Information', and Chapter 14: 'Multiple Functions of Grammatical Structures'.

Downing, Angela and Philip Locke (2006) *English Grammar: A University Course*, second edition, Abingdon, Oxon: Routledge.

Huddleston, Rodney and Geoffrey K. Pullum (2005) *A Student's Introduction to English Grammar*, Cambridge: Cambridge University Press.

Lyons, John (1968) *Introduction to Theoretical Linguistics*, Cambridge: Cambridge University Press; Chapter 7: 'Grammatical Categories', and Chapter 8 : 'Grammatical Functions'.

Robins, R. H. (1964) *General Linguistics: An Introductory Survey*, London: Longman; Chapter 6, sections 6.4 and 6.6: Grammatical classes, structures and categories.

Sinclair, John McH. (1990) *Collins COBUILD English Grammar*, London: Collins.

On gender

Chan Ho-yan, Clara (2009) 'Third Person Pronouns in Indigenous Chinese Texts and Translated Chinese Texts: The Westernization of Modern Written Chinese', *New Voices in Translation Studies* 5. Available at www.iatis.org/newvoices/issues/2009/article-chan-2009.pdf.

Clason, Marmy A. (2006) 'Feminism, Generic "He", and the TNIV Bible Translation Debate', *Critical Discourse Studies* 3(1): 23–35.

Hébert, Lyse (2009) 'Feminization: A Socially and Politically Charged Translation Strategy', in Raquel de Pedro, Isabelle Perez and Christine Wilson (eds) *Interpreting and Translating in Public Service Settings: Policy, Practice, Pedagogy*, Manchester: St. Jerome Publishing, 127–140.

Nissen, Uwe Kjaer (2002) 'Aspects of Translating Gender', *Linguistik online* 11(2). Available at www.linguistik-online.de/11_02/nissen.html.

Sánchez, Dolores (2007) 'The *Truth* about Sexual Difference: Scientific Discourse and Cultural Transfer', *The Translator* 13(2): 171–194.

Shurbanov, Alexander (2002) 'Translation Across Gender Discrepancies', *Textus, English Studies in Italy* 15(1): 45–63.

On person (including T/V distinction)

Beaton-Thome, Morven (2010) 'Negotiating Identities in the European Parliament: The Role of Simultaneous Interpreting', in Mona Baker, Maeve Olohan and María Calzada Pérez (eds) *Text and Context: Essays on Translation and Interpreting in Honour of Ian Mason*, Manchester: St. Jerome Publishing, 117–138.

Brown, Penelope and Albert Gilman (1960/1972) 'The Pronouns of Power and Solidarity', in Pier Paulo Giglioli (ed.) *Language and Social Context*, Harmondsworth: Penguin, 252–281.

Guillot, Marie-Nöelle (2010) 'Film Subtitles from a Cross-cultural Pragmatics Perspective: Issues of Linguistic and Cultural Representation', *The Translator* 16(1): 67–92.

Hatim, Basil and Ian Mason (1997) *The Translator as Communicator*, London: Routledge. Chapter 5: 'Politeness in Screen Translation'.

On tense and aspect

Cockerill, Hiroko (Shimono) (2003) 'Futabatei Shimei's Translations from Russian: Verbal Aspect and Narrative Perspective', *Japanese Studies* 23(3): 229–238.

Engel, Dulcie M. (2002) 'Radio Talk. French and English Perfects on Air', *Languages in Contrast* 2(2): 95–118.

Gadalla, Hassan A. H. (2006) 'Arabic Imperfect Verbs in Translation: A Corpus Study of English Renderings', *Meta* 51(1): 51–71.

Gentry El-Dash, Linda and JoAnne Busnardo (2003) 'Interaction of Semantic and Pragmatic Choices in the Translation of Verb Forms: English and Portuguese', *Journal of Pragmatics* 35(12): 1823–1841.

Lathey, Gillian (2003) 'Time, Narrative Intimacy and the Child. Implications of the Transition from the Present to the Past Tense in the Translation into English of Children's Texts', *Meta* 48(1–2): 233–240.

May, Rachel (1994) *The Translator in the Text: On Reading Russian Literature in English*, Evanston, IL: Northwestern University Press.

Polezzi, Loredana (1998) 'Rewriting Tibet: Italian Travellers in English Translation', *The Translator* 4(2): 321–342.

Williams, Christopher (2002) *Non-Progressive and Progressive Aspect in English*, Bari: Schena Editore.

On voice

Farghal, Mohammed and Mohammed O. Al-Shorafat (1996) 'The Translation of English Passives into Arabic: An Empirical Perspective', *Target* 8(1): 97–118.

Fujii, Yasunari (2008) 'The Asymmetrical Relationship between the Active and Passive Voice: Implications for Teaching Japanese-to-English Translation of Specialized Scientific Texts', *The Linguistics Journal* 3(1): 40–74. Available online: www.linguistics-journal.com/April_2008.pdf.

Kinsui, Satoshi (1997) 'The Influence of Translation on the Historical Development of the Japanese Passive Construction', *Journal of Pragmatics* 28(6): 759–779.

NOTES

1 A system is a set of options or contrasting choices.

2 See Chapter 5 for a discussion of word-order patterns and note 1 of the same chapter for an explanation of the functional elements **subject**, **predicator** and **object**.

3 The lexical item *late*, as in *the late Graham Greene*, can be used to convey a similar meaning in English. The difference is that this information is optional in English and the absence of *late* therefore does not necessarily indicate that a certain referent is alive.

4 And sometimes as masculine, feminine or neuter, as in the case of German. In some languages, the gender category is expressed in terms of animate vs inanimate rather than masculine vs feminine. Southern Paiute, an American Indian language, combines the animate/inanimate distinction with a further dimension, namely that of visibility (Sapir and Swadesh 1964). A given entity must be classified (a) as either animate or inanimate, and (b) according to whether or not it can be seen from the standpoint of the action's main setting.

5 A **determiner** is a word such as *the*, *this* or *some*, which is used with a noun to limit its meaning or specify its reference in some way.

6 Unmarked here means that it is the form normally used unless the speaker specifically wishes to highlight the distinction.

7 The reason that gender distinctions can be manipulated in this way in English is that they are not a regular feature of the grammar of English. An English speaker can convey certain expressive meanings by using *she* (rather than *it*) to refer to an inanimate object such as a *car* or *ship*, for instance. It would be difficult to transfer this type of manipulation into a language such as French, where gender is a regular grammatical feature. A French speaker has to use the feminine form for 'car', *voiture*, and the masculine form for 'ship', *bateau*; he or she has no other choice.

8 I am grateful to Monika Bednarek and her students for this information.

9 Elizabethan English made a distinction between *thou* (second-person singular) and *you* (second-person plural). The singular form was used to express familiarity and the plural form to express respect or distance. This distinction no longer exists in Modern English.

10 The most detailed study of this issue remains Brown and Gilman (1960/1972).

11 Brown and Gilman use *T* to refer to the familiar form and *V* to refer to the polite form in any language.

12 This classification is taken from St John (1983).

13 Distinguishing between the present and the future in non-past reference is achieved by adding a time adverbial such as 'now' or 'tomorrow' (Netsu 1981).

14 For a good, accessible summary of the functions of the passive in English, see *The Collins COBUILD English Grammar* (Sinclair 1990), sections 10.10 to 10.14 (pp. 404–405).

15 Reflexive structures involve a reflexive pronoun such as *myself* or *himself* as object. They suggest that the person or thing affected by the action is the same as the person or thing doing it, for example *I blame myself for not paying attention*, *He introduced himself to me* (examples from Sinclair 1990). Like passive structures, reflexive structures are sometimes used to suppress the agent. For example, 'the opportunity made itself available', which is a perfectly natural expression in Russian, allows the speaker to avoid specifying who made the opportunity available in much the same way as *The opportunity was made available*.

16 See Bennett (2007) for an interesting discussion of various features of English academic discourse, including the passive voice.

17 See Chapter 5 for a discussion of the role of voice in organizing messages.

18 This is still true to a large extent, even though passive structures are becoming more common in various contexts because of the influence of translation.

19 See Chapter 5, note 1, for an explanation of the functional elements **subject, predicator, object, complement** and **adjunct**.

20 For an excellent and accessible discussion of various considerations that impact on the translator's choice of strategy and degree of adherence to source- or target-culture norms, see Nord (1997).

21 This is not to say that equivalence at word level is not or should not be given priority in some contexts. The biblical or koranic translator, for instance, will often be at least equally concerned, if not more concerned, with equivalence at the level of the word or phrase.

22 I imagine that the extensive use of the passive in this particular text will not prove problematic in languages such as Japanese and Chinese, where the passive is associated with adversity. It may well be that the adversity function will be compatible with the tone of the text and the implications of cowardice and denial of responsibility.

CHAPTER 5

Textual equivalence: thematic and information structures

Given and new ... differ from theme and rheme ... in that 'given' means 'here is a point of contact with what you know' ... whereas 'theme' means 'here is the heading to what I am saying'.

(Halliday 1970:354)

There is a need for analysis of thematic progression in different languages over a range of text types. We know little about what patterns there are and how equivalence could be achieved between them. One thing of which we can be confident, nevertheless, is that the patterns are always employed in the service of an overriding rhetorical purpose. This is an aspect of texture which is of crucial importance to the translator.

(Hatim and Mason 1990:220)

We ended the last chapter with a brief discussion of **word order** and of **text**. It was suggested then that the linear arrangement of linguistic elements plays a role in organizing messages at text level. In this chapter, we resume our discussion of word order as a textual strategy (rather than a grammatical feature) and explore a number of ways in which its role in controlling information flow can be explained.

To illustrate what is meant by 'information flow', consider some possible formulations of sentence (2) in the following extract from Stephen Hawking's *A Brief History of Time* (1988:3).

(1) Ptolemy's model provided a reasonably accurate system for predicting the positions of heavenly bodies in the sky.

(2) a. But Ptolemy had to make an assumption that the moon followed a path that sometimes brought it twice as close to the

b. But an assumption that Ptolemy had to make in order to predict these positions correctly was that the moon followed a path that sometimes

c. But in order to predict these positions correctly, Ptolemy had to make an assumption that the moon followed a path that

| earth as other times, in order to predict these positions correctly. | brought it twice as close to the earth as at other times. | sometimes brought it twice as close to the earth as at other times. |

(3) And that meant that the moon ought sometimes to appear twice as big as at other times!

Sentences (2a–c) consist of the same elements, but the sequencing of elements is different in each one. The progression of links between each of the middle formulations and the preceding and following sentences can be visually represented as follows:

a. the positions ... an assumption ... the moon ... these positions ... that ... the moon

b. the positions ... an assumption ... these positions ... the moon ... that ... the moon

c. the positions ... these positions ... an assumption ... the moon ... that ... the moon

It should be clear from the above diagram that the sentence which forms the most readily accessible link between (1) and (3) is (2c) (it is also the one that appears in the actual text). The flow of information is smoother in (2c) because the progression of links is less messy and therefore easier to follow than in (2a) and (2b). Another factor which makes the extract easier to process if (2c) is selected is that sentences (2c) and (3) both start with an element that has already been established before presenting new information. The starting point of (2c), *these positions*, is already known to the reader because it occurs at the end of sentence (1). Similarly, the starting point of sentence (3), *that*, is *an assumption* already explained in the previous sentence.

Linear arrangement, then, has a role to play in processing information and organizing messages at text level. Of the numerous formulations available for expressing a given message, a speaker or writer will normally opt for one that makes the flow of information clearer in a given context. In order to appreciate the factors that motivate a writer or speaker to make this kind of selection, one needs to think of the clause as a message rather than as a string of grammatical and lexical elements. Over and above its propositional organization in terms of elements such as subject/object and agent/patient, a clause also has an interactional organization which reflects the addresser/addressee relationship. This interactional organization generally motivates us to make choices that ensure a clear progression of links is achieved and a coherent point of view is maintained throughout a text. But it also allows us to exploit word order occasionally in order to generate special effects, such as emphasis, by employing marked structures.

Clause as a message can be analysed in terms of two types of structure: (a) **thematic structure** (5.1.1) and (b) **information structure** (5.1.2). The Hallidayan approach to the analysis of the clause as a message treats thematic and information structures as separate, though often overlapping features of discourse organization. The two structures are seen to be essentially distinct from each other. Linguists belonging to the Prague School, on the other hand, by and large conflate the two structures and combine them in the same description (see section 5.2 below). The two approaches are often at odds with each other and can produce completely different analyses of the same clause. However, translators with different linguistic backgrounds should benefit from a brief exposure to both points of view. Here, as elsewhere, a translator would be well advised to use those explanations which are compatible with the languages that are of interest to him or her and ignore the rest.

Both approaches are outlined below, starting with a general overview which follows the Hallidayan or 'separating' approach. For a good overview of both positions, see Fries (1983), who refers to them as the 'separating' approach and the 'combining' approach.

5.1 A HALLIDAYAN OVERVIEW OF INFORMATION FLOW

5.1.1 Thematic structure: theme and rheme

One way of explaining the interactional organization of sentences is to suggest that a clause consists of two segments. The first segment is called the **theme**. The theme is what the clause is about. It has two functions: (a) it acts as a point of orientation by connecting back to previous stretches of discourse and thereby maintaining a coherent point of view, and (b) it acts as a point of departure by connecting forward and contributing to the development of later stretches. In *Ptolemy's model provided a reasonably accurate system for predicting the positions of heavenly bodies in the sky*, the theme is *Ptolemy's model*. This is what the clause is about. At clause level, a speaker announces the topic of his or her message by thematizing it, that is, by putting it in initial position.

The second segment of a clause is called the **rheme**. The rheme is what the speaker says about the theme. It is the goal of discourse. As such, it is the most important element in the structure of the clause as a message because it represents the very information that the speaker wants to convey to the hearer. It is the rheme that fulfils the communicative purpose of the utterance. In the above example, the rheme is: *provided a reasonably accurate system for predicting the positions of heavenly bodies in the sky*, which is what the writer has to say about *Ptolemy's model*. This basically means that every clause has the structure of a message: it says something (the rheme) about something (the theme).

Let us now look at a slightly more extended example of how a Hallidayan-style thematic analysis of a text might proceed in English. The following short extract selected for analysis is from Stephen Hawking's *A Brief History of Time* (1988:2):

Aristotle thought that the earth was stationary and that the sun, the moon, the planets, and the stars moved in circular orbits about the earth. He believed this because he felt, for mystical reasons, that the earth was the center of the universe, and that circular motion was the most perfect.

Suggested analysis:

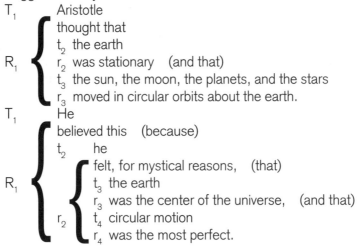

A number of interesting points arise from the above analysis:

(a) Thematic analysis can be represented hierarchically. Since sentences often consist of more than one clause, they will have several layers of thematic structure. Each clause will have its own theme–rheme structure which may be subordinate to a larger theme–rheme structure. The above visual representation of the hierarchical nature of theme–rheme structures is meant to illustrate the point without having to go through complex technical discussions.

(b) You will note that I have put some elements in parentheses, for example *because*, to suggest that they do not quite fit into the analysis. The reason is that, strictly speaking, some elements are not part of the basic thematic structure of the text because they are not part of the propositional meaning of the message. These include special linking devices such as *however, nevertheless, because* and *moreover*, which are called **conjunctions** (see Chapter 6, section 6.3). They also include items which express the attitude of the speaker, such as *unfortunately, in my opinion, frankly* and *clearly* (these are called **disjuncts**). Both conjunctions and disjuncts usually come at the beginning of English clauses; it is natural for the speaker to place in initial position an element which relates what he or she is about to say to what has been said before (conjunction) or an element which expresses his or her own judgement on what is being said (disjunct). In this sense, conjunctions and disjuncts are inherently thematic (Halliday 1985). However, because conjunctions and disjuncts are not part of the propositional content of the message, they are not considered thematic in the same way as the main clause elements **subject**, **predicator**, **object**, **complement** and **adjunct**.[1] There are ways of incorporating conjunctions and disjuncts into thematic analysis, but this type of detailed analysis is not necessary for our current purposes. For a fuller discussion of this subject, see Halliday (1985:Chapter 3, 'Clause as message').

(c) Conjunctions and disjuncts aside, there tends to be a very high correlation between theme/rheme and subject/predicate in the Hallidayan model (cf. the Prague position, section 5.2). The correlation does not hold in the case of **marked themes** as we shall see shortly (section 5.1.1.3), but, generally speaking, the distinction between theme and rheme is more or less identical to the traditional grammatical distinction between subject and predicate. In fact, Plato, who as far back as the fourth century BC had divided the sentence into what we now know as subject and predicate, used the terms **ónoma** and **rhema** (which originally meant 'name' and 'saying' respectively). However, the modern distinction between theme and rheme differs from Plato's original dichotomy in one important respect. The theme–rheme distinction is text-based. Its real value does not lie in explaining the structure of individual sentences but rather in shedding light on a number of important areas which control information flow. These are discussed briefly in sections 5.1.1.1– 5.1.1.3 below.

5.1.1.1 Thematic structure: grammaticality vs acceptability

Unlike the subject–predicate distinction, the notions of theme and rheme can be used to account for the acceptability (rather than grammaticality) of a given sequence in a given context. Theme and rheme are not grammatical notions. They have little to do with whether a given sequence is or is not grammatical.[2] Grammatical sequences are part of the abstract system of language. In context, grammaticality does not necessarily ensure acceptability or coherence. For example, the following text is well-formed grammatically, but is ill-formed in terms of its thematics:

> Now comes the President here. It's the window he's stepping through to wave to the crowd. On his victory his opponent congratulates him. 'Gentlemen and ladies. That you are confident in me honours me …'
>
> *(from Halliday 1978:134)*

A grammatical sequence such as *On his victory his opponent congratulates him* can be reordered in a number of different ways without affecting its propositional content. The writer could have selected a sequence such as *His opponent congratulates him on his victory* or *He is congratulated on his victory by his opponent.* The acceptability, rather than grammaticality, of any of these sequences in a given context depends on how it fits into its surrounding textual environment. Reasons for the thematic ill-formedness of the above extract will become clear as we explore various aspects of thematic organization. At this stage, it is sufficient to point out that it is difficult to see a link between the themes of the above clauses, or even between a rheme and a following theme, for instance. The result is that the text feels disjointed and lacks orientation. The individual clauses are perfectly grammatical but, taken together, they are not acceptable as a stretch of discourse.

The above text is fabricated for the purposes of illustration. Halliday argues that one does not normally meet non-text of this sort in real life (1978). Those of us who read a lot of translated texts of a particular type, for instance tourist brochures, know otherwise. Unlike the above constructed text, the following is an authentic advertisement for Mazda cars (most likely a translation of an Italian text) which appeared in the Alitalia inflight magazine (February 1991, 20–21).

> What inspired that rebellious young poet called Rimbaud? What drove him to reach into the innermost part of his soul in search of the undiscovered? It allowed him to take words that already existed and yet express himself in a completely new way. Some creators are brave enough to realise their dreams without compromise. It is men like this who created the MX-5 in 1989. By ignoring the rules they are constantly reshaping the future. Even now they are realising a new dream. They work for Mazda.

The Mazda text has the same feel of awkwardness and lack of orientation about it as Halliday's constructed example. To start with, none of the themes seem to link in with a previous theme or rheme; each sentence seems to stand on its own in a sort of vacuum. For instance, the theme of the third sentence, *It*, does not relate to either of the previous themes or rhemes. The theme of the fourth sentence, *Some creators*, relates to *Rimbaud* only indirectly on the basis that poets are some sort of creators, but it does not link in with the theme or rheme of the previous sentence. The reader initially gets the impression that the purpose of the text is to identify Rimbaud's source of inspiration. In the fourth sentence, the focus suddenly shifts to talking about creators in general and how they realize their dreams.

Another source of distraction is that the initial *what*-questions (first and second sentences) are followed not, as one might expect, by an identification of the thing that inspired Rimbaud and drove him to reach into his soul, but by the pronoun *It*. *It* suggests that the reader should know what inspired Rimbaud. But the reader has no way of knowing because the relevant information has not been given by the writer. The arrangement of given and new elements is discussed in detail under **information structure** (section 5.1.2).

The Mazda text illustrates that, quite apart from any considerations of grammaticality, it is necessary to take account of thematic structure and to maintain a coherent point of view in any act of communication.

5.1.1.2 Thematic structure: text organization and development

In addition to complementing the notion of grammaticality with notions of acceptability and naturalness, the theme–rheme distinction can also be useful in explaining methods of organization and development in different types of text; see Hatim and Mason (1990, Chapter 10) and Hatim (1997, Chapter 8) for extensive discussion of this issue.

In this area, a great deal of emphasis has traditionally been placed on theme rather than on rheme. By definition, theme represents the speaker's or writer's point of departure in each clause, which suggests that its organizational role is more important than that of rheme. The selection of an individual theme of a given clause in a given text is not in itself particularly significant. But the overall choice and ordering of themes, particularly those of independent clauses, plays an important part in organizing a text and in providing a point of orientation for a given stretch of language. It is no surprise, for instance, that travel brochures, at least in English, are characterized by a proliferation of place adjuncts in theme position. In the context of travel, location provides a natural point of orientation around which the text as a whole can be organized.

The following extract from Lonrho's *A Hero from Zero* shows how a series of homogeneous themes can provide a point of orientation and a method of development for a given stretch of language. The extract comes right at the end of the Foreword. Here, Tiny Rowland concludes his version of events leading up to the Fayed brothers' acquisition of the House of Fraser with a first-hand account of the situation in question against the background of his personal experience in business. The high frequency of *I* as theme helps to maintain a sense of continuity and a coherent point of view.

> *I* had nothing against his [Fayed's] being a wealthy commission agent – *I* had everything against his cheating his way into House of Fraser, helped by Kleinwort Benson and Norman Tebbit.
>
> It was bitter, but funny, to see that Professor Smith had doubled his own salary before recommending the offer from Fayed, and added a pre-dated bonus for good measure.
>
> *I* saw how Brian Basham of Broad Street Associates and the barrister, Royston Webb, helped venal journalists to turn a sow's ear into a golden purse, and how that golden purse was well received everywhere that it opened.
>
> *I* saw how the well-documented material containing the truth about Fayed that we began to put before the DTI was received in embarrassed silence.
>
> *I* saw how Leon Brittan, the incoming Secretary of State for Trade, was prepared to say he could find nothing wrong with the matter.
>
> *I* took my first job in the City in 1936, working for Kittel and Company at 5 Fenchurch Street. *I*'ve been a director of British public companies for thirty-one years. It is the worst thing I've ever seen in business, that deceits triumph

so well, and can even find apologists when they are exposed. *I am glad that after two years inspectors were appointed, and that they have expended 18 months upon investigating the take-over of House of Fraser.*

The above pattern can be reproduced in many, but not in all, languages. The Arabic translation adopts a very different pattern of organization.

ولم يكن لدى أى اعتراض على آونه و آيلاً بـلاعمولة من الأثرياء، ولكنى آنت أعارض تماماً سيطرته بـلاخداع على هاوس أوف فريزر، بمساعدة آلاينوورت بنسون و نورمان تيبيت.

وآن من المؤسف، بل ومن المضحك، أن يتمكن البروفسور سميث من مضاعفة راتبه مرتين قبل أن يتقدم بتوصيته لقبول عرض فايد، وأن يضيف الى ذلك مكافأة يتحدد سلفاً موعد حصوله عليها

ورأيت آيف أن براين باشام المسؤول فى برود ستريت اسوشييتس، والمحامى رويستن ويب قد ساعدا الصحفيين المرتشين على تحويل شىء مبتذل الى خزانة ذهبية، وآيف آانت هذه الخزانة الذهبية تُستقبل أحسن استقبال آلما فتحت.

ورأيت آيف أن المواد الحسنة التوثيق التى تشتمل على الحقيقة والصدق عن فايد، والتى بدأنا نعرضها على وزارة التجارة والصناعة، آيف أنها بدأت تُستقبل بصمت مشوب بـلاحرج.

ورأيت آيف أن ليون بريتن وزير التجارة الجديد آن مستعداً للقول بأنه لايجد أى خطأ فى الإجراءات.

لقد شغلت أول وظيفة لى فى حى السيتى بلندن سنة 1936، وذلك عندما التحقت بمؤسسة آيتل وشرآاه فى 5 فينانشرش ستريت. ومنذ ذاك اصبحت مديراً لشرآات بريطانية عامة على مدى إحدى وثلاثين سنة. ومن أسوأ ما عرفته فى المعاملات المالية والتجارية أن يفوز الإحتيال هذا الفوز الكبير، وأن يجد من يبرره حتى بعد فضحه. ويسعدنى أن تعين لجنة من المفتشين بعد انقضاء سنتين، وأن تقضى هذه اللجنة 18 شهراً للتحقيق فى واقعة امتلاك مؤسسة هاوس أوف فريزر.

The thematic structure of the Arabic translation of this extract deviates from the original for a number of reasons. First, Arabic rarely uses independent pronouns because Arabic verbs are inflected for person, number and gender. This means that any combination of pronoun plus verb, such as *I took* or *I saw*, is rendered by an inflected verb as theme in Arabic. It is important to bear in mind that while inflected verbs in languages such as Arabic, Spanish and Portuguese (to name but a few) do carry the same information as an English pronoun-plus-verb combination, the effect of placing them in theme position is not the same. The impact of a series of *I*s in theme position is not the same as the impact of a series of verbs inflected for first person, such as 'saw-I', 'took-I' and so on, where it is difficult to discern a theme line as clearly as in the pronoun-plus-verb combination. Second, Arabic negative particles come in front of the verb, so that an expression such as *I had nothing against* becomes literally 'not was for me any objection', thus pushing the 'me' further away from thematic position. Third, Arabic does not have an equivalent of the present perfect: *I've been a director* is rendered into Arabic as 'since then become-I', thus putting a temporal adjunct in theme position and pushing the inflected verb further towards the rheme. Here is a summary of the elements occurring in initial position in the English and Arabic versions of the extract. A literal translation is given of the Arabic themes to highlight the partial loss of orientation through discontinuity of theme.

> English: I, I, It, I, I, I, I, I, It, I.
> Arabic: not-was, but-I, was-it, saw-I, saw-I, saw-I, occupied-I, since
>   then, among the worst saw-I, pleases-me.

Having said that there is a partial loss of orientation in the Arabic version, it must be emphasized that it does display a reasonable level of thematic continuity in its own right. What gives the Arabic version its sense of continuity is not, as in the case of English, the use of a series of identical themes (I, I, I, . . .) but rather the frequent thematization of processes as expressed in verbs, mainly 'saw' but also 'occupied' and 'pleases'.

Attempting to analyse verb-initial languages such as Arabic in terms of Halliday's model highlights the fact that, for some languages, this type of analysis may not be as workable as it is in English. But whatever its status in other languages, exploring the thematic analysis of English is useful in illuminating certain areas of discourse organization. In so far as it applies to Arabic, for instance, it suggests that an ego-centred pattern which is perfectly feasible and natural in English has to be replaced in most contexts by a process-centred pattern which is far more typical of Arabic.

It seems to me that at this level of textual analysis translators generally face three main possibilities:

(a) You may find that you can preserve the thematic patterning of the original without distorting the target text. If the elements placed in theme position in the source text can easily and naturally be placed in theme position in the target text, the method of development of the two texts will be the same or very similar. The French translation of the above extract from *A Hero from Zero* manages to maintain 'I' as theme in all instances as the original and even adds one of its own: instead of *It was bitter, but funny*, the French literally goes 'I felt bitterness, but also amusement'.

> *Je* n'avais rien contre le fait qu'il fût un riche agent commissionné, mais *je* m'élevais fermement contre le fait qu'il ait obtenu House of Fraser par escroquerie, aidé par Kleinwort Benson et Norman Tebbit.
> *Je* ressentis de l'amertume, mais aussi de l'amusement, en voyant que le professeur Smith avait doublé son propre salaire avant de recommander l'offre de Fayed, et qu'il avait même ajouté un bonus antidaté pour faire bonne mesure.
> *Je* vis comment Brian Basham de Broad Street Associates et l'avocat, Royston Webb, aidèrent des journalistes mercenaires à transformer un tas de

cailloux en un sac d'or, et comment ce sac d'or fut bien accueilli partout où il était ouvert.

Je vis comment les documents constitués avec sérieux, que nous commen-çions à présenter au ministère du Commerce et de l'Industrie et qui révélaient la vérité sur Fayed, étaient accueillis par un silence gêné.

Je vis comment Leon Brittan, le nouveau ministre du Commerce et de l'In-dustrie, était prêt à déclarer qu'il ne trouvait rien à redire sur cette affaire.

J'ai commencé à travailler dans la City en 1936, chez Kittel and Company au numéro 5 de Fenchurch Street. *Je* suis administrateur de sociétés anonymes depuis trente et un ans. *La pire chose* que j'ai constatée dans les affaires, c'est la supercherie triomphant si facilement, et trouvant, même lorsqu'elle est démasquée, des apologistes. *Je* suis heureux qu'au bout de deux ans des inspecteurs aient été nommés, et qu'ils aient passé dix-huit mois à enquêter sur l'acquisition de House of Fraser.

Here is a summary of the elements placed in theme position in the French version:

Je, Je, Je, Je, Je, Je, J'ai, Je, La pire chose, Je.

The method of development in both extracts is therefore the same, and the French translation manages to retain the egotism of the original.

(b) You may find that you cannot preserve the thematic patterning of the original without distorting the target text. There are many factors which can restrict the choice and ordering of themes in translation. These factors may be grammatical; for instance it is ungrammatical to put verbs in theme position in English,[3] though not in Arabic or Spanish. On the other hand, the restriction on placing inde-pendent pronouns in theme position in Arabic is not, strictly speaking, gram-matical. An independent pronoun may occasionally be placed in theme position for emphasis, but a series of independent pronouns in theme position would be highly unnatural.

If the thematic patterning of the original cannot be reproduced naturally in the target language, then you will have to abandon it. If you do, you must ensure that your target version has its own method of development and maintains a sense of continuity in its own right.

(c) You may find that Halliday's model of thematic analysis does not apply to your language at all or does not apply to some of its sentence patterns. If this is the case, you may find the Prague model discussed in section 5.2 more helpful.

Whatever the difficulties involved in applying Halliday's model of thematic analysis to a given language, and irrespective of whether it is possible to reproduce the thematic patterning of the source text on a given occasion, one thing is certain: translators must not underestimate the cumulative effect of thematic choices on the way we interpret text. As Fries (1983:135) points out:

if the themes of most of the sentences of a paragraph refer to one semantic field (say location, parts of some object, wisdom vs chance, etc.) then that semantic field will be perceived as the method of development of the paragraph. If no common semantic element runs through the themes of the sentences of a paragraph, then no simple method of development will be perceived.

And this is why you have to ensure that whatever elements you put in initial-clause position in your target text or in a given part of your target text add up to something that can be understood as a method of development and that can provide a point of orientation for that part of the text.

5.1.1.3 Thematic structure: marked vs unmarked sequences

A further area in which the notions of theme and rheme have proved very useful relates to marked and unmarked structures. This particular aspect of thematic organization is of special relevance in translation because understanding it can help to heighten our awareness of meaningful choices made by speakers and writers in the course of communication.

Thematic choice involves selecting a clause element as theme. The main clause elements are **subject**, **predicator**, **object**, **complement** and **adjunct**.[4] In the Hallidayan model, thematic choice is expressed by placing one of these elements in initial position in the clause. Thematic choice is always meaningful because it indicates the speaker's/writer's point of departure. But some choices are more meaningful than others, because they are more **marked** than others.

Meaning, choice and markedness are interrelated concepts. A linguistic element carries meaning to the extent that it is selected. Meaning is closely associated with choice, so that the more obligatory an element, the less marked it will be and the weaker will be its meaning. The fact that adjectives have to be placed in front of nouns in English, for instance, means that their occurrence in this position has little or no significance because it is not the result of choice. On the other hand, putting a time or place adverbial, such as *today* or *on the shelf*, at the beginning of the clause carries more meaning because it is the result of choice: there are other positions in which it can occur. This is one aspect of the relationship between meaning, markedness and choice. A second aspect has to do with the degree of expectedness or unexpectedness of a choice. The less expected a choice, the more marked it is and the more meaning it carries; the more expected, the less marked it is and the less significance it will have. For example, it is possible but uncommon to place a complement in initial position in an English clause (as in *Beautiful were her eyes*, rather than *Her eyes were beautiful*). A complement is therefore highly marked in this position and indicates a more conscious effort on the part of the speaker or writer to highlight this particular element as his or her point of departure. It carries more textual meaning than an adverbial occurring in the same position. The more marked a choice the greater the need for it to be motivated. Conversely, unmarked options are those which are normally selected unless the context motivates the selection of another option from the same system.

It follows from the above discussion that placing a certain element in theme position does not necessarily constitute a marked thematic choice. The degree of markedness involved will depend on the frequency with which the element in question generally occurs in theme position and the extent to which it is normally mobile within the clause. A given type of clause will therefore have one unmarked thematic structure, variations of which will produce different types of marked theme. In English, it has been shown that an unmarked theme is one that signals the mood of the clause: in declarative clauses the unmarked theme is the subject (**Jane** *said nothing for a moment*); in interrogative clauses it is the *wh*-word (**What** *did Jane say?*), or the auxiliary in the case of polar questions (**Did** *Jane say anything?*); in imperative clauses it is the verb (**Say** *something*). These unmarked choices are a natural extension of the function of theme, which is to provide a point of departure and orientation. Speakers normally signal their point of departure by indicating whether they are making a statement, asking a question or giving an order. Thus, in the case of an imperative clause, for instance, the verb naturally occupies thematic position because that is what the message is about: getting the addressee to do something. Going back to the question of markedness, we can say that subject as theme in a declarative clause is not marked at all because this is the position it normally occupies in English declarative clauses. In other words, the subject is never *selected* as theme in an English declarative clause, it occupies that position by default.[5] By contrast, a predicator hardly ever occurs in theme position in English declarative clauses, and so, when it does, it is highly marked. The same cannot be said about languages in which the predicator frequently comes at the beginning of the clause and therefore represents an unmarked – or at least less marked – thematic choice.

So far so good, but what is the function of marked theme? Is it, as one might expect, a question of rejecting the default option (such as thematizing the subject in English declarative clauses) in favour of an element which provides a smoother link with the preceding discourse? This may partly explain why a speaker or writer opts for a marked theme in a given context. However, there are always unmarked options in every language which provide ways of changing the position of elements in a clause to fit in with the surrounding context. The passive is one such option in English (cf. *John gave me this book* and *This book was given to me by John*, which are both unmarked). This suggests that a marked theme has an additional or different function. A marked theme is selected specifically to foreground a particular element as the topic of the clause or its point of departure. This is often explained in terms of making the element in question more prominent or emphasizing it, an explanation which some may find confusing. I have already suggested (p. 133) that rheme, which comes in final position in the clause, is more important than theme, which comes in initial position. We might then expect that final rather than initial position in the clause is where prominence can be achieved. How can this statement be reconciled with the suggestion that in order to make an element prominent a speaker places it in theme position? The answer may lie in making a distinction between local prominence and overall discourse prominence (John Sinclair, personal communication). In marked thematic structures, theme position is associated with local prominence at the level of the clause. Rheme position, on the other hand, is prominent on an overall discourse level. In other words, placing an element in theme position gives that element local, temporary prominence within the clause. Putting an element in rheme position means that it is part of what the speaker has to say, and that is the very core of any message. Kirkwood, who adopts the Prague School rather than the Hallidayan definition of theme and rheme, suggests that placing an element in initial position will give it a certain prominence but that it will still 'carry less weight than the actual rheme' (1979:73).

It may be helpful at this point to illustrate the function of marked theme by discussing some examples of the way it works in one language, English. Hallidayan linguists identify three main types of marked theme in English: fronted theme, predicated theme and identifying theme. These are explained below with examples from translated texts where applicable.

(A) FRONTED THEME

Fronting involves 'the achievement of marked theme by moving into initial position an item which is otherwise unusual there' (Greenbaum and Quirk 1990:407). Taking an unmarked structure such as *The book received a great deal of publicity in China* as a starting point, we can suggest a number of possible thematic structures in English, starting with the least marked and ending with the most marked. Fronted thematic elements are underlined.

Fronting of time or place adjunct

> In China the book received a great deal of publicity.

This is a marked structure, but it is not highly marked because adverbials are fairly mobile elements in English. As I suggested earlier, thematizing place adjuncts is very common in certain types of text in English, such as travel brochures, where locative themes offer a natural method of text development. Enkvist (1987) found that the same is true of guidebooks. Thematizing temporal adjuncts is similarly common in any type of narrative text, that is, any text which recounts a series of events. In the following example from the Foreword to *A Hero from Zero*, Tiny Rowland presents a summary of the events leading up to the Fayed brothers' acquisition of the House of Fraser. Thematized temporal adjuncts are highlighted in bold.

> **On 4th March 1985**, the Fayed brothers made an offer of four pounds a share for House of Fraser. We applied twice more to the DTI for release.

> We immediately notified the Department of Trade that Mohamed Fayed's representations were incorrect, and gave what information we had at the time, which was sufficient to alarm, or at least give pause for basic investigations.
>
> **On 11th March** the merchant bank Kleinwort Benson announced on behalf of its brand new client, Fayed, that they had acceptances from House of Fraser shareholders for more than fifty per cent of the issued share capital.
>
> **Three hours later** a junior official of the DTI sent a note, uselessly releasing Lonrho from the undertakings not to bid.
>
> **In ten days**, the unknown Fayeds gained permission to own House of Fraser, and **throughout the ten days** they put continuous lies before the public to justify the Government permissions they had got with such ease.

Thematizing place and time adjuncts is less marked in some languages, such as Spanish and Portuguese, than in English. In German, a structure such as *Hier steigen wir aus* (literally: 'Here we get out') is totally unmarked (Kirkwood 1979). Similar choices in other languages may, on the other hand, be even more marked than in English. Wilkinson (1990) suggests that temporal adjuncts are rarely placed in theme position in Dutch. A temporal adjunct therefore represents a more marked thematic choice in Dutch than in English.

The series of marked themes in the above extract from *A Hero from Zero* basically foreground temporal sequence as the writer's point of departure. They can be reproduced with similar effect in French and Arabic. The French and Arabic translators of the above extract are therefore able to follow the same method of thematic development by placing the temporal adjuncts in theme position. This document has not been translated into Dutch, but I imagine that, had it been, extracts such as the one quoted above would have presented the Dutch translator with a problem – bearing in mind that the above is only a short extract and that a similar pattern of thematic development runs throughout the Foreword. On the one hand, placing all the above temporal adjuncts in theme position would be highly marked in Dutch; on the other hand, changing the thematic structure of the original may disrupt the natural development of the text – unless the translator finds a thematic element other than time which can provide a consistent point of orientation.

Fronting of object or complement

> Object: <u>A great deal of publicity</u> the book received in China.
> Complement: <u>Well publicized</u> the book was.

The fronting of objects and complements is much more marked than the fronting of adjuncts in English because objects and complements are fairly restricted in position. Again, the same is not true of other languages. Fronting an object is less marked in Chinese than in English. In German, it is totally unmarked if accompanied by a definite determiner (Kirkwood 1979).

Note that, unlike fronting, using the passive voice allows the speaker to select as theme what would have been the object of an active clause without making it marked. Fronting the object, on the other hand, foregrounds it and gives it local prominence (cf. *A great deal of publicity was received in China* and *A great deal of publicity the book received in China*).

You are unlikely to find a series of fronted objects or complements similar to the series of fronted temporal adjuncts quoted above. This is because, unlike adjuncts, objects and complements are not usually fronted to provide a point of orientation or method of development for a stretch of language. The effect of thematizing an object or complement in English is to provide contrast and to emphasize the speaker's attitude to the message.[6] It foregrounds the expressive meaning of the utterance. This can be seen in the following examples. The first, from John Le Carré's *The Russia House* (1989:19), illustrates a fronted nominal object:

> But Landau's clients were young and rich and did not believe in death. 'Niki boy,' said Bernard, walking round behind him and putting a hand on his shoulder, which Landau didn't like, 'in the world today, we've got to show the flag. We're patriots, see, Niki? Like you. That's why we're an offshore company. With the *glasnost* today, the Soviet Union, it's the Mount Everest of the recording business. And you're going to put us on the top, Niki. Because if you're not, we'll find somebody who will. Somebody younger, Niki, right? Somebody with the drive and the class.'
>
> The drive Landau had still. But the class, as he himself was the first to tell you, the class, forget it.

It is also possible to front a that-clause as object, as in the following example from Le Carré's *Our Game* (1995:150):

> But after a time my revulsion gave way to a furtive curiosity and the house attracted me despite myself. I would leave the tube a stop early and scurry across the Heath just to peer into its lighted windows. How do they live? What do they talk about, apart from me? Who was I when I lived there? That Diana had left the Office I knew only too well, for she had written Merriman one of her letters.

The next two examples illustrate a fronted complement. The first comes from Le Carré's *The Little Drummer Girl* (1983:19):

> In my next life I shall be a Jew or a Spaniard or an Eskimo or just a fully committed anarchist like everybody else, Alexis decided. But a German I shall never be – you do it once as a penance and that's it.

The following example comes from Le Carré's *Our Game* (1995:218):

<u>Crammed</u> against the stone wall stood the old school trunk I used as a filing box for my CC archive.

Fronting of predicator

They promised to publicize the book in China, and <u>publicize</u> it they did.

This is the most marked of all thematic choices in English. In addition to fronting the predicator, this choice also involves re-arranging other clause elements and adjusting the form of the verbal group. Authentic examples are hard to find because fronted predicators are rather uncommon in English. This one comes from Le Carré's *Our Game* (1995:30):

... He licked a finger and gaily flipped a page. 'Then all of a sudden you turn round and cut off the Doctor without a shilling. Well, well. No more incomings, no more outgoings, for three whole weeks. What you might term a radio silence. <u>Slammed</u> the door in his face, you did, Mr Cranmer, sir, and me and Oliver here were wondering why you did that to him. ...

In languages such as Arabic, verbs frequently occur in thematic position, and the fronting of a predicator is therefore not a marked thematic choice. In translating from a language such as Arabic to a language such as English, the unmarked predicator + subject structure would normally be translated by an equally unmarked structure such as subject + predicator, rather than by an identical but highly marked structure which places the predicator in initial position. Going in the other direction, say from English into Arabic, a translator should try to find some way of conveying the emphasis attached to a fronted predicator. I cannot comment on the devices available in other languages, but in Arabic, for instance, the particle *qad* may be used with the past tense of the verb to convey emphasis. A lexical item such as 'in fact' may also be used to convey even stronger emphasis. The effect would be similar to something like *and they did in fact publicize it* in English, except that the verb in Arabic would be in theme position (literally: *qad* publicize-they-it in fact).

(B) PREDICATED THEME

Predicating a theme involves using an ***it*-structure** (also called a **cleft structure**) to place an element near the beginning of the clause, as in *It was the book that received a great deal of publicity in China*, *It was a great deal of publicity that the book received in China* or *It was in China that the book received a great deal of publicity*. Apart from conjunctions and disjuncts which we have decided not to take into account for our current purposes, this is the only instance in which the theme of the clause is not the element that occurs in initial position. The theme of an *it*-structure is not *it* but rather the element which occurs after the verb *to be*. *It* simply acts as an empty subject which allows a certain element such as *the book* or *in*

China to be placed near the beginning of the clause and to be interpreted as its theme, that is, what the message is about.

Predicating an element foregrounds it by placing it in theme position. One of the options it allows a speaker is to select the element acting as subject as a marked thematic choice, an option not normally available since the subject is the unmarked theme of a declarative clause in English.

Like all marked themes, predicated themes often imply contrast. *It was in China that the book received a great deal of publicity* would generally suggest that *in China* contrasts with other places where the book did not receive a great deal of publicity. The predicated theme in the following example, from Thomas Bernhard's *Wittgenstein's Nephew* (translated into English by Ewald Osers),[7] fulfils a similar function by contrasting the years during which Wittgenstein didn't drink with the rest of his life:

> At the Obenaus, a small restaurant on Weihburggasse, he would drink several litres of white wine during an evening. He suffered for that. I believe <u>it was five or six years before his death</u> that he gave up drinking. Otherwise he would probably have died three or four years earlier, which, at least I think so, would have been a terrible pity.

The following example comes from an article entitled 'Rock that burns' (*New Internationalist* NI 431, April 2010, p. 16). The article discusses the practices of oil companies that extract crude oil from tar sands by methods that involve deforesting and subjecting the land to extreme temperatures. The reference in this specific extract is to the eastern desert of Jordan:

> Many Bedouin continue to live in the *badia*; the name itself means 'the place the Bedouin came from'. Small villages slide past, with tents, concrete block houses and large flocks of sheep and goats. Most Bedouin are 'settled' into these villages, but a significant number continue to live as nomads.
>
> <u>It is here</u> that Shell plans to introduce its tar sands extraction practices – well known from the images of torn up Alberta.

The predicated theme in this case effects spatial rather than temporal contrast: it foregrounds *here*, as opposed to other places. The implication is that the choice of location for such environmentally destructive practices is particularly relevant – specifically shocking from the writer's perspective.

Another important function of predicated theme is to signal **information structure** by presenting the element following *It* + BE in the main clause as the new or important item to which the hearer's or reader's attention is drawn. For a detailed discussion of information structure, see section 5.1.2. below.

(c) IDENTIFYING THEME

Identifying themes are very similar to predicated themes. Instead of using *It* (a cleft structure), an identifying theme places an element in theme position by turning it into a nominalization using a ***wh*-structure** (called a **pseudo-cleft structure**), as in *What the book received in China was a great deal of publicity*, or *What was received by the book in China was a great deal of publicity*. The following example comes from the March 2010 issue of *Cosmopolitan* (p. 125); *Cosmopolitan* is a woman's magazine that is regularly translated from English into a variety of languages, including Spanish, Hungarian, Russian and Thai:

> Whether you're a single mother or not, being a parent can be one of the most challenging, but rewarding, experiences of your life. What you need to do before you go ahead with finding a sperm donor is ensure that you're completely clear about what you're getting yourself into.

A second example comes from an article entitled 'I'll die doing this' which appeared in *New Internationalist* (NI 431, April 2010, p. 12), about the effect of tar sands pollution on indigenous people:

> Little is yet known about how the different toxic metals and petrochemicals interact, or how their effects could be magnified given that the flow of contam- inants into the rivershed during spring melt coincides with when fish fry are growing.
> What Fort Chipewyan needs, argues George, is a comprehensive, baseline health study that would do a thorough analysis of the entire community, and then track changes in the future based on that.

Both predicated and identifying themes are often associated with implicit contrast. They tend to imply that the item in theme position (in the case of predicated themes) or the item in rheme position (in the case of identifying themes) is chosen from a set of possible items as the one worthy of the hearer's or reader's attention: *It was the book* (rather than something else) *which received a great deal of publicity in China*; *What the book received in China was a great deal of publicity* (rather than bad reviews, for instance). In the example from *Cosmopolitan* above, the implication is that being clear about the consequences of becoming a parent is more important than other things (such as finding the sperm donor or the necessary cash to cover the relevant costs). In the example from *New Internationalist*, the implication is that the baseline health study is a priority: everything else is less important and less pressing than ensuring that this study is undertaken. Items in theme position are thus prominent in both structures – predicated and identifying. The difference is that in predicated themes, the thematic element is presented as new information; in identifying themes, the thematic element is presented as known information (see section 5.1.2 below for a discussion of known vs new information).

Predicated and identifying themes are marked but fairly common in English because they offer a thematization strategy that overcomes restrictions on word order. They also offer a way of signalling known vs new information independently of the use of intonation. Stress offers a reliable signal of information status in spoken English (see 5.1.2 below) but it is not available as a signalling device in written English. For this reason, predicated and identifying themes tend to be more common in written than in spoken English. By contrast, the two structures are of equal frequency in spoken and written Chinese because stress is not available as a device for signalling information structure in spoken Chinese (Tsao 1983).

Predicated and identifying themes must be handled carefully in translation because they are far more marked in languages with relatively free word order, such as German, than they are in English. Transferring all instances of predicated and identifying themes into a German translation would make it sound very un-German. An experienced German translator will normally replace all or most predicated and identifying themes with less marked German structures. An example of this can be found in the Morgan Matroc ceramics company brochure.

English original (*Morgan Matroc*):

> And yet there are some customers who in their search for a suitable material prefer to study complex tables of technical data. <u>It is for such customers that</u> we have listed the properties of Matroc's more widely used materials.

German translation:

> … **Für solche Kunden** haben wir die Eigenschaften der gängigsten Matroc Werkstoffe aufgelistet.

Back-translation:

> … **For such customers** have we the properties of the most popular Matroc materials listed.

Another example comes from an interview with the chairman of the Japanese Sony organization, Akio Morita, published in an edition of *Playboy* magazine and translated into Brazilian Portuguese.[8] Predicated themes are more marked in Brazilian Portuguese than they are in English:

English extract from the *Playboy* text:

> <u>It was about thirty years ago that</u> a young Japanese businessman visited the West and was deeply humiliated to learn that 'Made in Japan' was an international synonym for shoddiness – a phrase that produced jokes and laughter. Today, the laughter is heard mainly on

the way to the bank as Akio Morita, 61, the cofounder and the chairman of the Sony Corporation, continues to make his five-billion dollar corporation a fount of ever newer and more dazzling inventions.

It was Sony that gave the world mass-produced transistor radios, Trinitron television sets, Betamax video recorders and Walkman portable cassette players.

Portuguese translation:

Há trinta anos, um jovem homem de negócias japonês. exfabricante – malsucedido – de panelas de cozinhar arroz, visitou o Ocidente, e ficou profundamente humilhado ao perceber que a expressão 'Made in Japan' era um sinônimo internacional para mal-acabado. Era uma expressão que produzia piadas e risos. Hoje, os risos são ouvidos apenas quando se contabilizam os lucros de Akio Morita, 61 anos, co-fundador e presidente da Sony Corporation, que continua a usar a sua empresa de 5 bilhões de dólares (algo como um quarto das expor-tações brasileiras em 81) como fonte de novas e fantásticas invençôes.

Foi a Sony que deu ao mundo rádios transistorizados produzidos em massa, os inovadores aparelhos de televisão Triniton, os vídeo-gravadores Betamax e os toca-fitas portáteis Walkman.

Back-translation:

Thirty years ago, a young man of Japanese business …

Was Sony that gave to the world transistor radios …

In the Portuguese translation, the first cleft structure is rendered by an unmarked fronting of a time adjunct. The second cleft structure is rendered by a marked (but not highly marked) structure in which the verb is fronted.

Here is a further example, this time of identifying theme, from an article from the British newspaper the *Independent* (8 November 1988), attached to *A Hero from Zero*:

English extract from the *Independent* article:

The report had meanwhile been referred to the Serious Fraud Office. A reference to that office is made only where an inquiry concludes that an offence may have been committed. Lonrho has been informed that the report made no criticism of its conduct.

What Mr Rowland wants is the early publication of this report.

Arabic translation:

وقد أحيل هذا التقرير الى مكتب الإحتيالات الخطيرة. ولا تتم الإحالة الى هذا المكتب الا فى
حالة توصل التحقيق الى نتيجة تفيد بجواز حدوث مخالفة. وقد أبلغت مؤسسة لونرو بأن
التقرير لم يوجه أى انتقاد الى مسلكها.

ويسعى المستر رولاند الآن الى نشر هذا التقرير فى أقرب وقت.

And seeks Mr Rowland now to publish this report as soon as possible.

The Arabic predicator + subject structure is not marked at all, and it therefore fails to convey the emphasis signalled by the English identifying structure. It can be argued that 'normalizing' the marked English structure is not a good strategy in this instance and that a slightly different but similarly marked Arabic structure (using a particle such as *inna*) would have preserved the prominence given by the writer to the first part of the statement (*Mr Rowland wants*) and still sounded natural in Arabic:

إن السيد رولاند يسعى الآن الى . . .

Inna Mr Rowland seeks now …

Or

إن ما يسعى السيد رولاند اليه الآن هو نشر . . .

Inna what seeks Mr Rowland now is …

Generally speaking, languages with relatively free word order like German can thematize clause elements simply by fronting them. They therefore rarely use intricate structures that languages with relatively fixed word order resort to in order to thematize elements. Apart from being aware of the level of markedness of a given structure in the source and target languages, a translator should also learn to make use of the thematization devices available in each language. For instance, Wilkinson (1990:81) suggests that 'information which has been highlighted by being fronted in the Dutch clause lends itself to a translation in English using an IT cleft', but notes that trainee translators working from Dutch into English fail to make use of predicated and identifying themes in their English translations.

In addition to fronted, predicated and identifying themes, other types of marked theme exist in English, but they tend to be much more restricted and more likely to be used in informal language. These are **preposed theme** and **postposed theme** (Young 1980). Both involve using a gloss tag. In preposed theme, the gloss tag occurs at the beginning of the clause, in postposed theme, it occurs at the end of the clause. The following examples of both types are from Young (1980:145):

Preposed theme:	The fitter, he sent these documents to the office.
	These documents, the fitter sent them to the office.
Postposed theme:	He sent these documents to the office, the fitter.
	He sent these documents to the office, the fitter did.
	The fitter sent them to the office, these documents.

An authentic example of a preposed theme can be found in the extract from Le Carré's *The Russia House* quoted on page 145 above:

> With the *glasnost* today, the <u>Soviet Union</u>, it's the Mount Everest of the recording business.

The following two examples of postposed theme come from an interview with Sade, the well-known singer, published in *The Sunday Times Magazine* on 31 January 2010 (pp. 14, 17):

> It can be very hostile, <u>England</u>.
> He was a very strange man, <u>my father</u>, very boyish.

5.1.1.4 A brief assessment of the Hallidayan position on theme

Any approach to describing information flow in natural language will generally recognize that clauses are organized in terms of theme and rheme. But, as already noted, different linguists offer different accounts of the way in which theme and rheme are realized in discourse. Each account is naturally biased towards the native language of the linguist in question as well as other languages with which he or she may be familiar. One of the main differences between the Hallidayan and other approaches is that Halliday has always insisted that, at least in English, the theme–rheme distinction is realized by the sequential ordering of clause elements. Theme is the element placed by the speaker in first position in the clause; rheme is whatever comes after the theme. A rheme–theme sequence therefore has no place in Halliday's system.[9] This position contrasts sharply with that taken by Prague linguists, such as Firbas, who reject sentence position as the only criterion for identifying theme and rheme (see section 5.2 below).

   The attraction of the Hallidayan view is that, unlike the rather complex explanations of the Prague School, it is very simple to follow and apply. To some extent, it is also intuitively satisfying to suggest that what one is talking about always comes before what one has to say about it. Its disadvantages, on the other hand, include (a) its partial circularity:[10] theme is whatever comes in initial position and whatever comes in initial position is theme; and (b) its failure to relate descriptions of SVO languages,[11] particularly those with relatively fixed word order such as

English, to descriptions of languages with relatively free word order in which, for instance, the verb often occurs in initial position. If theme is whatever occurs in initial position we would have to acknowledge that some languages prefer to thematize participants (expressed as subjects in SVO and SOV languages) on a regular basis while other languages prefer to thematize processes (expressed as verbs in VSO languages). But Halliday does not attempt to address these preferences, nor does he discuss language features which restrict a speaker's choice of thematic elements. For instance, in Harway (a Papuan language) where the verb is always final, a speaker or writer does not have the option of thematizing processes.[12]

It is possible to see Halliday's view of theme – as whatever comes in initial position in the clause – as a reflection of (a) the nature of English as a language with relatively fixed word order,[13] and (b) his study of Chinese, this being a language with a special category of **topic** which always occurs at the beginning of the clause.

It may be useful at this point to explore the possible link between Halliday's notion of theme and the category of topic in Chinese and other topic-prominent languages. Apart from providing some insight into Halliday's view of the way in which theme is realized in discourse, the discussion of topic is also of particular interest here because it highlights an area of considerable potential confusion for translators interested in the thematic analysis of topic-prominent languages.

THEME AND CHINESE-STYLE TOPIC

Chinese has been identified by Li (1976) as a **topic-prominent** language. Unlike **subject-prominent** languages such as English, French and German, topic-prominent languages appear to have double subjects. Li gives the following examples from a variety of topic-prominent languages. The topic of each sentence is underlined:

<u>Animals</u>, I advocate a conservation policy.	(Mandarin)
<u>This field</u>, the rice is very good.	(Lahu)
<u>The present time</u>, there are many schools.	(Korean)
<u>Fish</u>, red snapper is delicious.	(Japanese)

Several questions need to be raised here to explore the relationship between theme and topic, if any exists. For instance, how do topics relate to themes? Do they behave in the same way syntactically, or, to put it more accurately, do topics, like themes, have no syntax? Does topic mean the same thing as theme, that is, what the message is about? Can topics be translated into languages which are not topic-prominent?

The topic of a clause in topic-prominent languages always occurs in initial position (Li 1976). In this respect, it coincides with theme in Halliday's model. If initial position is reserved for theme and if topic always occurs in initial position, then theme and topic are presumably the same thing.

In some languages such as Lisu, Japanese and Korean, topics are further marked by the addition of a morpheme: for example, the suffix -*nya* is always added to the topic of a sentence in Lisu. Japanese has two suffixes, -*wa* and -*ga*, the functions of which are explained in different ways by different linguists but which are said to mark, among other things, topic and non-topic respectively. Another syntactic feature of topic is that it controls anaphoric reference[14] so that (a) once an element is announced as topic, this element may be omitted altogether in subsequent clauses, hence the proliferation of subjectless clauses in languages such as Chinese and Japanese (see Chapter 6, p. 195, for an example of Japanese subjectless clauses), and (b) an element announced as topic overrides possible co-referential links with other elements in the sentence. Li gives the following example from Mandarin Chinese (1976:469):

Nèike   shù   yèzi   dà,   suǒyi   wǒ   bu   xǐhuān
that   tree   leaves   big   so   I   not   like
'That tree (topic), the leaves are big, so I don't like <*it*>.'

Topic–comment structures such as those given above are sometimes translated into English as, for instance, *Concerning animals ...*, *About this field ...*, *As for fish ...* and so on. There is, of course, a limit to how often this can be done in English. It is a marked structure in the sense of being relatively infrequent. Its overuse by Japanese and Chinese learners of English, for instance, is immediately noticeable. King (1990) similarly suggests that topicalization, as evident in the use of expressions such as *os pros*, *oson afora* and *oso ya* (all of which mean something like 'as for' or 'with regards to'), is more common in Greek than in English and that Greek learners of English tend to overuse this structure. Translators are in a position similar to that of advanced learners of a language in some respects, and pitfalls of this sort become more common when the direction of translation is into the non-native language rather than the translator's mother tongue.

Li (1976:484) suggests more natural structures for achieving something similar to topicalization in English:

Remember Tom?
Well, he fell off his bike yesterday.

You know Tom?

These structures may be natural in some situations, particularly in informal spoken exchanges, but they are undoubtedly inappropriate for many contexts. Like all the English structures suggested above for expressing Chinese-style topics, they remain far more restricted than the normal topic–comment structure in languages such as Chinese and Korean. In topic-prominent languages, these structures are the norm rather than the exception.

Chafe (1976) suggests that it is incorrect to translate a Chinese-style topic with an English expression such as *As for*. This is because the English expression suggests contrastiveness. A statement such as *As for animals, I advocate a conservation policy* implies that animals are being contrasted with something else for which the speaker perhaps does not advocate a conservation policy. The Chinese structure, on the other hand, need not imply any contrast, and Chafe therefore concludes that:

> Chinese seems to express the information in these cases in a way that does not coincide with anything available in English. In other words, there is no packaging device in English that corresponds to the Chinese topic device, and hence no fully adequate translation.
>
> *(1976:50)*

Syntactic behaviour and contrastiveness aside, it is tempting to interpret a Chinese-style topic in the same way as theme, that is, as meaning something like 'This is my starting point; this is what I am talking about'. But the scope of a topic is not restricted to the clause as the example on page 154 might suggest. Topic does not just control reference within clause boundaries, it controls reference outside clause boundaries as well. This is why once a topic is announced, the subject(s) of subsequent clauses can be omitted. Also, unlike themes (and subjects) which may be definite or indefinite, topics are always definite (Li 1976). This indicates a possible difference in meaning or function between the two. Chafe (1976:51) suggests that the function of topic is to specify some kind of framework, for instance in terms of time, location or individual reference, within which the main statement applies and that '"real" topics (in topic-prominent languages) are not so much "what the sentence is about" as "the frame within which the sentence holds"'. Li agrees with Chafe's interpretation of topic and links this to the observation that topics are always definite. A topic has to be definite because of its function of setting the framework for interpreting the sentence as a whole.

To my knowledge, no one has yet addressed the relationship between topic and theme in topic-prominent languages in a sustained fashion. These languages, presumably, have clause themes as well as sentence topics. Their organization into topic–comment structures must add to the complexity of their thematic analysis and to the difficulty of identifying signals of thematic status. There are, for instance, several conflicting claims concerning the function of the Japanese suffix -*wa*: some suggest that it is an obligatory marker of topic (this claim is implicit in Li 1976:465); others suggest that it marks given information (see 5.1.2. below for an explanation of given vs new information). Maynard (1981:124) seems to suggest that -*wa* marks topic, although she uses the term 'theme':

> -*WA* serves to create a theme by identifying NP's [i.e. noun phrases] that are to be placed on what we may call the 'thematic stage'. The thematic stage may be defined as the conceptual framework within which the story is told,

presented and performed. The choice of using -WA ... reflects the writer's thematic choice.

This is clearly an area of some difficulty for translators working from or into a topic-prominent language such as Korean, Japanese or Chinese.

The above discussion does not cover all aspects of thematic structure, but it is probably sufficient for our current purposes. We now turn our attention to the second aspect of the interactional organization of messages: information structure.

5.1.2 Information structure: given and new

The distinction between theme and rheme is speaker-oriented. It is based on what the speaker wants to announce as his or her starting point and what he or she goes on to say about it. A further distinction can be drawn between what is given and what is new in a message. This is a hearer-oriented distinction, based on what part of the message is known to the hearer and what part is new. Here again, a message is divided into two segments: one segment conveys information which the speaker regards as already known to the hearer. The other segment conveys the new information that the speaker wishes to convey to the hearer. Given information represents the common ground between speaker and hearer and gives the latter a reference point to which he or she can relate new information.

   Like thematic structure, information structure is a feature of the context rather than of the language system as such. One can only decide what part of a message is new and what part is given within a linguistic or situational context. For example, the same message may be segmented differently in response to different questions:

What's happening tomorrow?	We're climbing Ben Nevis.	
	NEW	
What are we doing tomorrow?	We're	climbing Ben Nevis.
	Given	New
What are we climbing tomorrow?	We're climbing	Ben Nevis.
	Given	New

(examples from Morley 1985:75)

The organization of the message into information units of given and new reflects the speaker's sensitivity to the hearer's state of knowledge in the process of communication. At any point of the communication process, a certain linguistic and non-linguistic environment will have already been established. The speaker can draw on this in order to relate new information that he or she wants to convey to elements that are already established in the context. The normal, unmarked order is for the speaker to place the given element before the new one. This order has been found to contribute to ease of comprehension and recall, and some composition specialists therefore explicitly recommend it to writers (Vande Kopple 1986).

The given-before-new principle influences other sequencing decisions in language. Greenbaum and Quirk posit a principle of **end-focus** to account for the tendency to process information 'so as to achieve a linear presentation from low to high information value' (1990:395). Moreover, they suggest that:

> Since the new information often needs to be stated more fully than the given (that is, with a longer, 'heavier' structure), it is not unexpected that an organization principle which may be called END-WEIGHT comes into operation along with the principle of end-focus.
>
> *(ibid.:398)*

In other words, the same principle which motivates speakers to place given before new information also motivates them to place longer and heavier structures towards the end of the clause, as in the following examples (*ibid.*):

> She visited him that day.
> She visited her best friend that day.
> She visited that day an elderly and much beloved friend.

A similar principle seems to operate in German where, Herbst *et al.* suggest, 'there is a stylistic tendency to place the more complex element (*ie* the one containing relatively more words) after the less complex' (1979:165).[15] At least one genre of Brazilian Portuguese, that of academic abstracts, also seems to follow the principle of **end-weight**. The results of a study carried out by Johns (1991) suggest that in this genre simple verbs without modals or closely linked prepositional phrases are regularly fronted while long and syntactically complex subjects are not. Problems arise in translation when a principle such as end-weight or end-focus seems to clash with more basic grammatical principles in the target language. For instance, one of the basic grammatical principles in English involves placing the subject before the predicate. In translating from Brazilian Portuguese, which allows the fronting of simple verbs, into English, a translator may be tempted to ignore the principle of end-weight in order to preserve the subject-before-predicate arrangement. The following example from a Brazilian Portuguese academic abstract illustrates the problem:[16]

Foram	estudados	os efeitos de luz,	de temperatura e	dos
were	studied	the effects of light,	of temperature and	of

tegumentos	na germinação	de	sementes	de limãocravo
presence/absence	in germination	of	seeds	of limão-cravo

(*Citrus limonia*, Osb.).	Foi	também	verificada a	influência da
(*Citrus limonia*, Osb.).	Was	also	verified	the influence of

velocidade	de	reidratação	de sementes	secas	artificialmente.
the speed	of	rehydration	of seeds	dried	artificially

The above extract was rendered as follows by the writer/translator:

> The effects of light, temperature and the presence or absence of the seed coat on limão-cravo (*Citrus limonia*) seed germination have been studied. The influence of rehydration rate on germination of artificially dried seed has been also verified.

Note that by adhering to the subject-before-predicate principle, the translator of the above extract has had to ignore the principle of end-weight. The result is awkward, unnatural and recognizably un-English. Each sentence consists of a very heavy subject followed by a very light verb. The clash between the end-weight and subject-before-predicate principles could have been avoided by switching from passive to active and inserting a subject such as *We* or *This paper*:

> This paper examines the effects of light, temperature and the presence or absence of the seed coat on limão-cravo (*Citrus limonia*). In addition, it verifies the influence of rehydration rate on germination of artificially dried seed.

5.1.2.1 How are given and new signalled in discourse?

As far as Halliday and Hasan are concerned, information structure is a feature of spoken rather than written English:

> The information systems are those concerned with the organization of the text into units of information. This is expressed in English by the intonation patterns, and it is therefore a feature only of spoken English.
>
> (*Halliday and Hasan 1976:325*)

Strictly speaking (for them), the domain of information structure is not the clause as a grammatical unit but the tone group as a phonological unit. Each information unit consists of either a combination of given-plus-new elements or of just a new element. This is realized phonologically as a tone group, with the peak of prominence or tonic accent falling on the new element. The new element on which the tonic accent falls carries the **information focus**. This is the device used by English speakers to highlight the core of a message. The tonic accent is what we normally perceive as stress. In the following examples (from Halliday 1985), the element which receives the tonic accent is underlined. The symbol // marks the boundary of a tone unit.

// now silver needs to have <u>love</u> //
// I haven't <u>seen</u> you for ages //

While clearly relevant to interpreting activities, this approach may seem of limited applicability in translation since it appears to rely heavily on phonological evidence. This, however, is not the case, for there is undoubtedly more to the distinction between given and new than the assignment of phonological stress.

Halliday (1985) explains that the boundaries of given and new elements are undecidable on phonological evidence alone. The tonic accent normally falls on the last item, but this does not tell us where the given element ends and the new one begins. To establish this, we have to look at other evidence in the surrounding context. For instance, by expanding the context of the first example above, we can establish which element is given: *In this job, Anne, we're working with silver. Now silver needs to have love.* The context, rather than phonological evidence, tells us that *silver* is given in the above example and that the new element therefore starts at *needs*. The analysis of the tone group is now as follows:

// now silver   needs to have <u>love</u> //

This is an example of a normal, unmarked structure (see sections 5.1.2.3 and 5.1.2.4 below for a discussion of marked information structure). Here, the tone unit coincides with the clause as a grammatical unit, theme coincides with given, and rheme coincides with new.

The importance of context in establishing the boundaries of given and new elements is worth noting because it suggests that analysing written language in terms of given and new is feasible. In written language, as in spoken language, one can refer to the context to establish whether a piece of information has or has not been introduced earlier. Moreover, many of the devices used to signal information status are common to both spoken and written language. For instance, in both spoken and written English definiteness is generally associated with given information and indefiniteness with new information. *The girl walked into the room* suggests, in most contexts, that the identity of *the girl* has already been established. This contrasts with *A girl walked into the room*, which suggests that a new entity is being introduced into the discourse. Similarly, in both spoken and written English given information tends to be grammatically subordinate to other information. In *Heseltine's appointment as Minister of the Environment came as no surprise*, the event of Heseltine's appointment is presented as given; the reader is assumed to know about it. Had it been new information, it would have been presented independently in the predicate, because this is where new information normally occurs in English: *Heseltine has been appointed as Minister of the Environment. This comes as no surprise.* The use of subordination as a syntactic device for marking given information may be a common feature of information structure in many languages: for instance, Maynard (1981) suggests that given information in Japanese also tends to be subordinate.

Some items are inherently given because of their meaning, and this generally applies not only to spoken and written English but also to most languages. Pronouns present the most obvious case, with first- and second-person pronouns being the prime example of items whose givenness is determined contextually.

Because stress is not available in written language, intricate syntactic devices have to be used to perform a similar function. For example, one of the most important functions of cleft and pseudo-cleft structures in English (discussed under predicated and identifying theme, section 5.1.1.3) is to signal information status. In cleft structures, the item in theme position is presented as new and the item in rheme position is presented as given. In the following extract from Morgan Matroc's brochure, the new item is underlined:

> And yet there are some customers who in their search for a suitable material prefer to study complex tables of technical data. It is <u>for such customers</u> that we have listed the properties of Matroc's more widely used materials.

A shorthand representation of the above structure would be 'It is for X that we have listed the properties …', where the element presented as given is 'we have listed the properties … for X' and the element presented as new is 'X = such customers'. Compare this with the following pseudo-cleft structure from the *Independent*:

> Lonrho has been informed that the report made no criticism of its conduct.
> What Mr Rowland wants is <u>the early publication of this report.</u>

Here, the information presented as given is that Mr Rowland wants something, and the information presented as new is that this something is the early publication of the report.

Failure to appreciate the functions of specific syntactic structures in signalling given and new information can result in unnecessary shifts in translation. The following example is from *Arab Political Humour* (Kishtainy 1985:x). The source text is English.

> The kind of joke related by any man is a good indicator of his character, mood and circumstance – a fact which is as valid when applied to the nation as a whole. <u>It is a general picture this book tries to depict</u> rather than the detailed idiosyncrasies of any political leader.

Arabic translation:

إن نوع الفكاهة التى يرويها رجل ما، دليل صالح على أخلاقه ومزاجه و ظروفه الخاصة. وهذا الواقع الفردى يصدق كذلك بالنسبة الى الأمة جمعاء. وهذه الصورة العامة هى، من باب أولى، تلك التى نحاول رسمها فى هذا الكتاب، لا الخصائص الشخصية التفصيلية التى تميز أياً من الزعماء السياسيين.

Back-translation:

> ... And **this general picture is**, primarily, **that which we attempt to draw in this book**, not the detailed personal characteristics which distinguish any of the political leaders.

An exact translation of the above English cleft structure would be very unnatural in Arabic but the structure opted for is also clumsy. Apart from being awkward, the Arabic version also distorts the information structure of the original by presenting the first element ('general picture') as given when the point of the cleft structure is to present it as the new information worth attending to. The cleft structure quite reasonably presents as given the assumption that the book is trying to depict something (all books do). The Arabic version, on the other hand, presents 'general picture' as given and offers as new information in the predicate a definition or identification of what this general picture is. The shift in information structure could have been avoided by using a pseudo-cleft structure (a marked but natural structure in Arabic). Rewording the message as:

إن ما نحاول رسمه فى هذا الكتاب هو صورة عامة، لا الخصائص ...

'What we are attempting to draw in this book is a general picture, not ...' could have preserved the given/new status of the relevant elements, although their order would have changed. This pseudo-cleft structure would signal that the first part, 'we are attempting to draw something in this book', is given and the second part, 'this something is a general picture', is new.

Although unavailable in written language, stress is often implicit in certain structures which involve emphasis. We generally assume that stress falls on DO when used for emphasis, as in *I **did** see him*. The same applies to the repetition of an auxiliary, particularly if it can be replaced by a contracted form.

> A: It's about time you went home.
> B: I *am* going. (cf. I'm going.)

Apart from syntactic structure, punctuation can also be used as a device for signalling information structure in written language.[17] It is used, for example, to distinguish between a defining relative clause such as *He was waving to the girl who was running along the platform* and a non-defining relative clause such as *He was waving to the girl, who was running along the platform*. In the first example, *who was running along the platform* identifies *the girl* and therefore does not add new information (if it did, it would be useless as a way of identifying the girl). In the second example, the comma is used to signal that the same clause represents new information.

The above discussion suggests that, when needed, clear signals of information status can be employed in written language. Different languages use different devices for signalling information structure, and translators must develop a sensitivity to the various signalling systems available in the languages they work with. This is, of course, easier said than done because, unfortunately, not much has been achieved so far in the way of identifying signals of information status in various languages. As is the case with most areas of textlinguistics, linguists tend to concentrate on the analysis of signalling devices in English and extrapolate from that to other languages. For example, Chafe sums up the expression of givenness as follows:

> The principal linguistic effects of the given-new distinction, in English *and perhaps all languages*, reduce to the fact that given information is conveyed in a weaker and more attenuated manner than new information. This attenuation is likely to be reflected in two principal ways: given information is pronounced with lower pitch and weaker stress than new and it is subject to pronominalization.
>
> *(1976:31; my emphasis)*

Brown and Yule reiterate Chafe's views in suggesting that 'speakers usually refer to current given entities with attenuated syntactic and phonological forms' (1983:189). These comments may well apply to English, and perhaps even a large number of languages, but they certainly do not apply to all. It is well known, for instance, that pronominalization is rare in Japanese, and it is therefore unlikely to play a significant role in signalling givenness. On the other hand, some languages (Japanese included) use special affixes to mark given and new information or thematic and non-thematic elements. This kind of feature is difficult to describe in terms of attenuation. In some languages, stress and intonation are not available as devices for signalling new information. They are not available, or not as readily available, in Chinese (Tsao 1983) or in French (Paula Chicken, personal communication). These languages rely on lexical and syntactic devices to signal information status. For instance, in Chinese definiteness and indefiniteness (which reflect given and new information respectively) are typically signalled by means of word order:

> The most usual way of showing definiteness [in Chinese] is by means of word-order arrangement. And the most general principle is: nominals occurring before the main verb of a sentence tend to be definite while those occurring after the main verb can be either definite or indefinite.
>
> *(Tsao 1983:104)*

Finnish is another language that does not have an article system. It uses case endings and word order to signal definiteness and indefiniteness (Sunnari 1990). This type of signalling does not seem to support the attenuation theory. Similarly, one could argue that the attenuation theory does not apply to languages such as Arabic, which have a definite article but no explicit marker of indefiniteness. Like

English, these languages tend to use definiteness as a signal of givenness and indefiniteness as a signal of newness. However, if anything, it is the new rather than the given entity which is regularly referred to by an attenuated syntactic structure.

5.1.2.2 How is givenness determined?

Identifying signals of information status is one area of information structure that is clearly relevant in translation. Another area which can pose problems in translation relates to the ability to determine when a certain item of information can and cannot be treated as given.

Most commonly, a given element is an element which is recoverable because it has been mentioned before. This is the basis on which the various elements in the answers to the questions given on page 156 have been labelled as given or new. But information may be treated by the speaker as given for a variety of other reasons. It may be predictable, or it may be contextually salient, as in the case of first-person pronouns. Rather than use a variety of notions such as recoverability, predictability and saliency to explain givenness, Chafe suggests that the key to givenness lies in the notion of consciousness:

> Given (or old) information is that knowledge which the speaker assumes to be in the consciousness of the addressee at the time of the utterance. So called new information is what the speaker assumes he is introducing into the addressee's consciousness by what he says.
>
> *(1976:30)*

> The fact that the speaker and addressee themselves are regularly treated as given (and pronominalized as *I* and *you* respectively) stems from the same consideration. The speaker is conscious of the addressee, and the addressee is conscious of the speaker.
>
> *(ibid.:31–32)*

An important question with implications for some translation-related activities such as abridging, expanding or any form of rewriting that introduces or deletes gaps between a certain item and its subsequent mention in a text is this: how long can an element be assumed to remain in the addressee's consciousness? In other words, under what circumstances would a previously mentioned item have to be re-introduced as new? Chafe suggests two variables which can be used to determine whether an item may or may not have left the addressee's consciousness:

> The number of intervening sentences in which the item was not mentioned is one obvious variable, but more interesting would be the effect of such discourse boundaries as a change of scene, where a whole set of items can

be assumed to enter the consciousness of the addressee, presumably pushing out old ones.

(ibid.:32–33)

The following example from *Autumn of Fury: The Assassination of Sadat* (Heikal 1983) illustrates the effect of both variables: number of intervening sentences and change of scene. This book was originally written in English and then later translated into Arabic (with considerable additions) by the author himself. Possible explanations for these additions are discussed in Chapter 7. The extract forms part of the description of events that followed the shooting of Anwar Sadat, former President of Egypt who was assassinated in 1981 (English version: p. 271; Arabic version: pp. 527–531). Items relevant to the present discussion of givenness are underlined.

According to Heikal, Sadat was put into a helicopter, accompanied by his wife Jihan. But instead of flying straight to the hospital, the helicopter first stopped by Sadat's residence:

> Jihan is known to have rushed into the house and put through two telephone calls to the United States. One was to her elder son Gamal, who was then in Florida. She learnt that Gamal had gone with some friends to an island off the coast of Florida, so she told the person who answered the telephone to get hold of him immediately at any cost and tell him to call his mother on a matter of the greatest urgency. Who the other call was to Jihan has never revealed, but it is certain that it must have been someone of the highest importance, and that her purpose was to obtain from the most authoritative source possible some outside indication of what was happening in Egypt. After these two telephone calls had been made Jihan rejoined the helicopter which continued its course up the Nile to the Maadi hospital.
>
> The official report from the hospital stated that when the President arrived he was in a state of complete coma, with no recordable blood pressure or pulse, 'the eyes wide open, with no response to light', and no reflexes anywhere. The report went on to list his injuries, which included two bullet entrances under the left nipple, one entering below the knee and exiting at the top of the left thigh, as well as several wounds in the right arm, chest, neck and round the left eye. There was 'a foreign substance which can be felt by touch under the skin of the neck', which was presumably the first and fatal bullet fired by Abbas Mohamed. The doctors detailed the attempts made at resuscitation, but by 2.40 it was concluded that there was no activity in either heart or brain and that the President must be declared dead. The cause of death was given as shock, internal haemorrhage in the chest cage, lesions in the left lung and all main arteries. The report was signed by twenty-one doctors.
>
> From the outset Jihan had realized that there was no hope of her husband's survival. As she waited outside the room where the doctors were operating the call came through from Gamal in Florida.

The middle paragraph, which summarizes Sadat's condition on arriving at the hospital and the doctors' report, is expanded into three pages in the Arabic version. Furthermore, the whole list of injuries is set aside as a sort of subsection, marked by three asterisks at the top and three at the bottom, so that the change of topic or scene is explicitly signalled to the reader. The following condensed extract (pp. 527–531 in the Arabic version, followed by a back-translation) illustrates the main differences:

وتقول بعض الروايات الموثوق بها أن زوجته السيدة جيهان هرعت الى التليفون تُجرى بعض الإتصالات بالولايات المتحدة، كان بينها اتصال مؤكد بابنها الوحيد جمال، والذى كان موجوداً فى ذلك الوقت فى ولاية فلوريدا بالولايات المتحدة. وقد عرفت أثناء اتصالها أن جمال قد ذهب مع بعض أصدقائه الى جزيرة أمام ساحل فلوريدا. وقد طلبت الى الشخص الذى اتصلت به أن يحاول العثور عليه بأسرع مايمكن، وأن يطلب اليه الإتصال بها فى القاهرة على الفور لأن هناك أمراً فى منتهى الخطورة تريد أن تحدثه فيه. وكانت هناك . . .

* * *

كانت السيدة جيهان تنتظر خارج غرفة الكشف وهى تعلم فى أعماقها أن زوجها قد فارق الحياة. وجاءتها مكالمة تليفونية من الولايات المتحدة، وكان ابنها جمال على الخط من ولاية فلوريدا.

… Some reliable sources report that the President's wife, Mrs Jihan, rushed to the telephone to make **some telephone calls** to the United States. Among these was definitely **a call to her only son Gamal**, who was then in Florida. During **the call** she discovered that Gamal had gone with some of his friends to an island on the coast of Florida. She asked the person who answered her to try and find him as soon as possible and to **ask him to contact her** in Cairo immediately as there is an extremely urgent matter she needs to talk to him about. There were other telephone calls that Mrs Jihan made to the United States …

* * *

The official report of the Maadi Hospital states that when Sadat arrived at the hospital and was examined he was in a state of complete coma. The official report issued by the Maadi Hospital was as follows:

[complete report quoted – three pages, ending with signatures of members of the medical team]

* * *

Mrs Jihan was waiting outside the examination room, knowing in her heart of hearts that her husband has departed. **A telephone call** came from the United States. It was her son Gamal on the line calling from Florida …

Unlike the English version, the last paragraph in the Arabic version reintroduces Gamal's telephone call to his mother as new information. This is signalled in Arabic through the use of an indefinite noun group: 'a telephone call' rather than 'the call'. It would have been unreasonable of the author/translator to expect this item of information to remain in the reader's consciousness after three intervening pages and an explicitly marked change of scene or topic.

A final point to bear in mind is that givenness is assigned by the speaker, and as such does not necessarily correlate with the reality of the linguistic or extra-linguistic situation. A speaker may decide to present an element as given even when there is no sufficient reason to assume that it is in the addressee's consciousness. This may be done for rhetorical purposes and is a common ploy in politics. Presenting a piece of information as given suggests that it is already established and agreed and is therefore non-negotiable. Similarly, an element which has been mentioned before may be presented as new because it is unexpected or because the speaker wishes to present it in a contrastive light.

5.1.2.3 Marked vs unmarked information structure

Unlike thematic structure (at least in English), information structure is not realized by the sequencing of elements. It is realized chiefly by tonicity. In unmarked information structure, the information focus falls on something other than the theme. It falls on the whole rheme or part of it; for example, in *John was appointed Chairman*, the tonic accent will normally fall on *Chairman*:

// John was appointed <u>Chairman</u> //

This information structure would give the message the meaning of a statement of what happened or what John was appointed as.

Other options are available to the speaker, depending on where he or she feels the burden of the message lies. For instance, the information focus may be placed on *John*, and in this case the message will be understood as a statement of *who* was appointed Chairman and may imply surprise or contrast:

// <u>John</u> was appointed Chairman //

Similarly, the focus may be placed on *was* to stress the truth of the utterance:

// John <u>was</u> appointed Chairman //

In written language, marked information structure is often signalled by means of typography or punctuation devices. In the following example from Agatha Christie's

Crooked House (1949/1989:61), italics are used to highlight the elements on which the information focus falls:

> 'The family! Beasts! I hate them all.'
> She looked at me, her mouth working. She looked sullen and frightened and angry.
> 'They've been beastly to me always – always. From the very first. Why shouldn't I marry their precious father? What did it matter to *them*? They'd all got loads of money. *He* gave it to them. They wouldn't have had the brains to make any for themselves!'
> She went on:
> 'Why shouldn't a man marry again – even if he is a bit old? And he wasn't really old at all – not in himself. I was very fond of him. I *was* fond of him.'
> She looked at me defiantly.

Here, the elements which are selected as focal (*them*, *he* and *was*) are not new in the sense of not having been mentioned before, but they are new in the sense of being in some way contrastive. For instance, the last item, *was*, contrasts with what the speaker thinks the hearer believes about her feelings. In the French translation of this extract, the italics are left out. As mentioned earlier, French does not generally use phonological stress to highlight a clause element; instead, lexical means are employed to signal what would normally be conveyed by means of intonation in English. Thus

> The <u>English</u> have changed

can be rendered as

> Les Anglais, eux aussi, ont évolué

where the lexical item *eux aussi* ('as well') replaces stress in highlighting the previous item *Les Anglais*. Instead of italics, the French translator of the above extract opts for repeating the last statement to achieve similar emphasis:

> ... D'ailleurs, il n'était pas vieux du tout! Il y a vieux et vieux. Je l'aimais bien.
> Comme me défiant des yeux, elle répéta:
> – Oui, je l'aimais bien. ...

The emphasis in the French version does not just come from the repetition of *je l'aimais bien*, which also occurs in the original, but rather from the fact that the repetition is labelled as repetition: *elle répéta*.

5.1.2.4 Marked information structure and marked rheme

To my knowledge, Hallidayan linguists have always concentrated on marked theme and do not seem to have considered that a rheme can also be marked. But the notion of marked rheme may prove helpful in accounting for the communicative force of some utterances. For instance, there are times when a speaker or writer seems to be deliberately highlighting a rheme by stripping the message of its initial element, that is, the theme. The following example illustrates the point.

> English extract from *A Hero from Zero* (p. v)
>
> House of Fraser shares were highly sensitive to any rumours of a bid, and we waited with caution and anxiety for the green light from the ministry. <u>And waited</u>.

It seems reasonable to suggest that the natural theme *we* is omitted in the second sentence in order to foreground the rheme. The rheme is all there is in the clause and thus receives the reader's undivided attention. To distinguish between the function of marked theme and that of marked rheme, we could say that marked theme gives prominence to an element as linking information, whereas marked rheme gives prominence to an element as the core of the message.

Another reason for the prominence of *And waited* in the above example is that it repeats verbatim information that has already been established in the previous sentence. It therefore has a surprise effect on the reader, who expects each new clause to move the discourse forward. In cases of this sort, the pure repetition of information and the reader's expectation that the discourse should be moving forward are reconciled by finding an indirect interpretation of the message. In this particular instance, we interpret *And waited* as meaning something like 'we went on waiting and nothing happened' or 'we waited in vain'. In French, it is impossible to reproduce the above themeless clause. A French verb has to be accompanied by an immediate subject. This is, of course, also true of English grammar (taken as an abstract system), but unlike French, English employs themeless sentences as a fairly common stylistic device which is both acceptable and effective in many contexts. The French translation overcomes the problem by spelling out the interpretation: *Nous attendîmes en vain* (literally: 'we waited in vain'), but loses the surprise element because it conforms to the given-plus-new pattern. The Arabic translation preserves the surprise element by employing a mixture of repetition and temporal signalling:

وانتظرنا ثم انتظرنا .

literally 'and waited-we then waited-we', that is, 'we waited and then we waited some more', meaning 'we waited in vain'.

Apart from deleting the theme in order to highlight the rhematic element, it is also possible to use punctuation in written language to signal an unusual arrangement of clause elements into tone groups. Consider the following example from Le Carré's *The Little Drummer Girl* (1983:8):

> As a further precaution, the addresses of Israeli staff were not printed in official diplomatic lists for fear of encouraging the impulsive gesture at a time when Israel was being a little hard to take. Politically.

The full stop before *Politically* does a number of things simultaneously. First, it forces an end of a tone group on the previous stretch of language, thus presenting what follows as a separate unit of information. A unit of information must include a new element (the given element being optional). The new element, a complete unit of information in this case, is a simple adverb: *Politically*. This in itself is unusual and therefore marked in English. Second, in order to interpret *Politically* as a unit of information, we have to assume that it is meant as a foregrounded rheme – foregrounded by omitting the thematic element *Israel was being a little hard to take*. Third, in forcing an end of a tone group at this point, the full stop also foregrounds the previous rheme. It gives greater rhematic emphasis to the previous chunk of information: *was being a little hard to take*.

Here is another example of marked information structure, this time from an advertising leaflet which accompanies a range of cosmetic products by Estée Lauder:

> Extraordinary new colors.
> Extraordinary new compacts.
>
> ESTÉE LAUDER SIGNATURE.
>
> Singular. Intense.
> Privileged. Provocative.
>
> Colors to astonish.
> Make resistance impossible.
>
> Consider them. Yours.
> Like a fingerprint.

The strategy used to foreground rhematic elements and to create highly marked information structures in the above extract is the same as that used by Le Carré in *The Little Drummer Girl* example. Thematic elements are omitted to foreground a rheme, for example *Make resistance impossible* (*They/These colors?*). Full stops are inserted in unexpected places to force the reader to treat certain elements as complete units of information. This is particularly effective in the case of *Consider them. Yours*, where one automatically gets the two interpretations: 'consider them' (i.e. think about them), 'they are yours' and 'Consider them yours'. Only the first interpretation is successfully conveyed in the French version of the leaflet (*Regardez-les. Elles sont à vous*).

Since information focus normally falls on the rheme or part of it, and since unmarked information structure involves placing the given element before the new one and unmarked thematic structure involves placing theme before rheme, it is not surprising that theme often coincides with given, and rheme often coincides with new. This is probably why, for most Prague linguists, part of the definition of theme is that it is given and part of the definition of rheme is that it is new. We will now look at this alternative view to explore its relevance to translation activities.

5.2 THE PRAGUE SCHOOL POSITION ON INFORMATION FLOW: FUNCTIONAL SENTENCE PERSPECTIVE

The Prague School position on theme/rheme and given/new is quite distinct from Halliday's and results in a significantly different explanation of how these categories are realized in discourse. This approach is generally referred to as **functional sentence perspective (FSP)**.[18]

The theory of functional sentence perspective was developed by a group of Czech linguists who pioneered most studies investigating the interaction between syntax and communicative function. The details of FSP theory are rather complex, and there are several distinct approaches within the Prague tradition itself. Nevertheless, it is important for translators to become familiar with at least one of the major models proposed within this alternative tradition. For one thing, a functional sentence perspective approach may prove more helpful in explaining the interactional organization of languages other than English, particularly languages with free or relatively free word order. For another, FSP theory often forms the basis for highly relevant discussions of translation problems and strategies (see, for example, Hatim 1984, 1987, 1988, 1989, Hatim and Mason 1990, Rogers 2006), and basic familiarity with this approach tends to be taken for granted by those exploring its relevance to translation studies. A simplified general outline of one FSP model is therefore given below in the hope that it will prove useful to translators interested in resolving, or at least identifying, translation problems relating to information flow.[19]

The main premise in FSP theory is that the communicative goals of an interaction cause the structure of a clause or sentence to function in different kinds of perspective. Jan Firbas,[20] one of the main proponents of this approach, gives the following example (1986). A sentence such as *John has been taken ill* has a certain syntactic structure which remains unchanged in different communicative settings. In context, it will function in a certain kind of perspective, depending on the purpose of communication; for instance, it may function as a statement of a person's state of health (*John has been taken **ill***), as an identification of the person affected (***John** has been taken ill*), or as an affirmation that the information conveyed is really valid (*John **has** been taken ill*). Note that what Firbas describes as functional sentence perspective in this example would be analysed purely in terms of information structure in Halliday's model.

The concepts of theme/rheme and given/new are supplemented in Firbas' model with a non-binary notion that determines which elements are thematic and which are not thematic in a clause. This is the notion of **communicative dynamism (CD)**. Firbas (1972:78) explains it as follows:

> communicative dynamism ... is based on the fact that linguistic communi-cation is not a static, but a dynamic phenomenon. By CD I understand a property of communication, displayed in the course of the development of the information to be conveyed and consisting in advancing this development. By the degree of CD carried by a linguistic element, I understand the extent to which the element contributes to the development of the communication, to which, as it were, it 'pushes the communication forward'.

In order to relate the notion of CD to the question of identifying theme/rheme and given/new in discourse, Firbas suggests the following. A clause consists of different types of element. Some elements lay the foundation on which other elements may convey a message. These foundation-laying elements are context-dependent and constitute the theme. They carry a low degree of CD because, being context-dependent, they do not play a major role in pushing the communication forward. If we take the example of *John has been taken **ill*** (as a statement of John's state of health), the foundation-laying element would be *John*. The remaining elements complete the information and fulfil the communicative purpose of the utterance. These core-constituting elements form the non-theme, are context-independent and carry a higher degree of CD.

What Firbas seems to be suggesting so far is that theme consists of context-dependent and rheme of context-independent items. He does, however, modify this position slightly in his later writings as we shall see shortly. It is also important to point out at this stage that Firbas' notions of context-dependence/independence are much more restricted than Halliday's notions of given/new:

> context dependence/independence is judged by a very narrow criterion. Any kind or aspect of information that is not present in the immediately relevant verbal or situational context is to be regarded as irretrievable and hence context-independent.
>
> *(Firbas 1987:30–31)*

Firbas' notions of context-dependence/independence are therefore purely linguistic and do not extend to the psychological aspect of communication as Halliday's notions do.

Firbas goes on to explain that the non-theme consists of two elements: the **transition** and the rheme. The transition consists of elements which perform the function of linking the foundation-laying and the core-constituting parts of the clause. It generally consists of the temporal and modal exponents of the verb, which are 'the transitional element par excellence: They carry the lowest degree of CD within the non-theme and are the *transition proper*' (Firbas 1986:54). In the example given above, *John has been taken **ill***, the transition would be *has been +* *-en*. The transition may also consist of a link verb such as *be* or *seem*, or any verb whose main function is simply to link the foundation-laying and core-constituting elements of a clause. In *The weather is fine*, for example, *is* would normally constitute the transition (assuming the communicative purpose of the utterance is to state what the weather is like). The rheme represents the core of the message and carries the highest degree of CD. It consists of the notional component of the finite verb and the rest of the message. In *John has been taken **ill***, the rheme is *take + ill*. In *The weather is **fine***, the rheme is *fine*.

Apart from the notion of transition outlined above, and unlike the Hallidayan approach, where the verb is generally considered part of the rheme, FSP theory assigns thematic or rhematic status to the verb depending on the context and the semantics of the verb itself. Semantically, the less of a notional component the verb has, the more naturally it goes with the theme as a foundation-laying element. Link verbs are a clear case of verbs with a very limited notional component whose function seems to be simply linking the theme to the rest of the message. In fact, in many languages (for instance, Arabic and Russian) equative sentences such as *The weather is fine* are verbless. It is also possible to omit a link verb in English in some contexts, as in the following example from Le Carré's *The Russia House* (1989:18):

> And in the corner of his eye – an anxious blue blur was all that she amounted to – this Soviet woman he was deliberately ignoring.

This seems to support the view that link verbs play little or no role in pushing the communication forward and therefore have no rhematic status.

Contextually, the notional component of the verb is assigned thematic status if it has already been mentioned. Scinto (1983:80) gives the following example:

> Consider the following utterance:
>   Leander bought a new book.
> To this sentence we can pose the wh-question: What did Leander buy? or, What did Leander do? In the case of the first question the response is 'a new book'. In the case of the second, 'bought a new book'. What these answers demonstrate is that the verb may be part of either Theme or Rheme proper. In the case of the first question the verb is thematicized; in the second it is rhematic and is substituted for by a categorical verb, i.e. to do.

Which question to ask will, of course, depend on whether the context already tells us that Leander bought something. Note that this approach tends, by and large, to equate theme with given (context-dependent) and rheme with new (context-independent) elements. However, Firbas does modify this position when he insists that, as far as he is concerned, this is not necessarily the case:

> I consider rhematic information to be always new, but thematic information old and/or new. On the other hand, old information is always thematic, but new information thematic or rhematic.
>
> *(1987:46)*

In other words, Firbas, like Halliday, acknowledges that a unit of information may consist of a given plus new element, or of just a new element. In the first case, the given element would be considered thematic and the new element would be considered rhematic. In the second case, a theme still has to be identified and, for Firbas, this would be the least context-independent element (i.e. the element with the lowest degree of CD).

So far, Firbas' approach to information flow can be summed up as follows. A clause consists of two types of element: foundation-laying/context-dependent elements and core-constituting/context-independent elements. The former have a lower degree of CD and are always thematic. The latter, however, may be thematic or rhematic. A clause may totally consist of context-independent elements and, in this case, the theme will be the element with the lowest degree of CD and the rheme will be the element with the highest degree of CD.

5.2.1 Linear arrangement and thematic status in FSP

It should be clear by now that, unlike Hallidayan linguists, FSP theorists do not see theme and rheme as being realized chiefly by their relative positions in the clause. This is not to say that they do not acknowledge the role played by sequential ordering in signalling the communicative function of an utterance. Firbas, for instance, suggests that 'the basic distribution of CD is implemented by a series of elements opening with the element carrying the very lowest and gradually passing on to the element carrying the very highest degree of CD' (1974:22). This is more or less the same as saying that theme normally precedes rheme. However, as can be seen from the above brief discussion of the verb as a thematic or rhematic element, FSP theorists also acknowledge semantic structure and context as factors which further determine the distribution of CD. Communicative dynamism is therefore assumed to be achieved by the interplay of these three factors: linear modification (i.e. gradation of position, syntax), semantic structure and context. Semantic structure and context 'operate either in the same direction as or counter to' linear modification (Firbas 1974:22), but both are hierarchically superior to it. For example, with the exception of contexts in which they are presented contrastively, pronouns, being context-dependent, always carry a low degree of CD irrespective of where they occur in the clause. In *I gave the book to him* or *I gave him the book*, *him* would normally be considered thematic in FSP theory. Similarly, definite expressions would be considered thematic and indefinite expressions rhematic in most contexts. The following examples, adapted from Firbas (1986:58) illustrate the priority given to context over linear arrangement. Rhematic elements are italicized.

(1) *A heavy dew* (Rh) had (TME) fallen (Th; TME).
(2) The grass (Th) was (TME) *blue* (Rh).
(3) *Big drops* (Rh) hung (TME) on the bushes (Th).

(Rh = rheme; TME = temporal modal exponent/transition; Th = theme)

The analysis of clause elements in terms of FSP is clearly a complex business. It is not as easy to apply or follow as Halliday's system. However, as explained earlier, a basic understanding of this approach may well prove helpful in some contexts.

5.2.2 Linear arrangement and marked structures in FSP

Since FSP theorists do not take sentence position as the only criterion for assigning thematic status to clause elements, it follows that two alternative formulations of the same message can have the same thematic analysis. For example, *In China the book received a great deal of publicity* and *The book received a great deal of publicity in China* would be analysed in the same way. *In China* would be considered rhematic in both formulations (unless stress is used to signal a difference in its thematic/rhematic status). Compare this with the Hallidayan approach, where *In China* would be considered rheme in the second and marked theme in the first example. It also follows that one cannot talk specifically about 'marked theme' in FSP theory, since the question of producing a marked theme by putting an element in initial position in the clause assumes that initial position is reserved for theme. FSP theorists do, however, acknowledge that there are marked and unmarked structures in every language. They also attempt to explain the difference in terms of theme/rheme, though their explanation is somewhat different from Halliday's.

Very briefly, according to Prague linguists such as Mathesius and Firbas, the nature of interaction suggests that the usual, unmarked order of message segments is that of theme followed by rheme. It is clearly easier to follow a message that announces its subject and then says something about it than the other way round. Weil (1844, discussed in Firbas 1974), one of the pioneers of this area of study, suggested that the movement from the initial notion of subject of utterance (theme) to the goal of utterance (rheme) represents the movement of the mind itself.[21] The organization of a message into a theme + rheme sequence therefore represents the unmarked, normal order. He further suggested that sequences which deviate from this normal order do occur, and he called a rheme–theme organization of a message the 'pathetic order' (Firbas 1974). The pathetic order is marked; its function is to convey emotion of some sort: it may be contrastive or contradictory, for example. Instead of conveying a message in a straightforward way, the pathetic order allows the speaker to add an emotional layer to it. An

English clause such as *Well-publicized the book was* would therefore be considered marked in both Hallidayan and Prague linguistics. However, a Hallidayan linguist would analyse it as a fronted theme + rheme sequence, whereas a Prague linguist would analyse it as a rheme–theme sequence.

What we have here, then, are two different explanations of the feature of marked organization of the clause as a message. The Hallidayan approach explains it in terms of the fronting of an element to make it thematic. The Prague linguists' approach explains it in terms of reversing the theme–rheme sequence. For the purposes of translation, what matters is that both types of analysis recognize the sequence as marked.

5.2.3 The tension between word order and communicative function: a problem in translation?

According to FSP scholars, restrictions on word order in various languages result in a linear arrangement that may or may not coincide with the interpretative arrangement of an utterance. Firbas (1986:47) gives the following examples (always assuming a neutral context for each utterance):

Interpretative arrangement	Linear arrangement
I him used to know.	I used to know him.
Ich ihn habe gekannt.	Ich habe ihn gekannt.
Je l'ai connu.	Je l'ai connu.

Irrespective of the specific examples used by Firbas, this view implies that, generally speaking, in languages with relatively free word order there will be less tension between the requirements of syntax and those of communicative function. Conversely, in languages with relatively fixed word order there will be greater instances of tension between syntax and communicative function.

Word-order patterns fulfil a number of functions in all languages: syntactically, they indicate the roles of subject, object and so on; semantically, they indicate roles such as actor, patient, beneficiary; communicatively, they indicate the flow of infor-mation (however we may wish to represent this: in terms of theme/rheme, given/new or communicative dynamism). Several linguists have suggested that different languages give different priorities to each of these functions, depending on the extent to which their system of word-order is fixed. Mathesius (quoted in Firbas 1974:17) compares English and Czech in this respect and concludes that in English, the grammatical principle (i.e. syntax) plays the leading role in the hierarchy of word order principles and that 'English differs from Czech in being so little susceptible to the requirements of FSP as to frequently disregard them altogether'. De Beau-grande and Dressler (1981:75) make the same assertion:[22]

> In English, the lack of a differentiated morphemic system in many areas places heavy constraints on word-order patterns. In Czech, with its richer

morphemic systems, word order can follow the functional sentence perspective much more faithfully.

Johns (1991:10–11) makes similar claims with respect to topic-prominent vs subject-prominent languages: 'in a topic-prominent language linear arrangement follows the scale of CD far more closely than it does in a subject-prominent language'. This is an interesting view of word order vs communicative function. It suggests that translating between languages with different priorities and different types of syntactic restriction necessarily involves a great deal of skewing of patterns of information flow. The question is: can translators do anything to minimize this skewing?

5.2.4 Suggested strategies for minimizing linear dislocation

A number of linguists have suggested a variety of strategies for resolving the tension between syntactic and communicative functions in translation and language learning. In this section, I will attempt to explore some of these strategies, with examples from translated texts where possible. The strategies discussed are drawn from two main sources: Johns (1991) and Papegaaij and Schubert (1988).

Strategy no. 1: voice change

This strategy involves changing the syntactic form of the verb to achieve a different sequence of elements. A good example of this is voice change in languages with a category of voice. The following examples, from Johns (1991), involve the substitution of active for passive. The reverse, the substitution of passive for active, is of course also possible.

Example A
Portuguese text (*Ciência e cultura* (1980), 32(7):936)

Neste trabalho são apresentadas observações fenológicas   sobre
In this paper   are presented   observations phenological about

Magonia pubescens St. Hil.
Magonia pubescens St. Hil.

English Text

This paper reports observations about the phenology of Magonia pubescens St. Hil.

Example B
Portuguese text (*Ciência e cultura* (1980), 32(7):941)

Estudaram-se	a	morfologia	e	a	histologia	do	aparelho
Were studied	the	morphology	and	the	histology	of	system

reprodutor	masculine	do	camarão	de	água	doce,
reproductive	male	of	prawn	of	fresh	water,

Macrobrachium acanthurus (Wiegmann, 1836).
Macrobrachium acanthurus (Wiegmann, 1836).

English text

This paper deals with the anatomy and histology of the male reproductive system of the freshwater prawn Macrobrachium acanthurus (Wiegmann, 1836).

Johns notes that the strategy of substituting active for passive raises the problem of providing a subject for the active clause. He rightly points out that the subject of the active clause must preserve the impersonality we normally associate with passive structures in many European languages. In the above examples, the choice of *This paper* as subject satisfies this condition of impersonality.

Ergative structures may provide a strategy similar to that of voice change in some languages. **Ergativity** involves using the object of a transitive verb as the subject of an intransitive verb: compare *An explosion shook the room* and *The room shook (with the explosion)*. This type of structure is very common in some languages, such as Finnish.

Strategy no. 2: change of verb

This involves changing the verb altogether and replacing it with one that has a similar meaning but can be used in a different syntactic configuration. Examples of pairs of verbs that describe an event from different perspectives in English include *give/get* and *like/please*. These often allow reordering the sequence of elements in a clause without a significant change of meaning (cf. *I like it* and *It pleases me*).

I have not been able to find any examples of this strategy in my data or in Johns' data. The reluctance of translators to use it is understandable to some extent. Expressions such as *I like it* and *It pleases me* are 'equivalent' only in theory. In real life, one of the options – in this case, *It pleases me* – tends to be very unnatural. Each language has its own phraseology, its own idiom which rules out many options that are potentially available as grammatical sequences.

Reciprocal pairs that offer more natural alternatives than *like/please* do exist, however. For instance, *I bought it from John* and *John sold it to me*, or *I received/ got a letter from John* and *John sent me a letter* are equally 'natural' as far as the phraseology of English is concerned; their 'acceptability' is, of course, determined by the context in which they occur.

Strategy no. 3: nominalization

Some languages allow the order verb + subject. If the translator wishes to maintain this thematic organization and, at the same time, adhere to an obligatory order of subject + verb in the target language, nominalization could probably provide a good strategy in many contexts. Nominalization involves replacing a verbal form with a nominal one (e.g. *describe* → *description*). This can then be followed by a semantically 'empty' verb such as *give* or *take* in the passive. For example, the Portuguese sequence:

Estudou-se	o	comportamento	de	*Drosophila sturtevanti*
were-studied	the	behaviour	of	*Drosophila sturtevanti*

can be turned into

A study was carried out of the behaviour of …

Alternatively, the nominalization can follow a 'weak' subject such as *This* in the following example (from Johns 1991):

This is a study of the behaviour of …

I have not found any examples of the use of this strategy in actual translations. Johns similarly confirms that, in his own data, this 'sophisticated strategy of nominalisation is under-represented' (1991:7). The fact that it is underrepresented highlights the need to draw translators' attention to it. If sophisticated strategies such as nominalization have not so far been recognized as viable options in resolving the tension between syntax and communicative function, this does not imply that they are not viable – just that they have been largely overlooked.

To illustrate the potential usefulness of the strategy of nominalization, we could perhaps look at how it might be used to improve an existing translation. Below is a Brazilian academic abstract (from *Ciência e cultura* (1980), 32(7): 857), followed by its existing English translation. Initial verbs are highlighted in the Portuguese text.

Analisou-se as relações da dopamina cerebral com as funções motoras. O trabalho discute as evidências de que drogas que incrementam a transmissão dopaminérgica central produzem aumento da atividade locomotora, estereotipia e hipercinesia, enquanto que drogas neurolépticas como o haloperidol, bloqueadoras de receptores dopaminérgicos centrais, induzem hipocinesia e rigidez. **Associou-se** o efeito do tratamento prolongado com neurolépticos e os sintomas das discinesias tardias ao desenvolvimento da supersensibilidade dopaminérgica central.

Existing English translation:

Dopamine and motor function. The relations between dopamine and motor functions were analyzed. Several references were presented suggesting not only that drugs that increase central dopaminergic transmission increase locomotor activity and induce stereotypy and hyperkinesia but also that neuroleptic drugs like haloperidol, that block dopamine receptors, induce hypokinesia and rigidity. The effects of long-term neuroleptic treatment and the symptoms of tardive dyskinesia were associated to the development of central dopaminergic supersensitivity.

Suggested version:

Dopamine and motor function. An analysis is carried out of the relations between dopamine and motor functions. Several references are presented which suggest not only that drugs that increase central dopaminergic transmission increase locomotor activity and induce stereotypy and hyperkinesia but also that neuroleptic drugs like haloperidol, that block dopamine receptors, induce hypokinesia and rigidity. An association is established between the effects of long-term neuroleptic treatment and the symptoms of tardive dyskinesia on the one hand and the development of central dopaminergic supersensitivity on the other.

With the exception of the use of nominalizations and a change from the past to the present tense, my suggested version is identical to the existing translation (the present tense is the correct one to use here because it signals that the abstract reports the contents of the paper, not the procedures undertaken in the research – see discussion of tense as a signalling device in academic abstracts, Chapter 4, section 4.2.4). The nominalizations offer a way of presenting the information from a perspective similar to that of the Portuguese text. This is not a question of adhering to the structure of the source text for the sake of preserving form. The placement of verbs in initial position in the Portuguese text has a communicative function: it thematizes processes as the writer's point of departure, an arrangement particularly suited to the reporting of academic research and scientific methods.[23]

Strategy no. 4: extraposition

Extraposition involves changing the position of the entire clause in the sentence, for instance by embedding a simple clause in a complex sentence. **Cleft** and

pseudo-cleft structures, discussed under predicated and identifying themes in 5.1.1.3 above, provide good examples. Papegaaij and Schubert (1988:182) explain that the main advantage of extraposition is that it 'provides an escape to a higher and, in this particular respect, freer level' when word order is relatively fixed at clause level. For various examples of cleft and pseudo-cleft structures, see sections 5.1.1.3 and 5.1.2.1 of this chapter.

The above strategies are potentially available for resolving the tension between word order and communicative function. In practice, syntactic and semantic considerations often override or interact with communicative considerations to produce structures that do not follow the arrangement of the source text.

I have to admit that it is very difficult indeed to find clear examples of any of the above strategies in authentic translations. If anything, the most common strategy by far seems to be to abandon the thematic organization of the source text in favour of adhering to whatever word-order principles may be operating in the target language. In other words, most translators seem to give priority to the syntactic principles of the target language rather than to the communicative structure of the source text. Generally speaking, this strategy does not, in itself, seem to interfere with the natural flow of information in the target text. In his study of Portuguese and English versions of Brazilian academic abstracts, Johns (1991:6) found that abandoning the thematic organization of the source language, in this case Portuguese, 'often gives a perfectly acceptable English text'. In outlining the strategies potentially available to a translator, I am therefore not suggesting that translators should necessarily follow the thematic organization of every clause in the source text. Nor am I suggesting that these strategies are in fact used by professional translators in any significant way; one has to acknowledge that, in spite of being available in theory, they are in fact rarely used in practice. What I am suggesting, however, is that an awareness of aspects of information flow and potential ways of resolving tension between syntactic and communicative functions is important in translation. The fact that certain strategies which can be shown to be useful in translation tend not to be made use of suggests that translators are simply not aware of them, rather than that they are familiar with them but consciously or subconsciously choose not to use them.

To sum up, a translator cannot always follow the thematic organization of the original. If at all possible, and unless the translation is designed to achieve a different effect, he or she should make an effort to present the target text from a perspective similar to that of the source text. But certain features of syntactic structure such as restrictions on word order, the principle of end-weight and the natural phraseology of the target language often mean that the thematic organization of the source text has to be abandoned. What matters at the end of the day is that the target text has some thematic organization of its own, that it reads naturally and smoothly, does not distort the information structure of the original (see 5.1.2 above) and that it preserves, where possible, any special emphasis signalled by marked structures in the original and maintains a coherent point of view as a text in its own right.

1. John Le Carré's novel *The Russia House* opens with the following three
    paragraphs (1989:17–18):

> In a broad Moscow street not two hundred yards from the
> Leningrad station, on the upper floor of an ornate and hideous
> hotel built by Stalin in the style known to Muscovites as Empire
> During the Plague, the British Council's first ever audio fair for
> the teaching of the English language and the spread of British
> culture was grinding to its excruciating end. The time was half
> past five, the summer weather erratic. After fierce rain showers
> all day long, a false sunlight was blazing in the puddles and
> raising vapours from the pavements. Of the passers-by, the
> younger ones wore jeans and sneakers, but their elders were still
> huddled in their warms.
>
> The room the Council had rented was not expensive but neither
> was it appropriate to the occasion. I have seen it – Not long ago, in
> Moscow on quite another mission, I tiptoed up the great empty
> staircase and, with a diplomatic passport in my pocket, stood in
> the eternal dusk that shrouds old ballrooms when they are asleep
> – With its plump brown pillars and gilded mirrors, it was better
> suited to the last hours of a sinking liner than the launch of a
> great initiative. On the ceiling, snarling Russians in proletarian
> caps shook their fists at Lenin. Their vigour contrasted unhelp-
> fully with the chipped green racks of sound cassettes along the
> walls, featuring *Winnie-the-Pooh* and *Advanced Computer English
> in Three Hours.* The sack-cloth sound-booths, locally procured
> and lacking many of their promised features, had the sadness of
> deck chairs on a rainy beach. The exhibitors' stands, crammed
> under the shadow of an overhanging gallery, seemed as blas-
> phemous as betting shops in a tabernacle.
>
> Nevertheless a fair of sorts had taken place. People had come,
> as Moscow people do, provided they have the documents and
> status to satisfy the hard-eyed boys in leather jackets at the door.
> Out of politeness. Out of curiosity. To talk to Westerners. Because
> it is there. And now on the fifth and final evening the great farewell
> cocktail party of exhibitors and invited guests was getting into its
> stride. A handful of the small *nomenclatura* of the Soviet cultural
> bureaucracy was gathering under the chandelier, the ladies in
> their beehive hairstyles and flowered frocks designed for slenderer
> frames, the gentlemen slimmed by the shiny French-tailored suits
> that signified access to the special clothing stores. Only their
> British hosts, in despondent shades of grey, observed the monotone
> of socialist austerity. The hubbub rose, a brigade of pinafored

governesses distributed the curling salami sandwiches and warm white wine. A senior British diplomat who was not quite the Ambassador shook the better hands and said he was delighted.

Imagine that you have been asked to translate Le Carré's novel into your target language. You have not yet read the whole novel – and you would normally read a text all the way through before you seriously get down to translating it. However, you decide that it might be helpful to 'warm up' to Le Carré by translating a few extracts to get the hang of his unusual style.

Translate the above extract into your target language and comment on any difficulties involved in maintaining the flow of information in terms of thematic and information structures. You should pay particular attention to marked information structures in the third paragraph. How does Le Carré's manipulation of English syntax foreground certain items of information? Can this be successfully conveyed in your target language?

2. The following extract is from Swee Chai Ang, *From Beirut to Jerusalem: A Woman Surgeon with the Palestinians* (1989:299–300). This book gives a first-hand account of death and suffering in Palestinian refugee camps in war-torn Beirut in the 1980s. Ms Ang, a surgeon, volunteered to provide medical assistance to Palestinians and was with them during the Israeli invasion of West Beirut in 1982. She also lived through the appalling 1982 massacres in the Sabra and Shatila camps. Since then, she has returned repeatedly to Lebanon and the Occupied Territories to help Palestinians.

Israeli bomber planes were breaking the sound barrier in south Lebanon. Villages in the south, as well as the Palestinian refugee camps, were attacked. In May 1988, two thousand Israeli troops crossed into southern Lebanon. People in Lebanon told me: 'The Israelis failed to stifle the uprising in the occupied territories, so they take it out on us by threatening to invade Lebanon again.'

It was a multi-pronged attack on the Palestinians in Lebanon. Saida and the south were bombed by Israeli aeroplanes, and shelled from the sea by Israeli gunboats. The Beirut camps were attacked from the mountains, not by the Israelis, but by anti-PLO forces. Shatila and Bourj el-Brajneh were shelled incessantly from the month of May 1988. Both camps were flattened; homes and hospitals demolished.

Shatila finally collapsed on 27 June 1988, followed by Bourj el-Brajneh a few days later. I got the news of the fall of Shatila in London, having just returned from a fund-raising trip in the Gulf countries. People all over the Gulf wanted to support the uprising and build hospitals and clinics to mend the wounds of the Palestinians. What can I say? Each time I think of Shatila, I still cry. It was nearly six years since I first met the people of Sabra and Shatila. My understanding of the Palestinians began with them. It was they who taught a naive woman surgeon the meaning of justice. It was they who inspired me to struggle incessantly for a better world. Each time I felt like giving up, they would strengthen me with their example.

the uprising:	commonly known in the West as the *intifada* – the Palestinian uprising against Israeli occupation in Gaza and the West Bank of Jordan
Saida:	Lebanese town
PLO:	Palestine Liberation Organization
Bourj el-Brajneh:	Palestinian refugee camp

Imagine that you have been asked to translate the above extract for inclusion in a review of the book, to be published in one of the leading newspapers in your country. Various reviews of the book in English papers have suggested that the poignancy of Dr Ang's narrative is enhanced by her unadorned style, by her awkward, artless prose which has the raw immediacy of everyday speech. Consider how this straight-to-the-point, free-from-rhetoric, 'artless' style is reflected in the simplicity of the thematic and information structures in the above extract. How does the contrast between this general feature and the build-up of emotion, culminating in marked thematic structures towards the end of the extract, enhance the emotional impact of the message? How successfully are these features reflected in your target version?

3. The Project for the New American Century is a neoconservative think tank that exercised considerable influence on US foreign policy between 1997 and 2006. Imagine that you have been asked to translate its Statement of Principles into your target language, for inclusion in a forthcoming volume of scholarly articles intended to critique American foreign policy under George W. Bush (2001–2009). The Statement, reproduced in full below, is available at www.newamericancentury.org/statementofprinciples.htm.

Statement of Principles

June 3, 1997

American foreign and defense policy is adrift. Conservatives have criticized the incoherent policies of the Clinton Administration.

They have also resisted isolationist impulses from within their own ranks. But conservatives have not confidently advanced a strategic vision of America's role in the world. They have not set forth guiding principles for American foreign policy. They have allowed differences over tactics to obscure potential agreement on strategic objectives. And they have not fought for a defense budget that would maintain American security and advance American interests in the new century.

We aim to change this. We aim to make the case and rally support for American global leadership.

As the 20th century draws to a close, the United States stands as the world's preeminent power. Having led the West to victory in the Cold War, America faces an opportunity and a challenge: Does the United States have the vision to build upon the achievements of past decades? Does the United States have the resolve to shape a new century favorable to American principles and interests?

We are in danger of squandering the opportunity and failing the challenge. We are living off the capital – both the military investments and the foreign policy achievements – built up by past administrations. Cuts in foreign affairs and defense spending, inattention to the tools of statecraft, and inconstant leadership are making it increasingly difficult to sustain American influence around the world. And the promise of short-term commercial benefits threatens to override strategic considerations. As a consequence, we are jeopardizing the nation's ability to meet present threats and to deal with potentially greater challenges that lie ahead.

We seem to have forgotten the essential elements of the Reagan Administration's success: a military that is strong and ready to meet both present and future challenges; a foreign policy that boldly and purposefully promotes American principles abroad; and national leadership that accepts the United States' global responsibilities.

Of course, the United States must be prudent in how it exercises its power. But we cannot safely avoid the responsibilities of global leadership or the costs that are associated with its exercise. America has a vital role in maintaining peace and security in *exercises*

Europe, Asia, and the Middle East. If we shirk our responsibilities, we invite challenges to our fundamental interests. The history of the 20th century should have taught us that it is important to shape circumstances before crises emerge, and to meet threats before they become dire. The history of this century should have taught us to embrace the cause of American leadership.

Our aim is to remind Americans of these lessons and to draw their consequences for today. Here are four consequences:

- we need to increase defense spending significantly if we are to carry out our global responsibilities today and modernize our armed forces for the future;
- we need to strengthen our ties to democratic allies and to challenge regimes hostile to our interests and values;
- we need to promote the cause of political and economic freedom abroad;
- we need to accept responsibility for America's unique role in preserving and extending an international order friendly to our security, our prosperity, and our principles.

Such a Reaganite policy of military strength and moral clarity may not be fashionable today. But it is necessary if the United States is to build on the successes of this past century and to ensure our security and our greatness in the next.

When you have translated the text, comment on the ease or difficulty of maintaining the contrastive thematic choices of *we* and *they* and any resulting loss or shift in thematic patterning. You might also like to consider the various senses of *we* (inclusive of the American nation, exclusive to the group which drafted the Statement) and whether these senses can be maintained in your translation while retaining the repetition of the same pronoun as theme.

SUGGESTIONS FOR FURTHER READING

On Halliday's model of thematic and information structures

Eggins, Suzanne (2004) *An Introduction to Systemic Functional Linguistics*, second edition, London: Continuum. Chapter 1: 'The Grammar of Textual Meaning: Theme'.

Halliday, M. A. K. (1985) *An Introduction to Functional Grammar*, London: Edward Arnold. Chapter 3: 'Clause as Message', and Chapter 8: 'Beside the Clause: Intonation and Rhythm'.

Young, David (1980) *The Structure of English Clauses*, London: Hutchinson. Chapter 12: 'Theme'.

On functional sentence perspective

Firbas, Jan (1986) 'On the Dynamics of Written Communication in the Light of the Theory of Functional Sentence Perspective', in C. R. Cooper and S. Greenbaum (eds) *Studying Writing: Linguistic Approaches*, New York: Sage, 40–71.

Firbas, Jan (1992) *Functional Sentence Perspective in Written and Spoken Communication*, Cambridge: Cambridge University Press.

For a general overview and discussion of aspects of information flow

Brown, Gillian and George Yule (1983) *Discourse Analysis*, Cambridge: Cambridge University Press. Chapter 4 : '"Staging" and the Representation of Discourse Structure', and Chapter 5 : 'Information Structure'.

Fries, Peter H. (1983) 'On the Status of Theme in English: Arguments from Discourse', in J. S. Petöfi and E. Sözer (eds) *Micro and Macro Connexity of Texts*, Hamburg: Helmut Buske, 116–152.

Ward, Gregory and Betty Birner (2005) 'Information Structure and Non-canonical Syntax', in Laurence R. Horn and Gregory Ward (eds) *The Handbook of Pragmatics*, Oxford: Blackwell Reference Online. Available to subscribers at www.blackwellreference.com/public/tocnode?id=g9780631225485_chunk_g97806312254859#citation.

On aspects of word order and information flow in the context of translation

De Regt, Lenart J. (2006) 'Hebrew Syntactic Inversions and their Literary Equivalence in English: Robert Alter's Translations of Genesis and 1 and 2 Samuel', *Journal for the Study of the Old Testament* 30(3): 287–314.

Fawcett, Peter (1997) *Translation and Language*, Manchester: St. Jerome Publishing. Chapter 8: 'Text Structure'.

Firbas, Jan (1999) 'Translating the Introductory Paragraph of Boris Pasternak's *Doctor Zhivago*: A Case Study in Functional Sentence Perspective', in Gunilla Anderman and Margaret Rogers (eds) *Word, Text, Translation*, Clevedon: Multilingual Matters, 129–141.

Hasselgård, Hilde (1998) 'Thematic Structure in Translation between English and Norwegian', in Stig Johansson and Signe Oksefjell (eds) *Corpora and Cross-linguistic Research: Theory, Method and Case Studies*, Amsterdam: Rodopi, 145–167.

Hatim, Basil and Ian Mason (1990) *Discourse and the Translator*, London: Longman. Chapter 10: 'Discourse Texture', pages 212–222: 'Thematisation: Functional Sentence Perspective'.

Lorés Sanz, Rosa (2003) 'The Translation of Tourist Literature: The Case of Connectors', *Multilingua* 22(3): 291–308.

Mason, Ian (1994/2010) 'Discourse, Ideology and Translation', in Robert de Beaugrande, Abdullah Shunnaq and Mohamed Heliel (eds) *Language, Discourse and Translation in the West and Middle East*, Amsterdam: John Benjamins, 23–34; reprinted, with a post-script, in Mona Baker (ed.) *Critical Readings in Translation Studies*, London: Routledge, 83–95.

Rogers, Margaret (2006) 'Structuring Information in English: A Specialist Translation Perspective on Sentence Beginnings', *The Translator* 12(1): 29–64.

Schmid, Monika S. (1999) *Translating the Elusive. Marked Word Order and Subjectivity in English–German Translation*, Amsterdam: John Benjamins.

Williams, Ian A. (2009) 'Discourse Style and Theme–Rheme Progression in Biomedical Research Article Discussions: A Corpus-based Contrastive Study of Translational and Non-translational Spanish', *Languages in Contrast* 9(2): 225–266.

NOTES

1   The **subject** of a clause is traditionally defined as the noun group which refers to the person or thing that does the action. More accurately, it is the noun group which usually comes in front of the verb group in English and with which the verb agrees in terms of number, person and, in some languages, gender:

> *Ellen* laughed.
> *Her sudden death* had surprised everybody.
> *Blue* suits you.
> *This view* has been challenged by a number of workers.

The **predicator** is the verb or verb group in a clause:

> Bob *coughed*.
> He *had* always *liked* Mr Phillips.
> What *am* I *doing*? I*'m looking* out of the window.

An **object** is a noun or noun group which refers to a person or thing, other than the subject, which is involved in or affected by the action of the verb:

> My questions angered *the crowd*.
> The trial raised *a number of questions*.
> She had *friends*.

The object of an active clause can often be made the subject of a passive clause:

> *The crowd* were angered by my questions.
> *A number of questions* were raised by the trial.

A **complement** is a noun group or an adjective which comes after a link verb such as *be*, *remain* and *look* and gives more information about the subject:

> The results of the experiment remain *a secret*.
> We were *very happy*.

A complement may also give more information about the object:

> They're driving me *crazy*.
> She painted her eyelids *deep blue*.

An **adjunct** is a word or group of words added to a clause to give more information about the circumstances of an event or situation, for instance in terms of time, place or manner:

> I've been *here all night*.
> Donald was lying *on the bed*.
> He acted *very clumsily*.

All examples from the *Collins COBUILD English Grammar* (Sinclair 1990).

2   But see section 5.2.3 for a discussion of the potential tension between word order and communicative function.
3   But see section 5.1.1.3 (c).
4   See note 1 above.
5   On the other hand, the noun or noun group functioning as subject can be selected as theme. This can be done by using an it-structure such as *It was John who told me about it*. The theme in it-structures is not *It* but the noun or noun group which comes after the verb to be. In effect, an it-structure selects what would have been the subject as a marked theme. See discussion of **predicated theme** later in this section.
6   Fronted adjuncts can also signal contrast: *In China, the book received a great deal of publicity* (but in other places it didn't).
7   Accessed through the Translational English Corpus. Available at www.llc.manchester. ac.uk/ctis/research/english-corpus/.
8   I am unable to trace the date of publication.
9   The only instance in which Halliday seems to depart from this position is in a brief discussion of **postposed theme**, which he calls **substitution** (1967). He gives examples such as *They don't match, these colours* and *He's always late, John is* and suggests that substitution 'reverses the normal sequence of theme–rheme and introduces a delayed theme after the remainder of the message' (*ibid.*:240). He further explains that the meaning of this structure 'is, as it were, "first I'll say what I have to say and then I'll remind you what I'm talking about"' (*ibid.*).
10 I use 'partial circularity' rather than 'circularity' because initial position is identified independently of theme. I am grateful to Mike Hoey for drawing my attention to this.
11 Languages are usually classified according to their normal ordering of clause elements. For instance, English is classified as an SVO language because the normal order of clause elements in English is subject–verb–object. Japanese is classified as an SOV language because the normal order in Japanese is subject–object–verb.

12 A verb in Harway can only be followed (optionally) by a locative (Comrie 1987).

13 It is fair to say that Halliday's view is also shared by some linguists interested in languages with relatively free word order, for example German. Herbst *et al.* (1979:166) report that 'some linguists … have suggested that the status of theme should be assigned to the element in initial position in all cases'.

14 **Anaphoric reference** involves using a word or phrase to refer back to another word or phrase that occurred earlier in the text, for example *John is a scientist. **He** studied physics at university*, where **He** refers back to *John*. For a detailed discussion of anaphoric reference, see Chapter 6, section 6.1.

15 For a specific discussion of problems associated with the principles of end-focus and end-weight in German–English translation see Snell-Hornby (1985).

16 I am grateful to the late Tim Johns, University of Birmingham, for providing all the data from Brazilian academic abstracts and for assisting me with the analysis of relevant extracts. This particular extract is from *Ciência e cultura* (1980), 32(8): 1094.

17 Halliday and Hasan recognize that punctuation plays a role in signalling information structure, but suggest that it cannot express it fully in English and that 'most punctuation practice is a kind of compromise between information structure (punctuating according to intonation) and sentence structure (punctuating according to the grammar)' (1976:325).

18 Functional sentence perspective is sometimes used as a cover term for any approach based on a theme–rheme or given–new type of analysis. For most linguists, however, it applies only to the work of Prague scholars such as Mathesius, Firbas and Daneš.

19 For a more detailed discussion of FSP theory, see Firbas (1974, 1986, 1999).

20 Jan Firbas is a Brno scholar, but he works within the Prague theoretical tradition.

21 Weil did not actually use the terms 'theme' and 'rheme'; Firbas only reports him as using 'initial notion' and 'goal of discourse'.

22 Halliday expresses a totally different view of the importance of FSP in English. For instance, when claiming that an unmarked theme in English is one that signals the mood of the clause (see 5.1.1.3), he says:

> It may not be unreasonable to suggest that the preference for the 'inverted' inter-rogative structure in English, by contrast with a number of other languages that have basically the same resources, is due to the relative importance assigned to thematic organisation in the syntax of the English clause.
>
> *(1976:180)*

23 Mike Hoey (personal communication) suggests that, compared to languages such as Portuguese and Arabic which can easily and naturally thematize verbs, that is processes, English is a rather clumsy language for reporting scientific research.

CHAPTER 6

Textual equivalence: cohesion

Each language has its own patterns to convey the interrelationships of persons and events; in no language may these patterns be ignored, if the translation is to be understood by its readers.

(Callow 1974:30)

The topic of cohesion ... has always appeared to me the most useful constituent of discourse analysis or text linguistics applicable to translation.

(Newmark 1987:295)

The last chapter dealt with one type of connectivity which helps to distinguish text from non-text, namely thematic and information structure. In this chapter, we resume our discussion of translation difficulties and strategies at the level of text by looking at cohesion, the second feature of text organization which was mentioned at the end of Chapter 4.

Cohesion is the network[1] of lexical, grammatical and other relations which provide links between various parts of a text. These relations or ties organize and, to some extent, create a text, for instance by requiring the reader to interpret words and expressions by reference to other words and expressions in the surrounding sentences and paragraphs.[2] Cohesion is a surface relation; it connects together the actual words and expressions that we can see or hear (cf. **coherence**, Chapter 7). This chapter draws heavily on the best known and most detailed model of cohesion available: the model outlined by Halliday and Hasan in *Cohesion in English* (1976). It is worth noting, however, that other models have been proposed by various linguists (see, for instance, Callow 1974, Gutwinski 1976, de Beaugrande and Dressler 1981, Hoey 1988, 1991).

Halliday and Hasan identify five main cohesive devices in English: **reference**, **substitution**, **ellipsis**, **conjunction** and **lexical cohesion**. Each device is explained below in some detail, followed by an attempt to explore its relevance to translation.

6.1 REFERENCE

The term **reference** is traditionally used in semantics for the relationship which holds between a word and what it points to in the real world. The reference of *chair* would therefore be a particular chair that is being identified on a particular occasion. In Halliday and Hasan's model of cohesion, reference is used in a similar but more restricted way. Instead of denoting a direct relationship between words and extra-linguistic objects, reference is limited here to the relationship of identity which holds between two linguistic expressions. For example, in

Mrs Thatcher has resigned. She announced her decision this morning

the pronoun *she* points to Mrs Thatcher within the textual world itself. Reference, in the textual rather than the semantic sense, occurs when the reader has to retrieve the identity of what is being talked about by referring to another expression in the imme-diate context. The resulting cohesion 'lies in the continuity of reference, whereby the same thing enters into the discourse a second time' (Halliday and Hasan 1976:31).

Every language has certain items which have the property of reference in the textual sense. These reference items have the potential for directing readers to look elsewhere for their interpretation. The most common reference items in English and a large number of other languages are pronouns. Third-person pronouns are frequently used to refer back (and occasionally forward) to an entity which has already been introduced (or is about to be introduced) into the discourse. Apart from personal reference, English also uses items such as *the*, *this* and *those* to establish similar links between expressions in a text. In

Mrs Thatcher has resigned. This delighted her opponents

the reader has to go back to the previous stretch of discourse to establish what *This* refers to.

Reference, then, is a device that allows the reader or hearer to trace partici-pants, entities, events and so on in a text. One of the most common patterns of establishing chains of reference in English and a number of other languages is to mention a participant explicitly in the first instance, for example by name or title, and then use a pronoun to refer back to the same participant in the immediate context. Languages that have number and gender distinctions in their pronoun system are less constrained in using this cohesive device, since different pronouns can be used to refer to different entities within a text with less possibility of confusion. The following example, from Agatha Christie's *Triangle at Rhodes* (1936), illustrates networks of personal reference in a short paragraph:

> Hercule Poirot sat on the white sand and looked out across the sparkling blue water. He was carefully dressed in a dandified fashion in white flannels and a large panama hat protected his head. He belonged to the old-fashioned *generation* which believed in covering *itself* carefully from the sun. Miss Pamela Lyall who sat beside him and talked carelessly, represented the modern school of thought in that she was wearing the barest minimum of clothing on her sun-browned person.
>
> (*Christie 1936: 196*)

Although Halliday and Hasan use a restricted notion of reference based on textual rather than extralinguistic relations, they still acknowledge that the relationship of reference may be established situationally. For example, a given pronoun may refer to an entity which is present in the context of situation rather than in the surrounding text. First- and second-person pronouns (*I*, *you*, *we* in English) are typical examples in that they do not refer back to a nominal expression in the text but to the speaker and hearer (or writer and reader) respectively. Third-person pronouns typically refer back (or forward) to a nominal expression in the text but may also be used to refer to an entity which is present in the immediate physical or mental context of situation. An utterance such as *He's not back yet* is perfectly feasible provided the speaker and hearer are clear about the identity of 'he', for example in the case of a couple referring to their son.

Another type of reference relation which is not strictly textual is that of **co-reference**. An example of a chain of co-referential items is *Mrs Thatcher* → *The Prime Minister* → *The Iron Lady* → *Maggie*. Halliday and Hasan do not discuss this type of referential linkage, and Hoey (1988:162) points out that co-reference 'is not strictly a linguistic feature at all but a matter of real-world knowledge'. It is of course true that recognizing a link between *Mrs Thatcher* and *The Iron Lady*, for instance, depends on knowledge of the world rather than on textual competence. However, it is generally difficult and, for the purposes of translation not particularly helpful, to attempt to draw a line between what is linguistic or textual and what is extralinguistic or situational. For example, in the following extract from an article entitled 'Cultural Revolutionary' (*The Economist*, 6–12 February 2010, p. 66), recognizing the co-referential link between *Google* and *the Silicon Valley firm* is based on both linguistic and situational knowledge:

> Now Mr Lu faces a new challenge. His job at Microsoft, where he moved a year ago, is to take on <u>Google</u> in the online search and advertising business, where <u>the Silicon Valley firm</u> rules supreme.

Here, we recognize *Google* as a *firm* partly because we know from real world experience that it is, and partly because the fact that it is capitalized makes it a good candidate for what is signalled, through the use of the definite article preceding *firm*, as an entity already identified in the text. The reference to *Silicon Valley*, on the other hand, relies heavily on our knowledge of the world.

It may be useful at this point to suggest, following Halliday and Hasan, that there is a continuum of cohesive elements that may be used for referring back to an entity already mentioned in the discourse. This continuum stretches from full repetition at one end of the scale to pronominal reference at the other. The following example is adapted from Halliday and Hasan (1976: 283) to illustrate the point:

> There's a boy climbing that tree.
> a. *The boy*'s going to fall if he doesn't take care. (**repetition**)
> b. *The lad*'s going to fall if he doesn't take care. (**synonym**)

    c. *The child*'s going to fall if he doesn't take care. (**superordinate**)
    d. *The idiot*'s going to fall if he doesn't take care. (**general word**)
    e. *He*'s going to fall if he doesn't take care. (**pronominal reference**)

Co-reference can be incorporated somewhere around the repetition/synonym level of the continuum if we decide to adopt a more flexible notion of reference for our current purposes.

Patterns of reference (also known as **anaphora**) can vary considerably both within and across languages. Within the same language, text type seems to be an important factor in determining the choice of pattern. Fox (1986) examined patterns of reference in three genres of American English: spontaneous conversation, written expository prose and written fast-paced popular narratives. She found that 'the distribution of pronoun versus full noun phrase differed dramatically from one discourse type to the next' (*ibid.*:27). Based on an extensive study of the language of advertising in English, Cook (1992:154) explains the preference in advertising for repeating the name of the product instead of using a pronominal reference such as *it* as follows:

> One obvious function of repetition is to fix the name of the product in the mind, so that it will come to the lips of the purchaser lost for a name. But nominal repetition is also an index of rank, esteem, intimacy or self-confidence: consider the repetition of names in ceremonies, prayers, by lovers, or by arrogant individuals who just 'like the sound of their own name'.

Each language thus has what we might call general preferences for certain patterns of reference as well as specific preferences that are sensitive to text type.

In terms of broad, language-specific preferences, Callow (1974) explains that Hebrew, unlike English, prefers to use proper names to trace participants through a discourse. So, where English would normally use a pronoun to refer to a participant who has already been introduced, provided there is no possibility of confusing reference, Hebrew is more likely to repeat the participant's name. Similarly, she explains, for the Bororos of Brazil the normal pattern is to refer to a participant by using a noun several times in succession before eventually shifting into a pronominal form.

Unlike English, which tends to rely heavily on pronominal reference in tracing participants, Brazilian Portuguese generally seems to favour more lexical repetition. In addition, Portuguese inflects verbs for person and number. This grammatical feature provides additional means of relating processes and actions to specific participants without the use of independent pronouns. The following example is from an article on Akio Morita, Chairman of the Sony Corporation. The article was published in the English and Portuguese editions of *Playboy* magazine. References to Akio Morita are highlighted in both extracts (and the back-translation), with the exception of verb inflections in Portuguese. Items in angle brackets are not in the Portuguese text – they are inserted to make the back-translation readable.

English text:

> Surrounded by the toys and the gadgets of <u>his</u> calling – tape recorders, mini television sets, world-band radios – <u>he</u> is the quintessential Japanese combination that has conquered the world: a tinkerer turned businessman.
>
> As the <u>eldest son</u> of a wealthy sake and soy-sauce producer in conservative Nagoya, <u>he</u> was expected to take over the family business – and perhaps become the 15th generation of Morita Mayors in the local community. Instead, <u>he</u> spent <u>his</u> time taking apart clocks and listening to Western classical music and preferred the study of physics to business. During World War Two, <u>he</u> went into naval research as a lieutenant, working on a thermal-guided missile and other projects, and it was there that <u>he</u> met his future partner, Ibuka. After the war, the two set up a business after a false start in the home-appliance market – manufacturing rice cookers. Total production: 100. Total sales: 0.

Portuguese text:

> Produto de uma cultura que valoriza a sutileza e as maneiras indi-retas, **Morita**, com **seu** jeito franco, é a ponte ideal entre o Japão e o Ocidente.
>
> **Filho mais velho** de um próspero produtor de óleo de soja e de saquê, em Nagoya, os pais de **Morita** esperavam que **ele** assumisse o controle dos negócios da famlia. Ao invés disso, **Morita** passava o tempo desmontando relógios, ouvindo música clássica ocidental e preferindo estudar Fisica a **se** meter em negócios. Durante a Segunda Guerra Mundial dedicou-**se** à pesquisa naval, como civil, e foi nessa época que fez a sociedade numa fábrica de panelas de cozinhar arroz. Produção total: 100 panelas. Total de vendas: 0.

> Product of a culture that values subtlety and indirect manners, **Morita**, with **his** frank way, is an ideal bridge between Japan and the West:
>
> **The eldest son** of a prosperous producer of soya oil and saki, in Nagoya, the parents of **Morita** expected that **he** should take over the control of the family business. Instead of this, **Morita** spent the time taking clocks apart, listening to Western classical music and preferring to study physics to putting **himself** into business. During the Second World War <he> dedicated **himself** to naval research, as a civilian, and it was in this period that <he> made a partnership in a factory of rice cooking pots. Total production: 100 pots. Total sales: 0.

The first sentence in each of the above extracts occurs at the end of the paragraph immediately before the one we are examining.[3] The two sentences are not 'equivalents' of each other, but they are quoted here to show that, in spite of the fact that the last mention of the particular participant being traced is by pronominal reference in the English version and by a proper noun in the Portuguese version, English still prefers to pick up the reference in the new paragraph by means of a pronoun while Portuguese prefers lexical repetition. Within the main paragraph under examination, Portuguese further repeats *Morita* twice while English persists in using pronominal reference. Note that the finite verbs in the Portuguese text establish additional cohesive links with *Morita* because they are marked for person.

In some languages, such as Japanese and Chinese, a totally different pattern seems to be in operation. Pronouns are hardly ever used, and once a participant is introduced, continuity of reference is signalled by omitting the subjects of following clauses. This is a sort of default mechanism which tells the reader that the participant last mentioned or, alternatively, the one in focus or the one that can be inferred on grounds of logic or context, is the subject of the following clause(s) unless otherwise indicated (see discussion of theme and Chinese-style topic in Chapter 5, section 5.1.1.4). In the following example from *Palace and Politics in Prewar Japan* (Titus 1974:23), we already know that the person addressed is the Emperor. The reader has to provide all the missing subjects and create his or her own chains of reference. Possible subjects and other pronominal references are inserted here in angle brackets for the reader's benefit – they do not appear in the Japanese text:

> いちばんむきつけだったのは、三等侍補の米田虎雄だった。「平素御馬術を好ませてもうほどに政治上に叡慮を注がせたまわば、今日のごとく世上より二三大臣の政治などいわるることはあるまじくとつねに苦慮つかまつりおれり」。

> The most blunt one was Komeda Torao who was the third Jiho. 'If the <Emperor/Your Majesty> pours <his/your> wise consideration into politics as much as <he/you> likes riding in <his/your> daily life, I would not think that <he/you/the government> would have been said as 'two three ministers' polities' by the public. So <I am> sincerely concerned.

The English translation (Titus 1974:20) naturally tries to approximate as much as possible to English patterns of cohesion:

> Komeda Torao, Jiho of the third rank, was the most blunt: 'If in the past [Your Majesty] had shown as much care for politics as he had passion for horsemanship, no such criticism from the public as "politics by two or three Ministers" would have occurred.'

Note the various rewordings and omissions in the English version. These allow the translator to use a chain of reference which is typical of English (*Your Majesty* → *he*) as well as avoid creating other chains which can only be inferred. The square brackets around *Your Majesty* in the English translation are presumably meant to alert the reader to the fact that the expression does not occur in the original, or that the translator is 'guessing' what might fill the subject slot in this case. Note also the use of the colon after *blunt* to provide additional cohesion.

The above examples illustrate that different preferences exist across languages for certain general patterns of reference. But these preferences can also be genre-specific; a good example of a pattern which is both language- and genre-specific is explained in Hatim and Mason (1990:97):

> It is a recognised text convention governing the field of discourse of news reporting/investigative journalism in French that a concept referred to in a noun phrase will not be expressed in the same way twice running in a text. Thus, *le dollar américain* will, in a subsequent lexicalisation, become *le billet vert*; *le Président de la République* will become, as well as the anaphoric *il*, perhaps *le chef de l'Etat* or even *l'Elyée see*.

6.2 SUBSTITUTION AND ELLIPSIS

Unlike reference, substitution and ellipsis are grammatical rather than semantic relationships. In **substitution**, an item (or items) is replaced by another item (or items):

> I like movies.
> And I do.

In the above example, *do* is a substitute for *like movies*. Items commonly used in substitution in English include *do*, *one* and *the same*, as in the following examples from Halliday and Hasan (1976:89, 105):

> You think Joan already knows? – I think everybody *does*. (*Does* replaces *knows*)
> My axe is too blunt. I must get a sharper *one*. (*One* replaces *axe*).

> A: I'll have two poached eggs on toast, please.
> B: I'll have *the same*. (*The same* replaces *two poached eggs on toast*).

Ellipsis involves the omission of an item. In other words, in ellipsis, an item is replaced by nothing. This is a case of leaving something unsaid which is nevertheless understood. It does not include every instance in which the hearer or reader has to provide missing information, but only those cases where the grammatical structure itself points to an item or items that can fill the slot in question. Here are some examples of ellipsis:

Joan brought some carnations, and Catherine some sweet peas. (ellipted item: *brought* in second clause)

Here are thirteen cards. Take any. Now give me any three. (ellipted items: *card* after *any* in second clause and *cards* after *any three* in third clause)

Have you been swimming? – Yes, I have. (ellipted items: *been swimming* in second clause)

(*Halliday and Hasan 1976:143, 158, 167*)

The following example of ellipsis comes from an article entitled 'Wolf Wars', by Douglas H. Chadwick, which appeared in the March 2010 issue of *National Geographic* (p. 38):

In 1995 and 1996, the U.S. Fish and Wildlife Service captured wolves in Canada and released them into 2.2-million-acre Yellowstone National Park and central Idaho's wilderness areas. The unprecedented federal action triggered such an eruption of hope, fear, resentment, lawsuits, and headline news that most people assume the whole return of the wolf to the West began that way. It <u>didn't</u>, but those reintroductions worked like a rocket booster. Populations grew, and the war escalated.

Halliday and Hasan give a detailed description of several types of substitution and ellipsis in English. Since substitution and ellipsis are purely grammatical relations which hold between linguistic forms rather than between linguistic forms and their meanings, the details are highly language-specific and are therefore not worth going into here.

Note that the boundary lines between the three types of cohesive device (reference, substitution and ellipsis) are not clear cut. Hoey (1991) gives the following example. A question such as *Does Agatha sing in the bath?* may elicit three answers, of which answer (a) is an example of substitution, answer (b) of ellipsis and answer (c) of reference:

(a) No, but I do.
(b) Yes, she does.
(c) Yes, she does it to annoy us, I think.

Answer (b) is an example of ellipsis because *does* cannot be said to be a substitute for *sing* in the above question. The ellipted items in *Yes, she does* are *sing in the bath*. The fuzziness of the boundaries and the technical differences between the three types of cohesive device need not concern us here; after all, they may not even operate in the same way in other languages. At this stage, the translator need only be aware that there are different devices in different languages for creating 'texture', and that a text hangs together by virtue of the semantic and structural relationships that hold between its elements. This has clear implications in practice. Every language has its own battery of devices for creating links between textual elements. Unless the translator is carrying out some kind of linguistic exercise, for instance for research purposes, transferring the devices used in the source text into the target text will not do. Under normal circumstances, what is required is a reworking of the methods of establishing links to suit the textual norms of the target language. The grammatical system of each language will itself encourage the use of certain devices in preference to others. The textual norms of each genre will further suggest certain options and rule out others that are grammatically acceptable and may, in other genres, be textually acceptable as well.

Here is an example of the way in which changes at this textual level are normally handled, consciously or subconsciously, by a professional translator. The original text is Arabic, the target text is English. It is part of a document explaining arbitration procedures at the International Centre for Arbitration in Cairo.

Arabic original:

اذا انقضى ثلاثون يوماً من تاريخ تسلم أحد الطرفين اقتراحاً قدم وفقاً للفقرة الأولى دون أن يتفق الطرفان على تعيين المحكم الواحد تولت تعيينه سلطة التعيين التى اتفق الطرفان على تسميتها. فإذا لم يكن الطرفان قد اتفقا على تسمية سلطة تعيين، أو اذا امتنعت السلطة التى اتفقا على تسميتها عن تعيين المحكم، أو لم تتمكن من اتمام تعيينه خلال ستين يوماً من تاريخ تسلم الطلب الذى قدمه لها أحد الطرفين فى هذا الشأن، جاز لكل من الطرفين أن يطلب من الأمين العام لمحكمة التحكيم الدائمة تسمية سلطة تعيين.

Back-translation of Arabic:

If thirty days elapse from the date on which one of the parties received a proposal submitted according to the first item without the parties agreeing to appoint the one arbitrator, his appointment is done by the appointing authority which the parties agreed to name. If the parties had not agreed on the naming of the appointing authority, or if the authority which they agreed on nominating declines to appoint the arbitrator or is unable to nominate him within sixty days of the date of receiving the request which one of the parties presented to it in this regard, each of the parties may ask the Secretary-General of the Permanent Arbitration Court to nominate an appointing authority.

English translation:

If thirty days elapse from the date on which either party received a proposal – submitted according to the first item [(a)] – without the two parties agreeing on appointing one arbitrator, the authority nominated by the two parties undertakes to appoint the arbitrator. If the parties had not agreed on nominating such authority, or if the nominated authority declines to appoint an arbitrator or is unable to nominate one within sixty days of its receipt of either party's request to that effect, both parties may ask the Secretary-General of the Permanent Arbitration Court to nominate an appointing authority.

The length and complexity of the sentences in the above extracts, and hence the potential difficulty of tracing participants, makes it necessary to use a variety of devices for establishing cohesive links in both texts. The level of linkage is quite dense in both extracts, but there are striking differences in the choice of devices used in each case. Arabic uses a number of devices which cannot be easily represented in back-translation. For instance, all verbs agree with their subjects in gender and number, which means that links between the two are clear even when they are separated by a number of embedded clauses with their own subjects and verbs. In addition to using the equivalent of 'which' to establish linkage, as in 'receiving the request which one of the parties presented to it', the verb that follows is further suffixed for pronominal reference (literally: 'which one of the parties presented-it-masculine to it-feminine'). With 'request' being a masculine noun and 'authority' a feminine noun in Arabic, the referential chains are not confused. The grammatical structure of Arabic therefore favours pronominal reference as a common device for tracing participants and establishing cohesive links in general.[4] In addition, however, this type of text tends to favour a high level of lexical repetition, and so the Arabic noun for 'parties', which is marked for duality, is repeated even in instances where no ambiguity would arise from using a pronoun or pronominal suffix.

English, like most languages, will generally use whatever means are necessary to reduce ambiguity in tracing participants. Unlike the Arabic grammatical system, the English system makes very few distinctions in terms of number, gender and verb agreement. Lexical repetition is therefore a much safer option in cases where ambiguity of reference may arise and in contexts which do not tolerate ambiguity in general and ambiguity of reference in particular. In legal and semi-legal texts, it has become the norm to use lexical repetition even in instances where no ambiguity might result from using pronominal reference. Although the Arabic text makes considerable use of pronominal reference, there are no instances of pronominal reference at all in the English text. It would be possible, but textually odd, to replace several of the lexical repetitions in the English text with the appropriate pronouns.

In addition to lexical repetition, the English version also uses substitution to establish cohesive links (*if the nominated authority declines to appoint an* **arbitrator** *or is unable to nominate* **one**). There are also several instances of ellipsis. In the example just quoted to illustrate substitution, the subject of the second clause ('the nominated authority/it') is elliptted.

To reiterate: every language has its own devices for establishing cohesive links. Language and text-type preferences must both be taken into consideration in the process of translation. With this in mind, let us now move on to examine other types of cohesive device that often require careful handling in translation.

6.3 CONJUNCTION

Conjunction involves the use of formal markers to relate sentences, clauses and paragraphs to each other. Unlike reference, substitution and ellipsis, the use of conjunction does not instruct the reader to supply missing information either by looking for it elsewhere in the text or by filling structural slots. Instead, conjunction signals the way the writer or speaker wants the reader or hearer to relate what is about to be said to what has been said before.

Conjunction expresses one of a small number of general relations. The main relations are summarized below, with examples of conjunctions which can or typically realize each relation.

(a) additive:	and, or, also, in addition, furthermore, besides, similarly, likewise, by contrast, for instance;
(b) adversative:	but, yet, however, instead, on the other hand, nevertheless, at any rate, as a matter of fact;
(c) causal:	so, consequently, it follows, for, because, under the circumstances, for this reason;
(d) temporal:	then, next, after that, on another occasion, in conclusion, an hour later, finally, at last;
(e) continuatives (miscellaneous):	now, of course, well, anyway, surely, after all.

A number of points need to be borne in mind here. First, the same conjunction may be used to signal different relations, depending on the context. Second, these relations can be expressed by a variety of means; the use of a conjunction is not the only device for expressing a temporal or causal relation, for instance. In English, a temporal relation may be expressed by means of a verb such as *follow* or *precede*, and a causal relation is inherent in the meanings of verbs such as *cause* and *lead to*. In fact, a language user will often recognize a semantic relation such as time sequence even when no explicit signal of such a relationship exists in the text. Third, conjunctive relations do not just reflect relations between external phenomena, but may also be set up to reflect relations which are internal to the text or communicative situation. For instance, temporal relations are not restricted to sequence in real time; they may reflect stages in the unfolding text. A good example is the use of *first*, *second* and *third* in this paragraph.

There is some uncertainty in the literature as to whether conjunctions which occur within sentences can be considered cohesive, since cohesion is considered by some linguists to be a relation between sentences rather than within sentences (see Halliday and Hasan 1976:232; see also note 2 of this chapter). This means that subordinators are not, strictly speaking, considered a type of conjunction. For example, Halliday and Hasan (*ibid.*:228) do not consider *after* a conjunction in

> After they had fought the battle, it snowed.

because it subordinates one part of the sentence to another but does not directly establish a link with another sentence. In the following example, by contrast, *afterwards* is considered a conjunction because it establishes a link between two sentences:

> They fought a battle. Afterwards, it snowed.

In this book, and for the purposes of translation, it makes more sense to take a broader view of cohesion and to consider any element cohesive as long as it signals a conjunctive-type relation between parts of a text, whether these parts are sentences, clauses (dependent or independent) or paragraphs. To reiterate, subtleties of technical definition are not the main issue here and are not likely to prove directly relevant in translation.

The following example from *A Study of Shamanistic Practices in Japan* (Blacker 1975:315) illustrates the use of conjunctions:

> The shamanic practices we have investigated are rightly seen as an archaic mysticism. On the basis of the world view uncovered by the shaman's faculties, with its vision of another and miraculous plane which could interact causally with our own, the more advanced mystical intuitions of esoteric Buddhism were able to develop.
>
> **Today, however**, this world view is fast disappearing. The vision of another plane utterly different from our own, ambivalent, perilous and beyond our control, has faded. **Instead** the universe has become one-dimensional; there is no barrier to be crossed, no mysteriously other kind of being to be met and placated.

Languages vary tremendously in the type of conjunctions they prefer to use as well as the frequency with which they use such items. Also, since conjunction is a device for signalling relations between chunks of information, it is naturally bound up with both the chunking of information, how much to say in one go, and with how the relations between such chunks of information are perceived and signalled. In fact, the use of conjunction provides an insight into the whole logic of discourse (Smith and Frawley 1983).

Some languages, such as German, tend to express relations through subordination and complex structures. Others, such as Chinese and Japanese, prefer to use simpler and shorter structures and to mark the relations between these structures explicitly where necessary. One noticeable difference in the use of conjunctions which is well documented in the literature is that between English and Arabic. Compared to Arabic, English generally prefers to present information in relatively small chunks and to signal the relationship between these chunks in unambiguous ways, using a wide variety of conjunctions to mark semantic relations between clauses, sentences and paragraphs. In addition to the types of conjunction discussed by Halliday and Hasan, English also relies on a highly developed punctuation system to signal breaks and relations between chunks of information. Unlike English, Arabic prefers to group information into very large grammatical chunks. It is not unusual for Arabic paragraphs to consist of one sentence. This is partly because punctuation and paragraphing are a relatively recent development in Arabic (Holes 1984). Moreover, Arabic tends to use a relatively small number of conjunctions, each of which has a wide range of meanings which depend for their interpretation on the context, thus relying heavily on the reader's ability to infer relationships which are only vaguely alluded to by the writer. The most frequently used conjunctions in Arabic are *wa* and *fa* (Al-Jubouri and Knowles 1988). According to Holes, '/wa/ can mark temporal sequence, simultaneous action, semantic contrast and semantic equivalence, amongst other things; /fa/ can be a marker of temporal sequence, logical consequence, purpose, result or concession' (1984:234). Short sentences, a varied array of conjunctions, and absence of the typical conjunctions (mainly *wa*, *fa* and a few other particles) are associated with translated Arabic texts – original Arabic texts do not normally display these features.

The following is an example of a fairly free translation into Arabic. The source text uses no conjunctions but relies instead on punctuation devices. The translated version conforms more to Arabic than to English norms of cohesion. Note, in particular, the use of typical Arabic conjunctions: *wa* (roughly: 'and'),[5] *hatha-wa* (literally: 'this and') and *kama* (roughly: 'also'/ 'in addition'). Note also that there are fewer sentence breaks in the Arabic version (sentence breaks are highlighted by slashes in both texts).

> English source text (*Brintons* – press release issued by carpet manufacturer):

> Brintons have been manufacturing fine quality woven carpet over 200 years /./ They are a privately owned company specializing in Axminster and Wilton carpets, using wool-rich blends /./ They have a totally integrated operation from the preparation of the yarn through to the weaving process /./ All their products are made on looms designed and built by their own engineers, and recognized as the most technically superior weaving plant in the World /./ Brintons are one of the largest weavers with a production capacity in excess of 100,000 square metres per week /./

> Arabic text:

> تقوم شركة برينتونز بتصنيع أرقى أنواع السجاد المنسوج منذ أكثر من 200 عام،
> وهى شركة خاصة، تتخصص فى انتاج سجاد أكسمنستر والويلتون الذى تدخله نسبة
> عالية من الصوف /./ هذا وتقوم الشركة بتنفيذ جميع خطوات الإنتاج بمصانعها، من
> إعداد الخيوط الى نسجها على أنوال من تصميم وصنع مهندسى الشركة، وتعتبر

مصانع برينتونز أكثر مصانع النسيج تقدما من الناحية الفنية فى العالم كله، كما تعتبر
شركة برينتونز من أكبر شركات النسيج بطاقة انتاجية تزيد عن 100,000 متر مربع
فى الاسبوع /./

Brintons company has been manufacturing the finest quality of woven carpets for over 200 years, **and** it is a private company which specializes in producing Axminster and Wilton carpets in which enters a high percentage of wool /./ **This and** the company carries out all steps of production in its factories, from preparing the yarn to weaving it on looms designed and manufactured by company engineers, **and** Brintons factories are considered the most advanced weaving factories from the technical aspect in the whole world, **also** Brintons company is considered among the largest weaving companies with a production capacity exceeding 100,000 square metres per week /./

The above example illustrates how conjunctions which are typically used in Arabic discourse are added to a translation to make it smoother, even when no conjunctions are used in the source text. But given the greater semantic generality of typical Arabic conjunctions, what does an Arab translator do when faced with an array of explicit conjunctions in the source text? Should preference be given to producing a smooth text with typical but semantically less precise conjunctions, or should the translator give priority to 'meaning' by opting for an equally varied array of conjunctions with precise meanings? What happens in practice is often something in between the two extremes outlined here. Most translators will try to do a bit of both. Here is an example from the preface to *Arab Political Humour* by Kishtainy (1985). Conjunctions are highlighted in both texts. Arabic conjunctions follow their English back-translations in italics to show the variety of items used.

English text:

Writing on the political humour of the Arab World, past and present, is a hazardous undertaking which I was resolved to risk, much against the advice of many friends. Some felt a shudder at the thought of tackling the sense of humour of the Prophet Muhammad and the holy imams of Islam, and counselled that the subject matter should be confined to modern times. Others, **however**, felt a similar shudder at the thought of telling and discussing the political jokes about contemporary leaders of the modern Arab World and advised me to confine myself to the days of the Prophet and the early imams. **After all**, these are men of God and are guided by his spirit of indulgence and forgiveness. They are, **furthermore**, dead and buried and have no recourse to the revenge squads despatched from the Middle East to the four corners of the world. **Yet**, a full picture of Arab political humour truly reflecting the psychology, thought and politics of the Arab peoples cannot be adequately drawn without covering the entire span of Arab history, at least from the rise of Islam.

Arabic text:

إن الكتابة فى موضوع الظرف السياسى فى العالم العربى، قديماً وحديثاً، مهمة محفوفة بالمخاطر. **لكننى** اتخذت قرار المجازفة فى اقتحامها، متحدياً نصائح العديد من الأصدقاء بمجانبة محاذيرها. **فقد** شعر بعضهم بصدمة عنيفة لمجرد تفكيرى فى اقتحام موضوع الحس الدعابى، عند النبى محمد وأئمة الإسلام الأبرار، ونصحوا لى بأن أحصر بحثى فى مجتمع العصر الحديث. **وأحس** آخرون بصدمة مماثلة لعزمى على التحدث عن الدعابات السياسية التى نسجت حول الزعماء المعاصرين فى العالم العربى الحديث، واقترحوا علىّ أن اقتصر من ذلك على ما خلفه زمن النبى والأئمة الأولين. **فهؤلاء، بعد كل اعتبار،** هم رجال الله وهم ينقادون فى انغماسهم وتسامحهم لروح الله. **ثم أنهم** فى عداد الأموات لا رجعة لهم الى صفوف المنتقمين فى الشرق الأوسط وفى جهات العالم الأربع. **ومع ذلك،** فمن المحال رسم صورة جامعة لظرف العرب السياسى تمثل نفسية الشعوب العربية، ومناحى تفكيرها، ومنازعها السياسية بصدق، دون أن نلقى نظرة شاملة على التاريخ العربى، ابتداءً من ظهور الإسلام على الأقل.

Writing on the topic of political humour in the Arab World, past and present, is a task full of danger. **But [laakin]** I made the decision of taking the risk, against the advice of a large number of friends to avoid the dangers involved. **For [fa]** some of them felt a strong shock just at my thinking of tackling the subject of the sense of humour of the Prophet Muhammad and the holy imams of Islam and advised me to confine my research to modern times. **And [wa]** others felt a similar shock at my intention to talk about political jokes relating to contemporary leaders of the modern Arab World and suggested that I should confine myself to the days of the Prophet and the early imams. **For [fa]** these, **after all considerations**, are men of God and they follow in their indulgence and forgiveness the spirit of God. **Furthermore [thumma anna]** they are dead and cannot come back to join the revenge squads in the Middle East and the four corners of the world. **And yet [wa ma'a thaalik]**, it is impossible to draw a full picture of Arab political humour, reflecting the psychology of the Arab peoples, their way of thinking and their politics without casting an overall glance on Arab history, beginning at least with the rise of Islam.

The translator of the above passage attempts, as most translators do in practice, to strike a balance between accuracy and naturalness. At the level of cohesion, naturalness is enhanced by using typical Arabic conjunctions such as *wa* and *fa*, sometimes at the expense of accuracy. For instance, using *wa* rather than something closer to English *however* (third sentence in the English text), reads smoothly in

Arabic but sacrifices some of the precision of the English conjunction. On the other hand, the direct translation of *After all* (Fourth sentence in the English text) into 'after all considerations', which is a paraphrase of the meaning of *After all* rather than an established conjunction in Arabic, represents a sacrifice of naturalness for the sake of accuracy.

You will have noted from the Brintons extract on page 202 that some English texts make little or no use of conjunctions. There are often pragmatic reasons for the preference for certain types of conjunction and the frequency with which conjunctions are used in general. Smith and Frawley's (1983) study of the use of conjunction in different genres of English suggests that some genres are generally 'more conjunctive' than others and that each genre has its own preferences for certain types of conjunction. Religion and fiction use more conjunctions than science and journalism. Religion displays a particular preference for negative additive conjunctions such as *nor*. Smith and Frawley explain this feature by suggesting that 'the high percentage of negative additive conjunctions ... indicates a tendency toward *falsification*, the most consistent method of proof' (1983:358). Religious texts also make heavy use of causal conjunctions such as *because*, *since* and *for*. In science and journalism, by contrast, conjunctions in general and causal conjunctions in particular are relatively infrequent. This is partly explained by the high level of assumed shared knowledge in science and by the need to give an impression of objectivity in both genres. Restrictions on space and the need to avoid giving an overt explanation of reported events which risks the danger of legal suits and liability further restrict the use of conjunctions, particularly causal conjunctions, in journalism.

Adjusting patterns of conjunction in line with target-language general and specific text-type preferences is less straightforward than adjusting patterns of reference. The problem with conjunction is that it reflects the rhetoric of a text and controls its interpretation. This suggests that adjustments in translation will often affect both the content and the line of argumentation. Let us look at an example of a German translation of an English text, the first page of Morgan Matroc's company brochure: *Technical Ceramics*. The German version conforms to German style to such an extent that it is generally taken by German speakers to be a very well written 'original'. Conjunctions are highlighted in both texts.

The English source text consists of six paragraphs; the German translation, on the other hand, consists of eleven paragraphs. This rechunking of the text may be an idiosyncratic adjustment on the part of the German translator, as it appears that German does not generally favour more breaks than English. Generally speaking, rechunking is done for two main reasons: (a) the source text is divided into chunks (whether sections, paragraphs, sentences or clauses) that are either too long or too short in terms of target-language average chunking of similar material; or (b) the nature of the target audience is different in terms of level of specialization, age and so on. A text addressing an audience of specialists will tend to group information into larger chunks than one addressing laymen or children, for instance. It may be that the target reader of the German translation is not envisaged to have the same familiarity with or interest in the ceramics industry as the prospective readers of the English version.

Moving on to the use of conjunctions, here is an initial breakdown of the ones used in each text:

English: *Today* (temporal);
so (causal);
because (causal), *but* (adversative);
and yet (additive + adversative), *however* (adversative);
and finally (additive + temporal);
however (adversative)

German: *Today* (temporal);
so (causal);
on the one hand (additive, comparison), *but on the other hand* (adversative + additive, comparison);
finally (temporal);
now (continuative, with additional force of adversative);
yet (adversative), *because* (causal);
and then (adversative), *for this purpose* (causal);
lastly (temporal);
now[6] (continuative or concession – see below);
however/in any event (adversative).

Source text – English:

Today people are aware that modern ceramic materials offer unrivalled properties for many of our most demanding industrial applications. **So** is this brochure necessary; isn't the ceramic market already over-bombarded with technical literature; why should Matroc add more?

Because someone mumbles, 'our competitors do it.' **But** why should we imitate our competitors when Matroc probably supplies a greater range of ceramic materials for more applications than any other manufacturer.

And yet there are some customers who in their search for a suitable material prefer to study complex tables of technical data. It is for such customers that we have listed the properties of Matroc's more widely used materials. Frankly **however** without cost guides which depend so much on shape such an exercise is of limited value.

There are others in the market place who simply want to know more about us and what we are doing. For them we offer illustrated commentaries on Matroc applications in many market sectors – from gas heaters to medical implants.

And finally there is a third class of customer who knows that a brief telephone conversation with a skilled Matroc engineer and the subsequent follow-up are more effective than 50 pages of technical data – such customers are our life blood – as we are theirs. For them this brochure is unnecessary.

Matroc like other Morgan subsidiaries acknowledges that customers and engineers will have a variety of approaches to problem solving. We hope that this publication will aid that process. We have no doubt about the most effective route **however** and suggest that the starting point should be the list of telephone numbers and addresses on the final page of this brochure.

Target text – German:

Heutzutage sind sich Fachleute völlig darüber einig, daß moderne Keramikwerkstoffe unerreichteEigenschaften für viele der anspruch-vollsten industriellenAnwendungen bieten.

Wir haben uns **daher** gefragt, ob bei der Flut von technischer Lite-ratur, die derzeit auf den Keramikmarkteinwirkt, dieser Katalog noch eine entsprechende Resonazfinden wird. Sollte Matroc das Seine noch hinzutun?

Einerseits meint so mancher: "das ist doch branchenüblich" aber erreichen wir **andererseits** unsere Kunden, in dem wir anderen nacheifern?

Schließlich bietet Matrocein größeres Keramiksortiment für mehr Anwendungen als manch andere Unternehmen.

Nun gibt es Kunden, die es auf der Suche nach geeigneten Werk-stoffen vorziehen,umfangreiche technische Datenblätter zu studieren. Für solche Kunden haben wir dieEigenschaften der gängigsten Matroc Werkstoffe aufgelistet.

Allerdings muß man bedenken, daß bei solchemVorgehen ohne Kostenerfahrung nur eine begrenzteAussagefähigkeit zu erwarten ist, **denn** der Fertigungsaufwand hängt wesentlich von der Geometrie der Teile ab.

Da gibt es andere in dem Markt, die einfach nur wissen wollen, was wir machen. **Zu diesem Zweck** haben wir illustrierte Kommentare aus den verschiedensten Marktbereichen von Matroc ausgewählt. – von Gasheizgeräten bis hin zu medizinischen Implan-taten. –

Letztlich gibt es für uns noch eine dritte Gruppe von Kunden, die wissen, daß ein kurzer Telefonanruf mit einem erfahrenen Matroc Techniker und der dann folgenden systematischen Bearbeitung wesentlich mehr bringt, als 50 Seiten technischer Daten. – Auf solchen Kunden fußt unsere Existenz – und umgekehrt!

Was bringt diesen Leuten noch eine Brochüre?

Nun, Matroc wie andere Morgan Tochterunternehmen bestätigen, daß Kunden und Techniker in der Regel mehrere Wege zur Problemlösung beschreiten.

Wir hoffen daß diese Publikation diesem Zweck dienlich ist. **Allerdings** haben wir eine feste Vorstellung über den effektivsten Weg und empfehlen bei Projektbeginn unbedingt die Liste mit den Telefonnummern und der Adressen auf der letzten Seite dieser Brochüre einzusehen.

Back-translation:

Today experts are fully agreed that modern ceramic materials offer unsurpassed qualities for many of the most demanding industrial applications.

So we asked ourselves whether this catalogue would still find a corresponding resonance, given the flood of technical literature which is currently circulating in the ceramics market. Should Matroc also add its contribution to this?

On the one hand, some would say: 'that is quite usual for business' **but on the other hand** will we reach our customers just by eagerly imitating others?

Finally, Matroc offers a greater range of ceramics for more applications than most other firms.

Now, there are customers who in their search for suitable materials prefer to study copious technical data sheets. For such customers we have listed the properties of the most popular Matroc materials.

Yet one must consider that such an undertaking without cost information can only be expected to give a limited explanation **because** the production yield depends considerably on the geometry of the articles.

And then there are others in the market who simply want to know what we make. **For this purpose** we have chosen illustrated commentaries from the most wide-ranging market sectors of Matroc – from gas heaters to medical implants.

Lastly we have a third group of customers who know that a brief telephone call with an experienced Matroc technician and the subsequent systematic processing would bring them significantly more than 50 pages of technical details. Our existence rests on such customers – and vice versa!

What does yet another brochure offer these people?

Now, Matroc like other firms in the Morgan Group acknowledge that customers and technicians as a rule follow more than one path in solving a problem.

We hope that this publication serves its purpose. **Yet/in any event** we have a firm idea about the most effective path and unreservedly recommend that at the beginning of the project one looks at the list of telephone numbers and addresses on the last page of this brochure.

There are noticeably fewer conjunctions in the English text (eight) than in the German (twelve). German seems to be generally more conjunctive than English.[7] The use of explicit conjunction makes the structure of the text more transparent. For instance, the 'reason' relation between the limited value of the brochure and cost information (English, third paragraph; German, sixth paragraph) is made more explicit in German by the addition of *denn* 'because'.

Both texts proceed by questioning the need for a company brochure. To start with, an attempt is made to find the answer by considering what Matroc's competitors do and weighing up two possibilities: (a) Matroc's competitors have company brochures and therefore Matroc has to do the same; and (b) Matroc does not need to imitate its competitors. The German conjunctions used to signal this structure (*Einerseits* 'on the one hand', *aber ... andererseits* 'but on the other hand') are more transparent than the mixture of causal *Because* and adversative *But* used in the English text. Both texts then seem to abandon the question of what Matroc's competitors do and move on to consider the types of customer in the market place and whether the brochure would be of any value to them. This departure is signalled more firmly in the German text through the use of *Schließlich* ('finally') and the additional paragraph break. None of this means that the German text is 'better' or 'worse' than its English counterpart. The two texts simply address different readerships and in so doing reflect different textual preferences. If the English text seems less straightforward than the German one so far, it is not without reason. The English text achieves a higher level of informality by appearing to consider various angles of the problem in a relaxed, casual way, as if the writer is simply taking up issues as they occur to him or her. The use of *And yet* in the third paragraph, for instance, gives the impression that the writer is thinking aloud, or perhaps just moving back and forth along the same line of argument – as one would do in chatting to a friend – rather than firmly wrapping up one stage in the argument before moving on to the next as is the case in the German text. Both styles, the chatty English and the formal German, seem appropriate to their particular contexts.

There are other interesting differences between the two texts. The German translation makes a further internal relation between two parts of the text clearer by using *Zu diesem Zweck* ('for this purpose'; seventh paragraph), instead of the English *For them* (fourth paragraph). However, it loses the contrast that is developed in the fourth and fifth paragraphs in English: 'There are others ... For them we offer ...' / 'And finally there is a third class of customer. ... For them this brochure is unnecessary.' In fact, this last sentence, 'For them this brochure is unnecessary', does not appear in the German text at all but is replaced by 'What does another brochure offer these people?' This is particularly interesting because the conjunction in the final paragraph of the German text, *Allerdings*, allows two alternative interpretations in this context:

We hope that this publication serves its purpose,
(i)   **However** (adversative) we know the most effective path …
(ii) **In any event** (concession: whether it does or not, implying it may do) we know the most effective path …

Deleting 'For them this brochure is unnecessary' ties in with the second interpretation. Germans have a reputation for being highly logical and systematic in their approach to things. In a way, it seems rather illogical to dismiss the value of the brochure altogether, for all types of customer, and at the same time suggest that the best way a customer can get the information he or she needs is to use a list of telephone numbers printed in the very brochure that is being dismissed.

Whether a translation conforms to the source-text patterns of cohesion or tries to approximate to target-language patterns will depend in the final analysis on the purpose of the translation and the amount of freedom the translator feels entitled to in rechunking information and/or altering signals of relations between chunks. Whatever the translator decides to do, every option will have its advantages and disadvantages. Following source-language norms may involve minimal change in overall meaning (other factors excluded). On the other hand, noticeable deviation from typical target-language patterns of chunking information and signalling relations is likely to result in the sort of text that can easily be identified as a translation because it sounds 'foreign'.

Apart from questions of naturalness, accuracy and the 'logic' of a text, there are sometimes stylistic considerations which may make the translation of conjunctions particularly difficult. For instance, Milic (1970) suggests that one of the most striking features of Jonathan Swift's style relates to the way he uses conjunction. Swift's favourite conjunctions, according to Milic, are *and*, *but* and *for*. He apparently makes 'unusually heavy use' of these items (*ibid.*:246). Moreover, he does not use them as precise logical connectives but only to indicate that 'one sentence is connected with another without reference to the nature of the connection' (*ibid.*:247). In other words, Swift's use of conjunction is very similar to that of Arabic (see page 202). In both cases, two or three 'favourite' items are used very frequently in a semantically 'imprecise' way. The question then arises as to how one might translate Swift into Arabic when the hallmark of his style is a commonplace feature of Arabic prose.

6.4 LEXICAL COHESION

Lexical cohesion refers to the role played by the selection of vocabulary in organizing relations within a text. A given lexical item cannot be said to have a cohesive function *per se* (cf. reference, conjunction), but any lexical item can enter into a cohesive relation with other items in a text. Whereas on encountering a pronoun such as *he* or *they* the reader will automatically look to the surrounding text for its referent, he or she will not automatically look for a link between an item such as *socialism* and other items in the following example (from the book jacket of *Arab Political Humour*, Kishtainy 1985):

Ready suppliers of fun throughout the thirties and forties were the decadent pseudo-sovereign regimes of the West. More recently people have turned East for their targets, reflecting the new contact with communist countries and also the growing disenchantment with socialism.

And yet, one intuitively recognizes a sort of lexical chain which links *socialism* with *communist* and *East*. Moreover, this chain stands in some kind of opposition to *the West* and, for some people, to *decadent* as well. We could say then that lexical cohesion covers any instance in which the use of a lexical item recalls the sense of an earlier one.

Halliday and Hasan divide lexical cohesion into two main categories: **reiteration** and **collocation**. **Reiteration**, as the name suggests, involves repetition of lexical items. A reiterated item may be a repetition of an earlier item, a synonym or near-synonym, a superordinate, or a general word. In this sense, reiteration can be placed along the same continuum presented on pages 192–3 (with the exception of pronominal reference). This is repeated below for convenience:

> There's a boy climbing that tree.
> (a) *The boy* is going to fall if he doesn't take care. (repetition)
> (b) *The lad's* going to fall if he doesn't take care. (synonym)
> (c) *The child's* going to fall if he doesn't take care. (superordinate)
> (d) *The idiot's* going to fall if he doesn't take care. (general word)

Reiteration is not the same as reference, however, because it does not necessarily involve the same identity. If the above sentence is followed by a statement such as '*Boys* can be so silly', the repetition of *boy* → *boys* would still be an instance of reiteration, even though the two items would not be referring to the same individual(s).

Collocation, as a sub-class of lexical cohesion in Halliday and Hasan's model, covers any instance which involves a pair of lexical items that are associated with each other in the language in some way. Halliday and Hasan (*ibid.*:285–286) offer the following types of association as examples, but admit that there are other instances where the association between lexical items cannot readily be given a name but is nevertheless felt to exist. In the final analysis, they suggest, it does not matter what the relation is as long as we are aware of it and react to it as a cohesive device.

> Various kinds of oppositeness of meaning: e.g. *boy/girl*; *love/hate*; *order/ obey*.
> Associations between pairs of words from the same ordered series: e.g.
>   *Tuesday/Thursday*; *August/December*; *dollar/cent*.
> Associations between pairs of words from unordered lexical sets: e.g.
>   part–whole relations: *car/brake*; *body/arm*; *bicycle/wheel*;
>   part–part relations: *mouth/chin*; *verse/chorus*;
>   co-hyponymy: *red/green* (colour); *chair/table* (furniture).

> Associations based on a history of co-occurrence (collocation proper – see
> Chapter 3): e.g. *rain, pouring, torrential, wet; hair, comb, curl, wave*; etc.

Lexical cohesion is not a relation between pairs of words as the above discussion might suggest. On the contrary, lexical cohesion typically operates through lexical chains (such as *socialism, communist, East*) that run through a text and are linked to each other in various ways. The following example shows how patterns of lexical cohesion might be traced in a relatively straightforward piece of text. Sentences are numbered for ease of reference in the following discussion.

> (1) I first met Hugh Fraser in 1977. (2) Charming, rather hesitant, a heavy smoker and heavy gambler, he had made such headway through his fortune that he had decided to sell his last major asset, the controlling shares in the business which his father had built up and named Scottish and Universal Investments. (3) Scottish and Universal had, among its assets, 10% of the British stores group, House of Fraser. (4) Lonrho bought 26% of Scottish and Universal.
>
> (5) It was part of Lonrho's understanding with Hugh that he would stay on as Chairman of House of Fraser, but it gradually became clear that Sir Hugh was not on terms of mutual respect with most of his Board, and that the loyalty of his colleagues had been to his formidable father rather than to him. (6) They did not welcome the sale of Hugh's shares to Lonrho – and it was only natural, as a change was obviously in the air. (7) Lonrho was an expanding and acquisitive company, and House of Fraser was a quiet and pedestrian one.
>
> *(from* A Hero from Zero, *Lonrho:i)*

Instances of lexical cohesion in the above text include the repetition of items such as *Scottish and Universal* (sentences 2, 3 and 4), *Lonrho* (4, 5, 6 and 7) and *assets* (2 and 3). There is a superordinate–hyponym relation between *assets/shares*, oppositeness of meaning between *sell/bought*, reiteration by general word: *Lonrho/company*, and a relation of synonymy or near-synonymy between *expanding/acquisitive*. *Smoker/gambler* are co-hyponyms of something like 'behavioural vice' and *respect/loyalty* are co-hyponyms of 'institutional virtue'. Most important of all, of course, is the main collocational chain which helps to establish and maintain the subject of the text: *fortune, shares, assets, business, Chairman, Board, sale, expanding, acquisitive, company* and so on. Many more cohesive relations can be traced in the above text, which illustrates the typical density of networks of lexical cohesion in any stretch of language.

Another example from a different genre will serve to demonstrate the sort of manipulation of lexical associations available to speakers and writers. The following extract is from John Le Carré's *The Russia House* (1989:40):

The whole of Whitehall was agreed that no story should ever begin that way again. Indoctrinated ministers were furious about it. They set up a frightfully secret committee of enquiry to find out what went wrong, hear witnesses, name names, spare no blushes, point fingers, close gaps, prevent a recurrence, appoint me chairman and draft a report. What conclusions our committee reached, if any, remains the loftiest secret of them all, particularly from those of us who sat on it. For the function of such committees, as we all well knew, is to talk earnestly until the dust has settled, and then ourselves return to dust. Which, like a disgruntled Cheshire cat, our committee duly did, leaving nothing behind us but our frightfully secret frown, a meaningless interim working paper, and a bunch of secret annexes in the Treasury archives.

Two main collocational chains are cleverly interwoven in the above passage. One has to do with high-powered official institutions and practices: *committees, enquiries, chairman, witnesses, Whitehall, ministers, Treasury, report, interim working paper* and so on. The other evokes the theme of intrigue: the word *secret* is repeated several times and expressions such as *name names* and *point fingers* are used. But this is not genuine intrigue, because the two collocational chains are overlaid with ironic descriptive expressions which ridicule the institutions and practices in question and give an impression of 'mock suspense': *frightfully secret committee, indoctrinated ministers, the loftiest secret of them all, like a disgruntled Cheshire cat, frightfully secret frown, meaningless interim working paper, a bunch of secret annexes* and so on.

The notion of lexical cohesion as being dependent on the presence of networks of lexical items rather than the presence of any specific class or type of item is important. It provides the basis for what Halliday and Hasan call **instantial meaning**, or text meaning (1976:289):

> Without our being aware of it, each occurrence of a lexical item carries with it its own textual history, a particular collocational environment that has been built up in the course of the creation of the text and that will provide the context within which the item will be incarnated on this particular occasion. This environment determines the 'instantial meaning', or text meaning, of the item, a meaning which is unique to each specific instance.

The importance for translators of the notion of instantial meaning is obvious. Lexical networks do not only provide cohesion, they also determine collectively the sense in which each individual item is used in a given context. As Hoey (1991:8) points out, 'the text provides the context for the creation and interpretation of lexical relations, just as the lexical relations help create the texture of the text'.

The idea that the meanings of individual lexical items depend on the networks of relations in which they enter with other items in a text is now taken as axiomatic in language studies in general and in translation studies in particular. Snell-Hornby stresses the importance of this approach in translation, arguing that in analysing a text a translator 'is not concerned with isolating phenomena or items to study them in depth, but with tracing a *web of relationships*, the importance of individual items being determined by their relevance and function in the text' (1988:69).

It is certainly true that individual lexical items have little more than a 'potential' for meaning outside text and that their meanings are realized and can be considerably modified through association with other lexical items in a particular textual environment. And yet, the potential for meaning which a given lexical item has is not totally unrestricted. You simply cannot make any word mean whatever you want it to mean. What this suggests, in effect, is that as hard as one might try, it is impossible to reproduce networks of lexical cohesion in a target text which are identical to those of the source text. If you cannot make a word mean what you want it to mean, you might have to settle for one with a slightly different meaning or different associations. Every time this happens it introduces a subtle (or major) shift away from the lexical chains and associations of the source text. Significant shifts do occur, even in non-literary text. They include, for instance, cases where the source text uses a play on idiom to create a lexical chain or a number of separate chains that are linked together by virtue of relating to the literal or non-literal interpretation of the idiom. An example of this was given in Chapter 3 (p. 73). A similar example comes from an advertisement promoting a woman's magazine (*Woman's Realm*) which shows a woman wearing a large hat, accompanied by the following caption: 'If you think Woman's Realm is old hat ... think again' (*Cosmopolitan*, October 1989). *Old hat* means 'boringly familiar/uninteresting', but the literal meaning of *hat* is used here to create a lexical/visual chain by tying in with the actual hat in the photograph. This type of chain often has to be sacrificed in translation because interweaving idiom-based chains can only be reproduced if the target language has an idiom which is identical to the source idiom in both form and meaning.

As the *Cosmopolitan* example demonstrates, cohesive links are often established between textual and other types of element,[8] including visual elements such as photographs and drawings, layout elements such as position on the page, and, in the case of multimodal environments such as web sites, elements of navigation such as hypertext links and widgets. The example in Figure 15, from *National Geographic Magazine*, features a clever play on an idiom/fixed expression, a visual play based on image and colour, and a layout format that foregrounds and strengthens the textual-visual network of cohesive links.

In the original, full-colour image, the lefthand column above the image of the orange is printed in the same colour as the apple (red), and the righthand column is printed in the same colour as the orange; the column in the middle is printed in regular black. The dense network of cohesive links further features a visual/textual play on the idiom 'like comparing apples and oranges' (used to indicate a false analogy, an attempt to compare two things that are quite different in nature) and the actual images of an apple and an orange, repetition of items such as *compare*, and the synonymy between *dissimilar* and *different*, among other cohesive relations.

SCIENCE

Not Beyond Compare

"That's like apples and oranges." The classic phrase sums up the impossibility
of comparing dissimilar objects or ideas. But are the two foods that different?
Each is a seeded fruit "you want to pick up and bite," notes Cornell University
horticulturist Ian Merwin. Yet each grows in "profoundly different ways."
That doesn't mean you can't compare them (below). But Merwin sees subtlety
in the cliché: "Apples and oranges may seem the same, but they're not." To cite
utterly unlike items, try Serbia's odd pair: "old ladies and frogs." —Marc Silver

57	Calories, raw fruit*	85
2.6 grams	Fiber*	4.3 grams
5 milligrams	Vitamin C*	96 milligrams
11.3 grams	Total sugars*	16.8 grams
Thin, with natural wax layer	Skin	Thick, with oil glands
Embedded in the core	Seed location	In the edible sections
Warm summer, cold winter	Prime growing conditions	Subtropical
Deciduous	Tree type	Evergreen

Figure 15 'Not Beyond Compare', *National Geographic Magazine*,
1 March 2010, p. 26

Apart from the challenge posed by the manipulation of idioms and visual elements in
a source text, the lack of ready equivalents will sometimes require the translator to
resort to strategies such as the use of a superordinate, paraphrase or loan word (see
Chapter 2). These naturally result in producing different lexical chains in the target
text. Likewise, the grammatical structure of the target language may require the
translator to add or delete information and to reword parts of the source text in a

variety of ways. Admittedly, in non-literary translation new networks of lexical relations created in the target text during the course of translation will often be very
close overall to those of the source text. But they will still be different, and the
difference, subtle though it may be, may affect the cohesiveness and coherence
(see Chapter 7) of the target text in varying degrees, depending on the skill and
experience of the translator. Whatever lexical and grammatical problems are encountered in translating a text and whatever strategies are used to resolve them, a good
translator will make sure that, at the end of the day, the target text displays a sufficient level of lexical and other types of cohesion in its own right. Subtle changes –
and sometimes major changes – are often unavoidable. But what the translator must
always avoid is the extreme case of producing what appears to be a random
collection of items which do not add up to recognizable lexical chains that make
sense in a given context.

The Brintons press release is an example of the sort of subtle changes that
typically take place on the level of lexical cohesion in non-literary translation. A
quick look at the two versions presented below reveals considerable differences in
patterns of reiteration and collocation. We do not have to analyse the two texts in
detail to see that there is far more repetition in the Arabic version than there is in
the English text. For instance, *company* occurs only once in the English text; its
Arabic equivalent, *sharika*, is repeated eight times. Similarly, *colour(s)* occurs
three times in the English text; its Arabic equivalent occurs seven times. Some of
the subtle associations created by a careful selection of lexical items in the English
text are inevitably lost in the translation. The choice of items such as *plant* (rather
than *factory*), *qualities* (rather than *kinds* or *types*), *complementary* (rather than
matching colours) and *select* (rather than *choose*) plays a role in creating a
certain image of Brintons and their products in the perception of the reader. These
items, plus others such as *discerning* in the final sentence, collectively enhance
the image of Brintons as a sophisticated company producing a select range of
products. These subtle associations are lost in the Arabic version because the
lexical structure of Arabic does not offer the translator the same range of choices;
for instance, the distinction between *plant/factory* or *choose/select* does not exist
in Arabic. Moreover, Arabic has no ready equivalents for *complementary* and
discerning. The first item, *complementary*, is paraphrased in the Arabic version as
'the colours of which match the rest of the colours of the collection'. A paraphrase
of course cannot create the same kinds of association as a lexical item. The
second item, *discerning*, is omitted altogether.

Source text (*Brintons* press release):

> Brintons have been manufacturing fine quality woven carpet for over
> 200 years. They are a privately owned company specializing in
> Axminster and Wilton carpets, using wool-rich blends. They have a
> totally integrated operation from the preparation of the yarn through
> to the weaving process. All their products are made on looms

designed and built by their own engineers, and recognized as the most technically superior weaving plant in the world. Brintons are one of the largest weavers with a production capacity in excess of 100,000 square metres per week.

The recently introduced New Tradition Axminster range is already creating great interest and will be on display at the Exhibition. New Tradition offers a fascinating series of traditional patterns in miniature using rich jewel-like colours that glow against dark backgrounds, suitable for a wide variety of heavy wear locations from hotels, restaurants and leisure areas to high quality residential situations.

The successful Finesse and Palace Design qualities will also be displayed. Both carpets have geometrically styled designs suitable for both residential and contract use. Palace Design also incorporates a border and plain range in complementary colours.

Other Brintons products suitable for the commercial world, such as Bell Twist, Heather Berber, Broadloop, Bell Trinity and Trident Tile will also be on display.

Brintons will be delighted to solve any carpeting problems as special designs and qualities can be produced for minimum quantities. Their standard range of colours offers over 200 possibilities for the discerning designer to select from.

Target text:

تقوم شركة برينتونز بتصنيع أرقى أنواع السجاد المنسوج منذ أكثر من **200** عام، وهي شركة خاصة، تتخصص فى انتاج سجاد الأكسمنستر و الويلتون الذى تدخله نسبة عالية من الصوف. هذا وتقوم الشركة بتنفيذ جميع خطوات الانتاج بمصانعها، من اعداد الخيوط الى نسجها على أنوال من تصميم وصنع مهندسى الشركة، وتعتبر مصانع برينتونز أكثر مصانع النسيج تقدماً من الناحية الفنية فى العالم كله، كما تعتبر شركة برينتونز من أكبر شركات النسيج بطاقة انتاجية تزيد عن **100،000** متر مربع فى الاسبوع.

اثارت مجموعة "نيو تراديشن اكسمنستر" درجة عالية من الاهتمام منذ أن قامت الشركة بتقديمها حديثاً، وهى من ضمن أنواع السجاد التى سيتم عرضها بالمعرض. تقدم مجموعة "نيو تراديشن" عدد من التصميمات التقليدية الممتعة بحجم مصغر، فى ألوان باهرة كألوان الجواهر، تزيد الخلفيات الداكنة من توهجها. وهى مناسبة للتركيب فى العديد من المواقع التجارية ذات الاستعمال الكثيف، مثل الفنادق والمطاعم والأماكن الترفيهية وبعض المواقع السكنية ذات المستوى الرفيع.

كما يتضمن المعرض نماذج من سجاد "فينس" و "بالاس ديزاين" اللذين تم تسويقهما بنجاح كبير. ويتسم هذان النوعان من السجاد بتصميماتهما الهندسية ويصلحا للاستخدام فى كل من المواقع السكنية والتجارية. هذا وتشتمل مجموعة "بالاس ديزاين" على عدة ألوان سادة وتصميمات فى شكل كنار تتماشى الوانها مع باقى الوان المجموعة.

هذا وسوف تقوم شركة برينتونز بعرض بعض عدة أنواع أخرى من السجاد المناسب للاستعمال التجارى، مثل "بل تويست" و "هاذر بربر" و "برود لوب" و "بل ترينتى" و "ترايدنت تايل".

يسر شركة برينتونز مساعدتكم على حل أى مشاكل خاصة بالسجاد، حيث يمكنها انتاج تصميمات و أنواع خاصة بكميات محدودة، كما أن مجموعة الألوان المتوفرة لدى الشركة تزيد عن مائتى لون مما يتيح لأى مصمم فرصة كبيرة للاختيار.

Brintons company has been manufacturing the finest quality of woven carpets for over 200 years, and it is a private company, specializing in the production of Axminster and Wilton carpets in which enters a high percentage of wool. This and the company carries out all steps of production in its factories, from preparing the yarn to weaving it on looms designed and manufactured by the company engineers, and Brintons factories are considered the most advanced weaving factories from the technical aspect in the whole world, also Brintons company is considered among the largest weaving companies with a production capacity which exceeds 100,000 square metres per week.

The 'New Tradition Axminster' collection has aroused a high degree of interest since the company undertook its introduction recently, and it is among the types of carpets which will be displayed at the exhibition. The 'New Tradition' collection presents a number of fascinating traditional designs in a reduced size, in dazzling colours like the colours of gems, the glowing of which is increased by the dark backgrounds. And it is suitable for fitting in many commercial locations with heavy use, such as hotels and restaurants and leisure places and some residential locations of fine standard.

Also the exhibition includes samples of 'Finesse' and 'Palace Design' carpets which have been marketed with great success. And these two types of carpet are characterized by their geometrical designs and are suitable for use in both residential and commercial locations. This and the 'Palace Design' collection comprises several plain colours and designs in the shape of a border, the colours of which match the rest of the colours of the collection.

This and Brintons company will undertake to display several other types of carpet suitable for commercial use, such as 'Bell Twist' and 'Heather Berber' and 'Broadloop' and 'Bell Trinity' and Trident Tile'.

Brintons company is pleased to assist you in solving any problems concerning carpets, as it can produce designs and special types in limited quantities, also the collection of colours available at the company exceeds 200 colours which allows any designer a big opportunity for choice.

The above differences in patterns of reiteration and collocation do not mean that the Arabic text lacks lexical cohesion. We have noted, for instance, that there is an increase in the repetition of items such as 'company' and 'colours'. The Arabic text, then, has its own networks of lexical cohesion, but these do not match the networks created in the English text and do not trigger the same kinds of association in the mind of the target reader. Note that part of the lexical cohesion of any text is inevitably obscured by back-translation because it derives from the morphological structure of the language. For instance, in the Arabic version of the above text, cohesive links exist between the Arabic words for 'display' and 'exhibition', because they are derived from the same root. Unfortunately, links of this sort cannot be easily shown in back-translation.

One point that should be borne in mind is that languages differ in the level of lexical repetition they will normally tolerate. The above example suggests that Arabic tolerates a far higher level of lexical repetition than English. Greek seems to behave more like Arabic than English in this respect. Consider, for instance, the following extract from Hawking's *A Brief History of Time* (1988:1–2):

> Most people would find the picture of our universe as an infinite tower of tortoises rather ridiculous, but why do we think we know better? What do we know about the universe, and how do we know it? Where did the universe come from, and where is it going? Did the universe have a beginning, and if so, what happened *before* then? What is the nature of time? Will it ever come to an end? Recent breakthroughs in physics, made possible in part by fantastic new technologies, suggest answers to some of these longstanding questions. Someday these answers may seem as obvious to us as the earth orbiting the sun – or perhaps as ridiculous as a tower of tortoises. Only time (whatever that may be) will tell.

If you examine the above extract, you will find that six lexical items (not including function words such as *the* and *where*) are repeated as follows:

know (3 times)	*universe* (4)	*time* (2)
answers (2)	*ridiculous* (2)	*tower of tortoises* (2)

The pattern in the Spanish translation is very similar:[9]

saber 'know' (2)	*universo* 'universe' (4)
tiempo 'time' (3)	*respuestas* 'answers' (2)
ridículo 'ridiculous' (2)	*torre de tortugas* 'tower of tortoises' (2)

Compare this with the Greek translation,[10] where the number of items repeated (13) and the number of times that some items are repeated, for example 'universe' (6), are both much higher than in the English and Spanish texts:

anthropi 'people'	(2)	*ikona* 'picture'	(2)
simpan 'universe'	(6)	*gnorizo* 'know'	(3)
iparkho 'exist'	(6)	*khronos* 'time'	(5)
arkhi 'beginning'	(2)	*apandisi* 'answers'	(2)
yi 'earth'	(3)	*evnoitos* 'obvious'	(2)
anoitos 'silly'	(2)	*stirizo* 'supported'	(2)
apiri sira apo trapulo kharta 'infinite series of cards'			(2)

As far as I can tell from talking to native speakers of Greek, the Greek version of Hawking's book reads extremely well. It may be that one of the reasons it reads like an original is that it uses patterns of reiteration that are typical of Greek discourse instead of copying those of the English source text.

Shifts in patterns of lexical cohesion can however have important ideological implications in some contexts. Mason (1994/2010:95) offers an excellent example from a text about Mexican history which appeared in Spanish and English translation in the April 1990 edition of the *UNESCO Courier*. Here are the two texts:

¿Tiene la historia un destino?
Miguel León-Portilla

Antiguos y prolongados esfuerzos por conservar la memoria de sucesos que afectaron a la comunidad integran el primer gran capítulo de la búsqueda del ser y del destino mexicanos. Así, ya en la época prehispánica se afirma una forma característica de interesarse por preservar la memoria de sí mismo y luchar contra el olvido. Esa memoria era indispensable a los viejos sacerdotes y sabios para prever los destinos en relación con sus cálculos calendáricos. Tal quehacer de elaboración y registro de una historia divina y humana perdura en miles de vestigios arqueológicos que abarcan más de veinte siglos antes de la llegada de los españoles en 1519. Así, por ejemplo, las estelas de 'Los Danzantes' en Monte Albán, Oaxaca, fechadas entre 600 y 300 a.C., constituyen en el Nuevo Mundo el más antiguo registro de aconteceres, con sus años y días, nombres de lugares, de reyes y señores.

El destino – o los destinos – de los muchos pueblos que han vivido y viven en tierras mexicanas tuvo tiempos propicios y tiempos funestos. Hubo épocas de gran creatividad y otras de crisis y enfrentamientos, que llevaron a dramáticas desapariciones de hombres y de formas de exisitir. Los mitos y leyendas, la tradición oral y el gran conjunto de inscripciones perpetuaron la memoria de tales aconteceres.

Del más grande y trágico de los encuentros que experimentó el hombre indígena habrían de escribir personajes como el propio conquistador Hernán Cortés en sus *Cartas de Relación* y el soldado cronista Bernal Díaz del Castillo en su *Historia verdadera de la Nueva España*. Pero también los vencidos dejaron sus testimonios. Entre otros, un viejo manuscrito fechado en 1528, que se conserva ahora en la Biblioteca Nacional de Par's, consigna en lengua náhuatl (azteca) la memoria de lo que fue para los antiguos mexicanos el más grande de los traumas.

History or Destiny?
Miguel León-Portilla

Mexicans have always exhibited an obstinate determination to safeguard the memory of the major events that have marked their society and this has coloured the way in which they view their identity and destiny. From pre-Columbian times they have been engaged in a continuous battle to save their history from oblivion. Knowledge of the past was the foundation on which their priests and diviners based their astronomic calculations and their predictions of the future. Countless archaeological remains from the two thousand years before the arrival of the Spaniards in 1519 bear witness to the Mexican desire to interpret and record the history of gods and man. The stelae known as danzantes ('dancers') at Monte Albán in the Oaxaca valley, on which are inscribed a record of the passing days and years, place-names and the names of kings and other notables, constitute the oldest known chronicle (600 to 300 BC) of the New World.

The people, or rather peoples, who succeeded one another on Mexican soil met with mixed fortunes. Bursts of creativity were punctuated by times of crisis and war which even led to the abrupt disappearance of entire populations and civilizations. The memory of these events lives on in the thousands of inscriptions and the legends of oral tradition.

The greatest and most tragic clash of cultures in pre-Columbian civilization was recorded by some of those who took part in the conquest of Mexico. Hernán Cortés himself sent five remarkable letters (*Cartas de relación*) back to Spain between 1519 and 1526; and the soldier-chronicler Bernal Díaz del Castillo (c. 1492–1580), who served under Cortés, fifty years after the event wrote his *Historia verdadera de la conquista de la Nueva España* ('True History of the Conquest of New Spain'). The vanquished peoples also left written records. A manuscript dated 1528, now in the Bibliothèque Nationale in Paris, recounts in Nahuatl, the language of the Aztecs, the traumatic fate of the Indians.

Mason shows how networks of lexical cohesion in the source text that rely on repetition of items such as *memoria* and *destino* and on the semantic relationship between items such as *esfuerzos* (efforts), *luchar* (struggle) and *quehacer* (task) are disrupted in the English translation, resulting in what he describes as a 'radical shift of values' (*ibid.*:89); see Table 2. As Mason explains, the Spanish source text concedes that 'the Spanish Conquistadors were the official chroniclers of Mexican history' but insists that 'there are indigenous voices, under-represented hitherto, which are equally worth listening to and which have preserved the precious legacy of "memory" in their own written records' (*ibid.*:91). Failure to reproduce the relevant lexical chain in the source text, Mason suggests, does not allow the reader of the English text to appreciate the link between the past and the present for the source community. The result is that '[m]emory as such is downplayed, and the active search for the past and the task of recording it turn into a passive view of the past and a *desire* to interpret it' (*ibid.*:88).

Table 2 Recurrence and collocational cohesion (adapted from Mason 1994/2010:88)

SOURCE TEXT	TARGET TEXT
memoria	memory
memoria	history
memoria	knowledge of the past
memoria	memory
memoria	------
destino	destiny
destinos	the future
destino	------
destinos	------
esfuerzos (efforts)	obstinate determination
búsqueda (search)	the way in which they view
luchar contra (struggle against)	to save ... from
quehacer (task)	desire
épocas de gran creatividad (ages of great creativity)	bursts of creativity

Reference, substitution, ellipsis, conjunction and lexical cohesion are the devices identified by Halliday and Hasan for establishing cohesive links in English. These devices are probably common to a large number of languages. However, different languages have different preferences for using specific devices more frequently than others or in specific combinations which may not correspond to English patterns of cohesion. For instance, pronominalization is very frequent in English but is rarely used in Japanese and Chinese. Lexical repetition is far more frequent in Hebrew than it is in English (Berman 1978, in Blum-Kulka 1986:19).

Cohesion is also achieved by a variety of devices other than those mentioned by Halliday and Hasan and discussed above. These include continuity of tense, consistency of style, and punctuation devices such as colons and semi-colons, which, like conjunctions, indicate how different parts of the text relate to each other. It is worth noting here that unmotivated shifts in style, a common pitfall in translation, can seriously disrupt the cohesion and coherence (see Chapter 7) of a text.

Some languages have different or additional devices: for example, some languages such as Aguaruna use 'chaining', where part of the preceding information, for instance the predicate of the preceding sentence, is repeated in the following sentence (Larson 1984), as demonstrated earlier in this chapter. Cohesion can also be established between textual and non-textual elements, including visual material, layout, and search and retrieval elements such as hypertext links on the internet.

Finally, the overall level of cohesion may vary from one language to another; even within the same language, different texts will vary in the density of their cohesive ties. Vieira (1984, quoted in Blum-Kulka 1986), suggests that Portuguese prefers a higher level of explicit cohesiveness than English. Cohesion contributes to patterns of redundancy, and these vary both across languages and across text types. Explicit markers of cohesion raise the level of redundancy in text; their absence lowers it. Blum-Kulka notes that there is a general tendency in translation to raise the level of explicitness, that is, increase the level of redundancy in the target text, and suggests that 'it might be the case that explicitation is a universal strategy inherent in the process of language mediation, as practiced by language learners, non-professional translators and professional translators alike' (1986:21). This claim has been subjected to close scrutiny in several studies since the mid-1990s, with varying results. See, in particular, Olohan and Baker (2000), Kenny (2004), Englund Dimitrova (2005) and Mauranen (2008).

exercises

1. Choose one cohesive device and explore its function in your source and target languages, preferably in a specific genre. To do this, start by looking at a number of original texts in the two languages and compare the use of the particular cohesive device in them. For instance, if you choose reference, note how participants and entities are typically traced in both texts: by pronominal reference, by repetition, by co-reference and so on. Next, look at a number of translated texts from the same genre. Compare patterns of cohesion in the translated target texts with those in the original ones. Comment on differences and, where necessary, suggest ways in which patterns of cohesion in the translated texts may be adjusted to reflect target language preferences.

   This is a time-consuming but useful exercise and is best done as a project. Its aim is to help you become familiar with cohesive devices typically used in your language and in the special types of text you hope to specialize in.

2. Imagine that you have been invited to join a team of translators to produce a version of the *Macmillan Encyclopedia* in your target language. Your assignment is to translate all the entries on people (rather than those on countries or political terms, for instance). You will

therefore need to be particularly careful about handling referential chains in your translated version. Below are a couple of typical entries from *The Macmillan Encyclopedia* (1986):

Elizabeth I (1533–1603) Queen of England and Ireland (1558–1603), daughter of Henry VIII and Anne Boleyn. Her mother's execution and Elizabeth's imprisonment by Mary I made her cautious and suspicious but her devotion to England made her one of its greatest monarchs. Her religious compromise (1559–63) established Protestantism in England (*see* Reformation). Several plots to place her Roman Catholic cousin, Mary, Queen of Scots, on the throne led to Mary's execution (1587). England won a great naval victory in 1588 by destroying the Spanish Armada. Elizabeth never married and was called the Virgin Queen, although her relationships with, among others, the Earl of Leicester and the 2nd Earl of Essex caused considerable speculation.

Van Gogh, Vincent (1853–90) Dutch postimpressionist painter, born at Zundert, the son of a pastor. He worked as an art dealer, a teacher in England, and a missionary among coalminers before taking up painting in about 1880. His early works were chiefly drawings of peasants. After a limited training in The Hague and in Antwerp, where he studied the works of Rubens and Japanese prints, he moved to Paris (1886). Here he briefly adopted the style of impressionism and later of pointillism. In Arles in 1888 he painted his best-known works – orchards, sunflowers, and the local postman and his family – but only one painting was sold during his lifetime. The visit of his friend Gauguin ended in a quarrel during which Van Gogh cut off part of his own left ear. In 1889 he entered a mental asylum at Saint Rémy. The ominous *Wheatfield with Crows* (Stedelijk Museum, Amsterdam) was painted shortly before his suicide. His letters to his brother (Theo) contain the best account of his life and work. *See* expressionism.

Translate the above entries into your target language, paying particular attention to the ways in which different participants are traced in each entry. Comment on any differences in patterns of reference in the source and target versions of each entry.

3. The following is an extract from a Minority Rights Group Report on Lebanon (McDowall 1983:7):

It might initially seem puzzling for a Minority Rights Group Report to examine a whole country as a minority problem. Yet there can be

few countries which can claim to be so deeply and intrinsically composed of minorities as Lebanon – especially one so small that it could fit into one quarter of Switzerland. There is not a single resident in Lebanon who cannot, in one sense or another, truthfully claim to belong to a minority. It is the conflicting aspirations and fears of these different components of Lebanese society confined in a small and rapidly urbanizing area which lie at the heart of the continuing crisis in Lebanon today.

Outside the Lebanon the international media have frequently portrayed the conflicts within this unhappy country as the product of Christian–Muslim hatred, or in the political arena as a contest between the Left and Right, or as the product of outside (normally Palestinian or Syrian) subversion. These interpretations can be crude and dangerously misleading, but they tend to be repeated time and again, doing little to assist international understanding of Lebanon's ills. The non-Lebanese ingredients to the conflict, the Syrian, Israeli and Palestinian armed presence and the interference of the two super-powers have certainly exacerbated the conflict, but none of them started it. Civil conflict feeds on internal divisions, and had these not existed the Lebanese people would undoubtedly have closed ranks against the behaviour of their neighbours. Despite the departure of the PLO from Beirut and south Lebanon, which some wishful thinkers believed would presage an end to the conflict in Lebanon, no such thing has happened and the main Lebanese contestants during the Civil War period 1975–77 seem as much at loggerheads as ever.

It is not the primary cause of this paper to explain the Civil War, or indeed the two Israeli invasions of Lebanon in 1978 and 1982. Rather, its purpose is to provide a background to the hopes, fears and aspirations of these communities which have, all of them, already suffered too much. People in Lebanon have very long memories indeed, and their outlook can be considerably influenced by community experience – even centuries ago. For this reason I have given what may, to some, seem like undue attention to the past.

Study the above extract carefully, paying particular attention to the use of (a) conjunctions and the way they structure the argument, and (b) networks of lexical cohesion and the images and associations they trigger off in the mind of the reader.

Imagine that you have been asked to translate the above extract for inclusion in a review of the MRG report, to be published in one of the leading newspapers in your country. Translate the text into your target language and comment on any differences in the use of cohesive

exercises

devices. If you decide to make adjustments that lead to noticeable departure from the content or structure of the argument, justify your decision by reference to the purpose for which the translation is required.

4. An Indian non-profit organization, Katha, wishes to commission translations of selected pages of its web site into a range of languages in order to enhance its presence on the web and encourage the involvement of potential supporters in other countries. Examine Figure 16 carefully: this was the home page of Katha (www.katha.org/) until the organization revamped its website in August 2010. Make a note of the main cohesive links you can identify, both textual and visual. Clicking on the 'ENTER OUR WORLD' slogan at the bottom would have taken you to the page depicted in Figure 17. Examine the cohesive links on that page.

Translate the homepage and the first four paragraphs of the sub-page into your target language, bearing in mind that visuals, headings and hyperlinks will also need to be copied over or translated for the new web site. Comment on any challenges you encounter and strategies you use to maintain or adapt different types of cohesive link, both within the textual material and between text and visuals, and within each page as well as between different pages. For example, how do you render (or compensate for) the cohesive link between *children* and *kids* (or rather *kidz* as it is spelled here)? How do you deal with instances of 'phonetic cohesion' (cohesive links established through sound patterns), such as

Warm greetings from Katha! Katha is a unique model that seamlessly connects grassroots work in education, urban resurgence and story. Since 1990, we've driven our education model on a single powerful idea: Children can bring change that is sustainable and real. We run 96 schools in slum communities. And work with the government to bring the joy of reading to more than 200,000 children. We see translation as a non-divisive tool in nation building. We are a "profit for all" social organization.

Figure 16   Homepage of Katha

Figure 17   Sub-page of Katha web site

the link between *Mission* and *Vision* (righthand section of the sub-page)? Would you retain *kidzzone* as a loanword, given that it appears on both pages – in the visuals, the main text and as a hyperlink on the sub-page?

SUGGESTIONS FOR FURTHER READING

Blum-Kulka, Shoshana (1986/2004) 'Shifts of Cohesion and Coherence in Translation', in Juliane House and Shoshana Blum-Kulka (eds) *Interlingual and Intercultural Communication: Discourse and Cognition in Translation and Second Language Acquisition Studies*, Tübingen: Gunter Narr, 17–35; reprinted in Lawrence Venuti (ed.) *The Translation Studies Reader*, London: Routledge, 290–305.

Brown, Gillian and George Yule (1983) *Discourse Analysis*, Cambridge: Cambridge University Press. Chapter 6 : 'The Nature of Reference in Text and Discourse'.

Callow, Kathleen (1974) *Discourse Considerations in Translating the Word of God*, Michigan: Zondervan. Chapter 3: 'Cohesion'.

Cook, Guy (1992) *The Discourse of Advertising*, London: Routledge. Chapter 7: 'Connected Text'.

de Beaugrande, Robert and Wolfgang Dressler (1981) *Introduction to Text Linguistics*, London: Longman. Chapter 6: 'Cohesion'.

Fawcett, Peter (1997) *Translation and Language*, Manchester: St. Jerome Publishing. Chapter 8: 'Text Structure'.

Giora, Rachel (1983) 'Segmentation and Segment Cohesion: On the Thematic Organization of the Text', *Text* 3(2): 155–181.

Halliday, Michael A. K. and Ruqaiya Hasan (1976) *Cohesion in English*, London: Longman.

Hasan, Ruqaiya (1984) 'Coherence and Cohesive Harmony', in James Flood (ed.) *Understanding Reading Comprehension: Cognition, Language and Structure of Prose*, Newark: International Reading Association, 181–219.

Hoey, Michael (1991) *Patterns of Lexis in Text*, Oxford: Oxford University Press.

Shlesinger, Miriam (1995) 'Shifts in Cohesion in Simultaneous Interpreting', *The Translator* 1(2): 193–214.

NOTES

1   Throughout this chapter, I use 'network' in its non-technical sense and not as a systemic term.

2   Halliday and Hasan (1976:9) suggest that while cohesive ties do exist within a sentence:

> it is the intersentence cohesion that is significant, because that represents the variable aspect of cohesion, distinguishing one text from another. But this should not obscure the fact that cohesion is not, strictly speaking, a relation 'above the sentence'. It is a relation to which the sentence, or any other form of grammatical structure, is simply irrelevant.

The definition of 'sentence' is problematic even in English, with its highly developed punctuation system. In some languages, the notion of sentence is even more elusive. For instance, full stops in Arabic often occur only at the end of paragraphs, so that a whole paragraph will often consist of one very long 'sentence'. Even Halliday and Hasan, who argue that the notion of sentence is essentially valid, admit that the punctuation system in general is very flexible and that 'the sentence itself is a very indeterminate category' (1976:232). The discussion of cohesion in this chapter will therefore not be restricted to intersentential ties.

3   The Portuguese text is much shorter than the English, possibly because of restrictions on space.

4   Arabic makes heavy use of pronominal suffixes but not of independent pronouns. All pronouns in this text are suffixed to verbs, nouns or prepositions; they are not free-standing as the back-translation suggests. Independent pronouns are not generally used to trace participants in Arabic discourse. They are mainly used to signal emphasis or contrast. Occasionally, they may be used to disambiguate reference, a function normally realized by lexical repetition in English.

5   The boundary between conjunctive *and* and coordinating *and* is generally fuzzy, but it is even more so in Arabic, where it is often very difficult to distinguish between the two.

6   Unlike the first *Nun* (fifth paragraph in the German text; see below), this second *Nun* is not adversative. The difference in meaning is highlighted by the use of a comma after the second *Nun*. Commas usually delineate clauses in German and are rarely used at phrase level, unless there is a good reason for doing so.

7   This may have something to do with the complexity of German syntax. It may be that conjunctions are needed to disentangle the relationships between chunks of text embedded in long and complex structures.

8   Halliday and Hasan do not engage with non-textual links.

9   La mayor parte de la gente encontraría bastante ridícula la imagen de nuestro universe como una torre infinita de tortugas, pero ¿en qué nos basamos para creer que lo conocemos mejor? ¿Qué sabemos acerca del universe, y cómo hemos llegado a saberlo? ¿De dónde surgió el universe, y a dónde va? ¿Tuvo el universo un principio, y, si así fue, qué sucedió con anterioridad a él? ¿Cuál es la naturaleza del tiempo? ¿Llegará éste alguna vez a un final? Avances recientes de la física, posibles en parte gracias a fantásticas nuevas tecnologías, sugieren respuestas a algunas de estas preguntas que desde hace mucho tiempo nos preocupan. Algún día estas respuestas podrán parecernos tan obvias como el que la Tierra gire alrededor del Sol, o, quizás, tan ridículas como una torre de tortugas. Sólo el tiempo (cualquiera que sea su significado) lo dirá.

10 Φυσικά, οι περισσότεροι θα έβρισκαν γελοία αυτήν την εικόνα για το Σύμπαν και τη Γη να στηρίζεται σε μία άπειρη σειρά από τραπουλόχαρτα. Θα μπορούσαν όμως να εξηγήσουν το γιατί; Θα μπορούσαν να περιγράψουν τη δική τους εικόνα για το Σύμπαν και να αποδείξουν πως είναι η σωστή; Τι γνωρίζουν οι άνθρωποι για το Σύμπαν και πως το γνωρίζουν; Από πού προέρχεται το Σύμπαν και που πηγαίνει; Υπήρξε αρχή του Σύμπαντος και, αν ναι, τι υπήρξε πριν από αυτήν; Θα υπάρξει τέλος του Σύμπαντος και, αν ναι, τι θα υπάρξει μετά από αυτό; Τι γνωρίζουν οι άνθρωποι για το χρόνο; Υπήρξε αρχή του χρόνου; Θα υπάρξει τέλος του χρόνου; Η σύγχρονη φυσική, με τη βοήθεια και των καταπληκτικών νέων τεχνολογιών, προτείνει απαντήσεις σε αυτά τα αιώνια ερωτήματα. Στο μέλλον αυτές οι απαντήσεις θα μας φαίνονται τόσο ευνόητες όσο μας φαίνεται σήμερα ότι η Γη είναι σφαιρική και κινείται γύρω από τον Ήλιο – ή τόσο ανόητες όσο ότι η Γη είναι επίπεδη και στηρίζεται σε μια άπειρη σειρά από τραπουλόχαρτα. Ευνόητες ή ανόητες; Μόνον ο χρόνος θα δείξει – ό,τι κι αν είναι αυτό που ονομάζεται «χρόνος».

CHAPTER 7

Pragmatic equivalence

translating is an act of communication, involving texts as sets of mutually relevant intentions, in which users (including translators) pre-suppose, implicate and infer meaning.

(Mason 1998:170)

All successful translation is premised on the fact that it is addressed within a specific language, and therefore also to a specific set of practices, a specific form of life.

(Asad 1986/2010:21)

In this chapter we move our discussion of language and translation forward with a brief look at how a given text comes to 'make sense' to a given readership. In doing this, we will be venturing beyond the textual level of connecting sentences and paragraphs together and identifying various textual features. Here, we will be concerned with the way utterances are used in communicative situations and the way we interpret them in context. This is a highly complex but fascinating area of language study, known as **pragmatics**. Pragmatics is the study of language in use. It is the study of meaning, not as generated by the linguistic system but as conveyed and manipulated by participants in a communicative situation. Of the variety of notions that are central to this particular area of language study, I have chosen two which I believe to be particularly helpful in exploring the question of 'making sense' and in highlighting areas of difficulty in cross-cultural communication. These are **coherence** and **implicature**. Those interested in exploring this area further will find references to other relevant notions in the notes at the end of this chapter.

7.1 COHERENCE

7.1.1 Coherence vs cohesion

Like cohesion, **coherence** is a network of relations which organize and create a text: cohesion is the network of surface relations which link words and expressions to other words and expressions in a text, and coherence is the network of conceptual relations which underlie the surface text. Both concern the way stretches of language are connected to each other. In the case of cohesion, stretches of language are connected to each other by virtue of lexical and grammatical dependencies. In the case of coherence, they are connected by virtue of conceptual or meaning dependencies as perceived by language users. Hoey (1991:12) sums up the difference between cohesion and coherence as follows:

> We will assume that cohesion is a property of the text and that coherence is a facet of the reader's evaluation of a text. In other words, cohesion is objective, capable in principle of automatic recognition, while coherence is subjective and judgements concerning it may vary from reader to reader.

We could say that cohesion is the surface expression of coherence relations, that it is a device for making conceptual relations explicit. For instance, a conjunction such as *therefore* may express a conceptual notion of reason or consequence. However, if the reader cannot perceive an underlying semantic relation of reason or consequence between the propositions connected by *therefore*, he or she will not be able to make sense of the text in question; in other words, the text will not 'cohere' for this particular reader. Generally speaking, the mere presence of cohesive markers cannot create a coherent text; cohesive markers have to reflect conceptual relations which make sense. Enkvist (1978:110–111) gives an example of a highly cohesive text that is nevertheless incoherent:

> I bought a Ford. The car in which President Wilson rode down the Champs Elysees was black. Black English has been widely discussed. The discussions between the presidents ended last week. A week has seven days. Every day I feed my cat. Cats have four legs. The cat is on the mat. Mat has three letters.

The possibility of creating a semblance of cohesion which is not supported by underlying semantic relations is sometimes exploited in a few restricted genres, for instance in comedy. However, the fact that we cannot normally make sense of stretches of language like the one quoted above, in spite of the presence of a number of cohesive markers, suggests that what actually gives texture to a stretch of language is not the presence of cohesive markers but our ability to recognize underlying semantic relations which establish continuity of sense. The main value of cohesive markers seems to be that they can be used to facilitate and possibly control the interpretation of underlying semantic relations.

7.1.2 Is coherence a feature of text or situation?

> No text is inherently coherent or incoherent. In the end, it all depends on the receiver, and on his ability to interpret the indications present in the discourse so that, finally, he manages to understand it in a way which seems coherent to him – in a way which corresponds with his idea of what it is that makes a series of actions into an integrated whole.
>
> *(Charolles 1983:95)*

The ability to make sense of a stretch of language depends on the hearer's or reader's expectations and experience of the world. Different societies, and indeed different individuals and groups of individuals within the same society, have different experiences of the world and different views on the way events and situations are organized or related to each other. A network of relations which is valid and makes sense in one society may not be valid in another. This is not just a question of agreeing or disagreeing with a certain view of the world but of being able to make sense of it in the first place. Whether a text is judged as acceptable or not does not depend on how closely it corresponds to some state of affairs in the world, but rather on whether the reader finds the presented version of reality believable, homogeneous or relevant.

The coherence of a text is a result of the interaction between knowledge presented in the text and the reader's own knowledge and experience of the world, the latter being influenced by a variety of factors such as age, sex, race, nationality, education, occupation, and political and religious affiliations. Even a simple cohesive relation of co-reference cannot be recognized, and therefore cannot be said to contribute to the coherence of a text, if it does not fit in with a reader's prior knowledge of the world. Consider, for instance, the following extract from *A Hero from Zero* (p. i) where Tiny Rowland gives an account of how he lost control of the House of Fraser:

> The purchasing power of the proposed fifteen hundred shop outlets would have meant excellent price reductions to customers across Britain and the United States. The flagship, Harrods, had never been integrated with the rest and would demerge to retain its particular character and choice.
>
> It's often written, as a handy journalist's tag, that I suffered from an obsession to control the splendid Knightsbridge store. It would be a very static and limited aim, I think. For Lonrho's purpose, it could have been any well-spread stores group. It was chance, and also roulette, that brought Hugh Fraser, the seller, and Lonrho, the buyer, together in 1977.

There is no explicit cohesive relation in the above extract which tells us that *Harrods* and *the splendid Knightsbridge store* refer to the same thing, except perhaps the use of the definite article in *the splendid Knightsbridge store* and the synonymy between *shop outlets* and *store* (but even that depends for its interpretation on recognizing that *Harrods* is a shop or store of some sort). There is no pronominal reference, for instance, or direct repetition. The relation between the two, and therefore the continuity of sense between the two paragraphs, is, of course, perfectly accessible to any British reader as well as to anyone who is familiar with the famous Harrods store and knows that it is located in Knightsbridge. In translating a document like this, however, one cannot take it for granted that the target reader will have the necessary background knowledge to interpret the co-reference successfully, unless, of course, the translation is aimed at expatriate or immigrant communities in Britain. The Arabic translation provides an explicit link through repetition of 'store'. This makes it clear that Harrods is a store and also establishes continuity of sense in the mind of the target reader by linking *Harrods* in the first paragraph and *the splendid Knightsbridge store* in the second:

Arabic translation:

وكانت القدرة الشرائية المتجمعة لدى 1500 متجر معناها تخفيضات ممتازة فى الأسعار بالنسبة للمشترين فى جميع انحاء بريطانيا والولايات المتحدة. أما **المتجر الرئيسى هارودز** فلم يُضم الى بقية المتاجر واحتفظ به منفصلا عن المجموعة للإبقاء على طابعه المتميز ومجالات الإختيار المتوفرة فيه.

وكثيراً ما كتب عنى فى الدوائر الصحفية أننى أعانى من الحاح مرضى يدفعنى دفعاً الى محاولة السيطرة على **متجر نايتسبردج الفاخر**. .

> The combined purchasing power of 1500 stores meant excellent reductions in prices for buyers in all parts of Britain and the United States. As for the main store Harrods, it was not integrated with the rest of the stores and was kept separate from the rest in order to retain its distinctive character and the areas of choice available in it.
>
> It has often been written about me in journalistic circles that I suffer from a sick obsession which pushes me to try and control the splendid Knightsbridge store …

We could perhaps say that texts are neither coherent nor incoherent by themselves, that whether a text coheres or not depends on the ability of the reader to make sense of it by relating it to what he or she already knows or to a familiar world, whether this world is real or fictional. A text which coheres for one reader may therefore not cohere for another. Different linguists have different views as to whether this phenomenon implies that meaning is a property of a text or a property of a communicative situation involving participants and settings in addition to a text. Blum-Kulka's definition of coherence as 'a covert potential meaning relationship among parts of a text, made overt by the reader or listener through processes of interpretation' (1986:17) implies that she sees meaning, or coherence, as a property of a text, even though it is only accessible through processes of interpretation. Sinclair (personal communication) similarly states that processes such as 'the recall of past experience and knowledge of the world … are not part of the meaning of a text, but part of the human apparatus for working out the meaning of a text', which again suggests that meaning exists in texts but can only be accessed through various processes of interpretation on the part of the reader. By contrast, Firth (1964:111) asserts that '"meaning" is a property of the mutually relevant people, things, events in the situation', and Kirsten Malmkjær (personal communication) does not accept the view that meaning is *in* text and suggests instead that 'meanings arise in situations involving language'.

Whether one holds the view that meaning exists in text or in situations involving text in addition to other variables such as participants and settings, one cannot deny that a reader's cultural and intellectual background determine how much sense he or she gets out of a text. In the final analysis, a reader can only make sense of a text by analysing the linguistic elements which constitute it against the backdrop of his or her own knowledge and experience. It therefore seems reasonable to suggest that, regardless of whether meaning is a property of text or situation, coherence is not a feature of text as such but of the judgement made by a reader on a text. As far as translation is concerned, this means that the range and type of difficulties encountered will not so much depend on the source text itself as 'on the significance of the translated text for its readers as members of a certain culture, or of a sub-group within that culture, with the constellation of knowledge, judgement and perception they have developed from it' (Snell-Hornby 1988:42). Even when addressing members of their own linguistic community, writers will word their messages differently depending on the nature of the audience they have in mind, whether it consists of adults or children, specialists or non-specialists, and so on. Like any writer, a translator has to take account of the range of knowledge available to his or her target readers and of the expectations they are likely to have about such things as the organization of the world, the organization of language in general, the organization and conventions of particular text types, the structure of social relations, and the appropriateness or inappropriateness of certain kinds of linguistic and non-linguistic behaviour, among other things. These are all factors which influence the coherence of a text in varying degrees because, as human beings, we can only make sense of new information in terms of our own knowledge, beliefs and previous experience of both linguistic and non-linguistic events.

7.2 COHERENCE AND PROCESSES OF INTERPRETATION: IMPLICATURE

Charolles (1983) suggests that a reader may see a certain continuity of sense between parts of an utterance and still fail to understand it fully (inasmuch as it is possible to understand any stretch of language 'fully'). Consider, for instance, the following stretch of language:

I went to the cinema.   The beer was good.

This is a perfectly coherent, if decontextualized, piece of language. Charolles explains that anyone who hears or reads it will reach the following interpretation: the speaker says that he or she went to the cinema, that he or she drank beer at the cinema and that the beer in question was good. Note that we naturally provide the necessary links to render the discourse coherent. There is nothing in the above utterance which tells us explicitly that the speaker drank the beer or that he or she did so at the cinema. Charolles calls this type of minimal coherence **supplemental coherence**. He suggests that there is another type of coherence, which he calls

explanatory coherence, which not only establishes continuity of senses but, unlike supplemental coherence, also *justifies* it. The difference between supplemental interpretations and explanatory interpretations, Charolles suggests (1983:93), is that:

> the former never lead to the explication of a thematic continuity (they indicate that an element is repeated from one segment to another), whereas the latter justify this continuity (they lead to the manifestation of the reason why a certain thing is said supplementally about an element).

Explanatory coherence is achieved when, given the right context and the necessary knowledge of setting and participants, one can reach an interpretation such as this: the speaker says he or she went to the cinema. The film the speaker saw was bad – so bad that the only good thing he or she can find to say about it is that the beer he or she drank there was good. But how does a speaker signal or a hearer interpret this kind of implied meaning? How do we achieve explanatory coherence?

One of the most important notions to have emerged in text studies in relatively recent years is that of **implicature** – the question of how it is that we come to understand more than is actually said. Grice (1975) uses the term **implicature** to refer to what the speaker means or implies rather than what he or she literally says. Implicature is not to be confused with non-literal meaning, for instance with idiomatic meaning. Idiomatic meaning is conventional, and its interpretation depends on a good mastery of the linguistic system in question rather than on a successful interpretation of a particular speaker's intended or implied meaning in a given context. For instance, in the following exchange

> A: Shall we go for a walk?
> B: Could I take a rain check on that?

the successful interpretation of B's response depends on knowing the conventional meaning of *take a rain check* in American English ('to decline to accept an offer or invitation immediately but indicate willingness to accept it at a later date'). No conversational implicature is involved here. Compare this with a similar exchange which does not involve the use of an idiom:

> A: Shall we go for a walk?
> B: It's raining.

How does A, or anyone observing the scene, know how to relate the utterance 'It's raining' – a mere comment on the weather – to the question of going for a walk? Why do we assume that 'It's raining' is meant as an answer to the above question? One answer which has already been suggested is that we do it in order to maintain the assumption of coherence. If we do accept it as an answer, how do we know how to interpret it? Does it mean 'No, we'd better not because it's raining', 'OK, but we'd better take an umbrella', or perhaps 'Yes – we both like walking in the rain'? Note also that the same utterance *It's raining* can mean something totally different in a different context:

> A: What is Jane up to these days?
> B: It's raining!

Here, Speaker A would probably interpret B's comment on the weather as meaning something like 'I don't want to talk about this subject' or possibly, depending on B's tone of voice and facial expression, 'You're out of line – you shouldn't be asking me this question'.

Grice suggests that a speaker can signal an implied meaning conventionally or non-conventionally. To signal an implied meaning conventionally, a speaker uses the textual resources which are conventionally understood to signal certain relationships between propositions. Conjunctions such as *therefore*, *because* and *in spite of* are one such textual resource. Grammatical structure is another. For instance, in 'It's money that they want' the grammatical structure itself conventionally presupposes what is expressed in the subordinate clause, in this case 'they want something' (see discussion of information structure in Chapter 5, section 5.1.2).[1]

But how does a speaker signal (or a hearer interpret) meaning which is not conventionally coded in the language? Before I proceed to give an account of Grice's answer to this question, I have to point out that Grice is not primarily concerned with written text. In fact, not only does he restrict his comments to spoken exchanges, he restricts them to a very small sub-set of these – namely question/answer sequences. There is no doubt that Grice's preoccupation with speech means that his views are sometimes difficult to relate to written communication. Although speech and writing share many features, they are not the same thing. Having said that, I believe that Grice's views do have important applications in translation. I therefore propose to play down the inadequacy of Grice's theory of implicature in terms of its application to written discourse in order to explore its general relevance to translation.

Grice suggests that discourse has certain important features: for instance, it is connected (i.e. it does not consist of unrelated sequences); it has a purpose; and it is a co-operative effort. These features give rise to a general principle of communication, the **Co-operative Principle**, which participants are expected to observe:

> Make your conversational contribution such as is required, at the stage at which it occurs, by the accepted purpose or direction of the talk exchange in which you are engaged.
>
> *(Grice 1975:45)*

Implied meaning which is not signalled conventionally derives from the Co-operative Principle and a number of maxims associated with it: Quantity, Quality, Relevance (Relation) and Manner:

1. Quantity
   (a) Make your contribution as informative as is required (for the current purposes of the exchange).
   (b) Do not make your contribution more informative than is required.
2. Quality
   'Try to make your contribution one that is true', specifically:
   (a) Do not say what you believe to be false.
   (b) Do not say that for which you lack adequate evidence.
3. Relevance
   Make your contributions relevant to the current exchange.
4. Manner
   Be perspicuous, specifically:
   (a) Avoid obscurity of expression.
   (b) Avoid ambiguity.
   (c) Be brief (avoid unnecessary prolixity).
   (d) Be orderly.

The principles outlined above provide points of orientation rather than strict rules which have to be followed by language users. We can and do refuse to adhere to the maxims in some situations: for instance, a participant may try to avoid adhering to one or more of the maxims in order to evade a topic or question. This is often the case in political interviews. In spoken discourse, the other participant can always request that the maxims be adhered to. Blum-Kulka (1983) gives several such examples from political interviews on Israeli television. When an interviewer says to Mr Peres 'Mr Peres, if we can get down to concrete facts …' (*ibid.*:138), he is in effect invoking the maxims of manner and relation by asking Mr Peres to address the point being raised. Grice's maxims thus provide a point of orientation for participants even when they are flouted, so that flouting them is recognized as a way of exploiting the convention in order to convey an intended meaning. This is explained in more detail below. For the moment, it is sufficient to note that conversational maxims and the implicatures that result from observing or flouting them are adapted to serve the purpose of the communication in hand. This purpose will vary according to the situation and participants: it may be conveying information, influencing the opinions or emotions of hearers, directing their actions and so on.

Now, if as language users we recognize and generally abide by something like Grice's Co-operative Principle, then the reason we assume that an utterance which follows a question provides an answer to that question becomes obvious: we assume that both addresser and addressee are operating the Co-operative Principle, and in particular the maxim of Relevance. We will therefore go out of our way to find an interpretation that will connect it to the previous utterance. We attribute relevance to what we hear and read even when it appears, on the surface, to be unrelated to the preceding discourse, and regardless of whether a relation is explicitly signalled. For example, on hearing or seeing the statement

> Elizabeth is putting on a lot of weight. She smokes very heavily.

we will naturally strive to relate the two propositions somehow. We may infer that the speaker implies that Elizabeth is putting on a lot of weight *because* she is smoking too heavily, or the other way round: that she is smoking too heavily because she is putting on a lot of weight, perhaps as a way of controlling her appetite. A less likely, but nevertheless feasible, inference is that Elizabeth is putting on a lot of weight *in spite of* the fact that she is smoking too heavily. Yet another possible inference would be that Elizabeth is letting herself go, her health is on the decline, she is not looking after herself as she should do. Pragmatic inferences of this type are essential to maintaining the coherence of discourse. Levinson (1983) overstates the case a little when he suggests that such inferences arise to preserve the assumption of co-operation and that without them many adjacent utterances would appear to be unrelated to each other or to the discourse in hand. Nevertheless, there is a great deal of truth in what he says. Which inferences we do draw will naturally depend on a variety of factors such as our knowledge of the world, of such things as the relationship between smoking, appetite and weight; our knowledge of participants in the discourse, of the speaker, and of Elizabeth; our knowledge of and fluency in the specific language being used, and so on.

Implicatures, then, are pragmatic inferences which allow us to achieve something like Charolles' explanatory coherence. They are aspects of meaning which are over and above the literal and conventional meaning of an utterance and they depend for their interpretation on a recognition of the Co-operative Principle and its maxims. Apart from observing the maxims, a language user can deliberately flout a maxim and in doing so produce what Grice calls a **conversational implicature**. For instance, if used as a genuine question the utterance *Do you know what time it is?* conveys the meaning 'I do not know the time; I wish to know the time'. Levinson (1983) calls this type of meaning a **standard implicature**. If the same utterance is used as a rhetorical question, in the right context and with the appropriate intonation, it could convey a meaning such as 'You are very late'. This is what Grice would call a **conversational implicature**. It is achieved by flouting the maxim of Quality which demands sincerity. Conversational implicature can be conveyed by flouting any or several of the maxims. To use one of Grice's examples: imagine that a professor of philosophy is asked to supply a testimonial for a candidate for a position in the field of philosophy. He or she replies that the candidate's manners are impeccable and his or her handwriting is extremely legible. How does the addressee interpret this testimonial? Knowing that the professor in question is in a position to comment directly on the candidate's strengths and weaknesses in the area of philosophy but apparently refuses to do so, he or she must still assume that the professor is observing the maxims, particularly the maxim of Relevance. According to Grice, what is implicated by the speaker 'would be what he might expect the hearer to suppose him to think in order to preserve the idea that the maxims are, after all, not being violated' (1981:185). The addressee therefore infers that the professor is implying something by his or her reply, in this case that the candidate is no good at philosophy.

The Co-operative Principle and its maxims can account for the fact that we do not abandon contributions such as those described above as irrelevant, but they do not directly explain how we arrive at a particular inference or, in Grice's terms, a conversational implicature.[2] This is a difficult topic which remains largely unresolved. For one thing, conversational implicatures are often indeterminate. For another, an utterance may be open to several possible interpretations. This may or may not be intentional on the part of the speaker. In either case, it complicates the task of the translator who may knowingly or unknowingly eliminate certain possible interpretations of the original from the target text. The translator may even inadvertently give rise to other interpretations which are not derivable from the original text. Both situations can arise because of constraints imposed on the translator by the structure of the target language, the nature of the target audience and the conventions of the target culture.

Indeterminacy aside, Grice details a number of factors which can contribute to our success or failure in working out implicatures. These are:

1. the conventional meaning of the words and structures used (i.e. a mastery of the language system), together with the identity of any references that may be involved;
2. the Co-operative Principle and its maxims;
3. the context, linguistic or otherwise, of the utterance;
4. other items of background knowledge; and
5. the fact (or supposed fact) that all relevant items falling under the previous headings are available to both participants and both participants know or assume this to be the case.

7.3 COHERENCE, IMPLICATURE AND TRANSLATION STRATEGIES

Let us now look at the above factors in some detail. Grice himself suggested them as, in his own words, 'data' on which 'the hearer will reply' in working out whether a particular conversational implicature is present (1975:50). But they also provide a good basis for exploring the whole question of coherence. The following discussion will therefore consider how these factors might relate not only to working out implicatures but to the question of coherence in general and to common problems and strategies in translation.

For an alternative view of inferential processes in communication see Sperber and Wilson (1986) and Gutt (1991/2000, 2005).

7.3.1 The conventional meanings of words and structures and the identity of references

7.3.1.1 The conventional meanings of words and structures

This is an obvious point. If we do not understand the meanings of the words and structures used in a text, we cannot work out its implied meanings. Knowledge of the language system may not be sufficient, but it is essential if one is to understand what is going on in any kind of verbal communication. This means that any mistranslation of words and structures in the source text may well affect the calculability of implicatures in the target text. An example of this was given in Chapter 3, repeated here for convenience. The example is from *A Hero from Zero* (p. 59):

> All this represents only a part of all that Forbes Magazine reported on Fayed in the March issue mentioned before. In 1983, he had approached the industrialist Robert O. Anderson under the cover of a commission agent. The industrialist had been struck by his appearance as someone with <u>modest means</u>. Mr. Anderson was therefore astonished by his sudden acquisition of a considerable fortune.

The mistranslation of the description of Mohamed Fayed's appearance in the Arabic text, where *modest means* was rendered as 'his appearance suggests modesty and simplicity', makes the original implicature quite incalculable. The reader of both source and target texts must assume that the writer's description of Fayed's appearance is relevant and is meant to be as informative as is necessary for the purposes of the communication. The writer cannot be disregarding the maxims of Relevance and Quantity unless the Co-operative Principle is not being adhered to, and there is no reason to suspect that it is not. Therefore, the writer is implying something by describing Fayed's appearance. Given the co-text and context of the above extract and the relevant background knowledge, most readers of the source text will infer that Fayed has come to wealth suddenly and, quite possibly, by dishonest means. This implicature is difficult to calculate in Arabic because of the mistranslation of *modest means*. The Arab reader is left feeling somewhat unsure of how to interpret the favourable description of Fayed as simple and modest in a context which otherwise seems to suggest that he is anything but a 'nice person'.

As well as the conventional meaning of words, each language also employs conventionalized expressions and patterns of conveying implicatures. In other words, in every language there will be conventional associations between certain linguistic patterns and certain inferable meanings. These patterns are identifiable and are sometimes recorded in grammars. They are not necessarily associated with the same range of meanings in other languages. For instance, rhetorical questions such as *Isn't that an ugly building?* (instead of 'This is an ugly building') or *How can you be so cruel?* (instead of 'You are very cruel') are regularly used in English to express a range of emotive meanings such as indignation, shock and amusement (*COBUILD*

English Grammar, Sinclair 1990:205–206). Fixed expressions modelled on rhetorical questions, such as *Haven't you done well?* or *Don't I know it?*, are often ironic.[3] Likewise, far from being a literal request for feedback, the expression *Correct me if I'm wrong* suggests 'I know I'm right' (Duff 1990) and can therefore be quite irritating.

Louw (1993, 2000) and Sinclair (1999) discuss a fascinating feature of language patterning which was first identified, without being named as such, by Sinclair (1987a, 1991). Now known as **semantic prosody**, this feature gives rise to very subtle implicatures which are often processed subliminally, without the speaker or hearer necessarily being conscious of the attitude being expressed by the item in question.[4] Louw (1993:157) defines semantic prosody as 'a consistent aura of meaning with which a form is imbued by its collocates';[5] this 'aura of meaning' can be positive or negative, but more commonly it is negative (Louw 2000). Sinclair (1999) considers it an aspect of 'attitudinal or pragmatic meaning' and gives the example of *happen* in English. Here are some of the concordance lines he uses to demonstrate that despite its standard, attitudinally neutral meaning of 'take place', *happen* is often imbued with negative meaning:

> Something is going to <u>happen</u> to him unless he pulls himself together.
> I knew something terrible would <u>happen.</u>
> Accidents can <u>happen</u> in spite of rules and regulations.
> What I had feared might <u>happen</u> was <u>happening</u>.
> I was worried about what would <u>happen</u> when the public realized this.
> I'm always expecting something calamitous to <u>happen</u>.

Semantic prosody is not restricted to single words such as verbs and nouns. The expression *with/to/by the naked eye*, for example, has a semantic prosody of difficulty (Sinclair 1991), as is evident in the following examples from the *Translational English Corpus*:[6]

> In painting, as in music and literature, what is often termed abstract strikes me as being simply representative of a more delicate and elusive reality which is barely visible <u>to the naked eye</u>. (Source: *Discovering the World*, by Clarice Lispetor; translated from Brazilian Portuguese by Giovanni Pontiero)

> Her eyesight was so strong that she was able to extract a tiny piece of glass, hardly visible <u>to the naked eye</u>, from Aziza's fingertip using a pair of eyebrow tweezers. (Source: *The Golden Chariot*, by Salwa Bakr; translated from Arabic by Dinah Manisty)

> ... the dislocation could not be observed, at this altitude a speed of seven hundred and fifty metres per hour cannot be captured <u>by the naked eye</u>, ... (Source: *The Stone Raft*, by José Saramago; translated from Portuguese by Giovanni Pontiero)

What is particularly interesting about this feature of language patterning is that departure from the typical prosody of an item can generate irony or sarcasm, among other rhetorical effects, as is evident in this example of *with the naked eye*, also from the *Translational English Corpus*:

> I was confronted with bags and boxes of provisions, and my mother tasting a bit of rice and saying, 'They're obviously mean. God help us! You can count the cardamon pods and cumin seeds <u>with the naked eye</u>.' (Source: *Women of Sand and Myrrh*, by Hanan Al-Shaykh; translated from Arabic by Catharine Cobham)

Translators need to be alert to the subtle implicatures conveyed by semantic prosody as well as those communicated when a prosody is exploited for rhetorical effect. Kenny (1998:520) explains why:

> There are instances, for example, where the reader of an original text and its translation may feel that the translation is somehow tamer than the original, or that it paints a less bleak picture of a situation than did the original. It is often difficult, however, to say precisely why one has this feeling. One might be able to put one's finger on particular points in the text where certain passages have been toned down ..., but one may be left with a vague suspicion that there is more to it than that; that there is somehow a different attitude dispersed over the pages of the target text.

Finally, typographic features also play a role in conveying certain implicatures. In English, the use of inverted commas around a word or expression in the body of a text can suggest a range of implied meanings. It can suggest disagreement with the way a word or expression is used, emphasis, irony or tentativeness about the appropriateness or applicability of an expression. Other languages may prefer to convey similar meanings lexically or grammatically. Problems arise in translation when the function of such patterns is not recognized and a literal or near-literal transfer of form distorts the original implicature or conveys a different one. For example, Loveday (1982b:364) explains that in Japanese 'it is generally regarded as unrefined to clearly mark the end of one's utterance, and so the ending is frequently left hanging with a word like "nevertheless"'. A literal translation of this type of pattern into English would no doubt confuse a reader and may encourage him or her to read more into the utterance than might be intended.

7.3.1.2 The identity and import of any references mentioned in the text

The ability to identify references to participants, entities, events and practices is essential for drawing inferences and for maintaining the coherence of a text. A proper name or even a reference to a type of food or gadget which is unknown to the reader can disrupt the continuity of the text and obscure the relevance of any statement associated with it. Many of the examples discussed under **translation by cultural substitution** in Chapter 2 illustrate the translator's awareness of this problem and offer one type of strategy for overcoming it. A further example is given below, from *A Hero from Zero*. The source language of this particular extract is French. It is the opening paragraph of an article on Mohamed Fayed which appeared in one of Haiti's leading daily newspapers, *Le Matin*. The article is translated into English and incorporated into the English source document. The Arabic version of the article may have been translated from the French original or the English translation:

French source text (p. 51):

> Il y avait nombre d'années qu'on avait pas entendu parler de lui. Et voilà que dans son numéro du 7 Mars 1988. Le Magazine Américain 'forbes' le campe sous son vrai visage. Le qualificatif 'd'aventurier oriental' que lui avait collé un journal Haitien édité par des membres de la diaspora à New-York n'est rien au regard de ce qu'il représente vraiment. En vérité, il ferait pâlir <u>Arsène Lupin</u>.

English translation (p. 57):

> It's been quite a few years since we have heard him mentioned. And then, in its 7th March 1988 issue, the American Forbes Magazine painted his true picture. The description of 'oriental adventurer' given to him by a Haitian paper edited by members of the 'Diaspora' in New York is nothing in relation to what he really is. Indeed, he would frighten even **Arsène Lupin. (A French version of Boris Karloff.)**

Arabic translation (p. 67):

> ‏. . . ‏فالحق أنه شخصية كفيلة بأن تخيف **أرسين لوبين** نفسه.

> For the truth is that he is a character capable of frightening **Arsène Lupin** himself.

The reference to Arsène Lupin in the above extract may not cause a problem to many Arab readers, or at least the Arab translator does not seem to think it would. Most of Arsène Lupin's stories are translated into Arabic and his name will probably suggest the familiar image of a resourceful and cunning thief. The Arabic translation therefore does not provide an elaboration of the reference.[7] By contrast, Arsène Lupin is virtually unknown to the average English reader. The English translator attempts to bridge the gap between the textual world and the world of the target reader by explaining the unfamiliar (Arsène Lupin) in terms of the familiar (Boris Karloff). The strategy itself is fine, but Arsène Lupin has very little in common with

Boris Karloff. The former is the hero of a series of French detective-type stories: a thief; flamboyant, resourceful and elusive, but nevertheless a thief. The latter is a British actor associated mainly with horror films.

Identifying reference is not just a question of identifying roughly who or what the referent is but, crucially, of knowing enough about the referent to interpret the particular associations it is meant to trigger in our minds in a given context. Referents are not featureless beings and entities; they have specific histories, physical and social features, and are associated with particular contexts. It is the ability to interpret the significance of a given reference and the way it links with other features of the context and co-text that contributes to the continuity of sense or coherence of a text and enables us to draw any intended implicatures. The distinction between identifying reference and other items of background knowledge (7.3.4. below) is perhaps not a useful one to draw.

The ability to identify a referent may also be influenced by one's perspective. In the following example from *China's Panda Reserves*, 'we' is ambiguous in the Chinese translation:

English source text:

> Many of the species growing wild here are familiar to <u>us</u> as plants cultivated in European gardens – species like this exotic lily.

Target text (Chinese):

> 这里野生的许多种类我们很熟悉，是欧洲园林内种植的种类 – 像这 – 奇异的百合花等种类。

> \<With> many varieties of the wild life here **we** are very familiar, \<they> are the kinds grown in European gardens – varieties like this strange unique lily flower.

The Chinese reader may find it difficult to identify the referent of 'we', particularly since it contrasts with 'European gardens'. It may not be clear whether the text is written from the European or Chinese perspective.

7.3.2 The Co-operative Principle and its maxims

Grice suggests that the Co-operative Principle and its maxims are not arbitrary but are a feature of any rational behaviour, be it linguistic or non-linguistic. He gives examples of non-linguistic events in which all the maxims are seen to apply as they would in any verbal encounter. If someone is assisting you to mend a car and you ask for four screws, you do not expect to be handed two or six (Quantity); if you are mixing ingredients for a cake you do not expect to be handed a good book (Relevance), and so on. This suggests that the Co-operative Principle and its maxims are universal, on the assumption that linguistic behaviour is just one type of rational behaviour and that all human beings are rational. Levinson (1983) seems to support this suggestion. However, not all linguists would accept it quite so readily, and there is, in fact, some evidence to the contrary. Bible translators who regularly work with languages and cultures considerably different from those at the centre of linguistic and academic enquiry are quicker to voice their suspicion and to consider the possibility that the Co-operative Principle and its maxims are not universal. Thomson (1982:11) considers the possibility that:

> a certain type of implicature, say quality implicature, is never used by the speakers of a particular language, or that the contexts in which a type of implicature will be used will differ from one language community to the next.

Even within the same cultural and linguistic community, there are sometimes special contexts in which one or more of the maxims do not apply. The maxim of Quantity is usually in abeyance in adversarial court questioning (Levinson 1983). Here, it is mutually understood that it is the legal counsel's job to extract damaging statements from the defendant and that the latter's job is to resist that. This is an example of a non-co-operative context in which one participant, the defendant, tries to be as unco-operative as possible.

There is also the question of whether the list of maxims proposed by Grice is exhaustive and whether the maxims have the same value in different cultures. Grice himself conceded that the four maxims do not represent an exhaustive list and suggested that other maxims such as 'Be polite' may be added. In some cultures, 'Be polite' indeed seems to override all other maxims. Loveday (1982b:364) explains that '"No" almost constitutes a term of abuse in Japanese and equivocation, exiting or even lying is preferred to its use'. If this is true, it would suggest that the maxims of Quality and Manner are easily overriden by considerations of politeness in some cultures. At any rate, it certainly seems to cause cross-cultural difficulties, with serious consequences in some cases. When President Nixon expressed his concern about excessive Japanese textile exports to the United States to Premier Sato in 1970, 'Sato answered *zensho shimasu*, a phrase literally translated as "I'll handle it as well as I can". To Nixon, this meant, "I'll take care of it", that is Sato would settle the problem and find some way to curtail the exports. To Sato, however, it was merely a polite way of ending the conversation' (Gibney, quoted in Loveday 1982a:14).

Different cultures have different norms of 'polite' behaviour. They also have different ideas about what is and what is not a 'taboo' area. Sex, religion and defecation are taboo subjects in many societies, but not necessarily to the same degree within similar situations. Whatever the norms of polite behaviour in the target culture, it is important to note that in some translation contexts being polite can be far more important than being accurate. A translator may decide to omit or replace whole stretches of text which violate the reader's expectations of how a taboo subject should be handled – if at all – in order to avoid giving offence. For example, if translated 'accurately' into Arabic, the following extract from *Arab Political Humour* by

Kishtainy would no doubt be very offensive to the average Arab reader, for whom God is not a subject of ridicule and sexual organs are strictly taboo:

> The intricate and delicate configuration of the characters of the Arabic alphabet together with the customary omission of the vowels helped to create endless jibes and jokes which are completely confined to the Arabic reader. You only need a tiny dot, for example, to turn the letter R into Z. With the playful or accidental addition of such a dot the word *rabbi* (my God) can be turned into *zubbi* (my penis)! The door was thus opened for one satirical wit to make his dutiful comment and correct an otherwise unwarranted statement. Some humble person married a rich widow with whose money he built himself an imposing mansion which he piously adorned with the legend, carefully engraved over the door, 'Such are the blessings of my God' (*Hada min fadl rabbi*). The local wit hastened under cover of darkness to put matters right by adding the missing dot to change the hallowed phrase into 'Such are the blessings of my penis'.
>
> *(1985:12–13)*

In the published Arabic translation, all reference to *rabbi* and *zubbi* is omitted. The above example is replaced by a much 'tamer' one[8] where, by adding and omitting dots on various letters, the local wit turns a poem which is originally written in praise of Arabs into one that ridicules them. A similarly offensive extract (p. 14 in the English text), does not appear in the Arabic translation at all:

> The sarcastic misuse of names has not been always as polite or free from resort to the equivalent of the English four-letter words. In the fierce and often bloody strife between the Ba'th Party and the Nasserists and Communists, the opponents of the Ba'th played on the strange name of the founder and leader of the Ba'th Party, Michel Aflaq. One of the latest exercises in this respect was the discovery in Al-Muhit lexicon that Aflaq meant in archaic Arabic 'wide and loose vagina and stupid, sluttish woman'.

The existence of the additional maxim 'Be polite' and the overriding importance it tends to assume in many cultures may explain intelligent decisions taken in the course of translation which could otherwise seem haphazard and irresponsible. For interesting discussions and exemplification of the notion of politeness in the context of translation and interpreting, see Berk-Seligson (1988), Hatim and Mason (1997, Chapter 5), Hickey (2000), Arnáiz (2006) and Glinert (2010).

Going back to the question of whether Grice's proposed maxims have the same value in different cultures, Headland (1981) explains that the Dumagats have great difficulty in understanding the scriptures because of what he calls 'information overload'. By Dumagat standards, the Bible apparently gives far too much information. He illustrates his point through an overstatement of the case (*ibid.*:20):

> A Koine Greek and a Dumagat would both describe the shooting of a duck, but in different ways. The Greek would say, in describing the event, 'A few minutes after dawn, a large and beautifully plumed white female duck flew overhead just south of my hiding place. I quickly fired two shells with number sixteen lead shot, and the duck dropped nicely in front of me just five yards away, at the edge of the lake.' A Dumagat who had had the same experience would say, 'Yesterday I shot a duck.'

If Headland's comments are accurate, then how does the phenomenon of 'information overload' relate to Grice's maxim of Quantity? For one thing, it seems to suggest that the instruction 'do not make your contribution more informative than is required' can be interpreted quite differently by different cultures. Hatim and Mason's comment on this particular maxim is that 'What is "required" for any given communicative purpose within a TL cultural environment is … a matter for the translator's judgement' (1990:94).

An important factor which seems to override Grice's maxims and support the possibility that they are both language- and culture-specific relates to norms of discourse organization and rhetorical functions in different languages. Clyne (1981) suggests that, unlike English, German discourse is non-linear and favours digressions. In some extreme cases, such as Fritz Schutze's *Sprache soziologisch gesehen*, there are 'not only digressions [*Exkurse*], but also digressions from digressions. Even within the conclusion, there are digressions' (*ibid.*:63). Not only does the maxim of Relevance need to be redefined in view of these comments, but the non-linear organization of German discourse also seems to require a reassessment of another maxim: 'Be brief'. Clyne (*ibid.*) explains how 'every time the author returns to the *main* line of argument, he has to recapitulate up to the point before the last digression, resulting in much repetition'. One wonders how an organizational feature such as this relates to the maxims of Relevance and Manner. Can this apparent violation of the maxims render a German text partially incoherent if it is not adjusted in translation? An English translation of a German book, Norbert Dittmar's *Soziolinguistik*, was apparently felt to be chaotic and lacking in focus and cohesiveness, although the original was considered a landmark in its field by Germans (Clyne 1981).

Arabic is well known to use repetition as a major rhetorical device. This includes repetition of both form and substance, so that the same information is repeated again and again in a variety of ways in an effort to convince by assertion. This style of argumentative prose is seen by non-Arabs as too verbose and certainly anything but brief. The Japanese favourite 'dot-type' pattern in which anecdotes are strung together without an explicit link or conclusion can infuriate western readers who demand relevance of a type familiar to them. Loveday notes that 'westerners often react to this with "so what!!", considering the presentation shallow' (1982b:364). Different rhetorical conventions are therefore seen to apply in different cultures, and they can override a maxim such as 'Be brief' or 'Be relevant'. In fact, these conventions provide a context for interpreting the maxims.

Grice's notion of implicature is extremely useful to anyone engaged in cross-cultural communication, but it cannot be taken at face value. The maxims on which the Co-operative Principle is based have rightly been criticized as vague and ill-defined by various linguists. Sperber and Wilson, for instance, suggest that 'appeals to the "maxim of relation" are no more than dressed-up appeals to intuition' (1986:36). One question which readily comes to mind is this: how does Grice's notion of Relevance relate to the issue of a participant's level of interest in a particular topic and the way this, in turn, relates to the maxim of Quantity? Does 'relevant' imply 'of personal interest' and does it control the interpretation of 'Make your contribution as informative as is required'? This issue is particularly important in any translation activity which involves some form of rewriting, such as editing or summarizing. It raises questions which are not easy to answer because they have to do with how well the maxims transfer from speech to writing, that is, from a context which involves a single receptor to one which often involves an undefined range of receptors. An example from a translation which involves a significant degree of rewriting may help to illustrate the problem.

A well-known Egyptian journalist, Mohammed Heikal, published a book in 1983 about the assassination of the former Egyptian president Anwar Sadat. He wrote the book, *Autumn of Fury*, originally in English and later translated it himself into Arabic. Being in the rather special position of author/translator, Heikal clearly felt free to make whatever changes seemed necessary to appeal to the Arab reader in the translated version. The Arabic version is significantly longer and more detailed than the English original. For instance, the description of Sadat's wounds and his state on arrival at the hospital is done in one paragraph in the English version (see Chapter 5, p.164) but is expanded into four pages in the Arabic version. A chapter entitled 'Organized loot' in the English version describes the systematic looting of Egypt's resources by Sadat's relatives and favourites. The description is far more detailed in the expanded Arabic version (twenty-nine pages compared with seventeen pages in the English version). How do writers/translators such as Heikal balance the two maxims of Relevance and Quantity in renegotiating a text for a different readership?

Weaknesses of definition aside, it is interesting that Grice's maxims seem to reflect notions which are known to be valued in the English-speaking world, for instance sincerity, brevity and relevance. Robinson suggests that they are even more restricted in their applicability, describing them as 'redolent of the white masculine professional middle-class culture of the past hundred-odd years in England and the U.S.' (2003:128). The values they encode do not necessarily have the same resonance or relevance in other cultures, nor should they be expected to represent any ideal basis for communication. Loveday (1982b:363) asserts that 'the highly cherished norm of linguistic precision in Western culture cannot be taken for granted and is not universally sanctioned by every society', and Clyne (1981:65) rightly suggests that the emphasis on relevance 'may impede cross-reference, one of the most important aspects of discourse', and wonders whether it might lead to the suppression of associations. 'Just as there are Anglo-Saxon readers who dismiss some German academic writings as "chaotic"', he suggests in another article, 'there are German readers who find English-language publications too "narrow" or conclude that they are not saying very much' (1983:43).

We have seen that the suggestion that Grice's maxims are universal is difficult to justify. A more plausible suggestion would be that all discourse, in any language, is essentially co-operative, and that the phenomenon of implicature (rather than the specific maxims suggested by Grice) is universal. In other words, the interpretation of a maxim or the maxims themselves may differ from one linguistic community to another, but the process of conveying intended meaning by means of exploiting whatever maxims are in operation in that community will be the same. This position is much more tenable, particularly since it seems to be a feature of language use in general that it is based partly on adhering to constraints and partly on manipulating constraints to produce special effects.

7.3.3 The context, linguistic or otherwise, of the utterance

The context in which an utterance occurs determines the range of implicatures that may sensibly be derived from it. Sperber and Wilson suggest that 'the context does much more than filter out inappropriate interpretations; it provides premises without which the implicature cannot be inferred at all' (1986:37). Apart from the actual setting and the participants involved in an exchange, the context also includes the co-text and the linguistic conventions of a community in general.

Tse (1988) explains that in translating a text which describes an experiment in which the medical histories of patients were recorded on micro-chip medical record cards, one of the main difficulties resulted from differences in the source and target contexts. The text, 'Patients test micro-chip medical record card' (the *Independent*, 28 April 1988), states:

> Dr. Robert Stevens, whose study in Wales involves one group practice and one pharmacy, said patients' reaction to the cards had been favourable.

In the United Kingdom, a pharmacy is an establishment which dispenses medicine on the basis of prescriptions signed by a doctor. For an English reader, therefore, it makes sense to suggest that both group practices (i.e. groups of doctors working through the same clinic) and pharmacies can be involved in recording the medical histories of patients. Tse explains that 'both in China and in Hong Kong, a patient can receive medical treatment and medicines from a doctor's surgery. A pharmacy is a place where one can buy tablets without prescriptions' (1988:38). It would thus not make sense to a Chinese reader to suggest that pharmacies can or should be involved in an exercise of this sort. If they do not dispense medicine on the basis of prescriptions, how can they be expected to monitor patients' medical histories?

The inability to relate a piece of information to his or her own context can lead the reader to draw the wrong inferences from a text. Rommel (1987) explains that whereas the size of a house or flat is indicated in Britain by the number of bedrooms, it is normally indicated in Switzerland by the total number of rooms. A German version of Oscar Wilde's *The Importance of Being Earnest* which was shown in Zurich some time ago drew what Rommel refers to as a 'vulgar snigger' from the audience when Lady Bracknell asked *Wieviel Schlafzimmer* (literally 'How many bedrooms?') instead of adjusting the question to the realities of the Swiss context. The sexual connotations inferred by the Swiss audience were not intended by Oscar Wilde.

In addition to the actual 'realities' of a situation, the context also includes certain strategies that people regularly employ in order to impose some kind of structure on the world around them. When a person describes something, recounts an event or lists a number of items, he or she will normally follow a preferred sequence rather than a random one. For instance, in recounting a series of events, one would normally follow a temporal order, listing events in the order in which they occurred. This temporal order can, of course, be modified or even reversed provided appropriate signals such as tense markers or time adjuncts are used to clarify the alternative ordering. It nevertheless represents a 'preferred' or 'normal' ordering strategy which is regularly employed by most people.

Levinson relates the question of normal ordering of events in the real world to the sub-maxim of Manner, 'Be orderly'. He suggests that it is because we expect participants in a discourse to respect the maxim 'Be orderly' that we expect them to recount events in the order in which they happened (1983:108). This explains why we would find an utterance such as *The lone ranger rode into the sunset and jumped on his horse* odd. Temporal order may be a widespread or universal ordering strategy, but there are other types of preference for ordering strategies which tend to be language- and culture-specific. If we accept that the linguistic conventions of a community can provide a context for interpreting a maxim, then the relation which exists between 'being orderly' and following a 'normal' ordering of events can also be said to exist between 'being orderly' and following whatever ordering strategies are considered normal in relation to such things as the listing of entities and linguistic items.

Brown and Yule suggest that constraints on the ordering of events and entities are usually followed by language users and that when the normal ordering is reversed 'some "special effect" (staging device, implicature) would be being created by the speaker/writer' (1983:146). It is generally conceded that it is impossible to determine exactly what 'natural orders' there are in different types of discourse and in different languages, though one intuitively knows when a deviant order is being used. Part of the problem is that the ordering of events and entities may be adapted to maintain point of view or thematic progression for instance. Nevertheless, it is worth noting that even though an occasional divergence from preferred ordering strategies may not noticeably affect the coherence of a text, repeated minor disturbances of preferred sequences may have a cumulative effect on the ease with which a reader can make sense of a stretch of language. The following examples illustrate adjustments made in the course of translation to fulfil target readers' expectations of normal ordering.

English source text:

In the Devon study, 8,500 patients will carry the cards, which can be both read and updated by <u>GPs, a pharmacist, a local dentist, and by hospital clinics at Exmouth and the Royal Devon and Exeter Hospital</u>.

Back-translation of target text (Chinese):

8,500 patients will take part in the Devon experiment, using the medical cards. **Royal Devon and Exeter Hospital, Exmouth Hospital clinic<s>, and doctor<s>, pharmacist, and local dentist**, may use a machine reader to read the medical card's content and store new information.

The source text ('Patients test micro-chip medical record card', the *Independent*, 28 April 1988) and its Chinese translation are cited in Tse (1988). Tse explains that the order of the nominal groups underlined in the English text is modified in the Chinese translation to fulfil the expectations of the Chinese reader, who is used to listing entities in order of size, from 'large' to 'small'. In this case, the normal ordering strategy in Chinese would be to start with the larger entities, that is, hospitals. The same strategy is used in listing addresses. An address in Chinese, as well as Russian, would start with the largest entity, the country, and work its way down to county, town, area, street, flat, name and so on. In English, addresses are presented in the reverse order, starting with the name and ending with the country of destination. Any deviation from this normal order would encourage a reader to search for some kind of implicature or to reassess the context in which a text is encountered.

Ordering strategies may also be influenced by physical or emotional factors. It is normal to expect entities which are closer to one's own environment to be mentioned first in a list. Note the different ordering of languages in the following example from the Euralex Circular:

English text:

Abstracts (approximately 1,000 words) in any of the Congress languages, <u>English. French, German or Russian</u>, should be sent to the Lecture Programme Organizer, …

German text:

Abstracts (etwa 1000 Wörter bzw. 80–100 Zeilen) in einer beliebigen Konferenzsprache (**Deutsch, Englisch, Französisch, Russisch**) …

We request abstracts (about 1,000 words or 80–100 lines) in any conference language (**German, English, French, Russian**) …

Russian text:

Краткие конспекты рефератов (с объемом до 1000 слов или до 100 строк) просим до 15 ноября 1987 г. на любом из официальных языков конгресса, т.е. на русском, английском, немецком или французском языках, высылать по выше-указанному адресу главному координатору конгресса Юдит Зигань или науч-ному организатору конгресса д-ру Тамашу Маган. Последующую корреспон-денцию просим адресовать гл. редактору Юдит Зигань.

We ask for a short abstract of papers (up to 1,000 words or up to 100 lines) by 15 November 1987, in any of the official languages of the conference, i.e. in **Russian, English, French or German**, …

Another point which may be subsumed under the vast heading of 'context' is the language user's sense of what is socially and textually appropriate or normal. This does not have much to do with what the reader thinks the world is like, but rather with what he or she is prepared to accept as an appropriate behaviour (linguistic or otherwise) in a given situation. This 'sense of appropriateness' could provide the context for interpreting the additional maxim 'Be polite' discussed earlier. The varied use of pronouns of address in different cultures is a good example (see Chapter 4, section 4.2.3). However, appropriateness is not restricted to the notion of politeness; it covers a multitude of other things. Even something as simple as the use of a particular calendar, where the reader has access to more than one, can be more or less sensitive to readers' expectations in a given context. Note, for instance, the use of the Japanese calendar in the following example:

English source text (*Palace and Politics in Prewar Japan*, Titus 1974:17):

The heads of the ministries created in <u>1869</u> were not directly responsible for 'advising and assisting' (hohitsu) the emperor, though they were to become so in <u>1889</u>. According to the <u>1871</u> reorganization of the ministries, for example, the privilege of assisting the throne directly was in theory limited to the Chancellor (Dajo Daijin), Minister of the Left (Sa Daijin), Minister of the Right (U Daijin), and the Councillors (Sangi).

Japanese text (p. 23):

明治二年につくられた諸省の長は、天皇「輔弼」の直接責任者ではない。そうなったのは明治二二年なのである。たとえば、明治四年の官制改革によれば、理論上、天皇を直接補佐する特権は、太政大臣、左大臣、右大臣、それに参議たちに限られていた。

The heads of ministries which were created in **Meiji 2nd** are not directly responsible for 'hohitsu' the emperor. It was in **Meiji 22nd** that it became so. For example, according to the government reformation of **the fourth year of Meiji**, theoretically, the privilege of assisting the emperor directly was limited to Dajo Daijin, Sa Daijin, U Daijin, and Sangi.

Because the above text relates directly to Japanese culture, the Japanese reader would expect any reference to dates to be based on the Japanese rather than western calendar. The translation fulfils this expectation and therefore does not convey any unwanted implicatures. Compare the above with the following translation of a more modern text:

English source text (*The Patrick Collection* – a leaflet produced by a privately owned museum of classic cars):

In the Mansell Hall – named after Britain's race ace Nigel Mansell, who opened the Hall in <u>1986</u> – there's a unique display of <u>eighties</u> supercars.

Japanese text:

マンセル・ホール（英国のレースのエースであるナイジェル・マンセルにちなんでつけられた名で、かれは１９８６年にこのホールを開館しました。）では、１９８０年代のスーパーカーのユニークな展示が見られます。

In the Mansell Hall (named after Nigel Mansell who is the ace in Britain's race, and he opened this Hall in **1986**) a unique display of super cars of the **1980s** can be seen.

For the Japanese reader, it is acceptable to use the western calendar in texts which relate directly to the western world. However, texts which deal with topics that are closer to home, such as Japanese heritage or history, are expected to use the Japanese calendar.

An interesting area in which a translator needs to be particularly sensitive to the reader's expectations in a given context concerns modes of address. This covers far more than the use of pronouns as discussed in Chapter 4. It includes the use of appropriate personal and occupational titles, various combinations of first names and surnames, title and surname, or title and first name, the use of nicknames, and even the use of terms of affection such as *dear* or *darling*. Certain linguistic items may be used to address certain types of participant in order to convey implicatures which are highly language- and culture-specific. The following widely quoted example first appeared in Ervin-Tripp (1972). It is used by Blum-Kulka (1981:94) in a discussion of the difficulties associated with the translation of indirect speech acts[9] (emphasis added):

> The scene takes place on a public street in contemporary U.S.
> 'What's your name, <u>boy</u>?' the policeman asked.
> '<u>Dr. Poussaint</u>, I'm a physician.'
> 'What's your first name, <u>boy</u>?'
> 'Alvin.'

As Blum-Kulka explains, anyone familiar with address rules in American English will know that Dr Poussaint is black. They will also realize that by refusing to accept the normal address of occupational title plus surname and by using the term *boy* and requesting Dr Poussaint's first name, the policeman means to insult the doctor. Blum-Kulka rightly suggests that the meaning conveyed by deliberately misusing a socio-cultural rule would be difficult to transfer into another language.

However, not all contexts in which modes of address are used will involve deliberate violation of socio-cultural norms to convey implicatures. As long as the translator is aware that the norms of the target language will not necessarily match those of the source language, an appropriate adjustment in the target text should solve the problem and avoid conveying unintended implicatures. In English, for instance, a common and acceptable form of address in a formal context such as a business letter consists of title plus surname, for example *Mr Brown*, *Mrs Keith*, *Dr Kelly*. This would normally be replaced in Arabic by a combination of title plus first name or title plus full name. Translators often make adjustments in this area to conform to their readers' expectations. Note the adjustment made by the Russian translator of the following text:

English text (Euralex conference circular, 1987):

> *Ms. Judit Zigany*
> Akademiai Kiado
> 1363 Budapest
> P.O. Box 24
> Hungary

Target text (Russian):

> Гл. редактор
> Юдит Зигань
> Издательство Академии наук ВНР
> 1363 Будапешт
> п/я. 24
> Венгрия

> Ch. editor
> Judit Zigany
> Hungarian Academy of Sciences Press
> 1363 Budapest
> P.O. Box 24
> Hungary

The equivalent of a title such as *Mr* or *Mrs* in Russian is to use the first name plus the patronymic (middle name derived from the father's name) in formal address to other Russians and people from former socialist countries. Another polite form of address is *tovarishch* (i.e. 'comrade', used for both sexes), but some intellectuals now feel uneasy about it because of its associations with the Marxist era. For foreigners, Russians will typically use the terms of address *gospodin* ('Mr') and *gospozha* ('Mrs'), or the loan words *Mister*, *Missis* and *Miss*. All these, however, suggest 'foreignness'. They would be inappropriate – and even insulting – to use in addressing another Russian or even someone from a socialist country such as Cuba or Hungary.[10] Only foreigners from capitalist countries are normally addressed by these terms, and when they are, the terms are neutral – they simply denote polite address. Since Judit Zigany was a member of a socialist country (Hungary) at the time the Circular was issued, the mode of address in the Russian text appropriately consists of occupational title, followed by full name; no personal titles are used.

7.3.4 Other items of background knowledge

In order to make sense of any piece of information presented in a text, the reader or hearer has to be able to integrate it into some model of the world, whether real or fictional. Text-presented information can only make sense if it can be related to other information we already have. A text may confirm, contradict, modify or extend what we know about the world, as long as it relates to it in some way.

As explained under 7.3.1 above, there is a great deal of overlap between identifying reference and accessing relevant background information. Whether a translator decides to explain a reference or not depends on whether the target reader is assumed to be familiar with it and the extent to which the translator feels inclined to intervene. In the following example, from *A Hero from Zero*, both the French and Arab translators of the English source document must have either assumed that *Clive of India* is familiar to the average French and Arab reader, or decided that it is inappropriate for them as translators to comment directly on the source text. The Sultan referred to in the extract below is the Sultan of Brunei who, according to this document, gave Mohamed Fayed a power of attorney which put a considerable amount of his (the Sultan's) funds under Fayed's control.

English source text (p. 27):

> The incident that destroyed the Sultan's trust in Fayed (which the Sultan discovered later) was Fayed's taking for himself the $86 million from Hirschmann upon the cancellation of the contract for the 747-SP aeroplane. According to Barican, the Sultan never agreed to this and it was this incident that cost Fayed the Sultan's confidence ...
>
> Like Clive of India, Fayed must have stood amazed at his own restraint. According to Barican, the Sultan's funds in Swiss banks

were around five billion dollars at the time, and the power of attorney unlocked the door to all of them.

French text (p. 27):

Tout comme Clive of India, Fayed a dû s'étonner de sa propre retenue.

… Just like Clive of India, Fayed must have been amazed at his own restraint.

Arabic text (p. 40):

وما من شك أن فايد – شأنه فى ذلك شأن كلايف أوف انديا – قد وقف مذهو لا أمام قدرته على ضبط النفس.

… There is no doubt that Fayed – like Clive of India – stood amazed at his ability to restrain himself.

Lord Clive, Proconsul of India, was a British soldier and statesman. He is remembered for defeating the nawab of Bengal and for reforming the British administration in India. Following the Bengal famine of 1769–1770, he was accused of famine profiteering, of creating monopolies in cotton and diamonds, and of taking presents from Indian leaders after the Battle of Plassey in 1757. When Clive was questioned about the presents, he made the following remark, to which the above extract alludes:

> Consider the situation in which the victory of Plassey placed me. A great prince dependent on my pleasure; an opulent city lay at my mercy; its richest bankers bid against each other for my smiles; I walked through vaults which were thrown open to me alone, piled on either hand with gold and jewels. Mr Chairman, at this moment *I stand astonished at my own moderation*.
> (Lawford 1976:393; emphasis added)

Interestingly enough, I have not yet found an English speaker who could recall any details in connection with Clive of India, except that he was a military leader who secured victory for the British in India. The above supposedly famous remark and the context in which it was uttered are highly unlikely to be recalled by, and may not even be known to, many British readers. I suspect that many will therefore be unable to interpret the relevance of the reference to Clive of India in the above passage. The writer seems to have misjudged the reader's access to details which are needed to establish the relevance of part of what he says to the discourse in hand. This is not uncommon. It is very difficult indeed – for writers and translators alike – to judge what the average reader may or may not have at his or her disposal in terms of background information. Moreover, in the majority of cases, the translator is likely to be not as knowledgeable as the writer but rather as ignorant as the average reader, so that the translator's judgement is further hampered by his or her own lack of knowledge. The translator should, in theory, be able to do the kind of research that I have done here to access the relevant background knowledge, but this is not always feasible. The quality of research facilities, for example, varies tremendously among different settings, be they countries or institutions.

A second example, with a different assessment of the target reader's access to background information, comes from *Autumn of Fury: The Assassination of Sadat* by Mohamed Heikal (1983:3). Speaking of Sadat, Heikal says:

> While fully conscious of his shortcomings I hoped that the responsibilities of office would strengthen the positive elements in his character and enable him to overcome the weak ones. <u>The example of Truman was always present in my mind</u>. I managed Sadat's campaign ...

Arabic translation (p. 6):

وأظن أيضاً أننى لم أكن غافلا عن بعض أسباب للقصور فيه، لكننى تصورت أن أعباء المنصب ووقار المسؤلية سوف تقوى كل العناصر الإيجابية فى شخصيته، وسوف تساعده فى التغلب على جوانب الضعف فيها. وكان فى ذهنى باستمرار نموذج **الرئيس الأمريكى "هارى ترومان" الذى خلف "فرانكلين روزفلت" فى مقعد الرئاسةالإمريكية قرب نهاية الحرب العالمية الثانية . فقد بدا "ترومان" فى ذلك الوقت ــ وبعد "روزفلت" ــ شخصية باهتة ومجهولة لا تستطيع أن تقود الصراع الإنسانى الكبير فى الحرب العالمية الثانية الى نهايته المطلوبة والمحققة، لكن "ترومان" ــ أمام تحدى التجربة العملية ــ نما ونضج وأصبح من أبرز الرؤساء الإمريكيين فى العصر الحديث. ولقد تصورت أن نفس الشىء يمكن أن يحدث للسادات ولقد أدرت حملته الإنتخابية** . . . . (ص. 6)

> I also believe that I was not unaware of some of his shortcomings, but I imagined that the burden of office and responsibility would strengthen all the positive elements in his character and help him to overcome the areas of weakness in it. In my mind there was always the example of **the American President Harry** Truman**, who succeeded Franklin Roosevelt towards the end of World War II. At that time – and after Roosevelt – Truman seemed a rather nondescript/bland and unknown character who could not lead the great human struggle in World War II to its desired and inevitable end. But Truman – faced with the challenge of practical experience – grew and matured and became one of the most prominent American presidents in modern times. I imagined that the same thing could happen to Sadat.** I managed his campaign ...

The additional background knowledge about Truman in the Arabic version is clearly there for the benefit of the Arab reader, who may well know that Truman was a former president of America but is not expected to know enough about him to draw the specific analogy between him and Sadat that the writer wishes him or her to draw. What is largely implied in the English version is spelt out in detail in the Arabic version. Heikal could, of course, have included this information in a footnote rather than in the body of the text. In this respect, it is interesting to note Thomson's advice about what should or should not be relegated to footnotes in translation (1982:30):

> The study of implicature may provide a practical solution to the well known problem of deciding what parts of the original shared context should be built into the text of the translation and what should be provided separately, for example in footnotes. *Information essential to the success of conversational implicatures should be included in the text* if the translation is to be coherent and sensible. It is unrealistic and working against the pragmatic nature of language to put such information into footnotes.

Without necessarily knowing anything about Grice or implicatures, Heikal may well have followed a similar course of reasoning in deciding to include the above information in the body of the text.

As well as expanding a text to provide the necessary background information, a translator may decide to delete information with which the target readership may be assumed to be familiar. In the same text, *Autumn of Fury*, Heikal explains the word *zamzam* in the following extract with a footnote:

> Another example of how the President could over-reach himself in his desire to accommodate his new friends came over his offer of Nile water to Israel. After his visit to Haifa in September 1979 Sadat confided to a group of Israeli editors that he was thinking of diverting some of the Nile waters through Sinai to the Negev: 'Why not? Lots of possibilities, lots of hope.' Jerusalem, he said, was a city sacred to the three faiths. What could be more appropriate in the new climate of peace than to supply all the believers in Jerusalem with a new *zamzam*.
>
> Footnote: The sacred well in the Haram of Mecca whose water is drunk by pilgrims. It was by tradition opened by the Angel Gabriel to prevent Hagar and her son Ismail from dying of thirst in the desert.

This footnote is omitted in the Arabic version. The author/translator rightly assumed that it would be redundant as far as the Arab (predominantly Muslim) reader is concerned.

The following example illustrates what happens when the translator anticipates a serious clash between assumed and actual background knowledge of the reader. What is involved here is the difficulty of dealing with a vast gap between source and target cultures' versions of the world. It is not, in fact, a translation, but rather a comment on the translation of a whole chunk of text. The source text is Arabic; the target text is English. It is the twelfth 'surah' (verse) of the Qur'an which recounts the story of Joseph. The story of Joseph also appears in the Bible. However, the story presented in the Qur'an is quite different from that presented in the Bible. The translator of the text anticipates the clash with the Christian reader's version of the story and provides the following comment in a separate introduction:

> *Yusuf* takes its name from its subject which is the life-story of Joseph. It differs from all other Surahs in having only one subject. The differences from the Bible narrative are striking. Jacob is here a Prophet, who is not deceived by the story of his son's death, but is distressed because, through a suspension of his clairvoyance, he cannot see what has become of Joseph. The real importance of the narrative, its psychic burden, is emphasized throughout, and the manner of narration, though astonishing to Western readers, is vivid.
>
> (The Holy Qur'an, *translated by Pickthall 1982:51*)

The above comment is clearly meant to warn readers that they are about to encounter a different view of the world. It is important to note that in translation, as in any act of communication, a text does not necessarily have to conform to the expectations of its readership. Readers' versions of reality, their expectations and their preferences can be challenged without affecting the coherence of a text, provided the challenge is motivated and the reader is prepared for it. Like creativity in literature, for example, radically different versions of reality need not result in incoherence. It is well within our capacity as human beings to make sense of versions of reality which differ greatly from our own provided the differences are motivated and adequately signalled.

7.3.5 The availability of all relevant items falling under the previous headings

The final factor on Grice's list of 'data' on which 'the hearer will reply' in working out an implicature is, in his own words, 'the fact (or supposed fact) that all relevant items falling under the previous headings are available to both participants and both participants know or assume this to be the case' (1975:50).

In order to convey an intended meaning, the speaker or writer must be able to assume that the hearer or reader has access to all the necessary background information, features of the context and so on, that is, items 7.3.1–7.3.4 above, and that it is well within his or her competence to work out any intended implicatures. The less the writer assumes that the reader has access to, the more he or she will provide in the way of explanation and detail. As previous examples demonstrate, translators often find themselves in the position of having to reassess what is and what is not available to target readers to ensure that implicatures can be worked out. Apart from filling gaps in the reader's knowledge (which would cover the availability of relevant items of background knowledge, non-linguistic context, identity of reference, etc.), there is also the question of the reader's expectations. These are part of the 'data' available to the reader under the various headings 7.3.1–7.3.4 above. In translation, anything that is likely to violate the target reader's expectations must be carefully examined and, if necessary, adjusted in order to avoid conveying the wrong implicatures or even failing to make sense altogether.

Among the strongest expectations we bring to bear on any communicative event involving verbal behaviour are expectations concerning the organization of language. Unless motivated,[11] a deviant configuration at any linguistic level (phonological, lexical, syntactic, textual) may block a participant's access to 'the conventional meaning of the words and structures used' – item 7.3.1 above – and can directly affect the coherence of a text. The main function of linguistic elements and patterning is to organize the content of a message so that it is easily accessible to a reader or hearer. Any disturbance to the normal organizational patterns of language must therefore be motivated, otherwise the reader will not be able to make sense of it. To repeat an example which was discussed in Chapter 3, collocations such as 'harmed hair', 'damaged hair' and 'breakable hair' which appear in the Arabic translation of the Kolestral text are so deviant that the Arab reader is unlikely to be able to make any sense of that part of the text. Being both deviant and unmotivated, such unexpected organization of the language tends to render a text incoherent to its readers.

Most professional translators appreciate the need to fulfil a reader's expectations about the organization of the target language in order to maintain the coherence of a text and avoid giving rise to unwanted implicatures. Some of the adjustments that a translator may need to make in order to conform to readers' expectations in this area have been discussed and exemplified in previous chapters. However, there are instances in which deviation from normal patterning is a feature of the source text itself. If deviation is motivated, and especially if it is necessary for working out an intended meaning, the translator may well decide to transfer it to the target text. As discussed above, readers' expectations do not necessarily have to be fulfilled. Writers, and translators, often appeal to their readers to modify their expectations if such modifications are required in a given context. We are normally prepared to accept a great deal of unusual and even bizarre linguistic behaviour provided it can be justified, for instance on the basis of poetic creativity or humour.

The suggestion that deviations from normal patterning have to be motivated implies that they have to occur in a context that is 'interpretable' by the hearer or reader. Blakemore suggests that a speaker or writer who wants his or her utterance to be interpreted in a certain way 'must expect it to be interpreted in a context that yields that interpretation' (1987:27). The following example illustrates a situation where deviation from normal organization of the language seems justified in translation and where the translator has to enlarge the shared context of writer and reader in order to accommodate this feature in such a way that its relevance is made explicit and coherence is therefore maintained. The extract is from a transcript of conversation which is appended to *A Hero from Zero* (p. 143) and translated from English into French and Arabic. The three people taking part in the conversation (Mohamed Fayed, Shri Chandra Swamiji and Kailish Nath Agarwal) are all non-native speakers of English. The conversation is conducted partly in English and partly in Hindi. The speakers, particularly Mohamed Fayed, have a rather poor command of English. Here is an extract from the conversation to illustrate Mohamed Fayed's level of competence in English:

M. Fayed:	Sultan, you know, he gets influenced. I can't go sit with him all the time, you know. It's impossible for me, you know. Because he has one terrible, evil man, his aide, Ibnu.
Mamaji:	Pardon?
M. Fayed:	General Ibnu.
Mamaji:	Uh-huh.
M. Fayed:	Terrible man. This man takes money from everybody, everybody.
Swamiji:	I think girls also.
M. Fayed:	Yeah.
Mamaji:	Girls?
Swamiji:	Girls.
M. Fayed:	Girls, everything, everything, everything. He is the big man, but the Sultan don't trust him at all. Bad man. And this Ibnu and Zobel are like that. Build the palace together. Ibnu gives permission to all those people go inside, take pictures of his bedroom, everything, anything. And he's a bad man, you know. But for me, I don't – you know, er I don't need the Sultan. Sultan doesn't need me. But I made so much good for him, you know, with support him with the British Government, you know.

The problem that the Arab translator faces in rendering this text into Arabic is that Mohamed Fayed is Egyptian; his first language is Arabic. To simply transfer the deviant syntax into Arabic without any comment would leave the Arab reader puzzled as to why a native speaker of Arabic should speak in 'broken' Arabic. To adjust Fayed's speech to reflect normal patterns of Arabic would considerably weaken the carefully structured argument put forward by Tiny Rowland, the 'jilted suitor' who wants to show that Fayed is unworthy of the privilege of owning the House of Fraser and incapable of running such a prestigious British concern. After all, Fayed is portrayed here, among other things, as a 'foreigner', not very bright and rather incoherent! The translator decides to compromise by transferring the deviant organization into Arabic in order to convey something of the 'stupid foreigner' image of Fayed, while at the same time explaining the situation to the reader so that he or she can make sense of it. The following comment is inserted by the translator at the beginning of the transcript of conversation (p. 139):

ملحوظة. يتضح من قراءة النص الانجليزى للمحادثة المسجلة على الشريط أن الأشخاص الثلاثة الذين اشتركوا فيها ليس لديهم إلمام كاف باللغة الإنجليزية، كما يتبين ذلك بكل وضوح من الجمل الركيكة والمفككة التركيب والتى لا تراعى قواعد اللغة. ولذلك فلابد من أن تنعكس نقاط الضعف هذه فى الترجمة العربية حرصاً على مراعاة الدقة، بقدر الإمكان، فى نقل المعنى.

> **Note**: It is clear from reading the English text of the conversation transcribed on the tape that the three people who participated in it do not have sufficient command of the English language. This is also very clear from the use of sub-standard and loosely structured sentences which do not conform to the rules of the language. Therefore, these points of weakness have to be reflected in the Arabic translation in order to maintain accuracy, as far as possible, in the transfer of meaning.

Coherence is a very problematic and elusive notion because of the diversity of factors, linguistic and non-linguistic, that can affect it and the varying degrees of importance a particular factor can assume in a given context. Even a single lexical item, if mistranslated, can have an impact on the way a text coheres. A polysemous item in the source text will rarely have an equivalent with the same range of meanings in the target language. If the source text makes use of two or more meanings of an item and the translation fails, for whatever reason, to convey any of those meanings, whole layers of meaning will be lost, resulting in what Blum-Kulka (1986) refers to as a 'shift in coherence'.

It is impossible to itemize the various factors that can contribute to or detract from the coherence of a text. The variables involved and the processes of interpretation we employ in trying to make sense of a text are far too numerous and often too elusive to be pinned down and described. The fact that many of these factors are language- and culture-specific adds to the complexity of the problem. What most of the examples given in this chapter seem to suggest is that in order to maintain coherence translators often have to minimize discrepancies between the model of the world presented in the source text and that with which the target reader is likely to be familiar. The extent of intervention varies considerably and depends in the final analysis on two main factors. The first is the translator's ability to assess the knowledge and expectations of the target reader – the more the target reader is assumed to know, the less likely that the translator will be inclined to intervene with lengthy explanations. Likewise, the more harmony is assumed to exist between the model of the world presented in the source text and the target culture's version of the world, the more inclined the translator will be to refrain from direct intervention. The second factor is the translator's own view of his or her role and of the whole question of where his or her loyalties ought to lie – whether they ought to lie with the source text or with the target reader.

I hope that the above discussion will provide the reader with some basis on which to detect and explore areas in which a translation may or may not succeed in making sense to its readers. The main difficulties seem to be concerned with the ability to assess the target readers' range of knowledge and assumptions about various aspects of the world, and to strike a reasonable balance between, on the one hand, fulfilling their expectations and, on the other hand, maintaining their interest in the communication by offering them new or alternative insights. Brown and Yule (1983:67) suggest that:

> the principles of analogy (things will tend to be as they were before) and local interpretation (if there is a change, assume it is minimal) form the basis of the assumption of coherence in our experience of life in general, hence in our experience of discourse as well.

This is true, but we must also remember that readers in general, and readers of translated texts in particular, are prepared to accept a great deal of change and a view of the world which is radically different from their own, provided they have a reason for doing so and are prepared for it. In attempting to fill gaps in their readers' knowledge and fulfil their expectations of what is normal or acceptable, translators should be careful not to 'overdo' things by explaining too much and leaving the reader with nothing to do.

exercises

1. The following is a short essay from J. B. Priestley's *Delight*, a small collection of personal essays:

   Giving advice
   Giving advice, especially when I am in no position to give it and hardly know what I am talking about. I manage my own affairs with as much care and steady attention and skill as – let us say – a drunken Irish tenor. I swing violently from enthusiasm to disgust. I change policies as a woman changes hats. I am here today and gone tomorrow. When I am doing one job, I wish I were doing another. I base my judgments on anything – or nothing. I have never the least notion what I shall be doing or where I shall be in six months time. Instead of holding one thing steadily, I try to juggle with six. I cannot plan, and if I could I would never stick to the plan. I am a pessimist in the morning and an optimist at night, am defeated on Tuesday and insufferably victorious by Friday. But because I am heavy, have a deep voice and smoke a

exercises

pipe, few people realize that I am a flibbertigibbet on a weathercock. So my advice is asked. And then, for ten minutes or so, I can make Polonius look a trifler. I settle deep in my chair, two hundred pounds of portentousness, and with some first-rate character touches in the voice and business with pipe, I begin: 'Well, I must say that in your place —' And inside I am bubbling with delight.

Try translating the above essay into your target language, paying particular attention to the question of implicature and the whole image that the writer draws of himself. If necessary, consider possible explanations (or other strategies) that could help the target reader draw the right inferences from the author's statements. Consider, for instance, whether an analogy such as changing policies as a woman changes hats is likely to have the same implicature in your target language.

This essay appeared in *Literature in English*, one of the English for Today Series, published by the National Council of Teachers of English (1964), McGraw-Hill. The editors provide the following explanations of key words and expressions in footnote form. You may find these helpful.

> *drunken Irish tenor*: A drunken singer is not in control of himself. Priestley is suggesting that he manages his own affairs badly.
> *flibbertigibbet on a weathercock*: A flibbertigibbet is a frivolous and giddy person. A weathercock is a wooden or metal rooster that turns on top of a building and shows the direction of the wind. The whole expression suggests a very undependable person.
> *Polonius*: a character in Shakespeare's *Hamlet*, noted for giving advice.
> *two hundred pounds of portentousness* …: In other words, a large man ('two hundred pounds') using an impressive voice and using impressive gestures with his pipe ('some first-rate character touches') gives grave ('portentous') advice. This is a humorous description of the author's pose.

2. The following extract from an article by Vanessa Baird which appeared in the *New Internationalist* (January/February 2010, special issue on population growth) raises similar challenges, but the article does not come with notes and explanations this time. You may therefore need to undertake some research of your own to ensure that you understand the references and relevant implicatures before translating it into your target language. A good starting point would be to visit the *New Internationalist* web site,[12] unless you are already familiar with the magazine, to

establish what type of publication it is and where the sympathies of its contributors are likely to lie, especially since the author in this case is also one of the editors of the magazine.

Too many people?

When she was young, my great aunt – a tiny sprightly woman who painted vast canvasses – had wanted to become a nun. Then she met a Flemish poet and they fell in love. She agreed to marry him on one condition: that they have 12 children. True to the old baking tradition, they made 13.

Her niece, my mother, also briefly flirted with the holy life. Her tryst with celibacy was equally convincing. As the eighth of her brood, I approach the subject of global population with a touch of trepidation. By anyone's standard of reasonable family size I really shouldn't be here.

But then the subject of population – and in particular population growth – is one that seems capable of provoking all kinds of emotions.

...

Often the cause of concern is the speed at which others – be they people of other races or social classes or religions or political allegiances – are reproducing themselves, threatening, presumably, to disturb the wellbeing of whatever dominant group the commentator belongs to.

This was epitomized recently by Michael Laws, Mayor of Wanganui District in New Zealand, who proposed that in order to tackle the problems of child abuse and murder, members of the 'appalling underclass' should be paid not to have children. 'If we gave $10,000 to certain people and said "we'll voluntarily sterilize you" then all of society would be better off,' he told the *Dominion Post* newspapers.

Most contemporary worries about population are less offensively expressed. For many, the issue is primarily an environmental one. The logic is simple. The more people there are, the more greenhouse gas is emitted, the more damage is done. Any attempts to reduce carbon emissions will be negated by runaway population growth.

This was echoed recently by the *Financial Times* when it called for an international debate on population. A leader column argued: 'World population growth is making it harder to achieve cuts in carbon emissions' and went on to quote a disputed London School of Economics study* maintaining that spending on family planning is 'five times more cost effective at cutting carbon dioxide emissions than the conventional low carbon technologies'.

The UK-based Optimum Population Trust goes further, suggesting that to achieve sustainability we should be aiming to reduce global population by at least 1.7 billion people.

...

* Since found to be the work of a student funded by the Optimum Population Trust.

Imagine that you have been asked to translate this article for an activist site that is committed to promoting global justice and wishes to make key counter arguments on sensitive issues such as population growth available in a wide range of languages. In this context, it is vital that you convey the attitude of the author to the topic. You therefore need to pay particular attention to linguistic and typographic signals of this attitude, such as *presumably* and the use of scare quotes. Note also the reference to 'work of a student' in the footnote. What implicature might the author be trying to communicate here, and how would you ensure its accessibility to the target reader? Similarly, how would you handle the reference to 'baker's dozen' and the use of 'made' (rather than 'have') at the end of the first paragraph? How do you ensure that the target reader will understand these references and associated implicatures?

3. Here is a particularly challenging extract to translate. It is part of the well-known scene in Shakespeare's *Othello* (Act III, Scene iii), in which Iago deliberately violates Grice's maxims, certainly the maxim of relevance, in order to convey certain implicatures. Othello recognizes the violations and tries to get Iago to spell out what he means.

Iago: My noble lord –
Oth: What dost thou say, Iago?
Iago: Did Michael Cassio, when you woo'd my lady, Know of your love?
Oth: He did, from first to last. Why dost thou ask?
Iago: But for a satisfaction of my thought; No further harm.
Oth: Why of thy thought, Iago?
Iago: I did not think he had been acquainted with her.
Oth: O, yes, and went between us very oft.
Iago: Indeed?
Oth: Indeed? Ay, indeed! Discern'st thou aught in that? Is he not honest?
Iago: Honest, my lord?
Oth: Honest? Ay, honest.

Iago: My lord, for aught I know.
Oth: What dost thou think?
Iago: Think, my lord?
Oth: Think, my lord? By heaven, he echoes me,
        As if there were some monster in his thought
        Too hideous to be shown. Thou dost mean something.
        I heard thee say even now, thou lik'st not that,
        When Cassio left my wife. What didst not like?
        And when I told thee he was of my counsel
        In my whole course of wooing, thou cried'st 'Indeed?'
        And didst contract and purse thy brow together,
        As if thou hadst shut up in thy brain
        Some horrible conceit. If thou dost love me,
        Show me thy thought.

Consider how Iago conveys his intended meanings, both conventionally and non-conventionally. What adjustments, if any, do you feel you have to make to the lexis, syntax, or the way in which the maxims are violated in order to convey similar implicatures in your translated version?

4. Stephen Hawking's popular science book, *A Brief History of Time from the Big Bang to Black Holes* (1988) includes a number of appendices, each giving an insight into the life and personality of a famous scientist. This is one of them:

Isaac Newton

Isaac Newton was not a pleasant man. His relations with other academics were notorious, with most of his later life spent embroiled in heated disputes. Following publication of *Principia Mathematica* – surely the most influential book ever written in physics – Newton had risen rapidly into public prominence. He was appointed president of the Royal Society and became the first scientist ever to be knighted.

Newton soon clashed with the Astronomer Royal, John Flamsteed, who had earlier provided Newton with much needed data for *Principia,* but was now withholding information that Newton wanted. Newton would not take no for an answer; he had himself appointed to the governing body of the Royal Observatory and then tried to force immediate publication of the data. Eventually he arranged for Flamsteed's work to be seized and prepared for publication by Flamsteed's mortal enemy, Edmond Halley. But Flamsteed took the case to court and, in the nick of time, won a court order preventing distribution of the stolen work. Newton was incensed and sought his revenge by systematically deleting all references to Flamsteed in later editions of *Principia*.

A more serious dispute arose with the German philosopher Gottfried Leibniz. Both Leibniz and Newton had independently developed a branch of mathematics called calculus, which underlies most of modern physics. Although we now know that Newton discovered calculus years before Leibniz, he published his work much later. A major row ensued over who had been first, with scientists vigorously defending both contenders. It is remarkable, however, that most of the articles appearing in defense of Newton were originally written by his own hand – and only published in the name of friends! As the row grew, Leibniz made the mistake of appealing to the Royal Society to resolve the dispute. Newton, as president, appointed an 'impartial' committee to investigate, coincidentally consisting entirely of Newton's friends! But that was not all: Newton then wrote the committee's report himself and had the Royal Society publish it, officially accusing Leibniz of plagiarism. Still unsatisfied, he then wrote an anonymous review of the report in the Royal Society's own periodical. Following the death of Leibniz, Newton is reported to have declared that he had taken great satisfaction in 'breaking Leibniz's heart.'

During the period of these two disputes, Newton had already left Cambridge and academe. He had been active in anti-Catholic politics at Cambridge, and later in Parliament, and was rewarded eventually with the lucrative post of Warden of the Royal Mint. Here he used his talents for deviousness and vitriol in a more socially acceptable way, successfully conducting a major campaign against counterfeiting, even sending several men to their death on the gallows.

Imagine that you have been asked to translate the above appendix into your target language. Your translated version is to be included in a portfolio of light-hearted but factual background material for science students in secondary education, designed to stimulate their interest in the world of science at large.

Comment on the strategies you decide to use to convey Hawking's implied meanings to your target audience. For instance, do you transfer typographic signals such as exclamation marks and the inverted commas around *impartial* (third paragraph), or are there better ways of signalling similar meanings in your target language? Does the text, as it stands, convey the same image of Newton in your target language as it does in English, or do you have to make adjustments to accommodate your target reader's cultural background?

exercises

5. Much of our discussion of pragmatics concerned ways of 'making sense' of a text or interaction and finding ways of communicating our interpretation to the target reader. But some texts deliberately set out to undermine sense – nonsense literature is a good, extreme example. Other texts stretch the limits of 'sense' in less radical ways, using structures and expressions that would normally fail to cohere in less experimental texts but that are part of the message being communicated in this context. With this in mind, try your hand at the following opening paragraph of Robert Young's article 'The Procrastinator' (Young 1999:7):

> Too close to call, whether I am yet beyond the real deadlines that followed the final deadline because of course with deadlines there is always the possibility of a later insertion, at proof stage or even second proof stage, or even perhaps – No. That is no longer procrastination, that is living dangerously, the very thing the procrastinator wishes to avoid. The procrastinator is no revolutionary, leaping into the future: every procrastinator is at heart a conservative creature, cautious, politic, wishing to live on without the jolt of completion and the rush of emptiness that follows the offering up of a piece of writing no longer just one's own, now exposed to the possibility of being read, ridiculed, rejected – and producing the inevitable question of what is coming next. Publish and perish. Unwilling to become the productive academic *prestigateur*, pulling ever more startlingly innovative writings out of a glamorous top hat, the procrastinator eyes the enfeebled mortar board warily. No key player he.
>
> Nor she – though there is something very gendered about procrastination, an inexorable maleness in the spirit of Tristram Shandy, Leopold Bloom or Saleem Sinai. Viagra falls. The procrastinator hangs over the past, furtively stealing time's proferred moments, seeking to retrieve what has already past, to delay what has not been done. He who hesitates is rarely lost. It may never happen. The present must live on into the future, at all costs it must be kept going, not detached from the past, but nurtured and maintained for its familiar comfort, recognisable, known, safe. Let us linger on, procrastinate that act of fulfilment that belongs to tomorrow, meanly measure out our lives as they unroll slowly through the debris of what has long since lapsed and elapsed. Stay with me, delay with me. Hang on a while.

Consider what Young is trying to achieve by the various structures he opts for. To what extent can you reproduce this effect in your translation, while still producing a coherent text that can make sense to the target readers?

SUGGESTIONS FOR FURTHER READING

Bednarek, Monika A. (2005) 'Frames Revisited – The Coherence-Inducing Function of Frames', *Journal of Pragmatics* 37: 685–705.

Blum-Kulka, Shoshana (1986) 'Shifts of Cohesion and Coherence in Translation', in Juliane House and Soshana Blum-Kulka (eds) *Interlingual and Intercultural Communication: Discourse and Cognition in Translation and Second Language Acquisition Studies*, Tubingen: Gunter Narr, 17–35; reprinted in Lawrence Venuti (ed.) *The Translation Studies Reader*, London: Routledge, 290–305.

Brown, Gillian and George Yule (1983) *Discourse Analysis*, Cambridge: Cambridge University Press. Chapter 7: 'Coherence in the Interpretation of Discourse'.

de Beaugrande, Robert and Wolfgang Dressler (1981) *Introduction to Text Linguistics*, London: Longman. Chapter 5: 'Coherence', and Chapter 6: 'Intentionality and Acceptability'.

Enkvist, N. E. (1985) 'Coherence and Inference', in Ursula Pieper and Gerhard Stickel (eds) *Studia Linguistica Diachronica et Synchronica*, Berlin: Mouton de Gruyter, 233–248.

Hickey, Leo (ed.) (1998) *The Pragmatics of Translation*, Clevedon: Multilingual Matters.

Valdés, Cristina and Adrián Fuentes Luque (2008) 'Coherence in Translated Television Commercials', *European Journal of English Studies* 12(2): 133–148.

On politeness

Arnáiz, Carmen (2006) 'Politeness in the Portrayal of Workplace Relationships: Second Person Address Forms in Peninsular Spanish and the Translation of Humour', *Journal of Politeness Research, Language, Behaviour, Culture* 2(1): 123–141.

Berk-Seligson, Susan (1988) 'The Impact of Politeness in Witness Testimony: The Influence of the Court Interpreter', *Multilingua* 7(4): 411–439.

Brown, Penelope and Stephen Levinson (1987/1999) *Politeness. Some Universals in Language Usage*, Cambridge: Cambridge University Press; excerpted as 'Politeness: Some Universals in Language Usage', in Adam Jaworski and Nikolas Coupland (eds) *The Discourse Reader*, London: Routledge, 321–335.

Cambridge, Jan (1999) 'Information Loss in Bilingual Medical Interviews through an Untrained Interpreter', in Ian Mason (ed.) *Dialogue Interpreting*, special issue of *The Translator* 5(2): 201–219.

Glinert, Lewis (2010) 'Apologizing to China: Elastic Apologies and the Meta-discourse of American Diplomats', *Intercultural Pragmatics* 7(1): 47–74.

Hatim, Basil and Ian Mason (1997) *The Translator as Communicator*, London: Routledge. Chapter 5: 'Politeness in Screen Translating'.

Hickey, Leo (2000) 'Politeness in Translation between English and Spanish', *Target* 12(2): 229–240.

House, Juliane (1998) 'Politeness and Translation', in Leo Hickey (ed.) *The Pragmatics of Translation*, Clevedon: Multilingual Matters, 54–71.

On semantic prosody (and attitudinal meaning in general)

Louw, Bill (1993) 'Irony in the Text or Insincerity in the Writer? The Diagnostic Potential of Semantic Prosodies', in Mona Baker, Gill Francis and Elena Tognini-Bonelli (eds) *Text and Technology: In Honour of John Sinclair*, Amsterdam: John Benjamins, 157–176.

Louw, Bill (2000) 'Contextual Prosodic Theory: Bringing Semantic Prosodies to Life', in Chris Heffer and Helen Sauntson (eds) *Words in Context, A Tribute to John Sinclair on His Retirement*, CDRom. Available at www.revue-texto.net/docannexe/file/124/louw_prosodie.pdf.

Munday, Jeremy (2010) 'Evaluation and Intervention in Translation', in Mona Baker, Maeve Olohan and María Calzada Pérez (eds) *Text and Context: Essays on Translation and Interpreting in Honour of Ian Mason*, Manchester: St. Jerome Publishing, 77–94.

Stewart, Dominic (2010) *Semantic Prosody: A Critical Evaluation*, London: Routledge.

NOTES

1   Conventionally signalled implicatures are also known as **presuppositions**. Like implicatures, presuppositions are pragmatic inferences. They are based on the linguistic structure of an utterance, though they are still context-sensitive. For a detailed discussion of presupposition, see Levinson (1983, Chapter 4).

2   Grice's notion of conversational implicature and his proposed four maxims overlap with several notions discussed by other linguists, most notably in **speech-act theory**. Speech-act theory complements Grice's approach to meaning. Like Grice, speech-act theorists attempt to go beyond the literal meaning of words and structures by classifying utterances according to their implicit rather than explicit functions. For instance, a speaker may use a declarative/assertive structure to make a request or an interrogative structure to express reproof. The notions of **illocutionary meaning** and **indirect speech acts** in particular highlight an obvious area of overlap. Illocutionary meaning has to do with the speaker's intentions rather than his or her actual words. An indirect speech act is an utterance whose 'literal meaning and/or literal force is conversationally inadequate in the context and must be "repaired" by some inference' (Levinson 1983:270). It is, in fact, the flouting of a maxim such as Quantity or Relevance which results in an utterance having an indirect illocutionary meaning.

There is also some overlap between the maxim of relevance and the principle of **local interpretation** which 'instructs the hearer not to construct a context any larger than he needs to arrive at an interpretation. Thus, if he hears someone say "Shut the door" he will look towards the nearest door available for being shut' (Brown and Yule 1983:59).

Finally, Grice's division of implicature into conventional implicature and conversational implicature also overlaps with Beekman and Callow's distinction between two major types of **implicit information**:

There is the implicit information conveyed in the written document itself by the vocabulary and grammatical constructions of the language, and there is the implicit information which lies outside the document, in the general situation which gave

rise to the document, the circumstances of the writer and readers, their relationship, etc.

(1974:48)

3 *Haven't you done well?* can also be patronizing, and *Don't I know it?* can be
self-recriminating.

4 As defined here and in the work of Sinclair, Louw and others, **semantic prosody** is not
the same as 'invoked attitudinal meaning' in appraisal theory (Martin and White 2005,
Munday 2010). Munday (2010:85–87) discusses *Victorian arcades* and *cobbled
streets* as examples of invoked attitudinal meaning: these items are perceived in a
particular communicative context (rather than the language at large) as having positive
values; for many people in the English-speaking world, they are associated with tradition,
authenticity and quality of life. Semantic prosody is a much more subtle feature of
language patterning. It is not dependent on specific communicative contexts and tends
to be less subjective in its interpretation.

5 Louw (2000) offers a more extended definition:

> A semantic prosody refers to a form of meaning which is established through the
> proximity of a consistent series of collocates, often characterisable as positive or
> negative, and whose primary function is the expression of the attitude of its speaker
> or writer towards some pragmatic situation. A secondary, although no less important
> attitudinal function of semantic prosodies is the creation of irony through the delib-
> erate injection of a form which clashes with the prosody's consistent series of
> collocates.

6 See www.llc.manchester.ac.uk/ctis/research/english-corpus/.

7 For a fascinating discussion of some aspects of the history of Arsène Lupin translations
into Arabic, specifically in Egypt, see Selim (2010).

8

قال الشعر مادحاً:

من نفسهِ فليأتِ أحلافَ الْعَـرَبْ	مَنْ رام ان يُلقى تباريحَ الْكُرَبْ
والشِّعرَ والاوتارَ كيفمــا انقلبْ	يرى الْجَمال والجَلال والْحَسَبْ
وأسمحُ النـاس وأجرى من يَهَبْ	أشرفُ أهل الارض عن أمّ وأبْ
ولا يُبالونَ باحـــــراز النشبْ	لا تُعرَفُ الاقذارُ فيهـم والرِّيَبْ

لكن يغارون على حفظِ النسبْ

فقال الظريف هاجياً:

من نفسهِ فليأتِ أجلافَ العـربْ	من رامَ أن يُلقى تباريــحَ الكُرَبْ
والشِّعر والاوبارَ كيفمـا انقلبْ	يرى الجمالَ والجِلالَ والخشبْ
واسمجُ الناس أخـزى من نَهَبْ	أسرقُ أهل الارض عن أم وأبْ
ولا يُبالونَ باحـــــراز النيربْ	لا تُعرَفُ الاقـدارُ فيهم والرتبْ

لكن يغارون على حفظِ النشبْ

والفروق بين النصين لا تتجاوز بعض النقاط والحركات. وغنيّ عن البيانِ أن امثال هذه الفروق لا تنقل الى لسان آخر.

9 See note 2 above: **an indirect speech act** is an utterance whose 'literal meaning and/
or literal force is conversationally inadequate in the context and must be "repaired" by
some inference' (Levinson 1983:270).

10 At the time when the Euralex Circular was prepared and circulated, Hungary was still a socialist country.

11 Motivation has to be seen from the point of view of the reader rather than the translator. In a sense, all deviant configurations are 'motivated' from the translator's point of view: they are 'equivalents' that can be slotted in at some point to allow the translator to get on with the rest of the job. This type of motivation, however, does not make a given configuration acceptable from the reader's point of view. To be justified, motivation has to be available to the reader.

12 www.newint.org.

CHAPTER 8

Beyond equivalence:
ethics and morality

Whatever the limitations on their social or interactional status in a given context, in situations where conflicting agendas arise or where the proper exercise of human or legal rights may be in doubt, translators' ethical and political judgments become as central to their task as cultural or linguistic competence. Translators cannot escape the burden of their moral proximity to others.

Inghilleri (2010a:153)

to become a point of contact can involve becoming a point of conflict.

(Maier 2007:256)

Various associations that represent translators and interpreters have long developed codes of practice, often referred to as codes of ethics, in order to ensure the accountability of their members to other parties involved in the interaction, particularly clients who pay their wages. In this chapter, we attempt to move beyond such codes in order to think critically about some of the concrete ethical choices and dilemmas that translators and interpreters often encounter and for which they are rarely prepared.

Of central concern in this chapter is the need to develop critical skills that can enable translators and interpreters to make ethical decisions for themselves, rather than have to fall back uncritically on abstract codes drawn up by their employers or the associations that represent them. This is important for at least three reasons. The first is that no code can ever predict the full range of concrete ethical issues that may arise in the course of professional practice, and hence translators – like other professionals – are often faced with situations in which it is difficult to interpret or apply the relevant code. Second, codes, like laws, are elaborated by people like us, and are therefore never infallible, ethically or otherwise. You might find yourself disagreeing with the code, perhaps because you believe it could result in tolerating certain types of injustice in some contexts. If so, it is your responsibility to question the code in order to avoid causing harm to others or perpetuating potential forms of injustice. And finally, it is in the interest of society as a whole for individuals to be accountable for their decisions, in professional life as elsewhere. Adopting the default position of applying a professional code unquestioningly undermines this accountability.[1]

We start, as elsewhere in this book, by defining the main concepts that will inform the discussion, including 'ethics' and 'morality'.

8.1 ETHICS AND MORALITY

Ethics and morality are generally understood to concern our ability to make decisions on the basis of what we believe to be morally right or wrong in a specific context. Those who follow what is known as **virtue ethics**, however, would argue that ethics is not just about knowing what to do on a given occasion. For them, rather than focusing on the question 'What should I do?', we must each be concerned with the question 'What kind of person should I be?' – or, more specifically, 'What kind of parent should I be?', 'What kind of politician should I be?', 'What kind of translator should I be?' and so on. As Cheney et al. explain, 'virtue ethics takes a long view of ethical issues, framing them not as merely momentary or episodic concerns but rather as issues relevant across all domains of life and one's entire lifespan' (2010:238). Ethics is thus understood as a lifelong process of learning and improvement, of nurturing the right virtues in ourselves and those in our care. But the two issues are clearly inseparable, since in striving to be a better person an individual must reflect on the same principles and ideals that inform his or her decision about what is ethical to do in a specific context.

The decision we take on any given occasion is generally judged as ethical or unethical to the extent that it affects others, for example in terms of their survival, freedom, well-being, comfort, happiness or success. Unethical behaviour thus causes harm *to others.* A person who behaves in a way that affects only him- or herself negatively is imprudent, not unethical (Driver 2007). It is unethical to torture, rape or deal in drugs. It is imprudent not to brush one's teeth regularly, or study for an exam, or save towards one's retirement. However, as is evident even from these examples, the distinction between the self and others is never straightforward; if it were, committing suicide would not be the subject of ethical debate. Because it is difficult to extract oneself from others, to act in a way that has no impact on the lives of at least those in our immediate vicinity, 'prudent' and 'ethical' are best thought of as points on a continuum rather than absolute values.

Cheney et al. (2010:3–4) reiterate a commonly held lay view, namely, that discussions of ethics revolve around 'dry, abstract' principles that are negatively formulated in the form of 'don'ts' rather than 'dos', while morality concerns everyday decisions, features prominently in public debates about the rights and wrongs of specific events, and therefore seems more relevant to our lives. Prado (2006) draws a similar distinction, adding that ethics has now come to be associated with the right conduct in professional life (hence our use of labels such as 'business ethics' and 'medical ethics'), whereas morality refers to the right conduct for everyone. Focusing on ethics in the context of translation, Koskinen (2000:11) makes the same distinction in slightly different terms:

> I see morality as a characteristic not of communities but of individuals, and ethics as 'collectivised' morality, as a collective effort of a community to formulate a set of rules or recommendations of accepted moral behaviour.

The common threads here are that ethics is collective, involves conscious elaboration of codes and principles that constrain the behaviour of those obliged to abide by them, and is increasingly associated with professional and institutional contexts, all of which explains why various institutions and associations have *codes of ethics*, rather than *codes of morality*. Despite its popularity, this distinction will not be maintained here: I will be using ethics, morality and their derivatives interchangeably, as they are often used in lay discussions. On the whole, I will also assume, with Cheney *et al.* (2010:237), that 'ethics is about the stream of life rather than just its turbulent moments', and that many default choices that do not necessarily give rise to conscious decision-making can have important ethical implications.

How do we decide what is ethical?

We might begin to address this question by drawing a broad distinction between teleological and deontological approaches to the issue of ethical decision-making. **Deontological** models define what is ethical by reference to what is right in and of itself, irrespective of consequences, and are rule-based.[2] Kantian ethics (discussed below) is a good example. A deontological approach would justify an action on the basis of principles such as duty, loyalty or respect for human dignity; hence: 'I refrain from intervening because it is my duty as a translator to remain impartial', or 'I intervene where necessary because it is the duty of a responsible interpreter to empower the deaf participant'. **Teleological** approaches, on the other hand, define what is ethical by reference to what produces the best results. Utilitarianism (also discussed below) is a teleological theory that is more concerned with consequences than with what is morally right *per se*. A teleological approach would justify an action on the basis of the envisaged end results; hence: 'Making a conscious effort [in community interpreting] to remain impartial can help avoid emotional involvement and possible burn-out' (Hale 2007:121–122), or 'I translate as idiomatically as possible because fluent translations receive good reviews'. The distinction between deontological and teleological approaches cuts across the various models of ethics discussed here, and others not dealt with in this chapter.

In the following discussion of specific approaches to ethics, you will note that different approaches can sometimes lead to the same decision, based on quite different arguments. As you reflect on each approach, it is important to bear in mind that the issue of *why* we opt for one decision rather than another is just as important as *what* decision we opt for. This is because the arguments we use to justify our actions to ourselves and others contribute to shaping the moral outlook of our communities. For example, whether we argue that torture is wrong because it produces what is referred to sometimes as 'low grade information'[3] or because it is a gross violation of human rights, whatever the quality of information it produces, is in itself a moral statement that reflects our attitude to others. The cumulative weight and balance of such arguments in any society will gradually incline its members to be more or less compassionate, more or less tolerant and so on. The arguments we use, like the specific linguistic choices we make (whether we call someone *disabled* or *a cripple*, for instance), are not without their own consequences.

The attempt to separate morality from ethics and to restrict it to the individual might suggest that what is moral is a matter of opinion, like an aesthetic judgement of beauty or elegance. This type of **relativism** can take various forms. Some relativists suggest that what is moral varies from one society to another and at different points in history, and that we must therefore refrain from judging others on the basis of our own, current values. This is like saying that different communities have different cultural beliefs, and that tolerance requires us to accept their way of life and expect them to accept ours. By this argument, societies that deny women access to education, for instance, would simply be abiding by a different moral code that we must not judge as wrong by our own values. Extending the same argument further, some relativists insist that each individual has his or her own set of moral values, and that no individual is in a position to judge the moral claims of another. Both of these positions are at the opposite extreme from any deontological model, since they offer no scope for defining an action as right in and of itself. But they are not teleological either, since they refrain from defining what is ethical for anyone other than the agent, with his or her own unique set of values. And it is precisely because they undermine the possibility of any moral judgement that both forms of relativism are intuitively unsatisfying for many people. If we follow them we would have to accept that slavery and apartheid practices should be tolerated, and that a paedophile who believes it is morally acceptable to rape children should not be punished. Moreover, belief in absolute relativism, whether at individual or collective level, would ultimately encourage conformity to the status quo and hence stifle critical thinking and action, to the detriment of society as a whole. As Driver argues, 'moral progress is often achieved through the efforts of rebellious individuals with beliefs that do not conform to popular cultural beliefs' (2007:18). Such individuals do not just hold different beliefs – they have the moral courage to act on them, to question the dominant beliefs of their societies and to resist practices that they consider ethically unacceptable. Martin Luther King in the United States, Mahatma Ghandi in India, Aung San Suu Kyi in Burma and Nelson Mandela in South Africa are good examples of individuals whose legacies challenge extreme relativism. At any rate, in practice relativism is a comfortable doctrine to hold on to only when the issue in question does not touch an aspect of our lives that really matters to us. As Blackburn explains, '[those] who say, "Well, it's just an opinion," one moment, will demonstrate the most intense attachment to a particular opinion the next, when the issue is stopping hunting, or preventing vivisection, or permitting abortion – something they care about' (2001:28).

Nevertheless, cultural relativism has many followers, and its main argument has a certain appeal in the context of translation and interpreting in particular, since it supports tolerance and cultural diversity. Relativism also alerts us to the fact that what is deemed controversial, and hence requires more sensitivity from a translator or interpreter to communicate, varies from one social environment to another. The right to wear the hijab is not a controversial issue in Saudi Arabia – if anything, it is the right not to wear the hijab that is controversial. A text about banning the hijab in, say, Belgium or France will therefore be more challenging to a mainstream Saudi audience than to the average Korean or Chinese reader. The extent to which one can challenge the values and expectations of readers and still maintain their involvement and treat them with dignity is an issue that occupies the minds of many translators and influences their choice of wording as well as what to include and what to omit, often with the involvement of their commissioner or other parties in the interaction.

Some aspects of relativism are thus helpful in thinking about certain issues in translation and interpreting. At the same time, we must remember that morality is not the same as good manners or socially approved habits, which do vary considerably from one cultural environment to another (Driver 2007:16). If translators are to behave in an ethically responsible manner, their decisions must be informed by principles that take account of the impact of their actions on others, principles such as 'do no harm' or 'do not acquiesce in injustice', irrespective of the prevailing moral code and social norms of the source or target culture. **Universalists** believe that such basic moral principles do exist and that they apply universally, but the way we interpret them can vary from one context to another. This context-sensitive version of universalism seems to strike a reasonable balance between pure, unbridled relativism and rigid, intolerant forms of moralizing, or as Blackburn puts it, 'between the saggy sands of relativism and the cold rocks of dogmatism' (2001:29). But this deontological approach does not solve all problems, partly because there is no general agreement about the set of relevant principles and partly because the principles often clash in real life. Causing no harm to one person can result in causing harm to another, and there are of course different types and degrees of harm.

Consequentialist theories, the best known among which is **utilitarianism**, bypass the issue of principles and their variation across cultures by assessing moral conduct purely on the basis of a cost-benefit analysis of the consequences of an action or behaviour. At one extreme, egoists maintain that an action is moral or ethical if its consequences are favourable for its agent. At the other extreme, altruists maintain that an action is moral if its consequences are favourable for everyone except the agent. Striking a middle course between the two, utilitarianism considers an action moral to the extent that its consequences are favourable for everyone, including the agent. Utilitarianism comes in two versions: act-utilitarianism and rule-utilitarianism.

Act-utilitarianists argue that an ethical decision is one that results in the most favourable consequences for the largest number of people *in a given context*. Torture would thus be acceptable if those authorizing it believed it could lead to information that would prevent death and injury to many innocent civilians. It is unacceptable by the same logic if, as Brigadier General David R. Irvine argued in 2005,[4] it is found to produce unreliable information, because those being tortured will say anything to put an end to their ordeal. The argument here is not concerned with the rights of those being tortured, but merely with the efficacy of the practice. In one of many such incidents reported in the media since 2001, the decision taken by the cabin crew and Spanish airport police on a flight from Malaga to Manchester in 2006 could be thought of as ethical in the same terms. In this case, several passengers who had 'overheard two men of Asian appearance apparently talking Arabic', according to the British newspaper the *Daily Mail*,[5] decided that they may be terrorists and refused to allow the flight to take off. The men were then removed, and the flight proceeded on its course. The decision to comply with the passengers' demands produced the 'best' consequences in the sense of avoiding major disruption to the plans of a large number of people and dealing effectively with their anxieties. However, many would consider it unethical, both because of its violation of the rights of two passengers who had committed no crime, and for its larger implications in terms of sustaining racism and vigilante practices.

In translation, act-utilitarian logic would support a decision that results in the largest number of participants, including the translator, achieving their objectives on a given occasion, even if the rights of one participant, perhaps an immigrant or the foreign author, are undermined. Like almost all ethical arguments, this statement is not straightforward and can be interpreted in a variety of ways. Someone could argue, for instance, that the 'participants' include not only those involved in the immediate interaction, but also the profession represented by the translator, the society in which translation takes place, the community to which the immigrant belongs and indeed the whole of humanity. This would fit in with the second version of utilitarianism, namely **rule-utilitarianism**, which considers that 'the right action is that action which is performed in accordance with a rule, or set of rules, the following of which maximizes utility' (Driver 2007:64).[6] Act-utilitarianism and rule-utilitarianism can thus yield quite different decisions based on utilitarian principles. The classic case here would be the typical hostage crisis: an act-utilitarian would probably opt for yielding to the hostage-takers' demands, while a rule-utilitarian would not, because doing so would not maximize utility overall. However defined, any form of utilitarianism can lead to some very questionable decisions. Following the rule 'don't steal' because it maximizes utility overall when one's family is starving and their lives can be saved by taking food from someone who has more than enough does not seem fair or realistic. Act-utilitarianism is similarly problematic and can lead to gross injustices, although it does reflect the decision-making processes that many people seem to adopt in real life.[7]

The ethical dilemmas that can lead many to adopt utilitarian decisions are brought to life vividly in Khaled Hosseini's bestselling novel, *The Kite Runner*. In the following scene, the main character returns to war-torn, Taliban-controlled Kabul to find his nephew and take him to safety. He is led by a taxi driver named Farid to the orphanage where his nephew was last seen. In talking to the director, Zaman, he discovers that like a number of other children his nephew had been handed over to the local war lords. The following exchange captures the ethical dilemma of the director, which he chooses to resolve on the basis of utilitarian principles (Hosseini 2003:235–236, 237):

> 'There is a Talib official,' he muttered. 'He visits once every month or two. He brings cash with him, not a lot, but better than nothing at all.' His shifty eyes fell on me, rolled away. 'Usually he'll take a girl. But not always.'
>
> 'And you allow this?' Farid said behind me. He was going around the table, closing in on Zaman.
>
> 'What choice do I have?' Zaman shot back. He pushed himself away from the desk.
>
> 'You're the director here,' Farid said. 'Your job is watch over these children.'
>
> 'There's nothing I can do to stop it.'
>
> 'You're selling children!' Farid barked.
>
> …
>
> Zaman dropped his hands. 'I haven't been paid in over six months. I'm broke because I've spent my life's savings on this orphanage. Everything I ever owned or inherited I sold to run this godforsaken place. You think I don't have family in Pakistan and Iran? I could have run like everyone else. But I didn't. I stayed. I stayed because of *them* [the children in the orphanage].' … 'If I deny him one child, he takes ten. So I let him take one and leave the judging to Allah. I swallow my pride and take his goddam filthy … dirty money. Then I go to the bazaar and buy food for the children.'

This is clearly an extreme case, but it captures the nature of ethical dilemmas and the appeal of utilitarianism in some contexts.

Particularly taxing ethical dilemmas, then, arise when the consequences of any decision we make are morally reprehensible, however small the number of people affected by them; in this rather exceptional case, the director cannot avoid doing serious harm to others, whatever his choice. It is worth noting here that one of the weaknesses of utilitarianism is that it does not take account of emotional factors, which come into play strongly when one or more of those who may be negatively affected by a difficult decision are very close to the agent: few people would in practice be able to sacrifice their son or daughter to save others, whatever the outcome of an abstract cost-benefit analysis.[8] But ethical dilemmas also arise if we follow universalist ethics, specifically when two or more of what we might think of as universal principles come into conflict, as when following the principle of truth or honesty would result in doing harm to someone.

Because of the difficulty of reconciling principles on the basis of consequences or universal values, some argue that **Kantian ethics** is a better option than both utilitarianism and universalism. Broadly speaking, Kantian ethics maintains that actions are right or wrong in and of themselves, irrespective of their consequences and of contextual considerations. A similar logic, or sentiment, is often expressed in the blogs and writings of professional translators. In an article which appeared in the journal of the Medical Division of the American Translators' Association, Michael McCann (2006), former Chairman of the Irish Translators' Association, insists:

> The principles of ethics governing a translator's work are applications of the great moral principles, based not on the quicksand of relativism, but solidly founded on the absolute foundation of what is good in itself, to the avoidance of what is wrong, for the pure, simple and unadulterated reason, that good is right, and that bad is wrong.

More specifically, however, Kantian ethics maintains that our actions must ultimately be motivated by a sense of duty. Some duties are so important that they admit of no exceptions: such is our duty to tell the truth at all times, because it is a necessary part of our duty to treat others with respect and dignity. Treating others with dignity means respecting their autonomy by allowing them access to all the information they need to make decisions that affect their lives and well-being. It requires us to acknowledge the right of all human beings 'to act for reasons they have formulated for themselves' (Benn 1998:208). Kantian ethics has had considerable influence on formulating ethical policy in several fields (Driver 2007), including medicine, where misleading patients about the nature of their treatment or their chances of recovery is no longer permissible in many parts of the world, irrespective of the negative psychological impact this can have on them or their loved ones.

Like all theories of ethics, taken individually, Kantian ethics falls short of offering us satisfying solutions in some situations which we might experience as morally taxing. It also does not reflect the way people often behave intuitively. In one of many such examples cited in the literature, the bilingual daughter of an Italian immigrant in Canada interprets between her father and an English-speaking Canadian in a business negotiation. When her father loses his temper and calls the Canadian businessman a fool (Digli che è un imbecile!), she renders this as 'My father won't accept your offer' (Mason 1999:156). Following Kantian principles, this must be considered unethical behaviour, because it violates the requirements of truth and autonomy. But we get different assessments if we draw on alternative models of ethical behaviour. Kantian ethics aside, whether we think the interpreter's behaviour is ethical or not will depend on at least two considerations. First, what we believe is likely to be the best outcome for all participants (both short term and long term), if we follow utilitarian logic. Second, whether we think the father's behaviour is guided by different norms and expectations operative in his own cultural setting, where perhaps calling someone a fool to express dissatisfaction does not carry the same weight as it does in the Canadian context – a partially relativist position. If so, there is no point in causing unintended offence (unnecessary harm), we might argue, and the young interpreter will have made an ethically responsible decision. An egoist, on the other hand, would consider the interpreter's behaviour ethical on the basis that she is protecting herself from being caught up in a stressful confrontation or being blamed for it. No doubt this kind of egoist logic motivates many decisions in translation and interpreting. As Donovan (2011) argues, conference interpreters' (and translators') insistence on 'professional neutrality and confidentiality as the pillars of their professional codes of practice' is at least partly motivated by the fact that 'this position protects them from awkward and even threatening criticism and deflects potential pressure from powerful clients'. Assuming we are not egoists, however, how ethical or unethical we think the resulting behaviour is will depend primarily on the extent to which we believe it impacts negatively on other participants, rather than merely on ourselves.

Other situations present different types of ethical challenge, for both Kantian and other approaches. What should a sign language interpreter do, for instance, when asked to make a phone call to a sex service on behalf of a deaf client?[9] On the one hand, the interpreter may feel that the sex industry is demeaning and exploitative, and that by supporting it he or she would be doing harm to others. On the other hand, it is possible to argue, in Kantian terms, that the interpreter has a duty to empower the deaf person, who should be able to make his or her own ethical decisions. Similarly, in a focus group study undertaken in several US hospitals in order to explore the difficulties encountered by interpreters in implementing standards drawn up by healthcare organizations in California, Angelelli (2006:182, 183–184) quotes two participants expressing quite different views, with different implications for the autonomy of the patient in a medical encounter:

> Let's say you are a good interpreter, right? And you are interpreting everything that is going on. All of a sudden, I am a nurse, I come in the room and I tell the doctor, 'you are giving the patient erythromycin and he is allergic to it. Do you still want to give him that or change it?' Now there is no need for you to interpret that. It has nothing to do with the patient.

> Sometimes when there is an English-speaking patient, the doctor and the nurse do not discuss certain things in front of the patient. They go outside. But when the patient is non-English-speaking, I have been in that situation. I had someone, an older person, come in and he was dying and the two doctors were standing in front of the patient saying 'he is going to keep coming here until he dies, until he gets pneumonia and finally …' I can't translate that for the patient. And I ask the doctors, 'Would you like me to translate that?' And they say, 'Oh, no. This is among ourselves.' 'Then please step outside.' That is what I said.

The first interpreter is clearly not aware of any ethical questions relating to the patient's right to have access to the full interaction in which he or she is not only involved but is also the subject of conversation and decision-making. The second interpreter finds it unethical to exclude a participant from an ongoing conversation in which he or she is physically present, and acts accordingly. A utilitarian approach would minimize the ethical implications here: there is no physical or psychological harm done to patients, as long as they do not find out that something was said about them to which they were not privy ('what you don't know can't hurt you' is a common, utilitarian saying in English that probably has its counterpart in many other languages). But a Kantian would point out that by allowing one participant to be excluded from the interaction and failing to inform him or her about an exchange that impacts his or her well-being, the interpreter has effectively failed to treat that participant with the dignity he or she deserves. A similar argument could be advanced with respect to significant shifts introduced in some forms of translation, such as literary translation, without the knowledge and consent of the author[10] and/or without alerting the target reader. A good example is the 1969 English translation of Milan Kundera's *The Joke*, in which the chapters of the book are reordered to reflect the chronological development of the plot, even though Kundera had specifically opted for a different order in the original (Kuhiwczak 1990). Kundera's subsequent outrage, expressed in a letter published in *The Times Literary Supplement* in the same year, is understandable in ethical terms on the basis that he remains a key participant in any interaction that involves a text which still bears his name, and as such is entitled to be treated with dignity and respect: his consent should have been sought for such a major form of intervention.

Whatever theory of ethics informs our thinking, when principles clash or our choices are severely restricted there will be no easy answer, no ready-made solution that can be extracted from any code. Ethical dilemmas are just that: dilemmas. As Goodwin explains in his discussion of the choice of subtitles in a politically charged documentary, 'like the technical question,[11] the ethical question does not admit of an easy answer' (2010:25). And yet, we have to be able to anticipate ethical difficulties in our professional life and to think of the various options available to us critically, because however difficult the decisions we have to make we are still accountable for them, to ourselves as well as others.

8.2 PROFESSIONALISM, CODES OF ETHICS AND THE LAW

Most professions have codes of ethics that regulate the behaviour of their members and demonstrate to those who depend on their services that they have mechanisms for ensuring accountability. In principle, professional codes can – and should – have a positive impact on the community to which they apply, and cannot be dismissed as irrelevant unless they prove to be out of touch with the realities of practice and with the moral outlook of practitioners. But they must always be approached critically, assessed on their own merits, and not used to 'deflect the necessity of ongoing personal and systemic reflection and adaptation' (Cheney *et al.* 2010:181).

Cheney *et al.* (*ibid.*:15) argue that the term 'professional' can have negative ethical implications, and may be used simply to constrain behaviour, to the detriment of moral standards in society. The phrase 'acting like a professional', they suggest, 'can be … code for not "rocking the boat" or not being fully human'. Moreover, in elaborating their codes of ethics, institutions sometimes negotiate the rules sensitively with their members and take account of their experience and values, but more often they impose these codes from the top down, as a response to some legal or public relations concerns. The resulting codes then tend to be 'oriented toward encouraging compliance with regulations far more than they are with elevating behavior' (*ibid.*).

Similarly, as Driver explains (2007:5), 'ethics and the law are distinct', and while one hopes that 'ethical norms will inform the content and enforcement of the law', we know that many laws have been used in the past and continue to be used today to discriminate against certain minorities, including women in some societies and blacks in many countries in the past, and to assist in various forms of colonial violence. This is perhaps why the World Medical Association's International Code of Ethics stipulates that 'a doctor's or investigator's conscience and duty of care must transcend national laws' (Godlee 2009). Consequently, where most professional codes of ethics understandably discourage members from breaking the law, some people will occasionally decide that it is unethical to do otherwise. In our specific context, some scholars have recently warned against 'restricting the notion of ethics in translation to questions … [of] contractual or legal obligations related to terms of employment' (Tymoczko 2007:219) because it turns translators into unthinking cogs in the wheel of an established social system rather than reflective and ethically responsible citizens.

Nevertheless, for many scholars and practitioners, professional codes of translation and interpreting are and must remain the reference point for ethical behaviour in the field. To resolve a range of ethical dilemmas for which the code offers no satisfying answers, some have argued that 'the code applies to the interpreted encounter, and not to any interactions before or after the professional encounter' (Hale 2007:130–131). Thus, the principle of confidentiality, which is central to all professional codes of interpreting and translation, does not necessarily have to apply when a patient tells an interpreter in the waiting room of a clinic that he or she intends to commit suicide but does not wish this to be revealed to the doctor. In deciding how to act ethically in this instance, the interpreter has to use his or her own judgement or appeal to some other code, perhaps the medical code, to resolve this dilemma. But this separation of pre/post-encounter and the encounter itself is arguably artificial and difficult to maintain in practice. At any rate, similar dilemmas often emerge during the professional encounter itself, and are no less ethically taxing for the translator or interpreter than those that arise outside the encounter proper.

When translators and interpreters are faced with serious ethical dilemmas, within or around the encounter proper, one way in which they might attempt to negotiate the need to abide by professional and legal codes on the one hand, and to act ethically on the other, is to reinterpret the key terms of the code. Almost all codes drawn up by associations that represent translators and interpreters consider impartiality to be a prerequisite for professional behaviour. Erik Camayd-Freixas was one of twenty-six interpreters called in to provide interpreting between US Immigration and Customs Enforcement officials and illegal immigrants arrested during a major raid on a slaughterhouse in Iowa in May 2008. In a long statement he published afterwards, he describes some of the harrowing scenes he witnessed when he and his fellow interpreters unexpectedly found themselves party to major abuses of the rights of these vulnerable immigrants. He quotes one of his fellow interpreters saying 'I feel a tremendous solidarity with these people', then comments: 'Had we lost our impartiality? Not at all: that was our impartial and probably unanimous judgment' (Camayd-Freixas 2008a). Rather than question the principle of impartiality, Camayd-Freixas thus chooses to interpret it as compatible with feelings of compassion and solidarity with the oppressed. His acceptance note when he was offered the Inttranews Linguist of the Year Award in 2008 further reveals his awareness of the potential conflict between various key principles that feature in almost all professional codes in the field:[12]

> We live in changing times where the canons of ethics are being redefined in many professions. For translators and interpreters, the prime imperative is Accuracy, followed by Impartiality and Confidentiality. In cases of conflict, Accuracy governs. And today there are cases in which Accuracy must be regarded as something more than mere literal correctness. If we are to be more than translation machines, more than automatons, if we strive to have a conscience and a heart, we must go beyond the words, to the deeper structures of meaning. For long, linguists have taken refuge in the comfort of formal correctness, but our world has closed that loophole. That ethical shelter is no more. Our Oath of Accuracy – we now realize – means a commitment to Truth.

Hale (2007:117–124) similarly accepts that impartiality does not mean lack of feelings on the part of the interpreter, but argues that interpreters must not allow their personal opinions or feelings to interfere with their work; if necessary, they can always declare a conflict of interest and decline the job. In Camayd-Freixas' case, however, things did not prove quite so straightforward, not least because he did not realize what was going on until he arrived on the scene and began interpreting.[13] He also had to weigh the ethical implications of ignoring injustice by simply walking away from it, as opposed to intervening to change the situation in the longer term. In an article about his experience that appeared in *The New York Times* (Preston 2008), he is reported to have 'considered withdrawing from the assignment, but decided instead that he could play a valuable role by witnessing the proceedings and making them known'. He then took 'the unusual step of breaking the code of confidentiality among legal interpreters about their work' (*ibid.*) by publishing a fourteen-page essay describing what he witnessed and giving interviews about his experience.[14] While maintaining his 'impartiality' during the assignment, to the best of his ability, he nevertheless arguably violated another professional and legal principle that could have had serious consequences for him personally, namely the principle of confidentiality.[15]

Donovan (in press) describes another situation that made adhering to the principle of impartiality ethically problematic, and that she chose to resolve by distancing herself from the utterance linguistically and justifying her intervention from a different perspective this time – not with reference to what occurs within or outside the encounter proper, but with reference to what might be considered standard practice within a specific type of event involving a conference interpreter. The 'interpreter' she refers to in the third person here is herself:

> During a lunch discussion, a Brazilian participant began to justify the assassi-nation of street children by paramilitaries. The interpreter, taken aback, intro-duced her rendition with 'the speaker seems to be saying that ...', thus distancing herself doubly from the content. This is a clear and deliberate break with standard practice. Thus, by using the third person the interpreter indicates disapproval and in effect comments on the speaker's remarks. ... This would generally be perceived as an unethical rendition by the standards of professional practice. The distancing was possible because the interpreter felt her obligation of complete, impartial rendition was weakened by the non-representational (i.e. personal) nature of the statement and its occurrence outside the official proceedings.

Commenting on the ethical implications of following the same principle in a very different context, Inghilleri (2010b) explains that impartiality for Sadi Othman, a trusted interpreter who worked with the US forces and local officials in Iraq following the invasion of the country in 2003, simply means that he does not side with one party or the other, whatever the nature of the interaction he mediates. As Inghilleri points out, what adherence to the principle of impartiality does in this case is 'to shield Othman, an avowed pacifist, from any moral responsibility for his direct participation in a war which has caused the deaths of thousands of innocent civilians' (*ibid.*: 191). Ultimately, then, impartiality, like almost any principle you will encounter in a legal or professional code, can be interpreted in different ways – by translators/interpreters and by other parties involved in the encounter or those who are in a position to comment on their behaviour.

8.3 THE ETHICAL IMPLICATIONS OF LINGUISTIC CHOICES

Accuracy, as already pointed out, is one of the principles included in most codes of ethics, and like impartiality and confidentiality can be difficult to adhere to for ethical reasons. But accuracy focuses specifically on the relationship between the source and target text, or source and target utterance in the case of interpreting.

The following extracts are from an article that appeared in the June 2010 issue of the KLM inflight magazine *Holland Herald* (Lapiere 2010:45–48). Translating this article would raise difficult ethical issues for many people, especially those who believe that some linguistic choices are demeaning for women and strengthen perceptions of them as objects to be possessed rather than equal members of society.

Tour of beauty

She was the loveliest baby any man could dream of marrying. The pale green, eight-cylinder Corniche I was contemplating in the window of London's Conduit Street Rolls-Royce showroom was the ultimate symbol of beauty and motor perfection.

... Driving throughout India aboard a Rolls-Royce and coming back home through Pakistan, Afghanistan, Iran and the whole Middle East at the wheel of such a mythical car was the ultimate dream I could think of. Though I did not possess a bowler hat and an umbrella to establish my credibility, I entered the showroom absolutely determined to make that Corniche my bride.
...
I had her spend her first Indian night in one of the majestic garages of the Royal Bombay Yacht Club that had formerly housed the Silver Phantoms and Silver Ghosts of the empire's high dignatories.
...
In a few months, I covered almost 20,000 kilometres throughout the former British Empire, often on terrible roads, under the pouring rains of the monsoon as well as in the blazing heat of summer. In spite of the filthy petrol with which I quenched her thirst, my Rolls-Royce never complained. She proudly sailed everywhere like her ancestors had in the times of the viceroys and the maharajas.
...
Since then, the beautiful car bought with the blessings of Lord Mountbatten has continued to be part of my life. Like an old couple that love has united for eternity, together we have covered many more thousands of kilometres across France and Europe. It is now 51 years old, and I am 78. She is parked under the red tiles of a garage just opposite the room where I have my work table. I have only to look up and glance out of the window to see the symbol of the greatest joys of my life, and draw from it the inspiration for further dreams.

This article, which is worth reading in full,[16] is problematic at more than one level – among other things, it paints a rather romantic and rosy picture of a colonial world that in reality was far from romantic for those at the receiving end of colonial violence. The car is explicitly associated with the 'grandeur' of that imperial past and referred to as 'she', 'loveliest baby' and 'bride'. Such gendered references and the idea of driving this obedient 'bride' who never complains through the lands of the former maharajas and viceroys are likely to trouble translators who are alert to the gender issue and to the violence of colonialism. For those who believe that such language and imagery can have negative ethical implications for society as a whole, and that it is therefore unethical to perpetuate this type of discourse through trans-lation, the answer is still not easy. They still have to address the implications of eliminating or even reducing the gendered references, downplaying the sexualized tenor of the original, or omitting some of the implicit praise of Britain's imperial past. Although it would be easy to achieve in many languages, without departing significantly from the content of the article, altering the tenor of the source text entails a certain disrespect for the autonomy of others involved in the encounter. In Kantian terms, we would have to acknowledge that the author has a right to express his own world view, and the reader has a right to access and judge that world view for him- or herself. Unfortunately, many contexts of translation do not afford translators the opportunity to include footnotes or even prefaces in which they might comment on unsavoury aspects of a source text that they wish to dissociate themselves from,[17] thus forcing them to make a decision that involves doing harm to one or more parties in the encounter: the author, the reader, their own values, a social or ethnic group, or even society as a whole. Some translators might attempt to resolve the dilemma by declining the assignment altogether. This option is available in principle to freelance translators, but a staff translator (someone employed by the *Holland Herald* in this case) cannot normally refuse to translate texts that raise ethical issues for him or her. In one real-life instance, a staff translator working for an agency was asked by her employer to translate a glossary of slaughterhouse terms. As a vegetarian and animal lover, she found this ethically taxing and asked to be relieved of the task. As she puts it, her employers:

> were quite happy to humour me in that instance (it was not a terribly long text) but ... the conflict between my ethical position and professional requirements would have been much more of an issue had my employers gained a substantial contract with the meat industry.
>
> *(Myriam Salama-Carr, personal communication)*

These examples bring us to the broader issue of our ethical responsibility as producers of language and discourse, irrespective of – or in addition to – the question of whether the wording we use in a translation is semantically 'accurate' in relation to the source text. Our wording will always, inevitably, be different from the wording of the source text, since it will be realized in a different language. Ultimately, however, '[w]hat is at stake' when we render a stretch of text or utterance from one language into another 'is not so much linguistic difference, as the social and cultural representations of the Other that linguistic difference invariably presupposes' (Lane-Mercier 1997:46). Like the decision to replicate or tone down the gendered language of the 'Tour of beauty' article above, the choice of a particular dialect, idiolect or register with which to render the speech of a character in the source text or the defendant in a courtroom is potentially an ethical choice, one that has an impact on the way our readers or hearers will perceive the character in question (and consequently the community he or she represents), the veracity of a defendant's testimony, the reliability of a witness's statement, the credibility of an asylum seeker's account of his or her persecution.

In 2001, BBC News published extracts from a purported English translation of secret Chinese official documents on the 1989 events in Tiananmen Square in Beijing.[18] The article which featured these extracts began as follows (bold in original):

Meeting between Premier Li Peng and paramount leader Deng Xiaoping, 25 April, 1989:

Li Peng: 'The spear is now pointed directly at you and the others of the elder generation of proletarian revolutionaries ...'

Deng Xiaoping: 'This is no ordinary student movement. A tiny minority is exploiting the students – they want to confuse the people and throw the country into chaos. This is a well-planned plot whose real aim is to reject the Communist Party ...'.

Li Peng, Premier of the People's Republic of China at the time, comes across in this translation as at best quaint and at worst incoherent, perhaps even eccentric. In deciding how to represent the speech of a character in another language, whether this character is fictional or real, we have to consider not only the semantics and aesthetics of the source and target utterances but also the values and attitudes we attribute to these characters and their communities through the choices we make. Do our choices make the character appear more or less intelligent than we might reasonably assume they are or than they appear to their own communities? Do they make the character and their community seem ordinary, human (like us), or radically different, and hence incomprehensible or even threatening? How far should we go to mediate the distance between the source and target cultures, to ensure that members of the former are understood and respected by members of the latter? These are not easy or straightforward questions, and different translators will want to draw the line at different points of the continuum between rigid adherence to the semantics of an utterance and active intervention in reformulating a character's speech to enhance their chances of being taken seriously or treated with empathy in the target context. Ultimately, however, as Lane-Mercier argues in the context of literary translation (1997:46):

Far from constituting a neutral operation, both the stylization process to which literary sociolects are exposed and the comic, picturesque or realistic effects they generate involve the authorial manipulation of real-world class determinations, ethnic and gender images, power structures, relations of hierarchy and exclusion, cultural stereotypes and institutional roles.

These observations are as pertinent to the translation (and interpreting) of political figures in the news and defendants and witnesses in the court as they are to literary characters in a novel.

8.4 CONCLUDING REMARKS

In an article about the importance of translators that appeared in the *Observer* newspaper in April 2010, Tim Parks, a well-known novelist and literary translator, writes:

> Occasionally, a translator is invited to the festival of individual genius as the guest of a great man whose career he has furthered; made, even. He is Mr Eco in New York, Mr Rushdie in Germany. He is not recognised for the millions of decisions he made, but because he had the fortune to translate Rushdie or Eco. If he did wonderful work for less fortunate authors, we would never have heard of him.

Leaving aside the fact that Parks assumes great novelists and their translators to be male by default, there is much truth in this statement. Nevertheless, I hope that our brief excursion into the creativity and ethics of translation in this book will encourage readers to think of translation and interpreting as diverse, challenging, exciting and highly consequential activities, whether undertaken for great literary writers or destitute immigrants, whether awarded with glamorous literary prizes or treated as run-of-the-mill, everyday jobs. Indeed, it is the largely invisible and the least glamorous aspects of translators' and interpreters' work that can often have the greatest impact on the lives of those around them, and hence require them to approach every assignment not just as a technical but as a primarily ethical challenge, one that calls on us to recognize the humanity of others and treat them accordingly. As you experience the highs and lows of your career as a translator or interpreter, it is important not to lose sight of this simple truth.

exercises

1. Goodwin (2010:26–27) proposes two ways of looking at the issue of ethics in translation:

> For one group, ethics may be regarded as important but *extrinsic* to translation itself, so that the latter should be ethically governed (as all human activities are) but, once it is set within an overall moral framework, can proceed without it. An analogy might be mining exploration: there is such a thing as the ethics of mining exploration, but mining itself is a technical activity quite separate from the ethical framework within which it is conducted. Thus, we might send a geological mission to a foreign country to explore the potential for mining its natural resources: on one piece of paper we could write technical instructions for mining, and on another, quite separately, we could write an ethical code of conduct we wished the mission to observe. In sympathy with such an approach would be any translator who regards the activity

itself as a technical procedure, in principle susceptible to remainderless scientific description.

The other way of thinking about translation ... is that it is *intrinsically* ethical: that the activity itself cannot proceed without an account (explicit or implicit) of how the encounter with the 'other' human being should be conducted. An analogy might be trade: suppose that instead of a mining mission, we sent a trade mission to our imagined foreign country. In this case, the activity involves the other human beings which the mission will encounter, and the activity must be consensual (non-consensual trade is not trade, but pillage), such that the activity itself cannot take place other than in the context of an ethical framework which provides a basis for concepts such as volition, consent and exchange. It would perhaps be possible in such a case to divide our instructions into the 'technical' and the 'ethical', but only with difficulty, and the latter would play a much more important and integral role in the activity itself.

Consider the two scenarios outlined by Goodwin. To what extent is the distinction he draws applicable to mining, trading or any other human activity? Would you consider yourself part of the first or second group he refers to? Playing the devil's advocate, irrespective of your own position, how would you explain to a potential client why translation is *extrinsically* or *intrinsically* ethical, in Goodwin's terms? What impact might each explanation have on different types of client and their trust in translators?

2.   Writing as a literary translator who had to make difficult ethical decisions about whether or not to translate different Serbian authors whose works 'could be used by nationalists to justify a campaign of hatred and genocide' (2004:719), Jones (*ibid.*:723) presents two opposing arguments – one he dubs 'Olympianism' and the other *Realpolitik*:

The former [Olympianism] argues that translators should remain true to texts that are artistically good, even in tainted social circumstances of production and reception – such as a source culture hijacked by extreme nationalism – in the knowledge or hope that the culture will recover. The latter [*Realpolitik*] claims that a text cannot remain separate from and thus untainted by its social context. Thus, for example, a translator should refuse to translate works whose imagery is being exploited to justify genocide, no matter how innocuous that imagery might have seemed at the time of first writing.

exercises

Discuss the ethical implications of both positions, bearing in mind that carefully considered ethical arguments can be presented in each case, and as Jones points out, the balance in such difficult situations may at times be tipped by the nature of the agent's personal relations, rather than abstract ethical considerations: 'In the end', Jones explains:

> a key reason that I did *not* break with Serbian and Croatian poetry was that it would have meant breaking personal ties built up over many years. I tended to be very wary of building up new ties, however, except on the rare occasions when I felt that my translation work supported some sort of opposition to the nationalist mindset.
>
> *(ibid.:719)*

3. A number of translation agencies in various parts of the world increasingly offer work to student translators, many of whom undertake this work either free of charge or for a low rate, as a way of gaining experience. Aurora Humarán, one of the founding members of AIPTI (Asociación Internacional de Profesionales de la Traducción y la Interpretación/ International Association of Professional Translators and Interpreters, based in Argentina), has this to say on the subject:[19]

> Does a dentistry student perform root canals? No. Does an architecture student build anything? Not a thing. Does a law school student defend anyone? No one.
>
> Students from any of those career fields can, of course, perform some sort of work 'within their areas' of study. A dentistry student can work as an assistant in a dental office. An architecture student can get a handle on his/her future profession by doing administrative work in an architect's office. And anyone in the legal field is certainly aware of how many law students act as paralegals, traipsing from one court to another every morning.
>
> In our profession, however, there is no place, really, in which translation students can learn to take their first steps. There is no such job as dictionary handler, word researcher, glossarist or anything of the kind for those who are trying their hand at these tasks for the first time. No such position exists. Well, let me correct myself: It *didn't* exist. It didn't, that is, until some slick operators threw together an agency – the way you might slap together a stand for a rummage sale – and (*voila!*) translation students suddenly had a place to work. So, let's translate! But translate just like a professional translator? No way! This is cut-rate translation in which students do the work professionals

usually do, but for ridiculous rates, turning themselves into veritable 'beggar translators'.

Compare the above statement with the following argument about volunteer translation and interpreting offered by ECOS, a socially committed group of lecturers and students of translation in Spain (Manuel *et al.* 2004):

> In the association ECOS, Translators and Interpreters for Solidarity, we perform volunteer work of translation and interpreting for NGOs, social forums and other nonprofit organisations with affinities to the philosophy of our organisation. In no case would we wish to accept a continuous role in the performance of a service which ought to be supplied by professionals under contract.
>
> In other words, we do not intend that the voluntary nature of work performed should serve as an excuse for the creation of what is beginning to be called a 'third sector,' which would amount to the utilisation of volunteer work and non-profit organizations together with private initiative to organise, at low cost, services which in our opinion ought to be supplied by the public sector, the only one capable of the coverage necessary. ... our work is like that of volunteers who supply medicines to third-world communities completely outside the trade network known as globalization.
>
> ... we consider it indispensable to broaden the concept of professional ethics in these times of neo-liberal globalization, which deepens the inequalities between peoples and within them. We can no longer limit our aims merely to defending decent working conditions and rejecting the intrusion of non-qualified persons into the profession. It would be hypocritical to bemoan the price per word paid by such-and-such a company, or the size of the interpreter's booths in this or that convention centre, while feeling no scruples at working for those who organise exploitation, misery and war in this world.

Would you argue that translating and interpreting by students and/or volunteers of various levels of expertise is (a) always, (b) never or (c) sometimes unethical? If the latter, under what conditions might it be considered ethical, in the sense of doing no harm, or doing positive good, to various parties in the interaction and to other professional translators and interpreters?

4. Based on research into actual practice in a pediatric outpatient clinic in Switzerland, Leanza (2005) draws up an extended typology of roles assumed by interpreters in this setting. Merlini (2009:64–65) offers the following potted summary of these roles:

    (1) *Translator*: the interpreter minimizes her/his presence and simply facilitates communication;
    (2) *Active translator*: the interpreter engages either primary party to clarify minor points or linguistic details;
    (3) *Cultural informant*: the interpreter addresses the service provider to inform her/him about the service user's cultural norms and values;
    (4) *Advocate*: the interpreter addresses the service provider to defend and promote the service user's interests;
    (5) *Culture broker* or *cultural mediator*: the interpreter negotiates between two conflicting value systems and helps parties arrive at a shared model;
    (6) *Bilingual professional*: the interpreter leads the interview with the service user and reports to the service provider;
    (7) *Monolingual professional*: the interpreter expresses her/his views on the matter at hand to the service provider, acting as her/his peer;
    (8) *Welcomer*: the interpreter welcomes service users before the service provider meets them;
    (9) *Support*: the interpreter meets the service users in the community, as a follow-up to the encounter.

    What are the ethical implications of each of the above roles, from the perspective of various participants, including the interpreter?
    If we replace *service provider* and *service user* with categories such as *author* and *target reader*, or *film producer* and *viewer* in the case of subtitling and dubbing, can a similar typology be drawn up for different types of translation, where we might, for instance, consider certain types of intervention or of footnotes added by the translator, as evidence that they are playing the role of *cultural informant* or *culture broker*? In the case of face-to-face interpreting, the immediacy of the interaction means that most of the above roles are performed, or otherwise, 'on the spot' (but note that item 9 refers to activities undertaken outside the interpreted encounter). In the case of translation, more activities might be undertaken outside the immediate context of translation. For example, literary translators often work as *advocates* for authors with whom they empathize, and this might involve acting as their 'agents' in some respects, as when they arrange for them to receive invitations to

speak at literary festivals or be interviewed by the press, and often accompany them and interpret for them on such occasions. How do all these activities relate to ethical principles as expressed in professional codes? How might a translator or interpreter argue that acting in any of these capacities is ethical (or unethical) despite (or because of) the ethical values that regulate the profession – including impartiality, neutrality and accuracy?

5. Consider the following two statements:

> **There is ... a category of texts which, at first sight, appear to be positively illegal. If a translator agreed to translate bomb-making instructions, would he be responsible for attacks committed with the bombs produced with the help of such instructions? He certainly would, in our view, if he did not take the trouble of finding out who needed the translation, and for what purpose it was required. If the nature of the client were sufficiently obscure to raise even the slightest concern, no translator in his right mind would accept such an order. However, if the translation was commissioned by a government authority as part of efforts to study terrorists' practices, the translator might actually contribute to a good cause by translating even the most reprehensible texts.**
>
> *(Simons 2010)*

> **The law may itself be unjust. It may not serve the common good, but the good of the tyrant or the party. The apartheid laws in South Africa were a case in point. Laws that in certain countries discriminate against women or against minority groups pose a problem and the moral dilemma of whether obedience is appropriate. Such dilemmas have to be faced and require more than a simple injunction to 'obey the law of the land'.**
>
> *(Wright, undated)*

What issues do these statements raise in relation to the link between ethics and legality? Are practices and objectives promoted by a government and enshrined in law necessarily ethical? Under what conditions do you believe the translator may be justified in breaking the law and entitled to receive support from fellow translators and the professional associations that represent them?

6. One of the cornerstones of all professional codes of ethics, including those relating to translation, is confidentiality. And yet, speaking of professional ethics in general, Cheney *et al.* argue that '[s]ometimes being morally responsible may mean resisting an order, going public with private information, or leaving a job or career altogether'

(2010:153). Reflect on this issue in the context of a real life case, like that of Katharine Gun, former translator working for a British intelligence agency who leaked secret documents to the press in 2003; the documents related to illegal activities by the United States and Britain in relation to the then impending invasion of Iraq. For this particular case, you can consult Solomon (2003), Burkeman and Norton-Taylor (2004), Tyler (2004), *BBC News* (2004), Davies (2004) and *Institute for Public Accuracy* (undated). Much more material on this case can be retrieved by searching for 'Katharine Gun' on the web.

7. Barsky (1996, 2010) notes that immigrants, refugees and asylum seekers are ill-served by a system that is inclined to criminalize them as a group, that treats them as 'guilty by virtue of being there' (2010:292). 'The intrinsic shortcomings of the system', he suggests, 'are such that the poor and the persecuted are disadvantaged from the outset' (1996:61). While accepting that interpreters cannot be expected to ensure justice for the vulnerable (*ibid.*), he argues that they:

> **can help redress the wrongs of the system to some extent. ... they can assist the persecuted by allowing them to articulate their claims and negotiate their 'difference' in an environment which is less sympathetic the more 'different' the claimant is seen to be. They can fill in cultural gaps and compensate for tactical errors to ensure that genuine stories of suffering and persecution are properly 'heard'.**

Consider the ethical implications of each type of assistance Barsky suggests an interpreter could offer. How would a Kantian balance the rights of different parties in the interaction, including the right of legal personnel to be allowed to assess each case on its own merits, and the rights of immigrants and asylum seekers to be treated with dignity? How would an interpreter's 'duty' be defined in Kantian terms in this instance? How would a utilitarian assess the various consequences of intervention and lack of intervention on the part of interpreters? On balance, what would you view as the more ethical approach to adopt, and why?

SUGGESTIONS FOR FURTHER READING

Ethics

Benn, Piers (1998) *Ethics*, London: Routledge.

Cheney, George, Daniel J. Lair, Dean Ritz and Brenden E. Kendall (2010) *Just a Job? Communication, Ethics and Professional Life*, Oxford: Oxford University Press.

Driver, Julia (2007) *Ethics: The Fundamentals*, Oxford: Blackwell.

Godlee, Fiona (2009) 'Rules of Conscience', *BMJ (British Medical Journal)*, 14 May. Available at www.bmj.com/cgi/content/full/338/may14_1/b1972. (In addition to the main article, scroll to the bottom of the page and read at least some of the rapid responses to it.)

Sternberg, Robert J. (2009) 'A New Model for Teaching Ethical Behavior', *The Chronicle Review (The Chronicle of Higher Education)*, 24 April. Available for purchase at http://chronicle.com/article/A-New-Model-for-Teaching-Et/36202/.

Ethical issues in translation and interpreting

Angelelli, Claudia V. (2006) 'Validating Professional Standards and Codes: Challenges and Opportunities', *Interpreting* 8(2): 175–193.

Baker, Mona (2008) 'Ethics of Renarration – Mona Baker is Interviewed by Andrew Chesterman', *Cultus* 1(1): 10–33. Available at http://manchester.academia.edu/documents/0074/9064/Baker_Ethics_of_Renarration.pdf.

Baker, Mona and Carol Maier (eds) (2011) *Ethics and the Curriculum: Critical Perspectives*, Special Issue of *The Interpreter and Translator Trainer* 5(1).

Batchelor, Kathryn (2009) *Decolonizing Translation: Francophone African Novels in English Translation*, Manchester: St. Jerome Publishing. Chapter 8: 'Exploring the Postcolonial Turn in Translation Theory'.

Chesterman, Andrew (2001) 'Proposal for a Hieronymic Oath', *The Translator* 7(2): 139–154.

Diriker, Ebru (2004) *De-/Re-Contextualizing Conference Interpreting: Interpreters in the Ivory Tower?* Amsterdam: John Benjamins. Esp. Chapter 2 'Broader Social Context in SI'.

Goodwin, Phil (2010) 'Ethical Problems in Translation: Why We Might Need Steiner After All', *The Translator* 16(1): 19–42.

Hale, Sandra (2007) *Community Interpreting*, Basingstoke: Palgrave Macmillan. Chapter 4: 'Analysing the Interpreter's Code of Ethics'.

Hermans, Theo (2009) 'Translation, Ethics, Politics', in Jeremy Munday (ed.) *The Routledge Companion to Translation Studies*, Abingdon, Oxon: Routledge, 93–105.

Inghilleri, Moira (2008) 'The Ethical Task of the Translator in the Geo-political Arena: From Iraq to Guantánamo Bay', *Translation Studies* 1(1): 212–223.

Inghilleri, Moira (2009) 'Ethics', in Mona Baker and Gabriela Saldanha (eds) *Routledge Encyclopedia of Translation Studies*, second edition, London: Routledge, 100–104.

Jones, Francis R. (2004) 'Ethics, Aesthetics and Decision: Literary Translating in the Wars of the Yugoslav Succession', *Meta* 49(4): 711–728.

Koskinen, Kaisa (2000) *Beyond Ambivalence: Postmodernity and the Ethics of Translation*, Tampere, Finland: University of Tampere.

Maier, Carol (2007) 'The Translator's Visibility: The Rights and Responsibilities Thereof', in Myriam Salama-Carr (ed.) *Translating and Interpreting Conflict*, Amsterdam: Rodopi, 253–266.

Manuel Jerez, Jesús de, Juan López Cortés and María Brander de la Iglesia (2004) 'Social Commitment in Translation and Interpreting; A View from ECOS, Translators and Interpreters for Solidarity'. Available at www.translationdirectory.com/article366.htm.

Pöchhacker, Franz (2004) *Introducing Interpreting Studies*, London: Routledge. Chapter 8: 'Practice and Profession'.

NOTES

1   It is also the case that some translation and interpreting activities take place in contexts where no codes are available for practitioners to fall back on. Inghilleri (forthcoming) notes that:

> [f]or interpreters in war zones, the absence of any official institutional location means that they cannot justify their actions through appeals to organizational rules and principles as can members of the military. They cannot claim to be just following orders. There are no professional codes of duty and service or of neutrality and impartiality to shield them from the consequences of their ethical subjectivity.

2   Being rule-based does not mean that one cannot or should not reflect critically on the rules and amend them on the basis of good reason and experience.

3   See discussion of act-utilitarianism below.

4   See www.alternet.org/rights/28585/. Brigadier General David R. Irvine is a retired Army Reserve strategic intelligence officer who taught prisoner interrogation and military law for eighteen years with the Sixth Army Intelligence School in the US.

5   'Mutiny as passengers refuse to fly until Asians are removed', the *Daily Mail*, 20 August 2006. Available at www.dailymail.co.uk/news/article-401419/Mutiny-passengers-refuse-fly-Asians-removed.html.

6   As Driver (2007:64) notes, act-utilitarians also recognize rules, but they are rules of thumb that can be overridden by the assessment of potential consequences in a given context.

7   One of the positive aspects of utilitarianism is that it stresses negative responsibility, that is, the idea that the individual is ethically responsible for maximizing the good and can therefore be held accountable for failure to act – not just for acting unethically (Driver 2007:72).

8   See exercise (2) at the end of this chapter for a concrete example of the impact of emotional factors on translators' decisions.

9   This example was discussed by Jeff McWhinney in his keynote speech at the third IATIS conference in Melbourne, July 2009. See www.iatis.org/content/conferences/melbourne.php.

10 Not all source texts have single authors, or even an identifiable set of authors. Similarly, dead authors cannot be made aware of changes introduced to their texts, though these changes are often quite significant, as when a Shakespearean play is adapted to a variety of political contexts (see Abend-David 2003).

11 By this he means the question of what strategy or lexical choice is the correct one to adopt, semantically and stylistically.

12 See www.prlog.org/10157687-dr-erik-camayd-freixas-is-elected-inttranet-linguist-of-the-year-for-2008.html.

13 'The more I found out', he says in his subsequent public statement, 'the more I felt blindsighted into an assignment in which I wanted no part. ... nothing could have

prepared me for the prospect of helping our government put hundreds of innocent people in jail' (Camayd-Freixas 2008a).

14 Camayd-Freixas has been quite critical of *The Times'* reporting on his case. In an article he subsequently published in *Proteus* (the Newsletter of the National Association of Judiciary Interpreters and Translators, Camayd-Freixas 2008b), he states the following:

> When I sent the essay to the *Times*, my intention was for them to conduct an investigative report on some of the problems mentioned therein. Instead, the *Times* journalist decided – which is her prerogative – to write an article about my speaking out, more than about the contents of my message. As such, the *Times* article raised a question that needed to be asked and answered before one could discuss the real issues documented in the essay. That question regarded the propriety of my decision to speak out despite the confidentiality clause in the interpreters' code of ethics.
>
> By so doing, the *Times* article adopted a polemical strategy designed to spark a general readership's interest, but not specifically addressed to the professional. As a result, it answered only partially the question it raised, and lacked the rigor that an interpreter readership would require.

15 Camayd-Freixas (2008b) offers a detailed rebuttal of the suggestion that his actions imply general support for intervention on the part of interpreters and, more importantly, that he broke the code of confidentiality:

> The interpreter code of ethics, in particular the clause of confidentiality, has as its meaning and rationale that the interpreter must *not influence the outcome of the case*. The Postville case had been closed, and its 10-day deadline for appeal had expired before I even began the essay. I do not mention any names and aside from anecdotal information of a general nature, all the facts mentioned are either in the public record or freely available on the internet. So I was careful not to break the code of confidentiality.
>
> Moreover, confidentiality is not absolute. There are other ethical requirements which override confidentiality. For example, a medical interpreter, in whom a patient confides that he has an epidemic disease, has the obligation to report it because it is in the public interest to do so. Similarly, in the Postville case, there were higher imperatives arising not only out of public interest but also out of the legal role of the court interpreter.

16 The full article is available at http://holland-herald.com/2010/06/the-silver-cloud/.

17 Hermans (2007) offers some interesting examples of such paratextual interventions, including prefaces to translations of Hitler's *Mein Kampf*.

18 The extracts are from *The Tiananmen Papers*, edited by Andrew Nathan and Perry Link. See http://news.bbc.co.uk/1/hi/world/asia-pacific/1106614.stm. The status and authenticity of this document remain highly contested (see, for example, Chan 2004).

19 See www.aipti.org/eng/articles/art7-iapti-decries-student-exploitation.html for the full article.

Glossary

Note: This glossary is offered as a quick look-up facility. It includes technical terms which are used repeatedly in the book and which can be defined in a straightforward way. Other technical terms which require more involved explanations have not been included. Their definitions can be traced through the subject index.

Words are quoted in block letters in the body of a definition if they appear as separate entries.

Act-utilitarianism See UTILITARIANISM.

active See VOICE.

adjunct A word or group of words added to a CLAUSE to give more information about the circumstances of an event or situation, usually in terms of time, place or manner, e.g. *I've known him **for years***.

anaphora The use of a word or group of words to refer back to someone or something that has already been mentioned in a text, e.g. ***The Chancellor*** *remarked that **he** had no inferiority complex about the Soviet Union.*

aspect A grammatical category which involves using affixes and/or changing the form of the verb to indicate the temporal distribution of an event, for example whether an event is completed, whether it is momentary or continuous.

case A grammatical category which indicates the function of a noun or noun group in a CLAUSE. For example, in Arabic *al-waladu* is in the nominative case (usually indicating that it is the SUBJECT of the CLAUSE), and *al-walada* is in the accusative case (usually indicating that it is the OBJECT of the verb). In some languages, such as English, similar functions are indicated mainly by word order.

clause A group of words which form a grammatical unit containing a SUBJECT and a verb.

coherence The network of semantic relations which organize and create a text by establishing continuity of sense.

cohesion The network of lexical, grammatical and other relations which provide formal links between various parts of a text.

collocation The tendency of certain words to co-occur regularly in a given language.

collocational restrictions Semantically arbitrary restrictions which do not logically follow from the PROPOSITIONAL MEANING of a word (cf. SELECTIONAL RESTRICTIONS).

complement A noun group or adjective which comes after a link verb such as *is*, *was* or *remain* and gives more information about the SUBJECT, e.g. *The child looked **neglected**.*

conjunction A word or phrase which links together two CLAUSES, groups or words. *And*, *but* and *on the other hand* are conjunctions. In the model of COHESION used in this book, conjunction is also the process by which this type of linkage takes place.

consequentialism An approach to ethics which assesses moral conduct on the basis of a cost-benefit analysis of the consequences of an action or behaviour. At one extreme, egoists maintain that an action is moral or ethical if its consequences are favourable for its agent. At the other extreme, altruists maintain that an action is moral if its consequences are favourable for everyone except the agent. Striking a middle course between the two, UTILITARIANISM considers an action moral to the extent that its consequences are favourable for everyone, including the agent.

deontological models of ethics define what is ethical by reference to what is right in and of itself, irrespective of consequences, and are rule-based (cf. TELEO-LOGICAL MODELS).

dialect A variety of language which has currency within a specific community or group of speakers.

duty ethics See KANTIAN ETHICS.

evoked meaning Meaning which arises from variations in DIALECT and REGISTER.

expressive meaning Meaning which relates to the speaker's feelings or attitude.

gender A grammatical distinction according to which a noun or pronoun (and some-times an accompanying adjective, verb or article) are marked as either masculine or feminine in some languages.

genre A set of texts, spoken or written, which are institutionalized in so far as they are considered by a given speech community to be of the same type, for example the genre of political speeches or the genre of editorials.

hyponym A specific word in a SEMANTIC FIELD. In the field of 'plants', *conifer* is a hyponym of *tree* and *tree* is a hyponym of *plant* (cf. SUPERORDINATE).

implicature A term used in PRAGMATICS to refer to what the speaker means or implies rather than what he or she literally says.

intransitive verb A verb which does not take an OBJECT, e.g. *The lorry **stopped*** (cf. TRANSITIVE VERB).

Kantian ethics A DEONTOLOGICAL, duty-based approach to ethics which is concerned with what is right or wrong *per se*, irrespective of consequences. A moral action, according to Kant, is one that is motivated by a sense of duty and respect for the autonomy and dignity of others.

lexical set This term has two meanings. It may refer to the actual words and expressions within a SEMANTIC FIELD. In lexical studies, a lexical set is also used to refer to a list of items which have a like privilege of COLLOCATION, i.e. items which collocate with a specific word or expression.

morpheme The minimal formal element of meaning in language. The word *unhappy* consists of two morphemes: *un-* and *happy*.

morphology The study of word structure, the way in which the form of a word changes to indicate contrasts in grammatical systems such as TENSE and GENDER.

object (of verb) A noun or noun group which refers to a person or thing, other than the SUBJECT, which is involved in or affected by the action of the verb, e.g. *They treated **him** for a stomach ulcer.* The object of an ACTIVE clause can often be made the subject of a PASSIVE clause: ***He** was treated for a stomach ulcer.*

passive See VOICE.

person A grammatical category which defines participant roles through a closed system of pronouns, such as *I, you, he, she* and *it* in English.

pragmatics The study of language in use: of meaning as generated by specific participants in specific communicative situations, rather than meaning as generated by an abstract system of linguistic relations.

predicator The verb or verb group in a CLAUSE.

presupposed meaning Meaning which arises from co-occurrence restrictions, namely SELECTIONAL RESTRICTIONS and COLLOCATIONAL RESTRICTIONS.

propositional meaning Meaning which arises from the relationship between a word or utterance and what it refers to.

range The set of collocates which are typically associated with a given word define its collocational range (see COLLOCATION).

reflexive Reflexive structures are structures in which the SUBJECT and the OBJECT of the verb are the same. The OBJECT is a reflexive pronoun such as *myself* or *himself*, e.g. *I blame myself.*

register A variety of language that a language user considers appropriate to a specific situation.

selectional restrictions Restrictions which follow logically from the PROPOSI-TIONAL MEANING of words (cf. COLLOCATIONAL RESTRICTIONS).

semantic fields Conceptual fields which reflect the divisions and sub-divisions imposed by a given linguistic community on the continuum of experience, e.g. the field of 'plants' with sub-divisions such as 'flowers', 'shrubs' and 'trees'.

semantic prosody Louw (2000) defines semantic prosody as 'a form of meaning which is established through the proximity of a consistent series of collocates, often characterisable as positive or negative, and whose primary function is the expression of the attitude of its speaker or writer towards some pragmatic situation. A secondary, although no less important attitudinal function of semantic prosodies is the creation of irony through the deliberate injection of a form which clashes with the prosody's consistent series of collocates.'

subject The noun or noun group which comes in front of the verb group in English and with which the verb agrees in terms of number and PERSON, e.g. *He had always liked her.*

superordinate A general word in a SEMANTIC FIELD. The meaning of a superordinate includes the meaning of all its HYPONYMS. In the field of 'trees', *tree* is the superordinate of *conifer*, *oak*, *maple* and so on (cf. HYPONYM).

syntax The study of the way in which classes of words such as nouns and verbs and functional elements such as SUBJECT and OBJECT combine to form CLAUSES and sentences.

teleological models of ethics define what is ethical by reference to what produces the best results (cf. DEONTOLOGICAL MODELS). See also UTILITARIANISM.

tense A grammatical category which involves changing the form of the verb to reflect the location of an event in time. The usual distinction is between past, present and future.

transitive verb A verb which takes an OBJECT, e.g. *Everyone **put their pens down*** (cf. INTRANSITIVE VERB).

utilitarianism is a DEONTOLOGICAL approach to ethics which assesses moral conduct purely on the basis of a cost-benefit analysis of the consequences of an action or behaviour (see CONSEQUENTIALISM). Act-utilitarianism considers an action or behaviour as ethical if it results in the most favourable consequences for the largest number of people *in a given context*. Rule-utilitarianism considers an action or behaviour as ethical if it follows a rule or set of rules that maximize utility overall.

voice A grammatical category which defines the relationship between a verb and its SUBJECT. In an active CLAUSE, the subject is the agent, e.g. *He never writes letters.* In a passive clause, the subject is the person or thing affected by the action, e.g. *Letters are never written in this way.* The difference is reflected in the form of the verb (cf. *writes* and *are written* in the above examples).

References

Aaltonen, Sirkku (2000) *Time-Sharing on Stage. Drama Translation in Theatre and Society*, Clevedon: Multilingual Matters.

Abend-David, Dror (2003) *Scorned my Nation: A Comparison of Translations of* The Merchant of Venice *into German, Hebrew, and Yiddish*, New York: Peter Lang.

Aixelá, Javier Franco (1996) 'Culture-Specific Items in Translation', in Román Álvarez and M. Carmen-África Vidal (eds) *Translation, Power, Subversion*, Clevedon: Multilingual Matters, 52–78.

Alexander, R. J. (1987) 'Collocation and Culture', mimeograph, University of Trier, West Germany.

Al-Jubouri, Adnan and Frank Knowles (1988) 'A Computer-assisted Study of Cohesion Based on English and Arabic Corpora: An Interim Report', in *Proceedings of the 12th International ALLC Congress, Geneva*, Geneva: ALLC.

Al-Wahy, Ahmed Seddik (2009) 'Idiomatic False Friends in English and Modern Standard Arabic', *Babel* 55(2): 101–123.

Anderman, Gunilla (2009) 'Drama Translation', in Mona Baker and Gabriela Saldanha (eds) *Routledge Encyclopedia of Translation Studies*, second edition, London: Routledge, 92–95.

Ang, Swee Chai (1989) *From Beirut to Jerusalem: A Woman Surgeon with the Palestinians*, Glasgow: Grafton.

Angelelli, Claudia V. (2006) 'Validating Professional Standards and Codes: Challenges and Opportunities', *Interpreting* 8(2): 175–193.

Arnáiz, Carmen (2006) 'Politeness in the Portrayal of Workplace Relationships: Second Person Address Forms in Peninsular Spanish and the Translation of Humour', *Journal of Politeness Research, Language, Behaviour, Culture* 2(1): 123–141.

Asad, Talal (1986/2010) 'The Concept of Cultural Translation in British Social Anthropology', in James Clifford and George E. Marcus (eds) *Writing Culture: The Poetics and Politics of Ethnography*, Berkeley, CA: The University of California Press, 141–164; reprinted in Mona Baker (ed.) *Critical Readings in Translation Studies*, Abingdon, Oxon: Routledge, 7–27.

Assis Rosa, Alexandra (2001) 'Features of Oral and Written Communication in Subtitling', in Yves Gambier and Henrik Gottlieb (eds) *(Multi)Media Translation*, Amsterdam: John Benjamins, 213–221.

Baker, Mona (ed.) (1998/2001) *Routledge Encyclopedia of Translation Studies*, first edition, London: Routledge.

— (2000) 'Linguistic Perspectives on Translation', in Peter France (ed.) *The Oxford Guide to Literature in English Translation*, Oxford: Oxford University Press, 20–26.

— (2006) *Translation and Conflict: A Narrative Account*, London: Routledge.

— (2008) 'Ethics of Renarration – Mona Baker is Interviewed by Andrew Chesterman', *Cultus* 1(1): 10–33. Available at http://manchester.academia.edu/documents/0074/9064/Baker_Ethics_of_Renarration.pdf.

— (2009) 'Norms', in Mona Baker and Gabriela Saldanha (eds) *Routledge Encyclopedia of Translation Studies*, second edition, London: Routledge, 189–193.

— (ed.) (2010a) *Critical Readings in Translation Studies*, London: Routledge.

— (2010b) 'Narratives of Security and Terrorism: "Accurate" Translations, Suspicious Frames', *Critical Studies on Terrorism*, 347–364.

Baker, Mona and Carol Maier (eds) (2011) *Ethics and the Curriculum: Critical Perspectives*, Special Issue of *The Interpreter and Translator Trainer* 5(1).

Baker, Mona and Michael McCarthy (1988) 'Multi-word Units and Things like That', mimeograph, University of Birmingham.

Baker, Mona and Luis Pérez-González (2011) 'Translation and Interpreting', *Handbook of Applied Linguistics*, London: Routledge, 39–52.

Baker, Mona and Gabriela Saldanha (eds) (2009) *Routledge Encyclopedia of Translation Studies*, second edition, London: Routledge.

Bandia, Paul (2008) *Translation as Reparation: Writing and Translation in Postcolonial Africa*, Manchester: St. Jerome Publishing.

Barnwell, Katherine (1974, 1980) *Introduction to Semantics and Translation*, High Wycombe: Summer Institute of Linguistics.

Barsky, Robert (1996) 'The Interpreter as Intercultural Agent in Convention Refugee Hearings', *The Translator* 2(1): 45–63.

— (2010) 'Assessing Contextual Assumptions in Dialogue Interpreting: The Case of Illegal Immigrants in the United States', in Mona Baker, Maeve Olohan and María Calzada Pérez (eds) *Text and Context: Essays on Translation and Interpreting in Honour of Ian Mason*, Manchester: St. Jerome Publishing, 288–302.

Bassnett-McGuire, Susan (1980) *Translation Studies*, London: Methuen.

Batchelor, Kathryn (2009) *Decolonizing Translation: Francophone African Novels in English Translation*, Manchester: St. Jerome Publishing.

Bauer, Laurie (2001) *Morphological Productivity*, Cambridge: Cambridge University Press.

BBC News (2004) 'GCHQ Translator Cleared over Leak', 26 February. Available at http://news.bbc.co.uk/1/hi/uk/3485072.stm.

Beaton-Thome, Morven (2010) 'Negotiating Identities in the European Parliament: The Role of Simultaneous Interpreting', in Mona Baker, Maeve Olohan and María Calzada Pérez (eds) *Text and Context: Essays on Translation and Interpreting in Honour of Ian Mason*, Manchester: St. Jerome Publishing, 117–138.

Becker, Annette (2009) 'Modality and Engagement in British and German Political Interviews', *Languages in Contrast* 9(1): 5–22.

Bednarek, Monika A. (2005) 'Frames Revisited – The Coherence-Inducing Function of Frames', *Journal of Pragmatics* 37: 685–705.

Beeby Lonsdale, Allison (2009) 'Directionality', in Mona Baker and Gabriela Saldanha (eds) *Routledge Encyclopedia of Translation Studies*, London: Routledge, 84–88.

Beekman, John and John Callow (1974/1976) *Translating the Word of God*, Michigan: Zondervan.

Bellos, David (1987) 'Summing up', in Catriona Picken (ed.) *ITI Conference 1: The Business of Translation and Interpreting*, London: Aslib.

Benn, Piers (1998) *Ethics*, London: Routledge.

Bennett, Karen (2007) 'Epistemicide!: The Tale of a Predatory Discourse', *The Translator* 13(2): 151–169.

Berk-Seligson, Susan (1988) 'The Impact of Politeness in Witness Testimony: The Influence of the Court Interpreter', *Multilingua, Journal of Cross-cultural and Interlanguage Communication* 7(4): 411–439.

Berman, R. (1978) 'Postponing Lexical Repetition and the Like – A Study in Contrastive Stylistics', *Balshanut Shimushit* 1(2): 3–26.

Billiani, Francesca (ed.) (2006) *Modes of Censorship and Translation: National Contexts and Diverse Media*, Manchester: St. Jerome Publishing.

Blackburn, Simon (2001) *Being Good: A Short Introduction to Ethics*, Oxford: Oxford University Press.

Blacker, C. (1975) *The Catalpa Bow: A Study of Shamanistic Practices in Japan*, London: George Allen & Unwin (Japanese translation by Satoko Akiyama, 1979).

Blakemore, Diane (1987) *Semantic Constraints on Relevance*, Oxford: Basil Blackwell.

Blum-Kulka, Shoshana (1981) 'The Study of Translation in View of New Developments in Discourse Analysis: The Problem of Indirect Speech Acts', *Poetics Today* 2(4): 89–95.

— (1983) 'The Dynamics of Political Interviews', *Text* 3(2): 131–153.

— (1986/2004) 'Shifts of Cohesion and Coherence in Translation', in Juliane House and Shoshana Blum-Kulka (eds) *Interlingual and Intercultural Communication: Discourse and Cognition in Translation and Second Language Acquisition Studies*, Tübingen: Gunter Narr, 17–35; reprinted in Lawrence Venuti (ed.) *The Translation Studies Reader*, London: Routledge, 290–305.

Bolinger, Dwight and Donald Sears (1968/1981) *Aspects of Language*, New York: Harcourt Brace Jovanovich.

Brennan, Mary (1999) 'Signs of Injustice', *The Translator* 5(2): 221–246.

Brown, Gillian and George Yule (1983) *Discourse Analysis*, Cambridge: Cambridge University Press.

Brown, Penelope and Albert Gilman (1960/1972) 'The Pronouns of Power and Solidarity', in Pier Paolo Giglioli (ed.) *Language and Social Context*, Harmondsworth: Penguin, 252–281.

Brown, Penelope and Stephen Levinson (1987/1999) *Politeness. Some Universals in Language Usage*, Cambridge: Cambridge University Press; excerpted as 'Politeness: Some Universals in Language Usage', in Adam Jaworski and Nikolas Coupland (eds) *The Discourse Reader*, London: Routledge, 321–335.

Burkeman, Oliver and Richard Norton-Taylor (2004) 'The Spy Who Wouldn't Keep a Secret', the *Guardian*, 26 February. Available at www.guardian.co.uk/politics/2004/feb/26/interviews.iraq.

Callow, Kathleen (1974) *Discourse Considerations in Translating the Word of God*, Michigan: Zondervan.

Camayd-Freixas, Erik (2008a) 'Interpreting the Largest ICE Raid in U.S. History: A Personal Account', *New America Media*, 11 July. Available at http://news.newamericamedia. org/news/view_article.html?article_id=dd3d7679d6579a9a883d376a80142456.

— (2008b) 'Statement to the Profession', *Proteus* (Newsletter of the National Association of Judiciary Interpreters and Translators) XVII(3). Available at www.najit.org/members_ only/proteus/Proteus_Fall08w.pdf.

Cambridge, Jan (1999) 'Information Loss in Bilingual Medical Interviews through an Untrained Interpreter', in Ian Mason (ed.) *Dialogue Interpreting*, special issue of *The Translator* 5(2): 201–219.

Carter, Ronald (1987) *Vocabulary: Applied Linguistic Perspectives*, London: Allen & Unwin.

Carter, Ronald and Michael McCarthy (1988) *Vocabulary and Language Teaching*, London: Longman.

Cary, Edmond and Rudolph W. Jumpelt (eds) (1963) *Quality in Translation: Proceedings of the International Congress on Translation*, Oxford: Pergamon Press.

Castellano, Lanna (1988) 'Get Rich – but Slow', in Catriona Picken (ed.) *ITI Conference 2: Translators and Interpreters Mean Business*, London: Aslib, 132–135.

Catford, J. C. (1965) *A Linguistic Theory of Translation*, London: Oxford University Press.

Celotti, Nadine (2008) 'The Translator of Comics as a Semiotic Investigator', in Federico Zanettin (ed.) *Comics in Translation*, Manchester: St. Jerome Publishing, 33–49.

Chafe, Wallace L. (1976) 'Givenness, Contrastiveness, Definiteness, Subjects, Topics, and Point of View', in C. N. Li (ed.) *Subject and Topic*, London: Academic Press, 25–55.

Chamizo Domínguez, Pedro J. and Brigitte Nerlich (2002) 'False Friends: Their Origin and Semantics in Some Selected Languages', *Journal of Pragmatics* 34(12): 1833–1849.

Chan, Alfred L. (2004) 'The Tiananmen Papers Revisited', *The China Quarterly* 177: 190–205.

Chan, Red (2007) 'One Nation, Two Translations: China's Censorship of Hillary Clinton's Memoir', in Myriam Salama-Carr (ed.) *Translating and Interpreting Conflict*, Amsterdam and New York: Rodopi, 119–131.

Chan Ho-yan, Clara (2009) 'Third Person Pronouns in Indigenous Chinese Texts and Trans-lated Chinese Texts: The Westernization of Modern Written Chinese', *New Voices in Translation Studies* 5. Available at www.iatis.org/newvoices/issues/2009/ article-chan-2009.pdf.

Charolles, Michel (1983) 'Coherence as a Principle in the Interpretation of Discourse', *Text* 3(1): 71–97.

Chaume Varela, Federic (1997) 'Translating Non-verbal Information in Dubbing', in Fernando Poyatos (ed.) *Nonverbal Communication and Translation*, Amsterdam: John Benjamins, 315–326.

Cheney, George, Daniel J. Lair, Dean Ritz and Brenden E. Kendall (2010) *Just a Job? Communication, Ethics and Professional Life*, Oxford: Oxford University Press.

Chesterman, Andrew (1997) *Memes of Translation*, Amsterdam: John Benjamins.

— (2001) 'Proposal for a Hieronymic Oath', *The Translator* 7(2): 139–154.

Cheung, Martha (ed.) (2006) *An Anthology of Chinese Discourse on Translation. Volume 1: From Earliest Times to the Buddhist Project*, Manchester: St. Jerome Publishing.

— (ed.) (2009) *Chinese Discourses on Translation*, Special Issue of *The Translator* 15(2).

Christie, Agatha (1936/1964) *Murder in the Mews*, Glasgow: Fontana/Collins.

— (1949/1989) *Crooked House*, Glasgow: Fontana/Collins. (French translation by Michel Le Houbie, 1951, Paris: Librairie des Champs-Élysées.)

Clason, Marmy A. (2006) 'Feminism, Generic "He", and the TNIV Bible Translation Debate', *Critical Discourse Studies* 3(1): 23–35.

Clyne, Michael (1981) 'Culture and Discourse Structure', *Journal of Pragmatics* 5: 61–66.

— (1983) 'Linguistics and Written Discourse in Particular Languages: Contrastive Studies: English and German', in R. B. Kaplan, R. L. Jones and G. R. Tucker (eds) *Annual Review of Applied Linguistics*, Rawley, MA: Newbury House, 38–49.

Cockerill, Hiroko (2003) 'Futabatei Shimei's Translations from Russian: Verbal Aspect and Narrative Perspective', *Japanese Studies* 23(3): 229–238.

— (2006) *Style and Narrative in Translations: The Contribution of Futabatei Shimei*, Manchester: St. Jerome Publishing.

Comrie, Bernard (1987) 'Grammatical Relations, Semantic Roles and Topic-comment Structure in a New Guinea Highland Language: Harway', in Ross Steele and Terry Threadgold (eds) *Language Topics: Essays in Honour of Michael Halliday*, Amsterdam: John Benjamins.

Cook, Guy (1992) *The Discourse of Advertising*, London: Routledge.

Cruse, D. A. (1986) *Lexical Semantics*, Cambridge: Cambridge University Press.

Culler, Jonathan (1976) *Saussure*, Glasgow: Fontana/Collins.

Curran, Beverly (2008) *Theatre Translation Theory and Performance in Contemporary Japan*, Manchester: St. Jerome Publishing.

Daneš, František (1974) 'Functional Sentence Perspective and the Organization of the Text', in František Daneš (ed.) *Papers on Functional Sentence Perspective*, The Hague: Mouton, and Prague: Academia.

Davies, Ben (2004) 'Interview: Whistleblower Katharine Gun', *BBC News*, 15 September. Available at http://news.bbc.co.uk/1/hi/uk_politics/3659310.stm.

Davies, Eirlys E. (2003) 'A Goblin or a Dirty Nose? The Treatment of Culture-Specific References in Translations of the Harry Potter Books', *The Translator* 9(1): 65–100.

— (2007) 'Leaving It Out: On Some Justifications for the Use of Omission in Translation', *Babel* 53(1): 56–77.

de Beaugrande, Robert and Wolfgang Dressler (1981) *Introduction to Text Linguistics*, London: Longman.

De Regt, Lenart J. (2006) 'Hebrew Syntactic Inversions and their Literary Equivalence in English: Robert Alter's Translations of Genesis and 1 and 2 Samuel', *Journal for the Study of the Old Testament* 30(3): 287–314.

Desmet, Mieke K. T. (2001) 'Intertextuality/Intervisuality in Translation: The Jolly Postman's Intercultural Journey from Britain to the Netherlands', *Children's Literature in Education* 32(1): 31–43.

Diriker, Ebru (2004) *De-/Re-Contextualizing Conference Interpreting: Interpreters in the Ivory Tower?* Amsterdam: John Benjamins

Donovan, Clare (2011) 'Ethics in the Teaching of Conference Interpreting', in Mona Baker and Carol Maier (eds) *Ethics and the Curriculum: Critical Perspectives*, special issue of *The Interpreter and Translator Trainer* 5(1).

Downing, Angela and Philip Locke (2006) *English Grammar: A University Course*, second edition, Abingdon: Routledge.

Driver, Julia (2007) *Ethics: The Fundamentals*, Oxford: Blackwell Publishing.

Duff, Alan (1990) *Translation*, Oxford: Oxford University Press.

Dunnett, Jane (2002) 'Foreign Literature in Fascist Italy: Circulation and Censorship', *TTR: Traduction, Terminologie, Rédaction* 15(2): 97–124.

Eggins, Suzanne (2004) *An Introduction to Systemic Functional Linguistics*, second edition, London: Continuum.

Engel, Dulcie M. (2002) 'Radio Talk. French and English Perfects on Air', *Languages in Contrast* 2(2): 95–118.

Englund Dimitrova, Birgitta (2005) *Expertise and Explicitation in the Translation Process*, Amsterdam: John Benjamins.

Enkvist, Nils E. (1978) 'Coherence, Pseudo-coherence, and Non-coherence', in Jan-Ola Östman (ed.) *Cohesion and Semantics: Report on Text Linguistics*, Abo: The Research Institute of the Abo Akademi Foundation.

— (1985) 'Coherence and Inference', in Ursula Pieper and Gerhard Stickel (eds) *Studia Linguistica Diachronica et Synchronica*, Berlin: Mouton de Gruyter, 233–248.

— (1987) 'Text Strategies: Single, Dual, Multiple', in Ross Steele and Terry Threadgold (eds) *Language Topics: Essays in Honour of Michael Halliday*, Amsterdam: John Benjamins.

Ervin-Tripp, Susan (1972) 'Sociolinguistic Rules of Address', in John B. Pride and Janet Holmes (eds) *Sociolinguistics,* Harmondsworth: Penguin, 225–240.

Farghal, Mohammed and Mohammed O. Al-Shorafat (1996) 'The Translation of English Passives into Arabic: An Empirical Perspective', *Target* 8(1): 97–118.

Fawcett, Peter D. (1981) 'Teaching Translation Theory', *Meta* 26(2): 141–147.

— (1997) *Translation and Language*, Manchester: St. Jerome Publishing.

Fenton, Sabine and Paul Moon (2003) 'The Translation of the Treaty of Waitangi: A Case of Disempowerment', in Edwin Gentzler and Maria Tymoczko (eds) *Translation and Power*, Amherst: University of Massachusetts Press, 25–44.

Fernando, Chitra (1996) *Idioms and Idiomaticity*, Oxford: Oxford University Press.

Fernando, Chitra and Roger Flavell (1981) *On Idiom: Critical Views and Perspectives* (Exeter Linguistic Studies 5), University of Exeter.

Findlay, Bill (2000) 'Translating Standard into Dialect: Missing the Target?', in Carole-Anne Upton (ed.) *Moving Target: Theatre Translation and Cultural Relocation*, Manchester: St. Jerome Publishing, 35–46.

Firbas, Jan (1972) 'On the Interplay of Prosodic and Non-prosodic Means of Functional Sentence Perspective', in V. Fried (ed.) *The Prague School of Linguistics and Language Teaching*, London: Oxford University Press.

— (1974) 'Some Aspects of the Czechoslovak Approach to Problems of Functional Sentence Perspective', in F. Daneš (ed.) *Papers on Functional Sentence Perspective*, The Hague: Mouton; Prague: Academia, 11–37.

— (1986) 'On the Dynamics of Written Communication in the Light of the Theory of Functional Sentence Perspective', in C. R. Cooper and S. Greenbaum (eds) *Studying Writing: Linguistic Approaches*, New York: Sage, 40–71.

— (1987) 'On Two Starting Points of Communication', in R. Steele and T. Threadgold (eds) *Language Topics: Essays in Honour of Michael Halliday*, Amsterdam: John Benjamins, 23–46.

— (1992) *Functional Sentence Perspective in Written and Spoken Communication*, Cambridge: Cambridge University Press.

— (1999) 'Translating the Introductory Paragraph of Boris Pasternak's *Doctor Zhivago*: A Case Study in Functional Sentence Perspective', in Gunilla Anderman and Margaret Rogers (eds) *Word, Text, Translation*, Clevedon: Multilingual Matters, 129–141.

Firth, J. R. (1957/1968) 'A Synopsis of Linguistic Theory, 1930–55 ', in *Studies in Linguistic Analysis* (Special volume of the Philological Society), Oxford: Philological Society, 1–32; reprinted in F. R. Palmer (ed.) *Selected Papers of J. R. Firth 1952–59*, London: Longmans.

— (1964) *The Tongues of Men and Speech*, Oxford: Oxford University Press.

Fox, Barbara A. (1986) 'Local Patterns and General Principles in Cognitive Processes: Anaphora in Written and Conversational English', *Text* 6(1): 25–51.

Freemantle, Brian (1985) *The Fix*, London: Michael Joseph. (Japanese translation by Tetsuo Shinshō).

Fries, Peter H. (1983) 'On the Status of Theme in English: Arguments from Discourse', in J. S. Petöfi and E. Sözer (eds) *Micro and Macro Connexity of Texts*, Hamburg: Helmut Buske, 116–152.

Fujii, Yasunari (2008) 'The Asymmetrical Relationship between the Active and Passive Voice: Implications for Teaching Japanese-to-English Translation of Specialized Scientific Texts', *The Linguistics Journal* 3(1): 40–74. Available at www.linguistics-journal. com/April_2008.pdf.

Gadalla, Hassan A. H. (2006) 'Arabic Imperfect Verbs in Translation: A Corpus Study of English Renderings', *Meta* 51(1): 51–71.

Gentry El-Dash, Linda and JoAnne Busnardo (2003) 'Interaction of Semantic and Pragmatic Choices in the Translation of Verb Forms: English and Portuguese', *Journal of Pragmatics* 35(12): 1823–1841.

Gentzler, Edwin (2008) *Translation and Identity in the Americas*, London: Routledge.

Gill, Rosalind M. and María Constanza Guzmán (2010) 'Teaching Translation for Social Awareness in Toronto', in Julie Boéri and Carol Maier (eds) *Compromiso Social y Traducción/Interpretación/Translation/Interpreting and Social Activism*, Granada: ECOS, 121–133.

Giora, Rachel (1983) 'Segmentation and Segment Cohesion: On the Thematic Organization of the Text', *Text* 3(2): 155–181.

Glinert, Lewis (2010) 'Apologizing to China: Elastic Apologies and the Meta-discourse of American Diplomats', *Intercultural Pragmatics* 7(1): 47–74.

Godlee, Fiona (2009) 'Rules of Conscience', *BMJ (British Medical Journal)*, 14 May. Available at www.bmj.com/cgi/content/full/338/may14_1/b1972.

Goodwin, Phil (2010) 'Ethical Problems in Translation: Why We Might Need Steiner After All', *The Translator* 16(1): 19–42.

Gottlieb, Henrik (1997) 'Quality Revisited: The Rendering of English Idioms in Danish Television Subtitles vs. Printed Translations', in Anna Trosborg (ed.) *Text Typology and Translation*, Amsterdam: John Benjamins, 309–338.

Grauberg, Walter (1989) 'Proverbs and Idioms: Mirrors of National Experience?', in Gregory James (ed.) *Lexicographers and Their Works* (Exeter Linguistic Studies 14), University of Exeter, 94–99.

Greenbaum, Stephen and Randolph Quirk (1990) *A Student's Grammar of the English Language*, London: Longman.

Gregory, Michael J. (1980) 'Perspectives on Translation from the Firthian Tradition', *Meta* 25(4): 455–466.

Gregory, Michael and Susanne Carroll (1978) *Language and Situation: Language Varieties in their Social Contexts*, London: Routledge & Kegan Paul.

Grice, H. P. (1975) 'Logic and Conversation', in L. Cole and J. L. Morgan (eds) *Syntax and Semantics*, Vol. 3: *Speech Acts*, New York: Academic Press, 41–58.

— (1981) 'Presupposition and Conversational Implicature', in P. Cole (ed.) *Radical Pragmatics*, New York: Academic Press, 183–198.

Guillot, Marie-Noëlle (2010) 'Film Subtitles from a Cross-cultural Pragmatics Perspective: Issues of Linguistic and Cultural Representation', *The Translator* 16(1): 67–92.

Gutiérrez Lanza, Camino (2002) 'Spanish Film Translation and Cultural Patronage: The Filtering and Manipulation of Imported Material during Franco's Dictatorship', in Maria Tymoczko and Edwin Gentzler (eds) *Translation and Power*, Amherst: University of Massachusetts Press, 141–159.

Gutt, Ernst-August (1991/2000) *Translation and Relevance. Cognition and Context*, Oxford: Blackwell; Manchester: St. Jerome Publishing, second edition.

— (2005) 'On the Significance of the Cognitive Core of Translation', *The Translator* 11(1): 25–49.

Gutwinski, Waldemar (1976) *Cohesion in Literary Texts*, The Hague: Mouton.

Hagfors, Irma (2003) 'The Translation of Culture-Bound Elements into Finnish in the Post-War Period', *Meta* 48(1–2): 115–127.

Hale, Sandra (1997) 'The Treatment of Register Variation in Court Interpreting', *The Translator* 3(1): 39–54.

— (2007) *Community Interpreting*, Basingstoke: Palgrave Macmillan.

Halliday, Michael A. K. (1964) 'Comparison and Translation', in Michael Halliday, Angus McIntosh and Peter Strevens (eds) *The Linguistic Sciences and Language Teaching*, London: Longman, 111–134.

— (1967) 'Notes on Transitivity and Theme in English', part 2, *Journal of Linguistics* 3(2): 199–244.

— (1970) 'Language Structure and Language Function', in John Lyons (ed.) *New Horizons in Linguistics*, Harmondsworth: Penguin, 140–165.

— (1974) 'The Place of "Functional Sentence Perspective" in the System of Linguistic Description', in František Danes (ed.) *Papers in Functional Sentence Perspective*, The Hague: Mouton; Prague: Academia, 43–53.

— (1976) 'Theme and Information in the English Clause', in Gunther R. Kress (ed.) *System and Function in Language: Selected Papers by M. A. K. Halliday*, London: Oxford University Press, 174–188.

— (1978) *Language as Social Semiotic: The Social Interpretation of Language and Meaning*, London: Edward Arnold.

— (1985) *An Introduction to Functional Grammar*, London: Edward Arnold.

Halliday, Michael A. K. and Ruqaiya Hasan (1976) *Cohesion in English*, London: Longman.

Hardwick, Lorna (2001) 'Who Owns the Plays? Issues in the Translation and Performance of Greek Drama on the Modern Stage', *Eirene* 37: 23–39.

Harvey, Keith (1995) 'A Descriptive Framework for Compensation', *The Translator* 1(1): 65–86.

— (1998) 'Compensation and the Brief in a Non-literary Translation: Theoretical Implications and Pedagogical Applications', *Target* 10(2): 267–290.

Hasan, Ruqaiya (1984) 'Coherence and Cohesive Harmony', in James Flood (ed.) *Understanding Reading Comprehension: Cognition, Language and Structure of Prose*, Newark: International Reading Association, 181–219.

Hasselgård, Hilde (1998) 'Thematic Structure in Translation between English and Norwegian', in Stig Johansson and Signe Oksefjell (eds) *Corpora and Cross-linguistic Research: Theory, Method and Case Studies*, Amsterdam: Rodopi, 145–167.

Hatim, Basil (1984) 'Discourse/Text Linguistics in the Training of Interpreters', in Wolfram Wilss and Gisela Thome (eds) *Translation Theory and its Implementation in the Teaching of Translating and Interpreting*, Tübingen: Gunter Narr, 298–307.

— (1987) 'Discourse Texture in Translation: Towards a Text-typological Redefinition of Theme and Rheme', in Hugh Keith and Ian Mason (eds) *Translation in the Modern Languages Degree*, London: CILT, 52–62.

— (1988) 'Discourse in the Translating and Interpreting Process', in A. Turney (ed.) *Applied Text Linguistics* (Exeter Linguistic Studies 13), University of Exeter, 69–78.

— (1989) 'Text Linguistics in the Didactics of Translation: The Case of the Verbal and Nominal Clause Types in Arabic', *IRAL* 27(2): 137–144.

— (1997) *Communication across Cultures: Translation Theory and Contrastive Text Linguistics*, Exeter: University of Exeter Press.

— (2001) *Teaching and Researching Translation*, Harlow: Pearson Education.

Hatim, Basil and Ian Mason (1990) *Discourse and the Translator*, London: Longman.

— (1997) *The Translator as Communicator*, London: Routledge.

Hawking, Stephen W. (1988) *A Brief History of Time from the Big Bang to Black Holes*, London: Bantam Press. (Spanish translation by Miguel Ortuño; Greek translation by Konstantinos Harakas.)

Headland, Thomas N. (1981) 'Information Rate, Information Overload, and Communication Problems in the Casiguran Dumagat New Testament', *Notes on Translation* 83: 18–27.

Hébert, Lyse (2009) 'Feminization: A Socially and Politically Charged Translation Strategy', in Raquel de Pedro, Isabelle Perez and Christine Wilson (eds) *Interpreting and Translating in Public Service Settings: Policy, Practice, Pedagogy*, Manchester: St. Jerome Publishing, 127–140.

Heikal, Mohammed (1983) *Autumn of Fury: The Assassination of Sadat*, London: Corgi. (Arabic translation by the author, Beirut: Sharikat Al Matbuaat Liltawzeei wa alnashr, 1984).

Herbst, Thomas, David Heath and Hans-Martin Dederding (1979) *Grimm's Grandchildren: Current Topics in German Linguistics*, New York: Longman.

Hermans, Theo (ed.) (2006) *Translating Others*, 2 vols, Manchester: St. Jerome Publishing.

— (2007) *The Conference of the Tongues*, Manchester: St. Jerome Publishing.

— (2009) 'Translation, Ethics, Politics', in Jeremy Munday (ed.) *The Routledge Companion to Translation Studies*, Abingdon, Oxon: Routledge, 93–105.

Hickey, Leo (ed.) (1998) *The Pragmatics of Translation*, Clevedon: Multilingual Matters.

— (2000) 'Politeness in Translation between English and Spanish', *Target* 12(2): 229–240.

Hinds, J. (1980) 'Japanese Expository Prose', *Papers in Linguistics* 13(1): 117–158.

Hockett, Charles (1958) *A Course in Modern Linguistics*, New York: Macmillan.

Høeg, Peter (1992/2005) *Miss Smilla's Feeling for Snow*, translated by F. David, London: Vintage.

Hoey, Michael (1988) 'The Clustering of Lexical Cohesion in Non-narrative Text', *Trondheim Papers in Applied Linguistics* 4: 154–180.

— (1991) *Patterns of Lexis in Text*, Oxford: Oxford University Press.

— (2005) *Lexical Priming: A New Theory of Words and Language*, Abingdon, Oxon: Routledge.

Holes, Clive (1984) 'Textual Approximation in the Teaching of Academic Writing to Arab Students: A Contrastive Approach', in John Swales and Hasan Mustafa (eds) *English for Specific Purposes in the Arab World*, Birmingham: University of Aston, 228–242.

Hosseini, Khaled (2003) *The Kite Runner*, London: Bloomsbury.

House, Juliane (1998) 'Politeness and Translation', in Leo Hickey (ed.) *The Pragmatics of Translation*, Clevedon: Multilingual Matters, 54–71.

Huddleston, Rodney and Geoffrey K. Pullum (2005) *A Student's Introduction to English Grammar*, Cambridge: Cambridge University Press.

Hung, Eva and Judy Wakabayashi (eds) (2005) *Asian Translation Traditions*, Manchester: St. Jerome Publishing.

Hunston, Susan and Gill Francis (2000) *Pattern Grammar: A Corpus-driven Approach to the Lexical Grammar of English*, Amsterdam: John Benjamins.

Inghilleri, Moira (2008) 'The Ethical Task of the Translator in the Geo-political Arena: From Iraq to Guantánamo Bay', *Translation Studies* 1(1): 212–223.

— (2009) 'Ethics', in Mona Baker and Gabriela Saldanha (eds) *Routledge Encyclopedia of Translation Studies*, second edition, London: Routledge, 100–104.

— (2010a) 'Afterword: Exploring the Task of the Activist Translator', in Julie Boéri and Carol Maier (eds) *Compromiso Social y Traducción/Interpretación / Translation/Interpreting and Social Activism*, Granada: ECOS, 152–155.

— (2010b) 'The Decision to Interpret', in Moira Inghilleri and Sue-Ann Harding (eds) *Translation and Violent Conflict*, Special Issue of *The Translator* 16(2): 175–196.

— (forthcoming) *Interpreting Justice: Ethics, Politics and Language*.

Institute for Public Accuracy (undated) 'The Katharine Gun Case'. Available at www.accuracy.org/article.php?articleId=1104.

Jakobson, Roman (1959) 'On Linguistic Aspects of Translation', in R. A. Brower (ed.) *On Translation*, Cambridge, MA: Harvard University Press.

Johns, Tim (1991) 'It is Presented Initially: Linear Dislocation and Interlanguage Strategies in Brazilian Academic Abstracts in English and Portuguese', mimeograph, University of Birmingham.

Johnson, Samuel (1755) *A Dictionary of the English Language*, 2 vols, London: Knapton.

Jones, Francis R. (2004) 'Ethics, Aesthetics and Decision: Literary Translating in the Wars of the Yugoslav Succession', *Meta* 49(4): 711–728.

Jüngst, Heike (2008) 'Translating Manga', in Federico Zanettin (ed.) *Comics in Translation*, Manchester: St. Jerome Publishing, 50–78.

Katamba, Francis (1993) *Morphology*, Basingstoke: Macmillan Press.

— (1994) *English Words*, London: Routledge.

Keith, Hugh A. (1987) 'Cohesion and Coherence and Communication in German–English Translation', in Hugh Keith and Ian Mason (eds) *Translation in the Modern Languages Degree*, London: CILT, 63–71.

Kenny, Dorothy (1998) 'Creatures of Habit? What Translators Usually Do with Words', *Meta* 43(4): 515–523.

— (2004) 'Parallel Corpora and Translation Studies: Old Questions, New Perspectives? Reporting "that" in Gepcolt: A case study', in Geoff Barnbrook, Pernilla Danielsson and Michaela Mahlberg (eds) *Meaningful Texts: The Extraction of Semantic Information from Monolingual and Multilingual Corpora*, London: Continuum, 154–165.

— (2009) 'Equivalence', in Mona Baker and Gabriela Saldanha (eds) *Routledge Encyclopedia of Translation Studies*, London: Routledge, 96–99.

Kim, Chul-Kyu and Geoff Thompson (2010) 'Obligation and Reader Involvement in English and Korean Science Popularizations: A Corpus-based Cross-cultural Text Analysis', *Text&Talk* 30(1): 53–73.

King, Philip (1990) 'The Syntax of Topic Organisation in English and Greek', mimeograph, University of Birmingham.

Kinsui, Satoshi (1997) 'The Influence of Translation on the Historical Development of the Japanese Passive Construction', *Journal of Pragmatics* 28(6): 759–779.

Kirkwood, Henry W. (1979) 'Some Systemic Means of Functional Sentence Perspective in English and German', in D. Nehls (ed.) *Studies in Contrastive Linguistics and Error Analysis*, Heidelberg: Groos.

Kishtainy, Khalid (1985) *Arab Political Humour*, London: Quartet Books (Arabic translation by Dr Kamal Al-Yaziji, London: Dar Al Saqi, 1988).

Koskinen, Kaisa (2000) *Beyond Ambivalence: Postmodernity and the Ethics of Translation*, Tampere, Finland: University of Tampere.

Kuhiwczak, Piotr (1990) 'Translation as Appropriation: The Case of Milan Kundera's *The Joke*', in Susan Bassnett and Andre Lefevere (eds) *Translation, History and Culture*, London: Pinter Publishers, 118–130.

Kwieciński, Piotr (1998) 'Translation Strategies in a Rapidly Transforming Culture. A Central European Perspective', *The Translator* 4(2): 183–206.

Lane-Mercier, Gillian (1997) 'Translating the Untranslatable: The Translator's Aesthetic, Ideological and Political Responsibility', *Target* 9(1): 43–68.

Lapiere, Dominique (2010) 'Tour of Beauty', *Holland Herald* (KLM inflight magazine), June, 45–48. Available at http://holland-herald.com/2010/06/the-silver-cloud/.

Larson, M. L. (1984) *Meaning-Based Translation: A Guide to Cross-Language Equivalence*, Lanham, MD: University Press of America.

Lathey, Gillian (2003) 'Time, Narrative Intimacy and the Child. Implications of the Transition from the Present to the Past Tense in the Translation into English of Children's Texts', *Meta* 48(1–2): 233–240.

Laviosa, Sara (2007) 'Learning Creative Writing by Translating Witty Ads', *The Interpreter and Translator Trainer* 1(2): 197–222.

Lawford, James P. (1976) *Clive: Proconsul of India: A Biography*, London: George Allen & Unwin.

Leanza, Yvan (2005) 'Roles of Community Interpreters in Pediatrics as Seen by Interpreters, Physicians and Researchers', *Interpreting* 7(2): 167–192.

Le Carré, John (1983) *The Little Drummer Girl*, London: Hodder & Stoughton.

— (1989) *The Russia House*, London: Coronet Books, Hodder & Stoughton.

— (1995) *Our Game*, London: Hodder & Stoughton.

Leech, Geoffrey (1974, 1981) *Semantics: The Study of Meaning*, Harmondsworth: Penguin.

Lehrer, Adrienne (1974) *Semantic Fields and Lexical Structure*, Amsterdam: North Holland.

Leppihalme, Ritva (2000) 'The Two Faces of Standardization: On the Translation of Regionalisms in Literary Dialogue', *The Translator* 6(2): 247–269.

Levinson, Stephen C. (1983) *Pragmatics*, Cambridge: Cambridge University Press.

Li, Charles N. (1976) 'Subject and Topic: A New Typology of Language', in C. N. Li (ed.) *Subject and Topic*, London: Academic Press, 457–490.

Li, Charles N. and Sandra A. Thompson (1981) *Mandarin Chinese: A Functional Reference Grammar*, Berkeley: University of California Press.

Li, Chris Wen-Chao (2007) 'Foreign Names into Native Tongues: How to Transfer Sound between Languages – Transliteration, Phonological Translation, Nativization, and Implications for Translation Theory', *Target* 19(1): 45–68.

Linder, Daniel (2004) 'The Censorship of Sex: A Study of Raymond Chandler's *The Big Sleep* in Franco's Spain', *TTR: Traduction, Terminologie, Rédaction* 17(1): 155–182.

Lorés Sanz, Rosa (2003) 'The Translation of Tourist Literature: The case of connectors', *Multilingua* 22(3): 291–308.

Louw, Bill (1993) 'Irony in the Text or Insincerity in the Writer? The Diagnostic Potential of Semantic Prosodies', in Mona Baker, Gill Francis and Elena Tognini-Bonelli (eds) *Text and Technology: In Honour of John Sinclair*, Amsterdam: John Benjamins, 157–176.

— (2000) 'Contextual Prosodic Theory: Bringing Semantic Prosodies to Life', in Chris Heffer and Helen Sauntson (eds) *Words in Context, A Tribute to John Sinclair on His Retirement*, CDRom. Available at www.revue-texto.net/docannexe/file/124/louw_prosodie.pdf.

Loveday, Leo J. (1982a) 'Communicative Interference: A Framework for Contrastively Analysing L2 Communicative Competence Exemplified with the Linguistic Behaviour of Japanese Performing in English', *IRAL* 20(1): 1–16.

— (1982b) 'Conflicting Framing Patterns: The Sociosemiotics of One Component in Cross-cultural Communication', *Text* 2(4): 359–374.

Lowe, R. (1985) *Basic Uummarmiut Eskimo Grammar*, Inuvik, Canada: Committee for Original Peoples Entitlement.

Lyons, John (1968, 1989) *Introduction to Theoretical Linguistics*, Cambridge: Cambridge University Press.

— (1977) *Semantics*, vol. I, Cambridge: Cambridge University Press.

— (1981) *Language and Linguistics*, Cambridge: Cambridge University Press.

McCann, Michael J. (2006) 'Translator Ethics and Professionalism in Internet Interactions', *Caduceus* (journal of the Medical Division of the American Translators' Association), Fall and Summer. Available at www.infomarex.com/pliki/1265729609Ethics_and_professionalism_in_internet_actions.pdf.

McCreary, Don R. (1986) 'Improving Bilingual Japanese–English and English–Japanese Dictionaries', *Papers in Linguistics* 19(1): 55–66.

McDowall, D. (1983) *Lebanon: A Conflict of Minorities*, Minority Rights Group report, no. 61. London: Minority Rights Group report.

Mackin, Ronald (1978) 'On Collocations: Words Shall Be Known by the Company They Keep', in Peter Strevens (ed.) *In Honour of A. S. Hornby*, Oxford: Oxford University Press, 149–165.

MacLaine, Shirley (1975) *You Can Get There from Here*, London: The Bodley Head.

The Macmillan Encyclopedia (1981/1986) London: Guild.

Maier, Carol (2007) 'The Translator's Visibility: The Rights and Responsibilities Thereof', in Myriam Salama-Carr (ed.) *Translating and Interpreting Conflict*, Amsterdam: Rodopi, 253–266.

Manuel Jerez, Jesús de, Juan López Cortés and María Brander de la Iglesia (2004) 'Social Commitment in Translation and Interpreting; A View from ECOS, Translators and Interpreters for Solidarity'. Available at www.translationdirectory.com/article366.htm.

Martin, James R. and Peter R. R. White (2005) *The Language of Evaluation: Appraisal in English*, Basingstoke: Palgrave Macmillan.

Mason, Ian (1982) 'The Role of Translation Theory in the Translation Class', *Quinquereme* 5(1): 18–33.

— (1994/2010) 'Discourse, Ideology and Translation', in Robert de Beaugrande, Abdullah Shunnaq and Mohamed Heliel (eds) *Language, Discourse and Translation in the West and Middle East*, Amsterdam: John Benjamins, 23–34; reprinted, with a postscript, in Mona Baker (ed.) *Critical Readings in Translation Studies*, London: Routledge, 83–95.

— (1998) 'Discourse Connectives, Ellipsis and Markedness', in Leo Hickey (ed.) *The Pragmatics of Translation*, Clevedon: Multilingual Matters, 170–184.

— (1999) 'Introduction', in Ian Mason (ed.) *Dialogue Interpreting*, Special Issue of *The Translator* 5(2): 147–160.

Mauranen, Anna (2008) 'Universal Tendencies in Translation', in Gunilla Anderman and Margaret Rogers (eds) *Incorporating Corpora: The Linguist and the Translator*, Clevedon: Multilingual Matters, 32–48.

May, Rachel (1994) *The Translator in the Text: On Reading Russian Literature in English*, Evanston, IL: Northwestern University Press.

Maynard, Senko Kuniya (1981) 'The Given/New Distinction and the Analysis of the Japanese Particles -WA and -GA', *Papers in Linguistics* 14(1): 109–130.

— (1986) 'Interactional Aspects of Thematic Progression in English Casual Conversation', *Text* 6(1): 73–105.

Mayoral Asensio, Roberto (2003) *Translating Official Documents*, Manchester: St. Jerome Publishing.

Merlini, Raffaela (2009) 'Seeking Asylum and Seeking Identity in a Mediated Encounter: The Projection of Selves through Discursive Practices', *Interpreting* 11(1): 57–92.

Meuss, A. R. (1981) 'Professional Translators' Examinations – A Pragmatic Model', in A. Kopczyński, A. Hanftwurcel, E. Karska and L. Rywin (eds) *The Mission of the Translator Today and Tomorrow: Proceedings of the IXth World Congress of the International Federation of Translators Warsaw 1981*, Warsaw.

Milic, Louis T. (1970) 'Connectives in Swift's Prose Style', in Donald C. Freeman (ed.) *Linguistics and Literary Style*, New York: Holt, Rinehart & Winston.

Miller, Katrina R. and Vernon McCay (2001) 'Linguistic Diversity in Deaf Defendants and Due Process Rights', *Journal of Deaf Studies and Deaf Education* 6(3): 226–234.

Moon, Rosamund (1998) *Fixed Expressions and Idioms in English*, Oxford: Clarendon.

Morley, George D. (1985) *An Introduction to Systemic Grammar*, Basingstoke: Macmillan.

Munday, Jeremy (2001/2008) *Introducing Translation Studies: Theories and Applications*, London: Routledge.

— (2010) 'Evaluation and Intervention in Translation', in Mona Baker, Maeve Olohan and María Calzada Pérez (eds) *Text and Context: Essays on Translation and Interpreting in Honour of Ian Mason*, Manchester: St. Jerome Publishing, 77–94.

Nedergaard-Larsen, Birgit (1993) 'Cultural Factors in Subtitling', *Perspectives: Studies in Translatology* 1(2): 207–241.

Netsu, Machiko (1981) 'The Theory of Tense and the Analysis of the Japanese Tense Markers -RU and -TA', *Papers in Linguistics* 14(2): 233–251.

Newman, Aryeh (1988) 'The Contrastive Analysis of Hebrew and English Dress and Cooking Collocations: Some Pedagogic Parameters', *Applied Linguistics* 9(3): 293–305.

Newmark, Peter (1987) 'The Use of Systemic Linguistics in Translation Analysis and Criticism', in R. Steele and T. Threadgold (eds) *Language Topics: Essays in Honour of Michael Halliday*, Amsterdam: John Benjamins, 293–303.

Nida, Eugene A. (1959) 'Principles of Translation as Exemplified by Bible Translating', in R. A. Brower (ed.) *On Translation*, Cambridge, MA: Harvard University Press, 11–31.

— (1964) 'Linguistics and Ethnology in Translation Problems' in Dell Hymes (ed.) *Language in Culture and Society: A Reader in Linguistics and Anthropology*, New York: Harper & Row, 90–100.

— (1975) *Exploring Semantic Structures*, Munich: Wilhelm Fink.

Nida, Eugene A. and Charles R. Taber (1969) *The Theory and Practice of Translation*, Leiden: E. J. Brill.

Nilsson, Anna-Lena (2005) 'False Friends and their Influence on Sign Language Interpreting', in Cynthia Roy (ed.) *Advances in Teaching Sign Language Interpreters*, Washington, DC: Gallaudet University Press, 170–186.

Nissen, Uwe Kjaer (2002) 'Aspects of Translating Gender', *Linguistik online* 11(2). Available at www.linguistik-online.de/11_02/nissen.html.

Nord, Christiane (1997) *Translating as a Purposeful Activity*, Manchester: St. Jerome Publishing.

Novák, P. (1974) 'Remarks on Devices of Functional Sentence Perspective', in F. Daneš (ed.) *Papers on Functional Sentence Perspective*, The Hague: Mouton; Prague: Academia.

Ó Cearúil, Micheál (1999) *Bunreacht Na hÉireann: A Study of the Irish Text*, Dublin: Government of Ireland.

Olohan, Maeve and Mona Baker (2000) 'Reporting *that* in Translated English: Evidence for Subconscious Processes of Explicitation?', *Across Languages and Cultures* 1(2): 141–158.

Palmer, Frank R. (1976, 1981) *Semantics*, Cambridge: Cambridge University Press.

Papegaaij, Bart and Klaus Schubert (1988) *Text Coherence in Translation*, Dordrecht: Foris.

Parks, Tim (2010) 'Why Translators Deserve Some Credit', the *Observer*, 25 April. Available at www.guardian.co.uk/books/2010/apr/25/book-translators-deserve-credit?utm_source=feedburner&utm_medium=feed&utm_campaign=Feed%3A+theguardian%2F books%2Frss+%28Books%29.

Pedersen, Jan (2007) 'Cultural Interchangeability: The Effects of Substituting Cultural References in Subtitling', *Perspectives: Studies in Translatology* 15(1): 30–48.

Pettit, Zoë (2005) 'Translating Register, Style and Tone in Dubbing and Subtitling', *JosTrans: The Journal of Specialised Translation* 4. Available at www.jostrans.org/issue04/art_pettit.php.

Pöchhacker, Franz (2004) *Introducing Interpreting Studies*, London: Routledge.

Pokorn, Nike K. (2005) *Challenging the Traditional Axioms*, Amsterdam: John Benjamins.

Polezzi, Loredana (1998) 'Rewriting Tibet: Italian Travellers in English Translation', *The Translator* 4(2): 321–342.

Prado, C. G. (2006) 'Ethics and Morality'. Available at http://personalethics.suite101.com/article.cfm/ethicsandmorality.

Preston, Julia (2008) 'An Interpreter Speaking up for Migrants', *The New York Times*, 11 July. Available at www.nytimes.com/2008/07/11/us/11immig.html?_r=2&ex=1216 440000&en=1a9a2b3b58e65cac&ei=5070&emc=eta1.

The Holy Qur'an, translated by Marmaduke Pickthall, New Delhi: Kitab Bhavan, 1982.

Queen, Robin (2004/2009) '"Du hast jar keine Ahnung": African American English Dubbed into German', *Journal of Sociolinguistics* 8(4): 515–537; reprinted in Mona Baker (ed.) *Translation Studies*, Volume III, London: Routledge, 169–192.

Robins, R. H. (1964/1989) *General Linguistics: An Introductory Survey*, London: Longman.

Robinson, Douglas (2003) *Performative Linguistics*, London: Routledge.

Rogers, Margaret (2006) 'Structuring Information in English: A Specialist Translation Perspective on Sentence Beginnings', *The Translator* 12(1): 29–64.

Rommel, Birgit (1987) 'Market-orientated Translation Training', in Hugh Keith and Ian Mason (eds) *Translation in the Modern Languages Degree*, London: CILT, 11–16.

Sánchez, Dolores (2007) 'The *Truth* about Sexual Difference: Scientific Discourse and Cultural Transfer', *The Translator* 13(2): 171–194.

Sapir, Edward and Morris Swadesh (1964) 'American Indian Grammatical Categories', in Dell Hymes (ed.) *Language in Culture and Society: A Reader in Linguistics and Anthropology*, New York: Evanston; London: Harper & Row.

Schmid, Monika S. (1999) *Translating the Elusive. Marked Word Order and Subjectivity in English–German Translation*, Amsterdam: John Benjamins.

Scinto, Leonard (1983) 'Functional Connectivity and the Communicative Structure of Text', in J. S. Petöfi and E. Sözer (eds) *Micro and Macro Connexity of Texts*, Hamburg: Helmut Buske.

Selim, Samah (ed.) (2009) *Nation and Translation in the Middle East*, Special Issue of *The Translator* 15(1).

— (2010) 'Fiction and Colonial Identities: Arsène Lupin in Arabic', *Middle Eastern Literatures* 13(2): 191–210.

Sheridan, Sarah (2009) 'Translating Idiomatic Expressions from English to Irish Sign Language (ISL): Theory and Practice', *The Sign Language Translator and Interpreter* 3(1): 69–84.

Shlesinger, Miriam (1995) 'Shifts in Cohesion in Simultaneous Interpreting', *The Translator* 1(2): 193–214.

Shurbanov, Alexander (2002) 'Translation Across Gender Discrepancies', *Textus, English Studies in Italy* 15(1): 45–63.

Simons, Fay (2010) 'Translation Ethics – Moral Issues in the Translation Business'. Available at www.articlesbase.com/ethics-articles/translation-ethics-moral-issues-in-the-translation-business-1698911.html#ixzzOoa7P1eHW.

Sinclair, John McH. (1966) 'Beginning the Study of Lexis', in C. E. Bazel, J. C. Catford, M. A. K. Halliday and R. H. Robins (eds) *In Memory of J. R. Firth*, London: Longman.

— (1987a) 'Collocation: A Progress Report', in R. Steele and T. Threadgold (eds) *Language Topics: Essays in Honour of Michael Halliday*, Amsterdam: John Benjamins.

— (1987b) *Collins COBUILD English Language Dictionary*, London: Collins.

— (1990) *Collins COBUILD English Grammar*, London: Collins.

— (1991) *Corpus Concordance Collocation*, Oxford: Oxford University Press.

— (1999) 'Concordance Tasks: Semantic Prosody'. Available at www.twc.it/happen.html.

Smith, Raoul N. and William J. Frawley (1983) 'Conjunctive Cohesion in Four English Genres', *Text* 3(4): 347–374.

Snell-Hornby, Mary (1985) 'Translation as a Means of Integrating Language Teaching and Linguistics', in C. Titford and A. E. Hieke (eds) *Translation in Foreign Language Teaching and Testing*, Tübingen: Gunter Narr, 21–28.

— (1988) *Translation Studies: An Integrated Approach*, Amsterdam: John Benjamins.

Solomon, Norman (2003) 'For Telling the Truth: The Strange Case of Katharine Gun', *Counterpunch*, 15 December. Available at www.counterpunch.org/solomon12152003.html.

Sperber, Dan and Deirdre Wilson (1986) *Relevance: Communication and Cognition*, Oxford: Basil Blackwell.

Sternberg, Robert J. (2009) 'A New Model for Teaching Ethical Behavior', *The Chronicle Review (The Chronicle of Higher Education)*, 24 April. Available for purchase at http://chronicle.com/article/A-New-Model-for-Teaching-Et/36202/.

Stewart, Dominic (2010) *Semantic Prosody: A Critical Evaluation*, London: Routledge.

St John, M. J. (1983) 'Summary Writing in Dissertations', MSc dissertation, Birmingham: University of Aston.

Sturge, Kate (2002) 'Censorship of Translated Fiction in Nazi Germany', *TTR: Traduction, Terminologie, Rédaction* 15(2): 153–170.

Sunnari, Marianna (1990) 'The Role of Information Structure in Translations: Its Implications for the Teaching of Translation', in Gunilla M. Anderman and Margaret A. Rogers (eds) *Translation in Language Teaching and for Professional Purposes*, Vol. III: *Translation in Teaching and Teaching Translation*, Guildford: University of Surrey.

Tan, T. (1980) 'Aspects of Translation Theory and Practice with Illustrations from Mao's vol. V', MA dissertation, Exeter: University of Exeter.

Thomson, Anne (1999) *Critical Reasoning in Ethics: A Practical Introduction*, London: Routledge.

Thomson, Gregory (1982) 'An Introduction to Implicature for Translators', *Notes on Translation* 1 (special edition).

Titus, David Anson (1974) *Palace and Politics in Prewar Japan*, New York: Columbia University Press (Japanese translation by Kenshirō Ōtani).

Tortoriello, Adriana (2006) 'Funny and Educational Across Cultures: Subtitling Winnie the Pooh into Italian', *JosTrans: The Journal of Specialised Translation* 6. Available at www. jostrans.org/issue06/art_tortoriello.php.

Toury, Gideon (1995) *Descriptive Translation Studies and Beyond*, Amsterdam: John Benjamins.

Trevelyan, R. (1965) *Italian Short Stories*, Vol. I, Harmondsworth: Penguin.

Trosborg, Anna (ed.) (1997) *Text Typology and Translation*, Amsterdam: John Benjamins.

Tsao, F. (1983) 'Linguistics and Written Discourse in Particular Languages: Contrastive Studies: English and Chinese (Mandarin)', in R. B. Kaplan, R. L. Jones and G. R. Tucker (eds) *Annual Review of Applied Linguistics*, Rowley, MA: Newbury House.

Tse, Y. (1988) 'A study of problems of coherence in translation', MA dissertation, Birmingham: University of Birmingham.

Tyler, Patrick E. (2004) 'Britain Drops Charges in Leak of U.S. Memo', *The New York Times*, 25 February. Available at www.nytimes.com/2004/02/26/international/europe/26BRIT.html?ex=1097726400&en=87ea4359da98cb9f&ei=5070.

Tymoczko, Maria (2007) *Enlarging Translation, Empowering Translators*, Manchester: St. Jerome Publishing.

Valdés, Cristina and Adrián Fuentes Luque (2008) 'Coherence in Translated Television Commercials', *European Journal of English Studies* 12(2): 133–148.

Vande Kopple, William J. (1986) 'Given and New Information and Some Aspects of the Structures, Semantics, and Pragmatics of Written Texts', in Charles R. Cooper and Sidney Greenbaum (eds) *Studying Writing: Linguistic Approaches*, New York: Sage, 72–111.

Venuti, Lawrence (1995) *The Translator's Invisibility*, London: Routledge.

— (2004) *The Translation Studies Reader*, second edition, London: Routledge.

Viaggio, Sergio (1996) 'The Pitfalls of Metalingual Use in Simultaneous Interpreting', in Dirk Delabastita (ed.) *Wordplay and Translation*, special issue of *The Translator* 2(2): 179–198.

Vieira, E. (1984) 'Comparative Stylistics Applied to Translation from English to Portuguese', paper delivered at AILA 1984.

von Flotow, Luise (1991) 'Feminist Translation: Contexts, Practices and Theories', *TTR: Traduction, Terminologie, Rédaction* 4(2): 69–84.

Ward, Gregory and Betty Birner (2005) 'Information Structure and Non-canonical Syntax', in Laurence R. Horn and Gregory Ward (eds) *The Handbook of Pragmatics*, Oxford: Blackwell Reference Online. Available to subscribers at http://www.blackwellreference.com/public/tocnode?id=g9780631225485_chunk_g978063122548 59#citation.

Wakabayashi, Judy and Rita Kothari (2009) *Decentring Translation Studies: India and Beyond*, Amsterdam: John Benjamins.

Whitaker, Brian (2006) *Unspeakable Love: Gay and Lesbian Life in the Middle East*, London: Saqi; translated into Arabic by F. Ibrahim as *Al-hubb Al-mamnu': Hayat Al-mithliyeen wa-l-mithliyaat fi Al-Sharq Al-Awsat*, London: Saqi, 2006.

Wilkinson, R. (1990) 'Information Structure Variability: Translating into the Foreign Language', in Gunilla M. Anderman and Margaret A. Rogers (eds) *Translation in Language Teaching and for Professional Purposes*, Vol. III: *Translation in Teaching and Teaching Translation*, University of Surrey.

Williams, Christopher (2002) *Non-Progressive and Progressive Aspect in English*, Bari: Schena Editore.

Williams, Ian A. (2009) 'Discourse Style and Theme–Rheme Progression in Biomedical Research Article Discussions: A Corpus-based Contrastive Study of Translational and Non-translational Spanish', *Languages in Contrast* 9(2): 225–266.

Winter, W. (1961, 1964) 'Impossibilities of Translation', in W. Arrowsmith and R. Shattuck (eds) *The Craft and Context of Translation*, New York: Anchor.

Wright, Clive (undated) 'Justice in Business'. Available at www.ridley.cam.ac.uk/documents/fib/justice.html.

Young, David (1980) *The Structure of English Clauses*, London: Hutchinson.

Young, Robert J. C. (1999) 'The Procrastinator', *Parallax* 5: 7–9.

Zgusta, Ladislav (1971) *Manual of Lexicography*, The Hague: Mouton.

Name index

Aaltonen, Sirkku 50 (n. 18)
Abend-David, Dror 298 (n. 10)
Aixelá, Javier Franco 50 (n. 16)
Alexander, R. J. 54
Al-Jubouri, Adnan 202
Al-Shorafat, Mohammed 128
Anderman, Gunilla 50 (n. 18), 186
Ang, Swee Chai 182
Angelelli, Claudia 282, 297
Arnáiz, Carmen 246, 270
Asad, Talal 231
Assis Rosa, Alexandra 48

Baker, Mona 8, 48, 50 (n. 17), 68, 91, 128, 187, 223, 271, 297, 297
Bandia, Paul 7
Barnwell, Katherine 48, 90
Barsky, Robert 296
Bassnett-McGuire, Susan 71
Batchelor, Kathryn 297
Bauer, Laurie 47
Beaton-Thome, Morven xiii, 107, 128
Becker, Annette 119
Bednarek, Monika xiv, 129, 270
Beeby-Lonsdale, Allison 59, 68
Beekman, John 48, 54, 90, 113, 127, 271
Bellos, David 2
Benn, Piers 281, 296
Bennett, Karen 130
Berk-Seligson, Susan 246, 270
Berman, R. 222
Bersianik, Louky 104
Billiani, Francesca 49
Birner, Betty 186
Blackburn, Simon 277–278
Blacker, C. 26, 34, 40, 118, 201
Blakemore, Diane 100, 260
Blum-Kulka, Shoshana 119, 222–223, 227, 233, 237, 253–254, 262, 270
Boéri, Julie xiv
Bolinger, Dwight 9, 19, 21, 47, 49 (n. 1), 52

Brennan, Mary 20
Brown, Gillian 121, 162, 186, 227, 250, 263, 270–271
Brown, Penelope 105, 107, 128, 129 (n. 10, 11), 270
Burkeman, Oliver 296
Busnardo, JoAnne 128

Callow, John 48, 54, 90, 113, 127
Callow, Kathleen 122, 190, 193, 227
Camayd-Freixas, Erik 284–285, 298–299 (n. 12, 13, 14, 15)
Cambridge, Jan 270
Carroll, Susanne 49
Carter, Ronald 16, 47, 90
Castellano, Lanna xv, 3
Catford, J. C. 105
Celotti, Nadine 32
Chafe, Wallace L. 155, 162–163
Chamizo Domínguez, Pedro 50 (n. 12)
Chan, Alfred L. 299 (n. 18)
Chan Ho-yan, Clara 127
Chan, Red 49 (n. 4)
Charolles, Michel 231, 234–235, 238
Chaume Varela, Federic 73–74
Cheney, George 275–276, 283, 295–296
Chesterman, Andrew 48, 297
Cheung, Martha 7
Christie, Agatha 106, 166, 191
Clason, Marmy 127
Clyne, Michael 247–248
Cockerill, Hiroko 7, 128
Comrie, Bernard 189 (n. 12)
Cook, Guy 193, 227
Cruse, D. A. 11, 47, 52
Culler, Jonathan 9
cummings, e. e. 94
Curran, Beverly 7

Daneš, František 189 (n. 18)
Davies, Ben 296

Davies, Eirlys E. 36, 50 (n. 23)
de Beaugrande, Robert 122, 175, 187, 190, 227, 270
De Regt, Lenart 186
Desmet, Mieke 50
Diriker, Ebru 6, 297
Donovan, Clare 282, 285
Downing, Angela 127
Dressler, Wolfgang 122, 175, 190, 227, 270
Driver, Julia 275, 277–278, 279, 281, 284, 297, 298 (n. 6), 298 (n. 7)
Duff, Alan 241
Dunnett, Jane 49

Eggins, Suzanne 186
Engel, Dulcie 128
Englund Dimitrova, Birgitta 223
Enkvist, Nils E. 143, 231, 270
Ervin–Tripp, Susan 253

Farghal, Mohammed 128
Fawcett, Peter 47, 186, 227
Fenton, Sabine 8
Fernando, Chitra 72, 75–76, 78, 90
Findlay, Bill 48
Firbas, Jan 152, 170–175, 186, 189 (n.18, 19, 20, 21)
Firth, J. R. xix, 234
Flavell, Roger 72, 75–76, 78
Fox, Barbara 193
Francis, Gill 57
Frawley, William 201, 205
Freemantle, Brian 97
Fries, Peter 133, 140–141, 186
Fuentes Luque, Adrián 270
Fujii, Yasunari 129

Gadalla, Hassan 128
Gentry El-Dash, Linda 128
Gentzler, Edwin 7
Gill, Rosalind xix
Gilman, Albert 105, 107, 128, 129 (n. 10, 11)
Giora, Rachel 227
Glinert, Lewis 246, 270
Godlee, Fiona 284, 297
Goodwin, Phil 283, 290, 297
Gottlieb, Henrik 48, 91
Grauberg, Walter 72
Greenbaum, Stephen 143, 157, 186
Gregory, Michael 49 (n. 3)
Grice, H. P. 235–239, 244–249, 258–259, 266, 271

Guillot, Marie-Noëlle 128
Gun, Katharine 296
Gutiérrez Lanza, Camino 49 (n. 4)
Gutt, Ernst-August 239
Gutwinski, Waldemar 190
Guzmán, María Constanza xix

Hagfors, Irma 50 (n. 16)
Hale, Sandra 48, 276, 284–285, 297
Halliday, Michael A. K. 5, 11, 92, 104, 121, 131, 133–136, 139–141, 143, 152–153, 158–159, 168, 170–175, 186, 188 (n. 9), 189 (n. 13, 17, 22), 190–192, 196–197, 200, 202, 211, 213, 222, 227, 228
Hardwick, Lorna 50 (n. 18)
Harvey, Keith 50 (n. 11), 86
Hasan, Ruqaiya 121, 158, 189 (n. 17), 190, 191–192, 196–197, 200, 202, 211, 213, 222, 228, 228 (n. 2, 8)
Hasselgård, Hilde 186
Hatim, Basil 5, 48, 123, 128, 131, 137, 170, 187, 196, 246–247, 270
Hawking, Stephen xvii, 24, 29–30, 46, 131, 133, 219–220, 267–268
Headland, Thomas 246–247
Hébert, Lyse 127
Heikal, Mohammed xvii, 164, 248, 257–258
Herbst, Thomas 157, 189 (n. 13)
Hermans, Theo 7, 297, 299 (n. 17)
Hickey, Leo 246, 270
Hockett, Charles 110
Høeg, Peter 126
Hoey, Michael xv, 90, 188 (n. 10), 189, 190, 192, 197, 213, 228, 231
Holes, Clive 202
Hosseini, Khaled 279–280
House, Juliane 227, 270
Huddleston, Rodney 127
Humarán, Aurora 292
Hung, Eva 6
Hunston, Susan 57

Inghilleri, Moira xiv, 8, 274, 286, 297, 298 (n. 1)

Jakobson, Roman 93, 96
Johns, Tim xv, 110, 111, 157, 176–178, 180, 189 (n. 16)
Johnson, Samuel 51
Jones, Francis 291–292, 297
Jüngst, Heike 22

Katamba, Francis 47
Kenny, Dorothy 5, 48, 51, 223, 242
Kim, Chul-Kyu 120
King, Philip xv, 154
Kinsui, Satoshi 129
Kirkwood, Henry 143–144
Kishtainy, Khalid 73, 160, 203, 210, 246
Knowles, Frank 202
Koskinen, Kaisa 275, 297
Kothari, Rita 7
Kuhiwczak, Piotr 283
Kundera, Milan 283
Kwieciñski, Piotr 50 (n. 16)

Lane-Mercier, Gillian 288–289
Lapiere, Dominique 286
Larson, Mildred 95, 116, 223
Lathey, Gillian 128
Laviosa, Sara 91
Lawford, James 256
Le Carré, John xvii, 56, 124, 145–146, 152,
    169, 172, 181–182, 212
Leanza, Yvan 294
Leech, Geoffrey 11
Lehrer, Adrienne 16, 18
Leppihalme, Ritva 48
Levinson, Stephen 105, 238, 245, 250, 270,
    271 (n. 1, 2), 272
Li, Charles 112, 153–155
Li, Chris Wen-Chao 48
Linder, Daniel 49 (n. 4)
Locke, Philip 127
Lorés Sanz, Rosa 187
Louw, Bill 56, 241, 271, 272 (n. 4, 5), 303
Lowe, R. 49 (n. 5)
Loveday, Leo 242, 245, 247–248
Lyons, John 49, 91 (n. 2), 101, 112–113,
    120, 127

McCann, Michael 281
McCarthy, Michael 16, 47, 68, 90
McCay, Vernon 48
McCreary, Don 20
McDowall, David xvii, 224–225
McWhinney, Jeff 298 (n. 9)
Mackin, Ronald 90
MacLaine, Shirley 55
Maier, Carol 274, 297
Malmkjær, Kirsten xv, 233
Manuel Jerez, Jesús de 297
Martin, James 272

Mason, Ian xii, 5, 48, 86, 123, 128, 131, 137,
    170, 187, 196, 220–222, 230, 246–247,
    270–271, 281
Mathesius, V. 174–175, 189 (n. 18)
Mauranen, Anna 223
May, Rachel 128
Maynard, Senko 155, 159
Mayoral Asensio, Roberto 22
Merlini, Raffaela 294
Meuss, A. R. 68
Milic, Louis 210
Miller, Katrina 48
Moon, Paul 8
Moon, Rosamund 56, 90
Morley, George 156
Munday, Jeremy 8, 48, 271, 272 (n. 4), 297

Nedergaard-Larsen, Birgit 50 (n. 16)
Nerlich, Brigitte 50 (n. 12)
Netsu, Machiko 129 (n. 13)
Newman, Aryeh 52
Newmark, Peter 190
Nida, Eugene A. 95, 108, 113
Nilsson, Anna-Lena 50 (n. 12)
Nissen, Uwe Kjaer 128
Nord, Christiane 130 (n. 20)
Norton-Taylor, Richard 296

Ó Cearúil, Micheál 101
Olohan, Maeve 128, 223, 271
Othman, Sadi 286

Palmer, Frank 16, 47, 52, 72
Papegaaij, Bart 176, 180
Parks, Tim 1, 2, 290
Pedersen, Jan 48
Pérez-González, Luis xiii, 8, 91 (n. 8)
Pettit, Zoë 48
Pöchhacker, Franz 8, 298
Pokorn, Nike 59, 68
Polezzi, Loredana 128
Prado, C. G. 275
Preston, Julia 285
Pullum, Geoffrey 127

Queen, Robin 48
Quirk, Randolph 143, 157

Robins, R. H. 97, 104, 120, 127
Robinson, Douglas 248
Rogers, Margaret 170, 186–187

Rommel, Birgit 249–250

St John, M. 129 (n. 12)
Salama-Carr, Myriam 297
Saldanha, Gabriela 8, 48, 50 (n. 18), 297
Sánchez, Dolores 128
Sapir, Edward 95, 108, 112, 129 (n. 4)
Schmid, Monika 187
Schubert, Klaus 176, 180
Scinto, Leonard 172
Scott, Howard 104
Sears, Donald 9, 19, 21, 47, 49 (n. 1), 52
Selim, Samah 7, 273
Sheridan, Sarah 91
Shlesinger, Miriam 228
Shurbanov, Alexander 128
Simons, Fay 295
Sinclair, John xiv, xvi, 49 (n. 9), 50 (n. 19), 52,
    54, 56, 90, 120, 127, 130 (n. 14, 15),
    143, 188 (n. 1), 233, 241, 271, 272 (n. 4)
Smith, Raoul 201, 205
Snell-Hornby, Mary 5, 189 (n. 15), 213, 234
Solomon, Norman 296
Sperber, Dan 239, 248–249
Sternberg, Robert 297
Stewart, Dominic 271
Sturge, Kate 49 (n. 4)
Swadesh, Morris 95, 108, 112, 129 (n. 4)
Sunnari, Marianna 162

Tan, T. 96, 109
Thompson, Geoff 120
Thompson, Sandra 112
Thomson, Gregory 245, 258
Titus, David Anson 39, 98, 111, 117–118,
    195, 252

Tortoriello, Adriana 49
Toury, Gideon 50 (n. 17)
Trevelyan, R. 32, 50 (n. 15, 20)
Trosborg, Anna 91, 123
Tsao, F. 149, 162
Tse, Y. 249, 251
Tyler, Patrick 296
Tymoczko, Maria 284

Valdés, Cristina 271
Vande Kopple, William 157
Venuti, Lawrence 8, 14, 91 (n. 14), 227, 270
Viaggio, Sergio 100
Vieira, E. 223
von Flotow, Luise 104

Wakabayashi, Judy 6–7
Ward, Gregory 186
Whitaker, Brian 50 (n. 10)
White, Peter 272
Wilkinson, R. 144, 151
Williams, Christopher 128
Williams, Ian 187
Wilson, Deirdre 239, 248–249
Winter, W. 92
Wright, Clive 295

Young, David 151–152, 186
Young, Robert 270
Yule, George 121, 162, 186, 227, 250, 263,
    270–271

Zgusta, Ladislav 11

Language index

Aguaruna 116, 223
Amuesha 95–96
Arabic 6, 7, 13, 17–19, 21–24, 35–37,
    39–41, 43, 50 (n. 10), 53–54, 58, 60–61,
    63, 65, 70–71, 73, 75, 77, 81–82, 85, 91,
    96, 98–103, 120, 128, 138–140, 144,
    146, 151, 160–162, 164–166, 168, 172,
    189, 198–199, 201–205, 210, 216, 219,
    228 (n. 2, 4, 5), 232–233, 240–243,
    245–248, 254, 256–262, 272, 279, 300
Aztec 95, 221

Bali 108–109
Brazilian Portuguese xv, 19, 110–111, 149,
    157, 178, 180, 189 (n. 16), 193, 241,
    286; see also Portuguese
British Sign Language

Chinese xiii, xv, 6–7, 18, 25, 27–28, 34, 38,
    41–43, 61–62, 72, 75, 78, 83–84, 94–98,
    100, 104, 108–110, 112, 116–117,
    119–120, 122, 127, 130, 144, 149,
    153–156, 162, 195, 201, 222, 244, 249,
    251, 278, 289; see also Mandarin
Czech 170, 175

Dagbani 121
Danish 22, 58, 91, 126–127
Dumagat 246–247
Dutch 144, 151, 224

Eskimo 120, 145; see also Inuit

Fijian 97
Finnish 120, 162, 177
French xiii, xv, 7, 9, 12, 22, 29, 32–34, 36,
    38, 42, 59, 66, 70–72, 76–78, 80, 82–83,
    91 (n. 2, 5), 95, 99–103, 105–106,
    112–114, 116, 128, 127 (n. 7), 139–140,
    144, 153, 162, 167–168, 170, 181, 196,
    243–244, 251–252, 255–256, 261

German xiii, xv, 7, 13, 22, 33, 35, 37, 40, 48,
    54, 66, 71–72, 79–80, 88, 100, 105, 107,
    108, 112–114, 116, 120, 129 (n. 4),
    144–145, 149, 151, 153, 157, 187, 189
    (n. 13, 15), 201, 205–207, 209–210, 228
    (n. 6, 7), 247–252, 268, 290
Greek xiii, xv, 7, 29, 30, 58, 93, 105, 154,
    219, 220, 247
Gujarati 107

Harway 153, 189 (n. 12)
Hebrew 119, 186, 193, 222
Hindi 107, 261
Hopi 110

Indonesian 19, 100, 105
Inuit 96–97, 126
Italian xv, 7, 13, 26, 29, 31–33, 49, 80, 100,
    105, 128, 136, 281

Japanese xiii, xv, 6–7, 10, 20–22, 26–27,
    33–36, 39–40, 50 (n. 21), 58, 80–81,
    84–85, 94–98, 105, 111, 116–118,
    128–129, 130 (n. 22), 149–150,
    153–156, 159, 162, 188 (n. 11),
    194–195, 201, 222, 242, 245, 247,
    252–253

Korean 95, 120, 153, 154, 156, 278

Lahu 153
Lisu 154

Malay 108
Mandarin 153–154; see also Chinese

Navaho 9–96
Nilotic languages 113

Polish 13

Portuguese 7, 128, 138, 144, 150, 176–180, 189, 193–195, 223, 228 (n. 3), 241; *see also* Brazilian

Russian xv, 7, 13, 18–19, 22, 64, 100, 104–105, 113–114, 116, 120, 125, 128, 130 (n. 15), 148, 172, 181, 251–252, 254–255

Scandinavian languages 22
Serbian 72, 291
Slavonic 96
Southern Paiute 129 (n. 4)
Spanish xiii, 7, 10, 22, 24, 73, 74, 80, 100, 105, 123, 138, 140, 144, 148, 187, 219, 220, 221, 224, 270, 279

Swahili 99
Swedish 22

Thai 116, 148
Tjolobal (Mexico) 113
Turkish xiii, 10, 112

Vietnamese 95–96, 116

Welsh 72
Wishram 108

Yana 95, 112
Yurok 108

Zapotec (Mexico) 108

Subject index

acceptability (vs. grammaticality) 52–57, 58, 60, 62, 64, 67, 76, 95, 113, 121, 122, **135–136**, 137, 168, 178, 180, 198, 232, 253–254, 263, 270, 273 (n. 11)

accountability xiii, 274–275, 283, 298 (n.7)

accuracy 11, 43, 57, 60, 61, 75, 80, 204, 205, 210, 245, 262, 285–286, 288, 295

active *see* voice

adaptation 32, 50 (n. 18), 298 (n. 10)

address *see* modes of address

adjunct 130, 135, **188**, 251, **300**; as theme 137, 139, 141, **143–144**, 145, 150, 188 (n. 6)

affixes 21, 46, 162, 300; prefixes 21; suffixes 21, 34, 46, 95, 96, 99, 111, 154–155, 199, 228 (n. 4); *see also* morpheme

AIPTI *see* Asociación Internacional de Profesionales de la Traducción y la Interpretación

American Translators' Association 281

analogy 3, 55, 214, 258, 264, 290; principle of **263**

anaphora/anaphoric 154, **189 (n. 14)**, 193, 196, **300**

Asociación Internacional de Profesionales de la Traducción y la Interpretación (AIPTI) 292

aspect **108–111**, 128, **300**

back-translation 6–**7**, 8 (n. 1); difficulties 199, 219

Bank of English 56

Bible (translation) xiii, 121, 127, 245–246, 259

borrowing 22, **79**; *see also* loan word

British National Corpus 50 (n. 13)

case (grammatical) 104, **120**, **300**

CD *see* communicative dynamism

censorship 15, 49 (n. 4)

chain, chaining 191, 192, 195–196, 199, 211–216, 223

chunking (of information) 169, 201–202, 205, 210

circumlocution 17, 60, 86, 105; *see also* paraphrase

cleft structures **146–147**, 148, 150, 160–161, 179–180; *see also* it-structures

COBUILD xv, 49 (n. 9), 50 (n. 19), 120, 127, 130 (n. 14), 188 (n. 1), 240

codes (of ethics, practice) 91 (n. 6), 97, 274–276, 282–286, 290–291, 295–296, 298 (n. 1), 299 (n. 14, 15)

cognates 22, 36

coherence 123, 135, 190, 216, 222–227, **230–234**, 235, 238–239, 242, 244, 250, 259–260, 262–263, 270, **300**; explanatory **235**, 238; supplemental **234–235**

cohesion 5, 123, **190**, 191, 195–196, 200–202, 204, 210, 213, 216, 222–224, 225, 228 (n. 2), 270, **301**; vs. coherence **230–231**; *see also* lexical cohesion, reiteration, collocation, reference, conjunction, ellipsis, substitution

collocation 15, 17, 47, 49 (n. 6), 51, **52–54**, 58, 59, 60–63, 67, 70–71, 86–87, 89–92, 94, 121–122, 126, 260, **301**; culture-specific **63–65**; markedness 54, **55–56**, 65–67; meaning **57–58**; range **54–55**; and register **56–57**, 89; restrictions **13**, **301**; as category of lexical cohesion **211–213**, 216, 219, 222

communicative dynamism (CD) **171**, 172–173, 175–176; *see also* Prague School

compensation/compensatory 21, 50 (n. 11), 86, 226

complement 130 (n. 19), 135, **188**, **301**; as theme **141**, **144–145**

confidentiality 282, 284–286, 295, 299 (n. 14, 15)

conjunction(s)/conjunctive 134–135, 146, 236, **301**; as cohesive device 190, **200–210**, 222, 225, 228 (n. 5, 7), 231

consequentialism 278, **301**; *see also*
    utilitarianism
conversational implicature *see* implicature
conversational maxims **236–238**, 239–240,
    244–250, 252, 266–267, 271 (n. 2); *see
    also* manner, quality, quantity, politeness,
    relation/relevance
Co-operative Principle **236**, 237–240,
    244–245, 248–249
co-reference 154, **192–193**, 223, 232
court interpreting xiii, 48, 270, 299 (n. 15)
cultural substitution **29–33**, 36, 243

definite(ness) 144, 155, 159, 162–163, 166,
    173–174, 192, 232
deontological **276**, 278, **301**
determiner 51, 99, **129 (n. 5)**, 144
dialect **13**, 44, 48, 70, 108, 288, **301**
direction of translation 6, 59, 68, 70, 105,
    146, 154
disjuncts 134–135, 146

ECOS (Translators and Interpreters for
    Solidarity) 293
egoism **278**, 281–282, 301; *see also*
    utilitarianism
ellipsis 190, **196–197**, 199–200, 222
end-focus **157**, 189 (n. 15)
end-weight 157–158, 180, 189 (n. 15)
ergative/ergativity **177**
ethics 5, 8, 68, 97, **274–299**; virtue ethics
    275; Kantian ethics **280**, 281–282; vs. the
    law 283–284; vs. morality 275–277; and
    professionalism 283–284; and linguistic
    choices 286–288; *see also* codes (of ethics,
    practice)
European Union/Commission/Parliament xiii,
    107, 108, 128
evoked meaning 11, **13–14**, 21, 40, 42,
    44–45, 62, 126, **301**
expressive meaning **11–12**, 20–21, 26–28,
    41, 46, 63, 101, 129 (n. 7), 145, **301**
extraposition **179–180**

false friends/faux amis **22**, 50 (n. 12), 91
feminist/feminism xiii, 22, 104, 127
field, of discourse **14**; semantic **16**, 47, **303**
fixed expressions 67, 90, 241; *see also*
    idioms
fronted theme **143–146**, 151, 157, 175, 188
    (n. 6); *see also* predicated theme
FSP *see* functional sentence perspective

functional elements 93, 120, 129 (n. 2), 130
    (n. 19)
functional sentence perspective
    (FSP) **170–176**, 186–187, 189 (n. 18)

gender 4, 10, 92–94, **99–104**, 105, 124,
    127–128, 129 (n. 4, 7), 138, 187, 191,
    199, 270, 287–289, **301**
general word 17, 19, 20, 23, 25–26, 35, 54,
    193, 211–212; *see also* superordinate
genre 50 (n. 18), 68, **123**,157, 193, 196,
    198, 205, 212, 223, 231, **302**; *see also*
    text type
given 131, 136, 155, **156–158**; determining
    givenness 163–166; signalling givenness
    158–163; *see also* known, new

humour 21, 55, 73, 100, 203–204, 260, 270;
    see also jokes
hyponym **17**, 19, 20, 25, 54, 212, **302**;
    co-hyponym 211–212

IATIS *see* International Association for
    Translation and Intercultural Studies
identifying theme 143, **148–152**, 160, 171, 180
idiolect 53, 288
idioms/idiomatic 15, 51, **67–91**, 177,
    214–215, 235, 276; *see also* fixed
    expressions
illocutionary meaning 271 (n. 2)
illustration (as translation strategy) 43–44
impartiality 276, 284–286, 295, 298 (n. 1)
implicature 123, 230, 234–260, 264,
    266–267, 271 (n. 1), **302**;
    conventional 271 (n. 2); conversational
    235, **238**, 239, 258, 271 (n. 2); standard
    238
implicit information 127, **271**
indefinite(ness) *see* definiteness
indicative verbs 110
indirect speech act *see* speech act
infer(ence) 96, 109–110, 195–196, 202, 230,
    238–240, 242, 249–250, 264, 270, 271
    (n. 1, 2), 272
information focus 158, 166–167, 170
information overload 246–247
information status 149, 159–163
information structure xv, 123, 133, 136,
    147–149, 151, 180, 182–183, 186–187,
    189 (n. 17), 190, 237; **156–170**
    (Hallidayan model), **171–176** (Prague
    model); information flow 131–133, 135,

152, 155, 170, 173, 175–176, 180, 182, 186; marked 159, 166–170; *see also* new information

information unit 156, 158

informative verbs 110

instantial meaning 213

Institute of Translation and Interpreting (ITI) xv, 2, 49 (n. 8), 91 (n. 6)

International Association for Translation & Intercultural Studies (IATIS) 298 (n. 9)

interpreting xx; interpreter roles 294–295

intonation 149, 158, 162, 167, 186, 189 (n. 17), 238

ITI *see* Institute of Translation and Interpreting

it-structures **146–147**, 188 (n. 5); *see also* cleft structures

jokes 67, 70, 73, 94, 140, 160, 203, 204, 246; *see also* humour

Kantian ethics *see* ethics

known 132, 148, 149, 156; *see also* given, new

lexical chain 211, 214–216; cohesion 190, **210–222**, 225; meaning **11–15**, 47–48, 52; networks 213; patterning 51; repetition 193, 195, 199, 219, 222, 228 (n. 4); set **16–17**, 49 (n. 6), 70, 211, **302**; unit 12

lexicalization 18, 36, 38

linear dislocation 176

loan word 22, 33–36, 40, 45, 79, 100, 215, 227, 255; *see also* borrowing

local interpretation, principle of 263, 271

manner 236, **237**, 245, 247, 250 *see also* conversational maxims

marked information structure 156, 159, 161, **166–170**, 182

marked rheme 168–169

marked thematic structure **141–156**, 170, 180, 183

marked theme 135, 143–152, 168, 174, 188 (n. 5), 189 (n. 22); function of 142–143

markedness (marked/unmarked) 91 (n. 2), 99, 100, 103, 129 (n. 6), 132, **141–142**, 187; in FSP 174–175; *see also* collocational markedness

maxims *see* conversational maxims

mode **14**, 49 (n. 3), 75

modes of address 105, 253–255

mood 120, 142, 189 (n. 22)

morality *see* ethics

morpheme **10–11**, 19, 47, 154, 175, 176, **302**; *see also* affixes

morphology/morphological 7, 19, 47, 93, 94, 96, 219, **302**

motivation 132, 142, 157, 222, 259–260, 273 (n. 11)

multimodal, multimodality 74, 214

neologisms 11, 50 (n. 10)

neutrality 282, 289, 295, 298 (n. 1)

new information 131–132, 136, 147–149, 155, 156, 157, 166–173, 175, 189 (n. 18); signalling of 158–163

nominalization 148; as strategy **178–179**

norms 14, 29, 33, 36, 50 (n. 17), 57, 103, 107, 113, 120–121, 130 (n. 20), 154, 198–199, 202, 210, 245, 247–248, 254, 278, 281, 284, 294

number 4, 92–95, **96–99**, 104–105, 138, 187 (n. 1), 191, 193, 199

object 93, 120, 129 (n. 2), 130 (n. 15, 19), 132, 135, 141, 175, 177, **187 (n. 1)**, 188 (n. 1, 11), **302**; as theme 141–146

omission 42–43, 50 (n. 23), 84–86, 96–97, 109, 216, 245–246, 258, 278, 288; of syntactic elements 154–155, 195–196; of theme 168–169; of link verbs 172

paraphrase 10, 21, 36–38, 41, 43, 46, 64, 80, 84–87, 205, 215–216; *see also* circumlocution

passive *see* voice

person 92, 99–100, 103, **104–108**, 112, 127–128, 129 (n. 9), 138, 160, 163, 187 (n. 1), 191–193, 195, 270, 286, **302**

politeness 63, 105–106, 119, 128, 129 (n. 11), 245–246, 252, 255, 270

postposed theme 151–152, 188 (n. 9)

Prague School 133, 135, 140, 143, 152, 170, 174–175, 189 (n. 18, 20)

predicated theme 143, **146–147**, 148–149, 151, 160, 180, 188 (n. 5); *see also* fronted theme

predicator 93, 120, 129 (n. 2), 130 (n. 19), 135, 187 **(n. 1)**, 302; as theme 141–142, **146**, 151

prefixes *see* affixes

preposed theme 151–152

presupposed meaning 11, **12–13**, 52, **303**

presupposition 236, **270 (n. 1)**
prominence 142–143, 145, 148, 151, 158, 168; topic-prominence 153–156, 176
pronominalization 162–163, 222
propositional meaning **11–12**, 13, 15–17, 20–23, 25, 29, 36, 40–41, 52, 99, 134, **303**
pseudo-cleft 148, 160–161, 179–180; see also wh-structures
punctuation 161, 166, 168, 189 (n. 17), 202, 222, 228 (n. 2)

quality see conversational maxims
quantity see conversational maxims
Qur'an 259

range see collocational range
reference (as cohesive device) 189 (n. 14), **190–196**, 197, 199–200, 205, 210–212, 222, 223–224, 228 (n. 4), 232, 287–288
reflexive 113, 116, 125, 130 (n. 15), **303**
register 11, **113–14**, 44, 48, 68, 76, 89, 112–113, 288, **303**; and collocation 56–57; see also field, mode, tenor
reiteration 211–212, 216, 219–220
relation/relevance 236–237, 239–240, 242, 244, 247–248, 256, 260, 266, 271 (n. 2); see also conversational maxims
relativism 277–278, 281
repetition 108, 161, 167–168, 185, 192–193, 195, 199, 211–212, 214, 216, 219, 221–222, 223, 228 (n. 4), 232, 247
rhematic status 172–174
rheme 131, 133–137, 139, 141–143, 148, 152, 156, 159–160, 166, 168–175, 187, 188 (n. 9), 189 (n. 18, 21); see also marked rheme, thematic structure

selectional restrictions 12–13, **303**
semantic field see field
semantic prosody 241–242, 271, 272 (n. 4, 5), **303**
sign language 20, 50 (n. 12), 91, 282
speech act 253, 271 (n. 2), 272 (n. 9)
stress (as signal of information status) 149, 158–162, 166–167, 174
subject 12, 93, 103, 112–113, 117, 120, 129 (n. 2), 130 (n. 19), 132, 135, 141, **187 (n. 1)**, 188 (n. 1, 5, 11), 195–196, 199, **303**; and thematic structure 142, 146–147, 151, 153–154, 157–158, 168, 174–175, 177–178

subject-prominent languages 153, 176; see also topic-prominent languages
substitution, grammatical 176, 188 (n. 9); as cohesive device 190, **196–197**, 199–200, 222; see also cultural substitution
suffixes see affixes
superordinate **17**, 19–20, 23, 25, 35, 38, 193, 211–212, 215, **303**; see also general word

teleological **276**, 277, **304**
tenor **14**, 20, 107, 288
tense 10, 94, **108–111**, 127–128, 146, 179, 222, 250, **304**
text type 5, 94, 119, **123**, 131, 193, 199, 205, 223, 234; see also genre
thematic choice 141–142, 144, 146–147, 156, 185
theme, thematic element/structure xv, 123, **133–156**, 162, 169–173, 178, 180, 182–183, 186; and grammaticality 135–136, 190, 228, 235; and markedness 141–152; progression 131, 166, 250; status (in FSP) **173–175**
topic (Chinese-style) 153–156, 195; see also topic-prominent languages
topicalization 154
topic-prominent languages 153–155, 176; see also subject-prominent languages
transition **171–172**, 174
Translational English Corpus 17, 49 (n. 7), 188 (n. 7), 241, 242, 272 (n. 6)
Translators' Guild 68, 70, 72

universalism 278, 280
utilitarianism 276, 278, 280–283, 296, 298 (n. 3, 6), 298 (n. 7), **304**; act-utilitarianism 279; rule utilitarianism 279; see also consequentialism

virtue ethics see ethics
voice (active vs. Passive) 103, 107, **112–120**, 124, 128, 129, 130 (n. 14, 15, 16, 17, 18, 22), 142, 145, 158, 176, 177, 178, 187, 222, **304**

websites/pages, translation of 74, 87, 214, 226–227, 264
wh-structures 148; see also pseudo-cleft structures